Pluralism and the Mind

Pluralism and the Mind
Consciousness, Worldviews
and the Limits of Science

Matthew Colborn

imprint-academic.com

Copyright © Matthew Colborn, 2011

The moral rights of the author have been asserted
No part of this publication may be reproduced in any form
without permission, except for the quotation of brief passages
in criticism and discussion.

Published in the UK by Imprint Academic
PO Box 200, Exeter EX5 5YX, UK

Published in the USA by Imprint Academic
Philosophy Documentation Center
PO Box 7147, Charlottesville, VA 22906-7147, USA

ISBN 9 781845 402211

A CIP catalogue record for this book is available from the
British Library and US Library of Congress

FOR MY PARENTS

Contents

Acknowledgements.................... viii
Introduction: The Persistent Question 1

Part One: *Historical Context*

1. From Animism to Mechanism 19
2. Vital Fluids, Darwin and Mechanical Men 31
3. Mind and Consciousness in the Late Nineteenth Century 43
4. Behaviourism, Computers and Exorcists 53

Part Two: *Philosophical Considerations*

5. Ontology 69
6. Epistemology......................... 87
7. The Problem of Biological Causation................ 105

Part Three: *Physicalism and its Limits*

8. The Computational Model of Mind 123
9. Some Theories of Consciousness 141
10. Neuroimaging and its Limits 159

Part Four: *Controversies and Speculations*

11. Pluralism and the Mind 179
12. Consciousness, Teleology and Evolution 197
13. Free Will............................. 215
14. The Hidden Portion and Our Selves 233
15. Limits of the Possible...................... 249
    Conclusion: Pluralism, Consciousness and Society 267
    Bibliography........................... 285
    Index 299

Acknowledgments

This book has many sources, but owes a significant part of its origin to the Master's course in cognitive science at the University of Birmingham, attended in 1996–7, where I first grappled with the baffling mystery that is consciousness. Thanks to all my tutors there. The most recent inspiration was reviewing Edward and Emily Kelly's *Irreducible Mind* for the *European Journal of Parapsychology* in 2009. This volume showed me that it was possible to formulate coherent alternatives to monistic physicalism, even though my views differ in some respects. Thanks also to the Society for Psychical Research for their support over the years.

I owe much to other's scholarship, but especially that of M.R. Bennett, Walter Elsasser, Paul Feyerabend, P.M.S. Hacker, Mary Midgley, Karl Popper, Steven Rose, Robert Rosen, Raymond Tallis and B. Alan Wallace. People who have read portions of the manuscript and/or have been significantly influential in shaping the ideas expressed here include Henry Bauer, Susan Blackmore, Stephen Braude, Richard Broughton, Edward F. Kelly, Emily Williams Kelly, Alan Gauld, Elisabet Sahtouris, Rupert Sheldrake, Aaron Sloman, Paul Stevens and Charles Tart. Help and encouragement has been supplied at various times by Michael Brown, Rita Carter, Cal Cooper, William Edmondson, David Luke, Robert McLuhan, Sarah Proud, Serena Roney-Dougal, Adrian Ryan, Christine Simmonds and all the others who have accompanied me on this exploratory journey. Thanks especially to Paul and Charla Devereux for inviting me to attend a study day on consciousness in spring 2010, which got me over a serious case of writer's block. Chapter five of this book owes a lot to that day. Thanks, too, go to Chris Roe and Simon Sherwood at the University of Northampton, who invited me to talk in the early stages of writing.

Thanks to my parents, who have supported me through some difficult times and especially my father, whose enthusiasm for this project has been one of the things that got me through to the end. Any mistakes, omissions or misinterpretations are my own. I have been as careful as possible with crediting sources, and any omissions will be corrected in future editions.

Introduction
The Persistent Question

> *The fundamental conceptions of psychology are practically very clear to us, but theoretically they are very confused, and one easily makes the obscurest assumptions in this science without realizing, until challenged, what internal difficulties they involve.*
> —William James, *Principles of Psychology*, 1890

Introduction

This is a book about the mind and its place in nature. It is an attempt to bridge the yawning gap between personal experiences of consciousness and the images of mind that frequently appear in the literature of the various cognitive sciences. There is also the need to understand better why such a gap exists in the first place, and whether it can — or should — ever be closed by a 'definitive' theory of consciousness that is satisfactory — or at least plausible — to all. But to begin, here are a few examples of subjective experience.

The Mystery of Consciousness

1. *'The sky is pale blue today, with fluffy clouds. The sun is bright, and there is a slight bite in the air. A wind is blowing the late-summer leaves and the flowers on the patio out of my window are bright red. Every so often, a nearby workman operates an electric cutter that makes the hairs on the back of my neck stand up. It's a relief when the motor stops, because you can hear the birds.'*

2. *'Yes because he never did a thing like that before as ask to get his breakfast in bed with a couple of eggs since the City Arms hotel when he used to be pretending to be laid up with a sick voice doing his highness to make himself interesting for that old faggot Mrs Riordan that he thought he had a great leg of and the never left us a farthing all for masses for herself and her soul greatest miser ever was...'* [1]

---

[1] Joyce, 1986/1922, p. 608.

3. *'About two years ago, while on holiday in Cornwall, I went for a walk with my sister along the beach... My sister walked on in front of me; I was left alone. It was as if time had stood still. I could think of nothing, I only felt I was "somewhere else." I was part of something bigger and absolutely beyond me. My problems and my life didn't matter at all because I was such a tiny part of a great whole.'*[2]

4. *'...And there were always choices to make. Every day, every hour, offered the opportunity to make a decision, a decision which determined whether you would or would not submit to those powers which threatened to rob you of your very self, your inner freedom; which determined whether or not you would become a plaything of circumstance, renouncing freedom and dignity to become molded into the form of the typical inmate.'*[3]

5. *'As the drug [an anaesthetic] began to work, I slipped down and lost awareness and feeling of my body. Visual impressions were relatively Spartan, but were mostly beige. Had experience of "white darkness" at one point, and complex patterns in dark brown against white beige very like the side-decorations in Tibetan art...*

'Reality felt gooey, or made of ice cream mixed with syrup. Feelings: at one point, I remember smiling and saying that I knew what the Buddhists were talking about. It was like I'd climbed a mountain to see a vast plain of "reality" and that it was good and light... These are metaphors; what I experienced, for fleeting moments, was ineffable.'

All five of the previous paragraphs describe different types of subjective experience. The first is a simple description of what lies outside my window. The second is a quotation from the novel *Ulysses* (1922) by James Joyce, which records the ramblings of the sleeping mind of Molly Bloom. The third is a description of a spontaneous mystical experience. The fourth is from Victor Frankl's *Man's Search For Meaning*, describing everyday life in Auschwitz, and the final one is an account of the extraordinary distortions of consciousness that occur when an hallucinogenic drug is administered. And these paragraphs are just pallid representations of the rich and various subjective experiences that are possible for a human being.

Scientists today are in many respects poorly equipped for the investigation of subjective experience,[4] and a cursory look at the literature reveals a mind that seems in some respects quite removed from the rich, organic and multifaceted experiences above. Compare 1–5 with the following quotes:

---

2 Witness quoted in Maxwell & Tschudin, 1990, pp. 46–47.
3 Frankl, 1992, p. 75.
4 Varela & Shear, 1999; see also comments in Midgley, 2001.

A. *'It seems to me to make no sense (in scientific terms) to try to distinguish sharply between acts that result from conscious intention and those that result from our reflexes or are caused by disease or damage to the brain.'*[5]

B. *'...the mind is fundamentally a sentient computing device, taking sentences as input from sensory transducers, performing logical operations on them, and issuing other sentences as output.'*[6]

C. *'...the [Robotic system] CADBLIND Mark I certainly doesn't have any qualia... So it does indeed follow from my comparison that I am claiming that we don't have qualia [i.e. private, ineffable, subjective experiences] either. The sort of difference that people imagine there to be between any machine and a human experiencer... is one I am firmly denying: There is no such sort of difference. There just seems to be.'*[7]

D. *'Big Ideas sometimes match the structure and function of the human brain such that the brain causes us to see the world in ways that make it virtually impossible not to believe them.'*[8]

E. *'...there is nothing more [than brain function], no magic, no additional components to account for every thought, each perception and emotion, all our memories, our personality, fears, loves and curiosities.'*[9]

If we take passages 1–5 to be reasonably accurate descriptions of their respective experiences, then they challenge the claims in A–E. It is true that there are some points of correspondence. For example, one could imagine *some* version of passage 2, which consists of garbled thoughts, being spewed out by a computer or 'sentient computing device' (statement B); although it's actually an expression of some complicated social intuitions, not to mention complaints.

But what about passage 4 and passage A? The writer of passage 4, a concentration camp inmate, describes constantly having to make internal decisions that could result in life or death. This seems completely at odds with the statement that there is essentially *no difference* between the behaviour caused by brain damage and that caused by a conscious decision.

Now compare passage B with passages 3 and 5, the mystical and drug-induced experiences respectively. Could a 'sentient computing device', or even a robot, possibly have such experiences? Maybe, maybe not — it really depends upon the ultimate nature of such experiences, which remain obscure (and dubbing them hallucinations begs the question of the hallu-

---

5   Blakemore, 1990, p. 270. Quoted in Tallis, 2004, p. 24.
6   Churchland, 1986, p. 36. Quoted in Tallis, 2004, p. 24.
7   Dennett, 1991, p. 375.
8   Liberman in Brockman, 2009, p. 89.
9   O'Shea, 2008, p. 12.

cination's nature). But at first sight, such experiences don't seem terribly compatible with the idea that the mind 'is' an information-processor.

Premature Certainty

Given these discrepancies and even contradictions, why do the authors of A-E come across as so certain of their ideas? If pressed, most or all of them would admit that there is an awful lot that we do not understand about the brain and/or nervous system.

One impetus for such surety might be to eliminate any occult or religious element from the study of the mind. This is clearest in statement E, with its reference to magic or 'additional components' (*aka* 'souls'). This eliminative drive can often reach the point of overkill, and one suspects that part of the resistance to free will is due to the concept's religious origin.

Another related factor is the entanglement of the mind-sciences with Scientism.[10] *Scientism* is the belief that science is or can be the only explanation of anything.[11] The followers of Scientism think that science can answer any question in any field, and that other modes of knowing—like art, spiritual practice or intuitive knowledge—are at best temporary stand-ins before a scientific explanation can be found. Followers will also tend to be almost comically blind to the problems and limitations of science and technology.[12] The problem with Scientism in this context is that it muddies the waters between what we actually know and what we only *think* we know. Another illustrative example:

F. *'If anyone says that will influences matter, the statement is not untrue, but it is nonsense... Such an assertion belongs to the crude materialism of the savage. Now the only thing which influences matter is the position of the surrounding matter or the motion of the surrounding matter.'*[13]

This is clearly similar in spirit to statements A-E, the only difference being that it was made in 1874, long before any in-depth examination of the brain had begun. And it is by no means the only such statement made during the Victorian period. At this period, there was enough physiological data to tie thinking in *some* way to the brain, but by no means enough to be making such definitive statements. Given that such pronouncements have not really changed significantly in over a century, *and* that they existed before

---

10   Tallis, 2004; Collins & Pinch, 1998.
11   Midgley, 2001.
12   See Dawkins, 2006, for a lengthy example. Dawkins has 20:20 vision for the numerous flaws of religion, but seems oblivious to problems generated by science and technology, e.g. the neutron bomb, poison gas, pollution, vivisection, the abuse of scientific knowledge in the name of profit, the common compliance of scientists to oppressive regimes, etc.
13   Thomas Huxley, quoted in Clifford, 1874, Body and Mind, *Fortnightly Review*, **16** (n.s.), pp. 714–736. Quoted in Kelly *et al.*, 2007, p. 53.

there could have been much evidence for their truth, *some* degree of wariness about them is surely warranted.

These claims remain moot to this day. Despite many assertions to the contrary, we are far from certain how the conscious mind fits into the wider world. To be sure, *some* portions of our subjective experience seem very closely tied to brain mechanisms. Baars notes that, for example, subjective experiences of light (brightness, hue and saturation) correlate pretty closely with the known neurophysiology of vision. Also, experiences of a mind's eye seem to correlate closely to specific functions in the visual cortex.[14] This close correlation between neural mechanisms and at least *some* subjective experiences should be conceded before we proceed.

But it's still true that we know far too little to conclude for certain that *every single* experience that we have is tied directly to some specific neural mechanism. In any case, the nature of said *relationship* remains far from clear. There have, of course, been attempts to close this gap, one of the most common being the assertion that subjective experiences are somehow illusory, and thus dissolvable into their correlating mechanism.

The Illusion Illusion

Look again at statement C, which denies qualia in machines and thus humans. Statement C is part of a larger argument that goes something like this: computer functions and human functions are comparable if they do the same job, like wine-tasting. We can reasonably say that computers or robots today do not experience *qualia*, or private, subjective experiences. But they can do *some* of the same 'functions' that we can. Since computers do not need *qualia* to successfully complete tasks like wine-tasting, *ergo* we don't either. QED.[15] Anyone who *thinks* they have qualia is subject to the 'Grand Illusion' of consciousness.[16]

The assertion that we are just fooling ourselves about qualia, free will, rational thought, the unitary sense of self, the self itself, and in fact just about any significant aspect of the human mind is a very routine response to any objections raised about the ideas in passages A–F. Our brains, the story goes, are 'designed by evolution' to *think* that we have qualia or free will, or purpose.

For example, Colin Blakemore, the author of passage A, goes on to say that the feeling of control we have is just a product of the machinery of the brain, put there by natural selection. Daniel Wegner has written an entire volume on how the feeling of conscious will is an illusion.[17] Similar stories, as I have said, have been made for a number of other mental attributes. In a

---

14 Kosslyn, 1994; Baars, 1999.
15 Dennett, 1991.
16 Blackmore, 2003.
17 Wegner, 2002.

like vein, resistance to these stories is generally rationalized as our in-built evolutionary drives kicking against unpalatable truths.

This rhetorical trick makes it very hard to dispute such ideas without seeming to be irrational and unscientific. If I argue that I certainly *feel* as if I have at least a measure of free will and *do* appear to make choices then the response will be that I am being 'fooled' by my own brain.

But such statements are often internally problematic. For example, Colin Blakemore seems to unwittingly exclude himself from the consequences of lacking free will. For one could argue that he has perceived that his brain is fooling him about free will and has decided *not* to be fooled. But this implies that he has a *choice* about whether he is fooled or not, which suggests that there *is* actually some choice about whether we accept the 'illusions' our brains serve up to us, which in turn suggests a wider form of freedom of choice. We will return to these sorts of dilemmas in the chapter on free will.

The words 'illusion' or even 'delusion' have become part of the standard lexicon in neuroscience. These words are often used in a very ill-defined way to effectively dismiss phenomena that are themselves often ill-defined. Thus we read that the self 'is' an illusion.[18] Well, maybe so, but there is hardly any common definition of the 'self', just as there is really no commonly agreed definition of 'illusion', and the same might be said of free will.

Susan Blackmore attempts a definition of such illusion as 'not something that does not exist but that is not what it seems',[19] using visual illusions to illustrate this. But this is hardly satisfactory either. Firstly, visual illusions, like conjuring tricks, are only illusions to the person apprehending them. Without the observer, there is no illusion. So if the self, or the visual world, or free will, really is an illusion, who, precisely, is being fooled?

One could attempt to move this illusion story to a neural level and claim that no one needs to experience an illusion if we imagine that the visual system is set up in such a way that the illusion just happens. But this only moves the story back a step, because one still needs an observer to apprehend the results of that neural quirk.

And as Popper and Eccles pointed out,[20] one has a choice about which way one sees such a figure. Examples include the ambiguous figure which can be seen as either two faces or a vase. Ah, but, that might just mean that there's a 'higher-order' computational switch that flips between the views.

But is such a higher-order switch *really* sufficient to account for such a choice? On the one hand, one could argue for a whole series of such dis-

---

18 Blackmore, 1993; 1999; 2003.
19 Blackmore, 1993.
20 Popper & Eccles, 1977.

crimination mechanisms that get steadily more sophisticated as we move into the brain. On the other, my instinct is that one *still* needs someone acting as a whole person to recognize an illusion and create or 'program' a new discriminatory switch.[21] Once more, we just have an *assertion* that an essentially mechanical system could do this.

We could also argue that virtually *anything* we observe is in a sense an illusion. A distant cow looks small because of the 'illusion' of perspective. The table on which I am writing seems solid but is, according to physics, mostly empty space. Light itself is 'nothing but' electromagnetic energy. The world appears flat most of the time but it is really round. The Sun appears to circle the Earth. These are all quite different sorts of illusions, which is really shorthand for saying that our senses very rarely, or even never, offer us up things that can be taken at face value. On this level, we might agree that our minds are not what they seem, but neither is anything else.

But quite often 'illusion' arguments have a specific, common function, which is to preserve the theoretical *status quo* against observations that seem to challenge it. Free will apparently contradicts determinism, so it 'must' be an illusion. The idea of a substantive self contradicts modular, functional theories of the human being, so *has* to be a phantom. The subjective sense of moving through a rich visual world does not tally with behaviouristically-inclined interpretations of the visual system, so the experience cannot be as it appears (however that is). In each case, our subjective experiences become subordinate to abstract theories, which are supposed more 'real' but discard much.

The frequency with which the 'illusion' argument is used seems to me suggestive. If our only way to explain a phenomenon is as an 'illusion', then maybe we need to go back to first principles and find out why we need to invoke such an explanation, so frequently. After all, without careful qualification, such a claim can come perilously close to a dismissal of the apparently illusory phenomena.

Consciousness as a Function of World-View

The major dilemma for Western science—and those who follow it—is how to fit subjective experiences into a larger world-view that at least appears to preclude them. As the philosopher John Searle put it; 'How can we square [the] self-conception of ourselves as mindful, meaning-creating, free, rational, etc., agents with a universe that consists entirely of mindless, meaningless, unfree, nonrational, brute physical particles?'[22] Searle is

---

21 The idea that we cannot just see thinking and perception as just brain-events but must look at the system—and observer—as a whole is discussed in Bennett & Hacker, 2003.
22 Searle, 2007, p. 5.

claiming that the background assumptions of Western science conflict in some fundamental way with our everyday view of ourselves.

Many writers in the mind-sciences are prepared to take the sort of assumptions Searle names for granted; hence the insistence that free will and subjective experiences are illusory. In other words, the 'illusion' arguments are predicated on the assumption that the 'fields and forces only' world-picture is correct in all essential respects. If such a world-picture is correct, then the *only* way to accommodate the problems of consciousness is by calling them somehow illusory.

Alan Wallace claims that these background assumptions have become so ingrained that they amount to a sort of secular faith that he calls 'scientific materialism'.[23] He claims that this faith creates a situation equivalent to medieval scholasticism, where arguments had to conform to a certain set of theological assumptions before they were accepted, and any that did not were considered heretical.[24] Opinions that diverge significantly from these assumptions are simply not taken seriously.

If one accepts Wallace's assertion that 'scientific materialism' has become a sort of substitute theology, then the statements A–F begin to look like expressions of dogma rather than value-free, objective, remarks. Statement D, which has not been discussed yet, is pertinent here. The 'sticky' Big Idea, which apparently adheres because our brains are 'wired' to believe it, turns out to be Cartesian dualism which, according to Lieberman, has not changed in thousands of years (although strictly speaking the kind of dualism Descartes advocated originated with him). Although he uses a number of neurological studies as evidence, the upshot is that this belief is characterized as yet another neurological illusion.

Two things need to be flagged here. First, that *any* kind of dualism has been traditionally reviled in the cognitive sciences since their inception, so this is far from a neutral assessment. We must, of course, beware of biases, neurological or otherwise, that might lead us to accept or reject an idea unfairly, but all this means is that we must try to use more than gut feelings to assess theories. After all, our brains might 'compel' us to accept that two plus two equals four, but this would not prevent it from being true, mathematically speaking.

Second, the question of consciousness remains open enough that *some* variety of dualism or pluralism cannot be fully ruled out and may even be necessary. Rosen pointed out that 'Science is built on dualities. Indeed, every mode of discrimination creates one'.[25] He meant that the very *nature* of science splits one phenomenon from another to facilitate explanation, and creates dualisms everywhere. This may, for all we know, be a 'neuro-

---

23 Wallace, 2000; Wallace & Hodel, 2008.
24 Wallace, 2000.
25 Rosen, 1991, p. 40.

logical' process itself, but even if that were true, it hardly renders science invalid. Again, it just means that we must use other means to confirm or deny scientific ideas. William James made the same point over a century ago.[26] But, if this is true, why have dualisms become such an anathema?

Insistent Monism

A central tenet of the belief system Wallace labels 'scientific materialism' is the insistence that the universe consists of one kind of stuff, sometimes known as 'matter', and that at least in principle everything can be reduced to the rules governing this 'stuff'. *Monism* is defined by Christof Koch as follows; 'The metaphysical position that all is the manifestation of a single underlying reality, principle, essence, or substance, and is governed by a universal set of laws... Monism is opposed to dualism, the belief that there are two domains, the physical and the mental.'[27] Physicalism is a variant, proposing that everything is derived from 'matter' (atoms and constituents) and energy and is governed by physical laws.

These assumptions have become so deeply ingrained in our culture that they have almost become truisms. But I will argue that it seems at *least* as plausible to see our universe as containing lots of 'realities' or 'principles'. For most intents and purposes, this *pluralistic* assumption is how physics already operates.[28] It will also be claimed that an *insistence* on materialistic monism — a component of the belief system entangled with science — has seriously distorted thinking and created an unnecessary fear of alternatives.

An additional problem highlighted by both Wallace and Stapp is that such 'materialism' (or 'physicalism') often proves to be shorthand for a particular *brand* of materialism based upon nineteenth-century assumptions. Both writers note that pretty much all of the assumptions upon which classical physics rested have been violated in some way by twentieth-century physics. This has serious, but mostly unnoticed, consequences for consciousness researchers.

The 'ground rules' of physics were significantly revised over the course of the twentieth century, and many in cognitive science have yet to take sufficient notice of this. The physicist Henry Stapp observed that 'philosophers of mind have isolated themselves in a hermetically sealed world, created by considering only what other philosophers of mind have said, or are saying, with no opening to the breezes that bring word of the highly pertinent revolutionary change that had occurred in basic science decades

---

26 James, 1902/1985.
27 From the Glossary pages of Koch's website: http://www.klab.caltech.edu/~koch/ accessed on 29/09/09.
28 Popper, 1959; Popper & Eccles, 1977.

earlier'.[29] According to Stapp, most philosophers of mind are trying to build their models in a world-picture that is thoroughly outmoded.

A Plethora of Theories

Paul Feyerabend noted that although it is *'possible* to create a tradition that is held together by strict rules… that is also successful to some extent… is it *desirable* to support such a tradition to the exclusion of everything else?'.[30] Feyerabend answers this in the negative, and this 'no' forms a central argument of his book. There are multifarious possibilities out there, and blinkering oneself in advance makes little sense.

It makes a good deal of sense, therefore, to consider multiple approaches to the study of consciousness, and fortunately, in at least some venues,[31] liberality has prevailed. There exist a plethora of views about consciousness, from the conservative to the radical. Some think that once we understand the brain or 'computational' mechanisms that supposedly underlie every subjective experience, then that is explanation enough. Others agree with the basic idea of neural mechanisms or 'information-processing' for completing tasks, but speak of a 'hard problem' which means that a subjective aspect, which seems to do nothing but watch, needs to be tagged on.[32] Still more think that such problems will disappear once we add a body to the brain and take social and physical interactions into account.[33]

Some — currently a minority — concur with Stapp and think that conventional science cannot handle subjective experience, placing their faith in some modification of quantum theory, or even claim that 'consciousness' is inherent in the universe and has somehow been around since the Big Bang. And on the fringe of psychology there are those who think that 'consciousness' can operate at a distance, influencing other minds and even the physical world directly.[34] Still more evoke strange entities like 'psychons',[35] 'shins',[36] or 'memes'.[37] We will take a brief look at some of these theories over the course of this book.

---

29 Stapp, 2009, Physicalism Versus Quantum Mechanics: http://arXiv.org/abs/0803.1625 accessed on 13/10/09.
30 Feyerabend, 1975, p. 19, his italics.
31 The *Journal of Consciousness Studies* being a good example of this. The *JCS* has included serious discussion of such *verboten* topics as psi phenomena and children's apparent memories of previous lives. At the same time, it also features many contributions from mainstream researchers on mainstream topics, with extensive mutual critiquing. Such liberality comes close to Feyerabend's demand that 'anything goes' in scientific research.
32 Chalmers, 1996.
33 Bennett & Hacker, 2003.
34 See Radin, 1997; 2006.
35 Eccles, 1994.
36 Stokes, 2007.
37 Dawkins, 1976.

It is terribly hard to work through this material in anything like a comprehensive manner and gain a coherent picture that does not contradict one or other of these opposing views. Each of these researchers comes to the table with different metaphysics, or underlying assumptions about how the world works. Each tends to highlight certain lines of evidence and to ignore or even deride others. But when the dust settles, it is often anything but clear who is right, who is wrong, or even if *any* of these conflicting theories has merit.

My contention, in fact, is that *none* of these ideas may prove definitive, and that to an extent, at least, a plurality of approaches could remain necessary. This is because any single approach or research programme will be inevitably partial and limited by its basic assumptions.

There is, however, a very human tendency to take our own partial, conceptual games for reality. As Sogyal Rinpoche noted, we tend to get 'confined in the dark, narrow [conceptual] cage'[38] of our own making and are liable to mistake the cage, game or approach for the whole of reality. But if we truly accept our own partiality or bias, then the drive to 'convert' everyone to one game, theory or cage becomes a highly suspect exercise.

A recent example of such urging occurred when the *Journal of Consciousness Studies* published work on the controversial remote staring experiments of Rupert Sheldrake. In a letter, Christof Koch expressed his surprise that 'JCS would give a platform to these sorts of ideas. It makes the job of those of us that seek to identify and study consciousness as a natural phenomenon, subject to known physical and biophysical principles, so much more difficult'.[39]

This seems to me a curious response. Koch's equation of 'consciousness as a natural phenomenon' with 'known physical and biophysical principles' strikes me as unreasonable because it implies that models of consciousness that evoke new principles or explanatory frames cannot by definition be natural or truly 'scientific'. This seems excessively conservative, because it assumes that contemporary physics and biophysics is complete, correct and all-encompassing. There are strong grounds for supposing this to be premature because contemporary physics has enough difficulty with *biological* systems, let alone conscious ones.[40]

Elsewhere, Koch with Francis Crick suggested that one should only consider alternatives to mainstream theories when one is forced to by anomalous experimental data, discovered in the course of a conventional research programme.[41] This suggestion has some merit in theory, but is probably less than airtight in practice. Historically speaking, psychology has proved more than capable of ignoring or rationalizing away research

---

38 Sogyal, 1992.
39 Koch, 2005. Quoted in the footnote in the *Journal of Consciousness Studies*, **12** (6), p. 6.
40 See Rosen, 1991; Elsasser, 1998; Dupré, 2001.
41 Crick & Koch, 2002.

anomalies; in the case of behaviourism, the mind itself was ignored for over half a century.

In contrast to these views, I wish instead to advocate an approach closer to Feyerabend, where 'anything goes'[42] and alternative views are not merely respected, but encouraged. We should not worry too much about contradictions between viewpoints or world-pictures, and focus instead on building alternative pictures in areas where currently dominant theory is weak. In the spirit of 'anything goes', I would like to question an often unconscious adherence to some logical principles which I believe creates a lot of confusion within the field.

Insights from General Semantics

In my view, many problems and disputes within consciousness studies can be traced to an often unconscious adherence to Aristotelian logic and essentialism.[43] Count Korzybski observed that much of Western thought seems to be based upon presuppositions that seem natural to us but are constructions of the Greek philosopher Aristotle. He believed that these presuppositions have an enormous impact upon the way we think about these problems. Korzybski's work has today mostly fallen into shadow, which is unfortunate, because in my view some of his insights could be of immense benefit to the field.

Aristotelian logic has a number of presuppositions.[44] The law of identity holds that a thing is what it is, so a tree is a tree and the truth is the truth. It also means that it is all what it is. The law of the excluded middle holds that something is EITHER true OR false. Either a person is a man or they are not; either something exists or it does not. From this follows the law of non-contradiction, which says that someone cannot be simultaneously, for example, a man and not a man, or a proposition cannot be simultaneously true AND false.

These laws imply permanent, polarized and static relationships that tend to force people to think of different categories as discrete things, even in places where this is inappropriate. To counter this, Korzybski invented a number of post-Aristotelian principles. He proposed that there are *no* identity relationships in nature, which was expressed by the statement 'the map is not the territory'. Similarly, words are not the things they represent. Secondly, he proposed the principle of not-allness. This is the idea that a label ('man', 'tree', 'true', 'false') does not convey a complete and exhaustive picture of the event, object or process so labelled. Third was the

---

42 Feyerabend, 1975.
43 Korzybski, 1994.
44 See Lance Strate's lecture notes on general semantics, undated, for a general summary, and Korzybski, 1994, for details: http://www.generalsemantics.org/learningctr/guides/lecture-notes-on-teaching-general-semantics-by-lance-strate.pdf

principle of self-reflexiveness, which holds that whilst the map is not the territory, a better map includes a map of the map and the observer.

Fourthly, he argued against the use of the verb 'to be' when making high-level abstractions, especially those of a very general nature (as in 'everything "is" matter', 'human brains "are" computers', 'everything "is" mind', 'biology "is" engineering', 'we "are" nothing but memes and genes', etc.) In statements like this, the word 'is' stands in for 'equals', within an Aristotelian system. It implies that the noun/s after the 'is' stands for concrete things, whereas in reality they often denote highly abstract, flexible, and even vague concepts. Korzybski suggested that we avoid the use of the verb 'to be' in these circumstances, and replace them with relational language and verbs suggesting processes. So the above statements may be rewritten; 'everything seems like matter to me', 'some aspects of the human brain may be usefully described in computational terms', 'everything seems like a mind to me', 'some aspects of biological systems can be usefully understood by using engineering metaphors', etc.) Unfortunately, the literature of cognitive science is replete with such totalistic 'is of' statements, as in interpretations of Artificial Intelligence that assume that 'cognition' in human brains and computers 'is' identical on some level.

Korzybski was not pressing for the *abolition* of Aristotelian logic, which still remains useful in some contexts, but he did question the use of such principles as a basis for thinking about many, or even most, situations in science and the outside world.[45] Korzybski's principles seem to me to allow us to build better and more reflexive maps within cognitive science and consciousness studies, and, to a degree, they will be applied in this book. His 'General Semantics' encourages multi-valued logic (truth values stated probabilistically in a spectrum between zero and one), avoids atomism or elementism (e.g. type-token Platonism, thoughts as atomic or granular, behaviour as reducible to a specific neural mechanism, etc.), and discourages sweeping 'allness' statements ('everything is...', etc.) Other advantages should become clear over the course of this book. The primary lesson I take from General Semantics is the principle of non-identity, especially with regards to words. So often in this field maps are mistaken for territories, even amongst philosophers who really should know better. This principle dovetails with my pluralistic approach, or the assumption that any map we make will tend to partiality.

The principles also allow us to be consciousness of the slippery and vague use of words. Words like 'mind', 'consciousness', 'matter', 'natural-

---

45 In a similar vein, I am not suggesting the wholesale rejection of all of Aristotle's ideas. On the contrary, we will see that a number of people have suggested that the adoption of an Aristotelian view of causation may afford us better understanding of biological systems; see chapter seven. A rejection or critique of *some* of a person's ideas does not imply a rejection of *all* of their ideas.

ism', 'physical', 'free will', 'determinism' are often used unreflexively in debates even though they are too wide-ranging and general to allow precise formulation. Other words that do have technical or precise definitions in some contexts are often used in loose and imprecise ways. Such words include; 'information', 'information-processing', 'representation', 'computation', etc. Where I use these words, I use them in provisional, relational and also metaphorical ways only.

The Current Context of the Debates

We seem to be living in a revolutionary era, where advanced neuroimaging techniques hold centre-stage in the hunt for consciousness. In the light of new data, some have urged that we should sideline theoretical or philosophical worries in favour of empirical investigation,[46] the underlying, rather positivistic, assumption seeming to be that technological advances will conquer all and inductively provide comprehensive solutions to most problems.

Neuroimaging has certainly resulted in a cascade of new data for the mind-sciences. By 2005, approximately 100,000 fMRI studies had been conducted,[47] and have led to some extravagant claims. The *Sun* newspaper for the 14th March 2009 published a quote from an fMRI researcher who claimed that we might be able to develop a 'mind reading' technology within ten years, and the futurist Ray Kurzweil thinks that, due to the improving resolution of scanning techniques, we will have complete models of the brain and will be able to fully 'reverse engineer' it within a decade or three.[48]

Spend long enough reading predictions like this and one gains the impression that the scientific juggernaut is indeed unstoppable. However, as the enthusiasts would no doubt be quick to remind us in different contexts, critical thinking remains an essential part of scientific practice. We should be entitled to ask some fairly penetrating questions about these claims — and, indeed, the wider claims of cognitive science, no matter how venerated our 'scientific' authority is held to be.

This is especially important because the influence of neuroscience, psychology and psychiatry is by no means entirely positive, and in some contexts has been quite pernicious. Wallace noted that while modern, Western approaches to the mind are 'remarkably empowering to those who create, market, and distribute... technology and drugs, [they are] profoundly disempowering to the individual'.[49] For example, some neuroscience pundits have suggested that we should change our criminal justice system

---

46 Koch, 2004.
47 Uttal, 2005.
48 Kurzweil, 2005.
49 Wallace, in Varela and Shear, 1999, p. 186.

because of what neuroscience has 'discovered' about the brain.[50] To quote the recent title of a book opposing such views, 'did my neurons make me do it?'[51]

A big problem, however, is that many of these views are based upon the problematic assumptions that we outlined above. Similarly, the neuro-imaging and other studies that purport to verify such views have been mostly conducted within this theoretical framework. Scientific work does not simply reveal what 'is' there; it remains, in part, manufactured knowledge that gets shaped by one's expectations, and this remains doubly true in the human sciences, where there is always a danger that a human being will shape themselves to fit social expectations, even in 'neutral' scientific experiments. Scientists, too, hardly constitute disinterested observers, because, to paraphrase Wittgenstein, one often sees what one wants to see. So there are both social and theoretical grounds to challenge such sweeping assertions about human nature. The social grounds concern how much power we wish to place in the hands of cognitive science, generally at the expense of the individual. The theoretical grounds are based upon the limits, biases or even serious deficiencies of current models of the person.

Plan of the Book

To understand where we are, it is often important to understand how we have got there. The first part of this book traces the changes in our views of minds and consciousness from early modern times to the present day. These chapters have been written in a revisionist spirit, challenging the view of relentless progress towards a 'true' view of human nature and emphasizing the multiplicity of various traditions within and without science. To this end, I have examined some byways of exploration, such as Mesmerism and psychical research. I will attempt to show that varieties of knowledge can bud, flower, and become forgotten as the collective attention system of societies change their orientation. I will also try to show that even 'pseudosciences' like phrenology can be instrumental in producing worthwhile science. Another issue, salient to the twentieth century and beyond, is how predominant ideologies can shape or even distort views of human beings.

Part Two, *Philosophical Issues*, begins with a survey of various ontologies of mind and nature. I then suggest a revised epistemology, after Feyerabend, Neurath and Cartwright, that questions the idea of 'Universal Laws' of nature and proposes instead a patchwork pluralism. This is needed to counter an unreflexive adherence to classical physics that underpins predominant views in the philosophy of mind and neurobiology (Wallace's 'scientific materialism'). Having established this

---

50   Especially Gazzaniga, 2005.
51   Murphy & Brown, 2007.

revised epistemology, I examine the problem of biological causation, which needs, in my view, to evolve beyond mechanistic models to better accommodate mental life.

The currently predominant metaphysic/ideology within science is monistic physicalism, which forms the basis of a range of research programmes. In Part Three, *Physicalism and its Limits*, I examine some of these research programmes and probe some of their limits. These approaches include the computational or information-processing approaches and questions of Artificial Consciousness. A number of theories have been proposed, which mainly seek to understand consciousness more accurately in terms of the operation of specific neural mechanisms, and these will be examined next. I will also look at the controversy behind quantum theory and its possible role in consciousness. Thirdly, I examine neuroimaging and its limitations.

In Part Four, I survey some select controversies and speculative theories concerning consciousness and the mind. I begin by moving slightly beyond physicalism, defending subjective experience as a primary reality and embracing a relational and phenomenological view of consciousness, similar in some respects to that of Protagoras and Buddha. This sort of approach might, I feel, be accommodated alongside an expanded and organismic view of living things. This leads to questions about how consciousness might emerge in the universe, and controversies about whether some form of teleological theory is needed to account for said emergence or whether conventional theories suffice. Thirdly, I examine the free will debate and, since free will is linked to the self and agency, what I term 'deep' and 'shallow' views of said self. Finally, I examine the difficult question of psychic phenomena and whether they may be considered commensurable with current science.

I make no apologies for examining both heterodox theories and controversial human abilities in the course of these discussions. This is partly because, if we are to expand beyond orthodoxy, we must be aware of at least some ordinarily excluded alternatives. In dealing with controversial material, I have tried to be as even-handed as possible, and to present and respect the views of experts with whom I might disagree. One should also be aware that the simple discussion of an idea does not denote unquestioning belief. At the same time, I believe that it is wrong to refrain from discussing areas of interest simply because one is afraid of what others might think, and that free thought should really mean free thought. With these basics out of the way, we can now begin our explorations.

Part One

Historical Context

Chapter One

From Animism to Mechanism

Our quest to understand the human mind is in part driven by the urge to spin stories about ourselves that make sense in light of our current knowledge about biology, evolution and the cosmos. Similar urges seem older than language, and are manifest in every age and culture. Since the dawn of language, human beings have told themselves stories about their origins and place in the universe. The Biblical story of Adam and Eve, the plucking of the fruit and original sin is one such story, but there are many others.

The cosmologist John Barrow sees most mythological accounts as having similar intentions. Pre-scientific world-myths provide 'completeness, confidence, and certainty... Nothing happens by chance. There are neither gaps nor uncertainties. No room for progress; no room for doubt'.[1] These frameworks help provide people with an idea of their position in a culture. They also guide behaviour, and suggest what is and is not possible in terms of physical, social and individual actions.

Although Barrow seeks to contrast such myths with scientific cosmologies, it is useful to see scientific stories as being closely allied to pre-scientific myth.[2] Here, the word is not meant pejoratively but in the philosopher Mary Midgley's sense, as 'imaginative patterns, networks of powerful symbols that suggest particular ways of interpreting the world'.[3] Myths provide meaning, and human beings seem incapable of living without such coherent stories about themselves. This is not a criticism, but an acknowledgment of a need as basic as food, shelter or companionship.

One of the key arguments in this book is that our overarching ideas about consciousness, human nature and our place in the universe can be understood as *myths*. That is, they are coherent (or even incoherent) stories that we weave to understand ourselves. These stories will inevitably go beyond the currently available evidence, because the sorts of results and

1 Barrow, 1991, p. 4.
2 Feyerabend, 1975.
3 Midgley, 2003, p. 1.

evidence science—or any other sort of empiricism—produces can never provide enough pieces to complete the jigsaw puzzle.

On the other hand, it would be quite false to suggest that myths are simply products of the imagination, with no basis in reality. For example, the medieval cosmos was based upon a mix of observation, classical and Christian thought, and served the needs of the medieval people by providing a coherent story for the kind of culture that then existed. We will also see that it began to change as culture changed, and new ideas and evidence about human nature came to light. This is to be expected, because myths are rarely static.

Medieval Self, Medieval Soul

Our ancestors lived in a very different personal and conceptual world from that which we inhabit. Primary sources from this time reveal a people who were moody, volatile and expressive. They were mostly illiterate, spent hours doing boring tasks, and lived in an endless present. They played simple, repetitive games, were attracted to bright colours, and could be very cruel.[4] Knowledge of the past was mostly limited to personal memories. Change was rare, and many people never moved beyond their villages.

Conceptions of the *self* were also very different. As Charles Taylor observed, 'The modern subject is self-defining, where on previous views the subject is defined in relation to a cosmic order'.[5] Medieval people defined themselves primarily in relation to their place in the wider social universe, rather than as atomic individuals who defined themselves.

Medieval people also lacked the solid conceptual barrier separating oneself from the outside universe. People of that time would sometimes credit outside sources with things that we would naturally credit to ourselves. One monk blamed all his sinful thoughts and even his farts on demons.[6] Dreams, erotic imaginings, and even extramarital affairs were also blamed on demons. Medieval people lived in a supernatural world, alive with angels, demons, fairies, werewolves and vampires. Humans had immortal souls that were destined for heaven, hell or purgatory.

Hierarchy was all. Peasants laboured under lords who served the King, whose ultimate authority stemmed from God. This hierarchy was mirrored in nature. The Great Chain of Being ordered the contents of the world, from inanimate matter at the bottom, through plants (which are living things), animals (which are living and sentient), and human beings (which have the capacity for choice as well as life and sentience).[7] The

---

4   Burke, 1985.
5   Taylor, 1975, p. 6.
6   Cohn, 1975.
7   Richards, 2000.

chain was promoted by the Ionian philosopher Aristotle (384–322 BC), whose writings formed the basis of much medieval thought.

The supernatural aspect of this hierarchy is perhaps best illustrated in the Florentine poet Dante's *Divine Comedy*, where the devil sits at the centre of the world at the bottom of a tiered hell, and purgatory and heaven are also ordered in stages up to God. Dante (1265–1321) imagined that human souls would be separated according to specific sins or virtues. As Margeret Wertheim noted, 'the world-picture of the Christian Middle Ages included the spaces of both the living and the dead... The Divine Comedy is the ultimate map of Christian Soul-space'.[8] Even in heaven, hierarchy was all.

This Christian soul-space was fitted around the ancient two-sphere universe. Medieval cosmology imagined an Earth-centred space, enclosed by the ultimate sphere of the stars (the 'two-sphere universe'; one sphere being Earth, the second being the sphere upon which the stars were fixed). A series of concentric crystal 'spheres' held the planets, allowing their motion around the Earth. In this scheme, the Sun was also classed as a 'moving star' that circled the Earth. Beyond this cramped universe was the *Empyrium* and God, who sat enthroned in the space beyond the celestial sphere.

The two-sphere universe was inherited from the ancients. The stars are the most distant things that ancient peoples could see, and they move together, suggesting that they are fixed upon the same surface. The Ancient Greek philosopher Plato of Athens (c.429–347 BC) had suggested that the 'fixed' stars moved on the surface of a sphere. Ancient arguments for a spherical Earth were in part based on the Platonic urge for symmetry. If the universe was a sphere, surely the place upon which humans lived was also spherical.[9] Aristotle incorporated this sphere idea into his cosmology, and his scheme came to dominate medieval thought. Then came Copernicus.

From Two Spheres to Infinity

> Behold now... the man who has pierced the air and penetrated the sky, wended his way amongst the stars and over-passed the margins of the world, who has broken down the imaginary divisions between the spheres... which are described in the false mathematics of blind and popular philosophy.[10]

This passage is a quotation from a dialogue by the ex-monk, heretic and hermetic magus Giordano Bruno (1548–1600). It describes a new vision of the universe, sweeping away the crystal spheres and cramped, outer

---

8 Wertheim, 1999, p. 43.
9 Kuhn, 1957.
10 Quoted in Yates, 1964, p. 237. Translation from Giordano Bruno's *Cena de la cenari* (1584), first dialogue.

sphere of fixed stars. Bruno's effusions were in response to the publication of Nicholas Copernicus's *De Revolutionibus* in 1543, outlining a mathematical scheme that transferred the Sun to the centre of the universe.

To comprehend the conceptual magnitude of this change, it is necessary to understand how completely our world-views *become* reality. Historian of science Thomas Kuhn noted that 'an astronomer who believes in the validity of the two-sphere universe will find that the theory not only provides a convenient summary of the appearances, but that it also *explains* them, enabling him to understand why they are what they are. Words like "explain" and "understand" apparently refer simultaneously to the logical and psychological aspects of conceptual schemes'.[11] For a pre-Copernican astronomer, an Earth-centred universe *was* reality.

Giordano Bruno, however, was a revolutionary. He interpreted Copernicus's theory as eliminating the need for an enclosed universe and imagined himself smashing the crystal on his ascent into the cosmos. Bruno went further, proposing an infinite universe with innumerable worlds, each inhabited. Such thinking seems very modern, and was celebrated as such by many nineteenth-century histories of science, and yet in actual fact, he was anything but a rationalist.

The Animistic Universe

Bruno was emphatically not a 'modern' thinker defying the 'darkness' of medieval thought. Koyne observed that 'Bruno's world-view is vitalistic, magical; his planets are animated beings that move freely through space of their own accord...'[12] The heliocentric universe just happened to accord with Bruno's interpretation of Hermetic philosophy, where the Sun was conceived as a secondary god, and it was appropriate that the Earth should revolve around a god.

Animism was central to medieval thought. Aristotle's universe was also animistic, and he ascribed intentions to plants and rocks. Natural phenomena were often explained in terms of sympathies and attractions between various natural substances. For example, Marsilio Ficino wrote that the parts of the world 'are united among themselves in the community of a single nature. From their communal relationship a common love is born'.[13] Even Johann Kepler (1571–1630), the astronomer and convinced Copernican, followed magical ideas when devising his laws of planetary motion.

Medieval views of causation were very different from modern views. Plato had believed that the reality we can see and touch was secondary to

---

11 Kuhn, 1957, p. 39.
12 Koyne, 1958, *From the Closed World to the Infinite Universe*, New York, p. 54. Quoted in Yates, 1964, p. 244.
13 Marsilio Ficino, *Commentaire sur le Banquet de Platon*, trans. Marcel, 1956. Quoted in Midgley, 2001, p. 58.

an unseen, primary world. His famous cave parable illustrates this idea. In this, prisoners in the cave are tied so they can only see shadows flickering, which give only the most indirect clues about the world beyond. These prisoners believe the shadows to be the only reality, and never guess the true nature of the cosmos.

To Plato, mathematical propositions like Pythagoras' theorem were true but not part of the physical world. He thought that such mathematical proofs existed in a separate, perfect world. Physical representations of triangles, circles, cubes or spheres could only approximate the perfection of the unseen world. Concepts such as 'beauty' or 'truth' also existed as perfect forms.

The idea of an unseen world that sits behind and influences the 'real' one is known as *hylomorphism*, a combination of the Greek *hyle* ('matter') and *morphe* ('form'). According to this view, every natural form consists of two intrinsic principles, one potential, matter and one actual, or substantial form.[14] It is as if there is a universe of blueprints sitting behind the observed world of physical forms.

Plato's views are the foundation stone upon which Western mathematics and science are laid, despite the fact that they are rooted in Pythagorean mysticism. Alfred North Whitehead was not exaggerating by much when he wrote that 'the safest general characterization of the European philosophical tradition is that it consists of a series of footnotes to Plato'.[15]

Plato actually split reality into *three* different worlds; the physical world, the abstract ideal world, and the mental world. Like the physical world, the mental realm was also held to be secondary to this unseen world of perfect forms.

In the *Phaedo*, he used arguments for Ideal Forms to support his belief in an immortal soul or psyche. This psyche was split into three subsections; the epithymia or appetite, the thymos ('spirited'), and nous or logos (reason). He thought that this soul existed before birth, and after death transmigrated to a different body.[16]

Although Plato remained a key influence in Western thought, Aristotle rejected his notion of an ideal world in favour of a theory that each substance could be analysed in terms of matter and its form. He proposed that each object had four causes; the material, efficient, formal, and final.[17] Appleyard illustrates this with a house analogy. The bricks and mortar would be the material cause, the efficient cause would be the building of the house, the formal cause the design or blueprint, and the final cause the creation of the object.

---

14 http://www.britannica.com/EBchecked/topic/279305/hylomorphism accessed on 21/09/09.
15 Quoted in Gardner, 1985, p. 3.
16 Russell, 1946/2004.
17 Russell, 1946/2004; Appleyard, 1992.

The material and final cause are the most relevant here. A brass statue could be analysed as both brass and its physical form or structure. But even before it is shaped, the brass holds the potential to become a statue.

This theory also held for living things. So as the brass holds the potential to be a statue, an acorn contains the potential to become a fully-grown oak. He also saw everything in nature as having a purpose. This sort of theory is also known as teleological (teleology), which is the idea that everything develops towards a final cause.

According to Aristotle, the form of an object, animal, plant or person was also its soul. Aristotle thought that this form gave an object its nature and that unformed matter was an abstraction that couldn't really exist. However, this implied that when an object or organism lost its particular form, then logically it would also lose its soul, which precluded life after death. This was a significant problem for medieval Christian scholars, who embraced Plato's doctrine of the eternal soul. Aristotle's rejection of Plato's ideas resulted in one of the great debates in medieval scholasticism.

Aristotle's ideas represent a variant, rather than a break, from hylomorphism. This ancient doctrine can be seen as an alternative theory of cause-and-effect, which was increasingly regarded with suspicion as we move from medieval to early modern times.

The Birth of Modern Science

Medieval science was, in Roger Bacon's words, 'the handmaiden of Theology'.[18] Bacon (1214-1292) was a thirteenth-century Franciscan brother and one of the founders of experimental science. He also thought that science could aid the interpretation of scripture. However, this view, which emphasized both the compatibility of science and religion and a mostly passive admiration of nature, did not survive the end of the medieval era.

Instead, the early modern founders of science emphasized the *control* of nature. The historical literature is full of passages that describe Nature as a female to be pursued, fought, courted, 'put to the question' (tortured), and forced to confess 'all that lay in her most intimate recesses'.[19] Francis Bacon (1561-1626) criticized the Aristotelians as being impotent before nature, never capturing the errant female.[20] Nature was characterized as a seductive female that must be aggressively tamed by men.

There are several possible sources for this attitude. Magicians like Bruno had also sought to control the physical cosmos, and Yates suggests that a combination of this very magical attitude with Greek rationalism and Baconian Empiricism helped kick-start the scientific revolution.

---

18 Quoted in Wertheim, 1999, p. 51.
19 Quoted in Midgley, 1992, p. 77.
20 *Op. cit.*, p. 77.

The Rise of Cosmopolis and the Cartesian Split

The seventeenth and eighteenth centuries saw the rise of a new vision of the world that sought to eliminate the occult and mysterious, and understand the world by rigorous mathematical reasoning as opposed to divine revelation. This movement, known as the Enlightenment, was in part founded by Rene Descartes (1596-1650).

Descartes wished to create a new, objective science that was untainted by opinion and subjective elements, but to do this he had to split the world into two. The observer and the observed were separated, a split that Descartes had deduced from first principles. He began by considering what would still exist if he had no senses or if there was a deceiver who wished to feed him false information via his sensory organs. He concluded that 'I am not more than a thing that thinks, that is to say a mind or soul...'[21] This was the only thing of which he felt certain.

There was a heavy price to pay for this split. On the one side was a philosophical system based on purely mechanical principles, and on the other was a purely mental world that could not be reduced to these mechanical principles.

This basic split was clearly inspired by both Platonic and Aristotelian thought. In his *Physiognomics*, Aristotle (or one of his pupils; authorship is unclear) had stated that 'soul and body... react sympathetically upon each other; a change in state of the soul produces a change in the shape of the body, and conversely: a change in the shape of the body produces a change in the state of the soul'.[22]

Descartes' immaterial mind was of a very specific sort, and was seen as the seat of reason. He characterized *understanding* as forming a set of symbolic representations that accurately described and predicted the phenomena of the observed, external world. These descriptions were built up out of primitive elements or ideas.[23] A modern analogy of this is the 'pure' symbol shuffling of a computer as it completes a chess game; and Dreyfus suggests that early attempts at Artificial Intelligence were inspired by Descartes' picture of the mind as a symbol-shuffler.

This basic idea of symbol-association was developed by subsequent generations of philosophers. An example of this development was *associationism*, a doctrine developed by philosopher David Hume (1711-1776) and the English psychologist David Hartley (1705-1757). The English philosopher John Locke (1632-1704) also proposed a variant of associationism. This doctrine was atomistic because ideas were thought to be discrete entities that associated within the psyche according to certain laws. This led to a law-based view of mental life in general that mirrored the atomistic,

---

21 In Descartes, 1997, p. 144.
22 Quoted in Popper & Eccles, 1977, p. 176.
23 Dreyfus, 1992.

Emotion and Memory Excluded and the Interaction Problem

Descartes excluded both emotion and memories from his isolated, reasoning mind. He believed that human beings were a mix of reasoning minds and unreasoning (and materially caused) bodily emotions. In his *Treatise of the Passions*, he wrote that the experience of being 'at the mercy of one's emotions' meant that one's (mental) rationality was overpowered by one's (physical, deterministic) emotional make-up.[25] But the reasoning mind was still superior, because it stood outside the physical universe.

Descartes also proposed a purely mechanical system for memory. Memory traces are 'nothing else than the circumstances that the pores of the brain through which the spirits [fluids] have already taken their course on presentation of the object, have thereby acquired a greater facility than the rest to be opened again the same way by the spirits which come to them...'[26] This recalled the ancient idea that memory traces were like impressions in wax or clay. So some aspects of phenomena we would term mental were accounted for in mechanical ways.

Human beings were the only living things to possess true minds. Animals (and women) were only mechanisms. Animal systems were, he believed, totally deterministic and mechanical.[27] For this reason, Descartes suggested that it might one day be possible to build mechanical animals or golden wind-up birds that sang and behaved just like the real thing.[28]

However, it remained very unclear how the substance of such an isolated mind could possibly interact with the substance of brute matter. Various successors to Descartes proposed ways round this problem, but these often invoked mind/body parallelism not unlike the Aristotelian statement of the soul affecting the body and vice versa.[29] This 'interaction problem' was to echo down the centuries to the present day and was something that Descartes never really solved.

---

24 Philosophy Professor webpage: http://www.philosophyprofessor.com/philosophies/associationism.php accessed on 21/09/09.
25 Toulmin, 1990.
26 Quoted in Sheldrake, 1988, p. 160.
27 Sparks, 1982.
28 Sahtouris, 1999.
29 Popper & Eccles, 1977.

MIND	MATTER
Interacts with brain via pineal gland	Mechanical 'pushing' causation only
Thinking, non-spatial, private	Non-thinking, extended in space, public
Logic, reason	Emotion, memories
ACCEPTS	**REJECTS**
Biblical miracles	Aristotelian & Platonic causation
	Most supernatural (ghosts, demons, fairies)

Table 1. Descartes' Conceptual Scheme.

Descartes' *ontology* appears a little strange to modern eyes (*ontology* is the study of the nature of being or existence, and includes questions like 'into what categories, if any, can we sort existing things?')[30] In this case, Descartes decided that there were two fundamental sorts of 'things', mind and matter, but he classified some of the things we would probably count as mind — memory and emotion — as matter. Descartes' decision was to have long-term conceptual consequences in the study of both the mind and life, which we will examine more closely in the next chapter. But first, we need to understand better his conception of the physical universe.

Descartes' External Universe

In Descartes' view, the external, physical universe ran on laws that were strictly determined from the time of the creation. He claimed that 'there exists nothing in the whole of nature which cannot be explained in terms of purely corporeal causes, totally devoid of mind and thought'.[31]

This is one form of the closure principle, which denies the possibility of non-material entities affecting anything in the natural world. This meant that one could not use an 'act of God' as an explanation of natural phenomena. But Descartes went further, explicitly exorcizing Aristotelian animism. 'There exist no occult forces in stones or plants. There are no amazing and marvellous sympathies and antipathies…'[32] The sole example of this type of interaction was, as we have seen, between the brain and the mind. At a stroke, the cosmos moved from being Aristotelian, animated and living to Cartesian, mechanistic and dead.

---

30 http://en.wikipedia.org/wiki/Ontology accessed on 11/11/09.
31 Quoted in Midgley, 1992, p. 84.
32 Descartes, *The Principles of Philosophy*, in Alquie (ed.) *Oevres Philosphiques*. Quoted in Midgley, 2001, p. 59.

Descartes and another Enlightenment philosopher, Thomas Hobbes (1588–1679) assumed that matter or 'extended substance' fills space and can push another body. As Popper notes, 'push, or impact, becomes the explanation of causal interaction ("action by contact"). The world is a clockwork mechanism of bodies that push each other like cogwheels'.[33]

In Descartes' scheme, this 'pushing' would be the only permitted form of causation, but this entirely mechanical world-picture never completely worked. For a start, the concept of gravitation, proposed by Sir Isaac Newton (1642–1727), was not strictly speaking mechanical because it implied 'action at a distance', which was the sort of thinking that Descartes had sought to abolish. The mutual 'attraction' of heavenly bodies was not at first considered an explanation at all, but the evocation of an 'occult force'.

Descartes himself favoured a system of 'vortices' to explain planetary movements, but he could not really get it to work. Newton's gravitation theory was subsumed into the clockwork universe because it worked better than any of its competitors. So even from the start, a purely mechanistic world-picture proved to be impractical, and some 'occult' elements were needed to get it to work. As Popper noted, brute materialism was forced to transcend itself.[34]

Despite this occult taint, Newton's theories of motion became a keystone of science. At a stroke, thousands of years' worth of observations in both the astronomical and terrestrial realms were reduced to a few simple laws of motion. It was a triumph of both reductionism and materialism, and showed how powerful science could be as a tool for understanding the universe.[35] The picture that emerged was of a universe that could ultimately be understood by reason and controlled observation.

A Political Agenda

In the seventeenth century, there were good reasons for favouring reason over emotion, or thinking over feeling. Descartes formed his views during a period of long, bloody, religious wars, at a time when people desperately needed truths that were free of the strictures of religious beliefs. His 'Quest for Certainty' was no abstract proposal, but a response to a specific historical challenge, which was the political, theological and social chaos of his time. The Enlightenment was similarly seen as a *social* programme that provided a new vision of a rational society as well as nature.[36]

Descartes was by no means the only advocate of such social reform. A number of the founders of the Scientific Revolution, like Hobbes, Bacon, Leibniz and Locke, promoted variants. The common trend was the cre-

---

33 Popper & Eccles, 1977, p. 6.
34 Popper & Eccles, 1977.
35 Jones, 1982.
36 Toulmin, 1990.

ation of abstract, eternal world-pictures which could be understood in explicit, mechanical terms and which transcended the messiness and uncertainty of everyday life.

The allure of this picture was strong, and was consolidated over the course of the eighteenth and early nineteenth centuries. Perhaps the ultimate expression of this mechanistic theory can be found in Laplace's demon. Pierre-Simon, Marquis de Laplace (1749–1827) envisioned in 1814 a thought experiment involving an intellect who knew the precise position and momentum of all the atoms in the universe. This intellect, Laplace argued, could in theory work out the complete past and future of the cosmos by an application of Newton's laws.

At the beginning of the chapter we quoted the cosmologist John Barrow, who stated that some of the cardinal characteristics of pre-scientific myth were completeness, confidence, and certainty, that nothing happened by chance, that there were neither gaps nor uncertainties: 'No room for progress; no room for doubt.'

Although Barrow meant to contrast this with a scientific outlook, where there *is* supposed to be room for doubt, uncertainty and progress, these same attributes also apply to Laplace's Newtonian universe, where there is also no room for doubt or uncertainties and where nothing happens by chance. Despite significant revisions of our ideas of causation, Laplace's deterministic dream — or nightmare — remains influential to this day.

In this chapter, we have moved from the closed, medieval two-sphere universe into an open universe that runs like a clockwork machine. The price was the exclusion of mental attributes from a cosmos that simply could not accommodate them. This split was to have serious repercussions when natural philosophers turned their attention to physiology and the brain.

Chapter Two

Vital Fluids, Darwin and Mechanical Men

It is easy to underestimate the long-term consequences of the Cartesian split between mind and matter, and many of the debates of the eighteenth and nineteenth centuries can really only be understood with reference to this divide. Two debates should be highlighted here. The first is between mechanists and vitalists, and the second is over the place of specifically human minds in nature. The first debate was between those who accepted Descartes' assertion that non-human living things were pure mechanism and those who viewed organisms as mechanisms who also possessed an insubstantial but essential vital force or soul. The second focused mainly on the place of the human mind in nature. As Wozniak states, 'the history of philosophizing about the relation of body and mind since Descartes is the history of attempts to escape the Cartesian impasse',[1] and the various nineteenth-century approaches to the mind/body dilemma were attempts to deal with this impasse. The key point is that both sides in these debates tacitly accepted the fundamental Cartesian type-difference between *mechanisms* and *qualities* like mental states, intentions and purposiveness.

These debates became more complex and involved as studies by physiologists began to demonstrate apparently close connections between the mind and the brain. Some even thought that precise mental attributes could be localized at very specific points in the brain. At the same time, the mechanical understanding of matter seemed to preclude the possibility of purposive, intentional behaviour being 'real'.

First, we need to understand some changes in scientific culture that occurred between the time of Descartes and the 'second' scientific age of the early nineteenth century. The Enlightenment had conceived of the universe as a system that could be entirely and explicitly understood by rational means. By the early nineteenth century, the mysterious and obscure

---

1   Wozniak, 1995.

side of nature had been rediscovered. One particular obscurity was the inner nature of human beings. Another was the basic nature of life itself.

Romanticism, the Vitalism Debate and the Growing Diversity of Science

The popular stereotype of Romanticism is of a movement that was opposed to science and reason; thus Keats' lament that to unweave, or understand rationally, a rainbow, is to 'clip an angel's wings'. But consider this quote:

> Though we can perceive, develop, and even produce by means of our instruments of experiment, an almost infinite variety of minute phenomena, yet we are incapable of determining the general laws by which they are governed; and in attempting to define them, we are lost through sublime imaginings concerning unknown agencies.[2]

Although this invocation of the sublime or mysterious in science can be seen as essentially Romantic, the speaker is not a scientific 'nay-sayer', but Sir Humphrey Davy (1778–1829), one of the foremost scientists of his time.

The relationship between Romanticism, science and the Enlightenment is far more complex than commonly supposed. By the time Romanticism emerged, in the late eighteenth and early nineteenth century, the world had seen the French Revolution, where many had been guillotined in the name of a new world dominated by the Goddess Reason. To the Romantics, it was unclear whether this revolution exemplified or parodied Enlightenment ideals.[3]

Romanticism is better seen as an encompassing movement that, whilst criticizing the excesses of Enlightenment thought, nevertheless remained in uneasy agreement with the liberating ideals of progress through rationalism, equality and learning. It is thus quite possible to conceive of a Romantic sort of science, and in fact the first person to refer to a 'second scientific revolution' was the poet Coleridge in his *Philosophical Lectures* of 1819.[4] So the stereotype of Romantics as 'anti-science' is not really fair.[5] It *would* be fair to say that the vision of some of the more Romantically inclined scientists differed from their fellows. These differences become clear when one examines the debates over putative life forces.

In this period, the nature of life—or the difference between living and dead matter—was a cause of continuing speculation. The experiments of Luigi Galvini (1737–1798) provide an example of this. Galvini had noticed that the shock from an electric ray fish was similar to that from a Leyden jar, and between 1780 and 1786 he experimented on frogs' legs, which

---

2   Sir Humphrey Davy, quoted in Heath & Boreham, 1999, p. 19.
3   Heath & Boreham, 1999.
4   Quoted in Holmes, 2008.
5   See Dawkins, 1998, for a recent characterization of Romantic poets in this way.

would jerk when the nerves and muscles were brought into contact with two types of metal. Thus were born speculations that the 'vital fluids' were related to electricity.[6]

These theories spread to fiction, including Mary Shelley's novel *Frankenstein* (1818), where the monster is brought to life by electricity. Mary Shelley was inspired to write the novel after discussions with Lord Byron and the poet Shelley concerning galvanism. That night, she had a dream in which she saw 'a pale student of the unhallowed arts kneeling beside the thing that he had put together'. She saw 'the hideous phantasm of a man stretched out, and then, on the working of some powerful engine, show signs of life...'[7] In the novel, the young Frankenstein is first inspired by lightning striking a tree, so the association of vital forces and electricity — at the time commonly characterized as a fluid — seem clear.

Mesmeric Influences

A similar sort of fluidic metaphor inspired the activities of the controversial Viennese physician, Franz Anton Mesmer (1734-1815). Mesmer is today widely regarded as a crank, and yet the craze he inspired can also be seen as part of the prehistory of analytical psychology.

Mesmer believed that he had found a fundamental type of fluidic energy that was subtle enough to have previously escaped detection. In 1779, Mesmer speculated that this fluid pervaded the cosmos, Earth and all life. It was 'so continuous as not to admit of a vacuum, and incomparably subtle'.[8] In proposing this fluid, Mesmer was putting forward a specifically *physical* theory, compatible with the physics of the time, and was actually suspicious of what he saw as occult or magical elements creeping into the Mesmeric movement.[9] He thought that 'animal magnetism' governed the health and well-being of every individual.

At first, Mesmer used magnets to affect his patients' inner force, but eventually he discovered that he could affect cures by stroking or making hand-passes across the patients' body.[10] The Mesmerists can claim a remarkable number of cures, no matter how these were achieved, and many of these cures were worked upon patients who had proven unresponsive to more conventional treatments.

Mesmerism entered a new phase with the discovery that the treatment could induce a trance-like state not unlike somnambulism or sleep-walking. Those in this state were often insensible to pain, even during surgical operations. In 1784 the Marquis de Puységur, a disciple of Mesmer's, was

6 Burke, 1985.
7 From the Introduction to the 1818 edition of *Frankenstein*.
8 Quoted in Inglis, 1992, p. 142.
9 Crabtree, 1993.
10 Gauld, 1992.

treating a 23-year-old peasant by the name of Victor Race, who suffered from an inflammation of the lungs. Victor responded by entering a trance, during which time his personality significantly changed from a dull-witted peasant to a fluent and articulate individual who even took over the management of his own case.[11] In this state, he even advised on Puységur's other cases and exhibited apparent clairvoyance during his trances.

In 1784, Puységur published *Memoire pour servir à l'histoire et à l'établissement du magnétisme animal*, in which he detailed his researches. In this, he described five characteristics of 'magnetic sleep':[12]

- *Sleep-walking consciousness*: Victor's magnetically induced conditions seemed very similar to sleep-walking, or a state that was neither sleep nor waking.
- *Rapport and suggestibility*: the state allowed a close rapport between subject and magnetizer; it was as if their will became one.
- *Lack of memory and divided consciousness*: the subject rarely remembered what had occurred during the sessions, but there was continuity of memory in that the somnambulist would remember waking states and during the magnetic states. So the sleep-walker's memory chain is separate from the memory chain of the waking person. The personality also altered significantly during the magnetic states.
- *Paranormal phenomena*: Victor exhibited many examples of apparent clairvoyance.
- *Healing effects*: Puységur used the state psychotherapeutically and for providing relief during the healing process.

Crabtree notes that unlike Mesmer, Puységur emphasized the psychological aspects of the 'magnetic sleep', and Puységur's writings show that he was equivocal about the existence of the fluid. We may also note the occurrence of many features of hypnotism, a term coined by James Braid (1795–1860) who had observed Mesmerism in 1841, but was sceptical of the fluid theory. He sought instead to explain magnetic sleep as a psychologically induced psycho-physiological state.[13]

Although it might seem strange today, Mesmerism was more than a fringe medicine fad, and in some ways was a forerunner of dynamic psychiatry.[14] However, it retains a poor reputation in part because of the conclusions of a Royal Commission of 1784, led by Benjamin Franklin, who conducted some experiments and concluded that the Mesmeric effect was probably due to the 'power of the imagination'.[15]

---

11 Gauld, 1992.
12 Detailed in Crabtree, 1993, chapter three.
13 Crabtree, 1993; Gauld, 1992.
14 Ellenburger, 1970/1994; Crabtree, 1993.
15 Quoted in Beloff, 1993, p. 35.

However, Gauld argues that this cannot be the whole answer. Many of Mesmerism's patients were rejects from a medical profession who could do nothing for them. If the credentials and status of the doctors did not work on these patients, then why were the Mesmerists successful?[16] Gauld's speculation is that maybe the 'stroking' movement triggered the release of the brain's natural opiates and so calmed the patients. And the commission's conclusions do not explain the numerous reported instances of clairvoyance and other apparently paranormal abilities.

Abernathy the Vitalist

The story of Mesmerism and its handling by the scientific authorities of its day is a curious one that finds a parallel with the vitalism debate. This was sparked by a series of lectures by John Abernathy (1764–1831). Abernathy was a physician and surgeon at Bart's hospital in London, and he proposed a theory of human life based upon an unseen life force. This 'Vitality' was a 'subtle, mobile, invisible substance, super-added to the evident structure of muscles'.[17] He compared this substance to the magnetism exhibited by iron, and suggested that this force must have been added by a power outside man.

Abernathy's ideas were denounced by one of his pupils, William Lawrence. Lawrence attacked his former master on the grounds that science must avoid 'clouds of fears and hopes, desires and aversions', that it should 'discern objects clearly', and dispel myth and 'absurd fables'. He further asserted that 'The theological doctrine of the soul… has nothing to do with the physiological question…'[18]

Lawrence was attempting to remove any question of a soul—something that he identified with religion—from the realm of science. So the vitalism debate should be seen as far more than a debate over technical details; the fight was over the fundamental nature of human beings. It was also a conflict over the blurry divide between religion and science. Abernathy's ideas were seen as an attempt to bring the soul into the scientific arena, something that Lawrence fiercely resisted. But once more, the lines of battle were drawn on thoroughly Cartesian lines. Questions of physiology, which were essentially mechanical questions, were perceived as 'scientific', whereas questions of animation and vitality (beyond mechanical movements) were seen as attributes of another realm.

Vitalism did not die after 1820. The chemist Liebig made a vitalist statement in 1844, and a form of vitalism was championed by Hans Dreisch at the beginning of the twentieth century.[19] Rupert Sheldrake's theory of

---

16 Beloff, 1993; Gauld, 1992.
17 Quoted in Holmes, 2008, p. 309.
18 Quoted in Holmes, 2008, p. 313.
19 Sheldrake, 1981/2009.

morphic resonance, propounded in 1981, can also be characterized as a sort of vitalistic theory.[20] However, debates of this sort were increasingly to become a *leitmotif* as nineteenth-century materialism grew in strength and sought to exclude such speculations. Instead of accommodating the purposive aspects of organisms, some believed that it might be possible to eliminate purpose altogether.

Machine-Men

One attempt to do without a 'vital spark' can be seen in La Mettrie's *L'Homme Machine* (1747), which expounded the idea that humans were nothing but mechanisms. This basic idea is actually a very old one; the first author to come up with the idea of robots was Homer.[21] Like Lawrence, La Mettrie also aimed to exclude theological discussions of the soul and redefine the mind in a way that could be handled by physicians and surgeons.

Although he saw man as mechanical, La Mettrie did not deny conscious experience. He also believed that given sufficient training, apes and maybe other animals could learn human traits like language.[22] This idea might in part be derived from the ideas of the Enlightenment philosopher John Locke (1632-1704), who believed that the human being entered the world as a *tabula rasa*, or blank slate, and if humans were a blank slate, who was to say that other animals were not? Those opposing such a doctrine were known as *nativists*, who believed that humans were born with many or most of their faculties in-built.

Investigating the Brain

La Mettrie's basic conclusion that the mind was a side-effect or product of brute matter came to seem more plausible as physiological experiments on the nervous system advanced. In 1812, Jean Cesar Legallis identified the region of the medulla essential for respiration, and Marie-Jean Pierre Flourens (1794-1867) performed a number of experiments on animals that showed that behaviour was tied to a functioning nervous system.

Flourens gave the following account of a pigeon with no cerebral lobes: 'It held itself upright very well; it flew when it was thrown into the air, it walked when it pushed; the iris of its eye was very mobile but nevertheless it did not see; it did not hear, it never moved spontaneously, it nearly always assumed the appearance of a sleeping or drowsy animal...'[23] From

---

20 Sheldrake, 1981/2009; 1988. Although Sheldrake terms his theory organismic rather than vitalist.
21 Popper & Eccles, 1977.
22 Hothersall, 2004.
23 Quoted in Hothersall, 2004, p. 97.

experiments like this, Flourens concluded that the cerebral lobes were not only the seat of perception but also the area of will and memory.[24]

Flourens' conclusions were shown to apply to human beings by an accident on a railroad construction site. On September 13th 1848, near Cavendish in Vermont, Phineas P. Gage was the victim of a terrible accident where a tamping iron was blown through his skull by gunpowder. Although the local doctors found the story initially hard to believe, Gage had an entry and exit wound to match the story witnesses told, and the iron was found, complete with brain-matter.[25]

Gage not only survived this accident, but also was conscious and began to talk only a few minutes afterwards. But the accident had a terrible, dramatic effect on his personality. Before, he had been described as hard-working, pleasant, and shrewd. Afterwards he became fitful, irreverent and indulged in 'gross profanities'. He lost his regard for his fellows, and often devised plans which were quickly abandoned. His friends came to see him as a different person. Hothersall notes that these characteristics are typical in people with frontal lobe damage; such people lack foresight, are highly distractible, frivolous and unreliable. But Gage's unfortunate accident cemented Flourens' conclusion that the brain was the organ of the mind.[26]

Bumps on Heads

Two German physicians, Franz Gall (1758–1828) and Johann Spurzheim (1776–1832) had anticipated Flourens' conclusion in the previous generation by inventing the 'science' of phrenology. If the brain was the organ of the mind, with different faculties located in different areas on its surface, then surely the relative strength of such faculties would be reflected in the skull that overlaid it? These faculties included cleverness, educability, sense of purpose, vanity, tendency to steal, instinct for murder, numeracy, poetry, amativeness, and so on.[27]

Phrenology is today regarded as pseudoscience, but it was very popular in its day and also spurred some neurophysiological experiments. At the time phrenology was popular, there was little practical need for medicine and surgery to examine the brain's function and structure, but the phrenologists' claims focused attention these areas. This attention led to the

---

24 Hothersall, 2004.
25 Hothersall, 2004.
26 Hothersall, 2004.
27 Burke, 1985. It's quite striking to compare the phrenological faculties with those supposedly determined by our genes, which include homosexuality, alcoholism, criminality, and even homelessness! (Rose, 1997.) One suspects that similar conceptual assumptions are being applied in both cases.

discovery of Broca's and Wernike's areas on the surface of the brain, areas that are associated with language production and comprehension.[28]

Neurologist Pierre-Paul Broca (1824–1880) made his discovery in 1861. One of his patients had lost his speech and, after his death, Broca performed an autopsy that showed a cavity the size of a small egg on the side of his brain. A second patient with the same symptoms showed damage to the same area. The conclusion that Broca came to was that speech production was linked to this specific part of the brain.[29]

This conclusion was itself controversial, in part because of the association of localization with phrenology, and it was at first rejected by the more conservative researchers who thought the brain always acted as a whole. Points were scored on both sides, and the controversy over language localization continues to this day.

Evolution

In the second half of the nineteenth century the quest for naturalistic accounts of mental functioning took on a new urgency because of the rise of evolutionary theory. Darwin's theory of natural selection was foreshadowed in a number of places, including by his grandfather, Erasmus Darwin, in a poem of 1803. Erasmus had written how 'organic life beneath the shoreless waves/Was born and nurs'd in ocean's pearly caves', and how 'as successive generations bloom/New powers and larger limbs assume'.[30] The idea that life changes over time, first proposed by the Ancient Greeks, had re-emerged.

It is worth mentioning the quasi-theological idea of progressivism because it was remarkably close to later, teleological evolutionary theories, including those of Frederick Myers, Henri Bergson and Tielhard de Chardin. Progressivism was based upon the observation of the 'progress' in the fossil record from simple invertebrates early on to more complex animals later.[31] Everything in existence had developed from inferior forms — life from a protoplasmic globule to coral, fish, reptiles, mammals, to man, and then maybe on to something superior. Robert Chambers' book *The Vestiges of the Natural History of Creation*, which promoted progressivism, was a bestseller when it was published in 1844, fifteen years before Darwin.[32]

Darwin's theory had significance because it provided a mechanism for evolution that seemed to preclude the need for divine intervention or an ordering, progressive force. Darwin's theory was described in his 1859

---

28 Burke, 1985; see also Hothersall, 2004.
29 Hothersall, 2004.
30 Quoted in Elsdon-Baker, 2009, p. 25.
31 Elsdon-Baker, 2009.
32 Elsdon-Baker, 2009.

book, *The Origin of Species*, and utilized an idea put forth by Thomas Malthus in the 1798 *Essay on the Principle of Population*. In this gloomy essay, Malthus argued that population would always overrun food supply because of the way in which humans reproduced, and that famine was inevitable.

Darwin's theory follows from Malthus's observation that population will always grow geometrically and inevitably outstrip its food supply. At this point, many of the organisms will die. But 'how will [this] struggle for existence', Darwin asked, 'act in regard to variation?'[33] His conclusion was that in the struggle for resources, any individuals with an advantage, however slight, would tend to survive and reproduce. 'This preservation of favourable variations and the rejection of injurious variations', he wrote, 'I call natural selection.'[34]

Darwin's discovery/invention of natural selection had serious implications for those of religious faith, because it eliminated the need for a 'designer' of organisms. Darwin suggested that natural selection could account for much of the variation that could be seen in that natural world. It could also account for the progression in the fossil record, where simple animals were found in ancient rocks and more complex ones in newer rocks.

There was also mounting evidence of the great antiquity of man, which contradicted the Biblical account of creation. Shortly before, human remains of great antiquity had been discovered in a cave near Dusseldorf, which had been named 'Neanderthal' after the valley in which they had been found.[35] The implications were clear: human beings were not part of a special creation, but had evolved as part of nature.

Many religious people reacted to the theory in horror. For example, the 1871 *Family Herald* stated that 'Society must fall to pieces if Darwinism is true'.[36] In the States, the theory triggered a surge of fundamentalism and public baptisms. Outside the sphere of religion, Darwinism inspired numerous political and social movements; George Bernard Shaw commented that 'Darwin had the luck to please anybody with an axe to grind…'[37] – a statement that remains true to this day.

X-club Legacy

One of those with an 'axe to grind' was Thomas Henry Huxley. Huxley was known as 'Darwin's Bulldog', and had defended evolution against religion at the great debate in Oxford in 1860. Huxley's ambitions went

---

33 Darwin, 1859, p. 63.
34 Darwin, 1859, p. 64.
35 Burke, 1985.
36 Quoted in Burke, 1985, p. 260.
37 Quoted in Burke, 1985, p. 261.

beyond the defence of science against religion. Along with eight others, he formed the 'X-club' (one of the members of which was Herbert Spencer, the social Darwinian who coined the term 'survival of the fittest'). The X-club promoted science as superior to any other way of knowing the universe. And Huxley claimed that science could achieve 'dominion over the whole realm of the intellect'.[38] This group even advocated a 'Church of Science' that might take over the functions of religion.

These extreme views were *not* the orthodox view of science, and were contested by a number of Huxley's peers.[39] However, the Huxleyan idea that mental phenomena were causally ineffectual epiphenomena, like the sound from a steam-whistle, was to become very influential in scientific thought.

The Mind as Steam-Whistle

If humans had evolved by natural selection within a mechanical universe, then it followed that their minds were a product of mechanism only. Allied to this problem was the continued headache of mental causation, still unresolved from Descartes' day. How could something as insubstantial as thought possibly move or influence matter?[40]

Huxley's response to this question was that it didn't. In 1874, he advanced the idea that mental events are caused by brain events, but are themselves incapable of causing anything: 'Consciousness... would appear to be related to the mechanism of [the] body, simply as a... [side] product of its working as the [sound of a] steam-whistle which accompanies the work of a locomotive... is without influence upon its machinery.'[41] Just as a steam-whistle is an effect of the steam locomotive's operations and lacks any causal influence on it, so mental events are mere side-effects of the brain mechanisms underlying behaviour.

The problem with Huxley's solution was that the view of the mind as causally ineffective or even non-existent clashes violently with everyday experience. Human beings seem purposive and wilful, and we at least appear to make decisions that directly affect the world all the time. But this language implies that mental phenomena are themselves causal factors in a universe.

This sort of thinking was for Huxley just wrong: 'If anybody says that the will influences matter, the statement is not untrue, but it is nonsense...'[42] In fact, by the late nineteenth century, it was quite possible to construct an unremittingly gloomy cosmology where humans were the

---

38 Quoted in Wallace & Hodel, 2008.
39 Noakes, 2007.
40 Emily Williams Kelly, in Kelly *et al.*, 2007, chapter two.
41 Huxley, 1901, p. 240. Quoted in Popper & Eccles, 1977, p. 72.
42 Huxley, 1887/1892. Quoted in Kelly *et al.*, 2007, p. 53.

helpless product of chance in a cold, mechanical universe. William James summarized (whilst not endorsing) this pessimistic viewpoint thus:

> Science... has ended by utterly repudiating the personal view... Our Solar System with its harmonies, is seen now as but one passing case of a certain sort of moving equilibrium in the heavens, realized by a local accident in an appalling wilderness of worlds here no life can exist... The Darwinian notion of chance production, and subsequent destruction, speedy or deferred, applies to the largest as well as smallest facts... Our private selves are like those bubbles,—epiphenomena... their destinies weigh nothing and determine nothing in the world's irremediable current of events.[43]

Conclusions like these would be contested in a number of different ways by several important thinkers in psychology. The alternative world-views that they formed in opposition would include some of the richest psychologies in the history of science.

Descartes' Boundary

The boundary that Descartes erected between the world of mind and matter may have been expedient in terms of the creation of a mechanistic theory of everything, but it had the result of effectively excluding mental, and a good portion of biological, phenomena from science. This dilemma became ever more acute as science became increasingly committed to the mechanistic view. Rosen, whose work we will encounter later, observed that this commitment to a basically Newtonian epistemology ran so deep that it remains closely identified with science to this day.[44] Indeed, to many, a Newtonian kind of epistemology *is* the only possible science.[45]

The price was that this created a dilemma concerning anything that did not fit neatly into such a restricted universe. We have seen that some suggested nineteenth-century solutions were a reduction of said problematic phenomena to mechanism, the addition of a different kind of 'stuff' to life that contained the excluded phenomena, or, as in Huxley's solution, the rendering of the problematic phenomena to acausal by-products of the primary mechanism. But however this dilemma was resolved, *each party tacitly accepted the sharp divide between phenomena that could be accounted of in mechanical terms and those that could not*. This dilemma, with accompanying tacit acceptance, would continue to play out as psychology came into its own in the latter half of the nineteenth century.

---

43 James, 1902/1985, p. 491.
44 Rosen, 1991.
45 See Metzinger, 2009, for a statement along these lines. See also the discussion in chapter fourteen.

Chapter Three

Mind and Consciousness in the Late Nineteenth Century

The later nineteenth century was in many ways a golden period for the mind-sciences. A number of schools emerged and developed diverse methods for investigating the mind and the brain. These included techniques that would not be out of place in a psychology laboratory today. There was also a wide breadth of opinion on the mind, and significantly more tolerance for subjects that today are often dismissed out of hand. Psychical researchers investigated the claims of mediumship, cases of apparent telepathy, and sought evidence for the survival of personality beyond death. Some of these investigations were taken seriously by leading figures in the emergent discipline of psychology.

The Founding of Psychology

The first psychological research laboratory was opened at Leipzig University in 1879 by the physiologist and psychologist Wilhelm Wundt (1832–1920).[1] Wundt saw the mind as a creative, dynamic force and emphasized the chemistry of the brain rather than clockwork-type mechanisms.[2] Unlike a number of his contemporaries, who attempted to create periodic tables of the mind, Wundt did not believe that thought could be understood by trying to identify basic elements or structure. His view of the mind was also naturalistic, and he was against the idea that the 'mind' and the 'body' were two distinct substances or things. He saw psychology as studying a different aspect of physiological functioning.

Wundt's investigatory technique was predicated on the assumption of a form of internal perception or *innere Wahrnehmung* that could be used to understand the human mind. This technique is otherwise known as introspection and relies upon the subject of the experiment reporting his subjec-

---

1 Hothersall, 2004.
2 Hothersall, 2004.

tive experiences. His studies were confined to perception and sensation, excluding the observation of thought processes themselves.[3]

Wundt tried to refine this introspective technique to achieve results that would be comparable to well established scientific observations of external phenomena. One way to do this was to present subjects with simple stimuli, like a green triangle, and get them to report their sensations according to strict rules. The stimuli were presented for brief and timed periods by means of a machine called a tachistoscope, and the reaction time between the subjective report and measurement was also timed.[4]

Wundt's methods have been called 'woolly' and his experimental methods have been said to have 'hopelessly bogged down' psychology,[5] but even the cursory description above should be enough to show that these accusations are not entirely justified. It is true that he ran into problems with more complex mental phenomena like thoughts, volitions and feelings,[6] but so did the forms of psychology that eventually eclipsed the introspectionist schools after about 1900.

Wundt represented one of several rival schools in Germany. Another was headed by Hermann Ebbinghaus (1850–1909) who pioneered *psychophysics*, or the measurement of sensation. For example, Ebbinghaus used nonsense syllables to investigate memory. A participant had to read out lists of these syllables and repeat them back in time to a metronome. Ebbinghaus would record the number of repetitions it would take to learn these syllables. He would then retest the subject twenty-four hours later. He found that the more a subject had had to repeat these syllables in the first session, the less time they would take to re-learn them.

Ebbinghaus's experiments were the prototype for cognitive psychology, the branch that looks at the processes of memory and perception. His laboratory experiments aimed to filter out 'pure' memory that was unencumbered by variables like interest or motivation.[7] This model of the mind owed a significant amount to Descartes' idea that mind and emotion were somehow divorced.

Hayes suggests that here also was born the notion of lab work as an ideal mode of study. Laboratory experiments came to be seen as pure and 'uncontaminated' by the mess of everyday experiences. She observes that to this day 'this is the research program into which students of psychology are first inducted: it is held up as an ideal, and encourages the student to discount real-world experience as somehow invalid'.[8] Although this even-

3   Wallace, 2000.
4   Wallace, 2000.
5   Sparks, 1982, p. 151.
6   Wallace, 2000.
7   Hayes, 1995.
8   Hayes, 1995, p. 108.

tually became the predominant attitude in psychology, it was not to go uncontested.

William James

William James (1842–1910) was born of a wealthy Irish-American family. His life was very cosmopolitan, and as a young man he met many of the great people of his time.[9] In 1864, he went to Harvard to study medicine, but was not very committed, seeing much nonsense within the subject. From 1867 to 1868, James fell into a deep depression that was in part triggered by the view that our subjective, mental experiences have no causal effect on the outside world. Recovery began when he read the works of philosopher Charles Renouvier, who affirmed the possibility of mental causation.[10]

James went on to become one of the founders of experimental psychology in America. In 1874, he offered a Harvard course on the relationship between physiology and psychology. James's psychology was mostly self-taught from studying his own self-consciousness and the behaviour of people around him. In 1878, he signed a contract to write his *Principles of Psychology*. He thought it would take two years, but eventually it took twelve.[11]

In this important work, James defined psychology as 'the science of mental life, both its phenomena and their conditions'.[12] He also made a number of important observations about consciousness, which remain salient today:

(1) It is personal. My consciousness is mine alone, not part of a group-mind.
(2) It is constantly changing, so we continually experience a stream of seeing, hearing, willing, recollecting.
(3) It is continuous in that it is not chopped up into atomistic bits. It is a flowing stream.
(4) It is selective in that it takes only parts of the totality of the experiential world to make sense of them.[13]

James thought that attempts to analyse consciousness by breaking it up into component pieces would fail. If the stream was continuous, then it made no sense to think of it in little pieces.

He also incorporated the idea of mental efficacy into his ideas, in line with his belief about free will. He proposed that 'no mental modification ever occurs which is not accompanied or followed by a bodily change', and that 'mental states occasionally also changes in the calibre of blood-

---

9 Hothersall, 2004.
10 Hothersall, 2004.
11 Hothersall, 2004.
12 James, 1890, Vol. I, p. 1.
13 James, 1890, Vol. I, p. 225. Quoted in Hothersall, 2004, p. 340.

vessels, or alteration in the heartbeats, or processes more subtle still, in glands and viscera'.[14] James also made extensive use of introspection to try and understand the nature of thought, although his methods differed from Wundt's. Using these techniques, he came up with a theory of volition and attentional 'pulses'.[15]

James also developed his own brand of philosophy that formed the basis of his views on consciousness itself. His view was that there was no fixed external world to be discovered by one's mind but instead a stream of thoughts that one organizes through experience. The universe and one's knowledge of it is continuously evolving, but since one's knowledge can never be complete, the cosmos cannot be reduced to a single underlying substance. As such, he rejected notions that the universe only consists of 'matter' or 'mind'.[16] This is a viewpoint known as *pluralism*.

In line with this, he also thought that consciousness as such had no inherent existence. He put it this way:

> I believe that 'consciousness,' when once it has evaporated to this estate of pure diaphaneity, is on the point of disappearing altogether. It is the name of a nonentity, and has no right to a place among first principles. Those who still cling to it are clinging to a mere echo, the faint rumour left behind by the disappearing 'soul' upon the air of philosophy.[17]

He went on to explain that he only meant to deny

> that the word stands for an entity, but to insist most emphatically that it *does* stand for a function. There is, I mean, no aboriginal stuff or quality of being…[18]

In taking this position, James was rejecting Descartes' suggestion that mind or matter could be understood in substantial terms.

James thought it wrong to suppose that there was any separate 'mind-stuff' operating the brain, and in this his ideas were very modern. But unlike the materialists, James's philosophy led him to think that 'matter' was just as much a conjectural substance as 'mind'. Both 'mind' and 'matter' were metaphors drawn from observations that one made, rather than substances inherent in the world. So he was emphatically not joining the materialists in eliminating the mind in favour of matter. Instead, he was trying to reframe the question so that the paradoxes of mind and matter might seem less insoluble.

---

14 James, 1890, Vol. I, p. 5.
15 Wallace, 2000; Stapp, 2007; James, 1892/1992.
16 Wallace, 2000. His views also come very close to the Middle Way philosophy of Tibetan Buddhism; see chapter eleven and discussions in Wallace, 2000; Wallace & Hodel, 2008.
17 James, 1912, online edition at http://web.archive.org/web/20060104095543/spartan.ac.brocku.ca/~lward/James/James_1912/James_1912_01.html accessed on 25/09/09
18 James, 1912, *op. cit.*

By the 1890s, James became more closely concerned with the mind/body question. This was in part because of his investigations into psychical research and the influence of Frederic Myers. He came to consider the possibility that thought, rather than simply being produced by brain function, might instead either be *permitted* or *transmitted* by the brain. To illustrate the idea of permission or releasing function, he used the analogy of the crossbow; in removing the obstacle that holds the string, the bow flies back to its natural shape.[19] The transmission idea he illustrated by the analogy of a prism that split white light into rainbow colours. He claimed that all the physiological evidence might be compatible with these two alternative views of the mind, rather than just the idea of basic physiological dependence.

James expanded on his idea thus:

> When the brain-activities change in one way, consciousness changes in another; when the currents pour through the occipital lobes, consciousness sees things; when through the lower frontal region, consciousness says things to itself; when they stop, she goes to sleep, etc. In strict science, we can only write down the bare fact of concomitance... Ask for any indication of the exact process either of transmission or of production, and Science confesses her imagination to be bankrupt.[20]

To James, all we are observing is a correlation of brain function and thought, and the relation between subjective experience and any third-person observation of brain function remained a mystery. And we face an identical dilemma today, despite over a century of technological advances. The relationship between subjective experiences and brain function remains a *correlative* rather than a *causative* one.

Of course, such 'transmission' or 'permission' theories tend to raise a number of problems, the primary one being what, exactly, the brain is supposed to be filtering or reducing. If one says the 'mind', or 'consciousness', then we are back where we started; it isn't really an answer, because it begs the question of the nature of that consciousness. But one also needs to bear in mind the metaphorical nature of 'mind' and 'matter'. As James said:

> An absolute phenomenalism, not believing such a dualism to be ultimate, may possibly end by solving some of the problems that are insoluble when propounded in [substance dualist] terms.[21]

The filter metaphor is also, in its way, as mechanistic and suggestive as other metaphors for consciousness (steam-whistles come to mind). Filters generally filter fluids like water or air, and sometimes—as in water filters—they strain out impurities. Despite James's repudiation of substance

---

19 James, 1898/1900, *Human Immortality*, online edition, http://www.religion-online.org/showchapter.asp?title=541&C=624 accessed on 02/10/09.
20 *Op. cit.*
21 *Op. cit.*, note 3.

dualism, the word brings to mind a sort of fluid-like mind, in accordance with nineteenth-century speculations about the 'aether', the medium thought to allow the transmission of light-waves in nineteenth-century physics.[22]

James's stance on the mind/body problem reflects his interest and participation in psychical research. This was a Victorian movement to research phenomena that we would today term 'paranormal', and it started in earnest in the 1870s. One key figure in such research was a friend of James, Frederic Myers.

Frederic Myers

Frederic William Henry Myers (1843-1901) was a poet and classicist who became a psychical researcher. His Magnum Opus, *Human Personality and its Survival of Bodily Death* (1903), remains one of the widest ranging surveys of extraordinary human experience ever written.[23]

Myers was the son of a clergyman. Raised in a religious environment, he retained his Christianity into young adulthood, although he was subject to passionate swings of emotion in his early twenties. In the New Year of 1869, he collapsed and visited church for the last time in 1871.[24]

Myers' crisis of faith was not atypical for his time. Frank Turner saw Myers as one of several Victorian figures who can be found between the realms of science and religion, because whilst he had become disenchanted with the Christian faith, he was also unable to fully accept the tenets of scientific naturalism.[25] With the encouragement of his friend and colleague Henry Sidgwick, he began to investigate the phenomena of spiritualism, and eventually became one of the founders of the Society for Psychical Research.

Later, Myers wrote an account of the founding of the society:

> In about 1873 — at the crest of perhaps the highest wave of materialism which has ever swept over these shores — it became the conviction of a small group of Cambridge friends that the deep questions thus at issue must be fought out in a way more thorough than either the champions of religion or materialism had yet suggested.[26]

This initiated an intense programme of investigation into 'whether anything could be learnt as to an unseen world or no'.[27]

The Society for Psychical Research (SPR) itself was founded in 1882 by a number of singular but very able individuals. Their aim was to investi-

---

22 Gribbin, 1984.
23 See Hamilton, 2009, for a biography of Myers, and Gauld, 1968, for his part in the founding of psychical research.
24 Hamilton, 2009.
25 Alvarado, 2009.
26 Myers, 1903/2001, p. 3.
27 *Op. cit.*

gate, in as unprejudiced manner as possible, 'those faculties of man, real or supposed, which appear to be inexplicable on any generally recognised hypothesis'.[28]

And investigate they did. The early years of the society are widely regarded as some of its most productive. Their first major work, *Phantasms of the Living* (1886), which chronicled apparent telepathic communications between those in distress and a distant friend or relative, came in two volumes totalling 1,300 pages. In this, 702 cases are examined, classified and analysed with impressive clarity and care. Gauld observed that 'to pass from even the ablest of previous works to *Phantasms of the Living* is like passing from a medieval bestiary or herbal to Linnaeus' *Systema Naturae*'.[29]

The context of the SPR's formation is important, especially given the contemporaneous rise of spiritualism. This religious movement began in Hydesville, New York state, in 1848. In Hydesville, two sisters aged twelve and fourteen apparently began communicating with a spirit. This sparked spiritualism's rapid spread across America and its eventual arrival in England.[30]

Gauld suggests that there are some grounds for suspecting a religious resurgence in Britain at the same time, and that religious belief was stronger in 1851 than it had been fifty years previously.[31] The rise of Romanticism is a possible factor, although as Gauld notes, 'a theory which can link Hannah More with Madam de Stael is surely capable of explaining anything'.[32] The spread of Methodism and Evangelism might also have played a part.

At the same time, the achievements of science had led to an atmosphere of doubt which was a challenge to blind religious faith, although as Hamilton points out, it is too simplistic to picture Victorian England as a pious land shaken by the advances of materialist science.[33]

The Evolutionary Potential of the Subliminal Mind

Myers' major contribution to psychology was to attempt an inclusive theory which accommodated the full range of human experiences, including 'rogue phenomena' like psychic effects, mind/body interaction, mystical experience, and others. This was developed in many papers in the *Journal* and *Proceedings* of the SPR and posthumously in his *Human Personality and its Survival of Bodily Death*. The central idea was the subliminal mind,

---

28 Quoted inside the front cover of the SPR's Journal.
29 Gauld, 1968, p. 164.
30 Gauld, 1968; Inglis, 1992.
31 Gauld, 1968.
32 Gauld, 1968, p. 32.
33 Hamilton, 2009.

which has to be understood in terms of Myers' wider, evolutionary cosmology.

Myers' cosmology owed much to the evolutionary ideas of Spencer.[34] He conjectured that a number of different possibilities or evolutionary propensities resided in a latent form in the primordial stuff of the universe and came to be expressed as cosmic history unfolded. To him, evolution was an active process and not just a matter of chance. This directional process was not complete, and Myers interpreted genius and paranormal phenomena as the emergence of higher evolutionary abilities. Myers' theory was therefore strongly teleological, and owes much to the pre-Darwinian idea of progressivism, which saw progress written in the fossil record.[35]

The human evolutionary potential was expressed via the subliminal mind. The subliminal mind existed below the threshold of conscious life and was at base, Myers believed, profoundly unitary. The personality of normal, waking, consciousness was merely a fragment of this far larger, mostly hidden personality. The subliminal mind, which was divided from ordinary or supraliminal consciousness by a permeable boundary, expressed itself via a range of means; during hysterical fits, via automatisms and hallucinations, and during moments of inspiration (a fuller description is provided in chapter fourteen). Negative potential also exists, and is exhibited when a personality 'disintegrates'. So Myers' subliminal mind contained the potential for genius as well as pathology and the emergence of what he termed 'supernormal phenomena' — things that apparently belonged to a more advanced stage of evolution.

This notion of latent potential has some intuitive appeal. Most of us are probably capable of far more than we ever realize. Conversely, we also contain the potential for depression, dissociative or hysterical illness, or more destructive reactions to the environment. To Myers, these states were expressions of previously latent aspects of personality, which could be either progressive or regressive.

One of the most significant aspects of the work is Myers' classification of mental phenomena. As Gauld notes, *outré* phenomena like apparitions of the dead or telepathy are presented not as isolated oddities, but as phenomena that have continuities with less disputed observations. Myers arranges his case studies so that there is a gradation, which means that it is hard to draw the line between normal and 'paranormal' phenomena.

For example, Myers presents accounts of apparitions of the dead as the end-point of an examination of: images; telepathic transmission of images; dreams; telepathy and clairvoyance in dreams; hallucinations; hypnotic

---

34 Kelly *et al.*, 2007. Pages 59–115 by Emily Kelly provide a fuller introduction to the theories and methods of Myers than can be given here.
35 See chapter twelve for a discussion of teleological theories in the context of the emergence of consciousness.

hallucinations; crystal visions; and crisis apparitions.[36] Although some modern readers may reject these experiences out of hand, both Myers and James thought that a truly comprehensive psychology must be able to accommodate them. And thanks to the SPR, many of these experiences were as well documented as more 'acceptable' phenomena.

Myers' theories were heterodox at the time and have become even more so today. Many of the research tools he used—automatic writing, hypnosis, crystal gazing—raised eyebrows at the time, and his theories were expressed in highly metaphoric and florid ways. Myers' wider cosmology seems even harder to swallow, because he postulated that a sort of Platonic 'self' existed both before and after life. He asserted that this soul, after death, progressed through a number of spheres and eventually merged with an 'ultimate principle'. In this respect, his philosophy was much like the spiritualists.[37] Despite this, Myers, along with James, should be seen as a founding figure of psychology. It is also quite possible to accept or build upon *some* of Myers' insights without necessarily accepting his framing cosmology.

Myers and James were attempting, however tentatively, to build bridges between science and some form of religious or spiritual faith. They did this in as thorough and comprehensive a manner as possible. One reason was that they thought that an acceptance of the hard-line picture promoted by Huxley and others would make life unliveable for many. James's observations about the shallow nature of the received materialist doctrines have some relevance here. He pointed out that any world-view, no matter how scientific, was necessarily secondary to pure sensory experience. Scientific objects and concepts are abstractions, and only individual experiences were concrete.[38] Such abstractions might guide our philosophies and actions, but should not be over-inflated beyond the abstractions that they are.

The influence of James was to wane during the first decade of the twentieth century, although he was remembered as an important founder of the discipline of psychology. Myers was virtually forgotten by conventional science, but he was hardly alone in this, as the European schools of psychology also became eclipsed by a new doctrine called behaviourism. As we will see in the next chapter, the subject-matter of psychology was to narrow sharply, partly because of the dominance of a school that rejected mind and consciousness altogether.

---

36 Gauld, 1968, p. 277.
37 Hamilton, 2009.
38 James, 1902/1985.

Chapter Four

Behaviourism, Computers and Exorcists

As the twentieth century dawned, psychology was steadily narrowing its subject matter. The 1900 congress of psychology was the last to consider psychical research, part of a process that amounted to a separation of 'the acceptable from the unacceptable in psychology'.[1] An American school, the behaviourists, subsequently accelerated this narrowing to an overzealous degree. In this chapter we shall look at the rise and fall of the behaviourists, and the subsequent rise of the Computational Theory of Mind, or CTM, which, despite some battering, predominates today.

Behaviourism, and its Legacy

The behaviourists were a group of young, mostly American, scientists who thought that researchers should restrict themselves to strictly public, 'third-person' methods of observation, which could be quantified and generally applied. They thought that any scientifically respectable phenomenon should be potentially observable by all, and so rejected both introspection and the psychoanalytic speculations of Freud and Jung.

Many contemporaries saw behaviourism as a basically optimistic view of human nature, significantly more so than the pictures offered by Wundt, James, or the psychoanalysts. In the early twentieth century, social orders were changing fast, and behaviourism seemed to suggest that new human societies could be built from scratch.[2] This new movement was seen as the antithesis of the stuffy, class-based psychology of the Europeans. Psychologist Mary Cover Jones recalled that Watson's ideas 'shook the foundations of traditional European-bred psychology, and we welcomed it. That was in 1919; it pointed the way from an armchair psychology to action and reform and was therefore hailed as a panacea'.[3]

---

1   Le Malefan, 1995, p. 624. Quoted in Alvarado, 2009, p. 159.
2   Hayes, 1995.
3   Quoted in Hothersall, 2004, p. 474.

John B. Watson (1878-1958), the founder of behaviourism, came to see organisms as blank slates whose nature could be entirely accounted for by chains of learned behaviour. His initial experiments were on rats, who of course could not report their inner experiences. Watson was therefore forced to come up with an alternative way of assessing their learning. These initial experiences still strongly shaped the orientation of his research even after he began work on human beings.

By 1919, he had concluded that instincts did not exist and that habits were predominant. Anything that *seemed* like an instinct — maternal care, gregariousness, aggression, etc. — could be accounted for in terms of learning during life. Watson's preconceptions led him to an alternative interpretation of behaviour that others had concluded was innate, because the psychology he had created was not congenial to such ideas.

Similarly, any talk of 'mind' or 'consciousness' had no place in scientific practice. He claimed that 'the time has come when psychology must discard all reference to consciousness... Its sole task is the prediction and control of behaviour, and introspection can form no part of its method'.[4]

Behaviourism was essentially a reductionist enterprise, and Watson's views of psychology were inspired by the tremendous successes of physics. The late nineteenth and early twentieth centuries had seen significant advances in physics in part because researchers had come to understand the behaviour of smaller and smaller blocks of matter. Their picture of atoms had shifted from Hobbesian billiard-balls, to a sort of round pudding with 'plum' electrons embedded in the surface, to the more familiar picture of a nucleus made up of protons and neutrons, with orbiting electrons.[5]

Watson's ambition was to acquire the precision of physics for psychology, in the hope of making comparable achievements. Psychology, therefore, needed its own 'atom',[6] and so animals were reconceptualized as 'black boxes' and 'stimulus-response' (S-R) machines. A *stimulus* was applied to an animal and its *response* to the stimulus was measured in precise terms.[7]

A prime example of such an S-R response could be seen in Ivan Pavlov's dogs. Pavlov (1849-1936) taught dogs to associate a bell ringing with feeding time. Subsequently they would salivate whenever they heard a bell, even if no food was present. The bell was the 'stimulus', the salivation the 'response'. The stimulus-response (S-R) unit was to be the 'atom' of a scientific psychology. According to behaviourists, even complex behaviours could be 'explained' by chains of these *reflex arcs*. Some of the more sophis-

---

4 Watson, J.B., 1913, *Psychological Review*, pp. 158-67. Quoted in Koestler, 1967, p. 5.
5 Gribbin, 1984.
6 Hayes, 1995.
7 Sparks, 1982.

ticated behaviourists, anticipating functionalism, speculated that some of the 'chains' might be internal.[8]

Watson's vision of science significantly differed from those of James or Wundt. Both the latter had defined science in terms of the method of investigation used, and had developed rigorous methodologies to investigate mental phenomena, which included introspection. Watson, however, saw science in terms of absolute laws, basic units, and rules of combination. The mind had no place in this vision because it was seen as a metaphysical entity with no inherent existence. An atomistic view of behaviour also contrasted with James's view of the continuous flow of experience.

Watson did not want for ambition. In 1924, he argued that if he were given 'a dozen healthy infants... and my own specified world to bring them up in', that he would 'guarantee to take any one at random and train him up to become any type of specialist I might select—doctor, lawyer... and yes, even beggarman and thief...'[9] Like animals, humans were truly *tabula rasa* and could be moulded in any desired way.

B.F. Skinner (1902–1990), a disciple of Watson's, eventually took this vision one step further, and in his book, *Beyond Freedom and Dignity*, outlined a society governed by behaviourist principles. His later novel, *Walden Two* (1948), dramatized such a society in which fear, rage and hate are unknown and competitiveness had vanished. Exceptional achievement was not admired either, because it reflected badly on the unexceptional achievement of others.[10] The general effect is totalitarian and it never seems to occur to Skinner to ask who conditions the *designers* of such a society (or indeed, if they are truly are so mechanical, how they could have designed such a society in the first place).

These overblown claims did not stop behaviourism from becoming the dominant school in psychology for a number of decades, but its copy-book was also blotted with some fairly appalling abuses of power. Watson himself had induced several phobias in a young boy,[11] and in the 1950s, the doctor Ewen Cameron performed a number of CIA-funded experiments on sensory deprivation in the belief that humans were slates that needed their learning 'wiped' to affect cures. He ended up severely traumatizing a number of his patients, and it is alleged that the techniques he pioneered have been used in Iraq.[12] A third example is the use of aversion therapy on gay men, a practice that left a number of men badly traumatized and even

8   Gardner, 1985.
9   Quoted in Hayes, 1995, p. 22.
10 An excerpt is included in the *Faber book of Utopias*, edited by John Carey (London: Faber & Faber, 1999). The book contains Utopias by such diverse thinkers as the Marquis de Sade, George Orwell, and Adolf Hitler.
11 Hothersall, 2004.
12 Klein, 2007.

led to deaths. The behaviourist psychologist, H.J. Eysenck, who pioneered this therapy, reportedly said that it was 'for the patient's own good'.[13]

These allegations, along with Skinner's social programmes, illustrate the inherently political nature of psychology. It shows that knowledge — even misconceived or false knowledge — is open to abuse by those with sufficient money, equipment and power over others. It is hard also to completely absolve the behaviourist belief system from some responsibility for its adherents' actions.

An uncharitable observer might, in fact, characterize behaviourism as something of a fad. It was heavily preached, had many followers who ruthlessly suppressed other modes of research, and who carried out procedures that are today seen as ethically dubious. Arthur Koestler characterized its doctrines as like a virus which 'first causes convulsions, then slowly paralyses the victim'.[14]

It's not clear that psychology has ever really recovered from the behaviourist 'virus'. Many branches retain 'physics envy', which includes an over-reliance on narrow laboratory experiments and a tendency to behavioural atomism (e.g. a complex behaviour is 'caused' by a specific underlying neural mechanism or gene). Another consequence is the remaining taboo of subjectivity.

Midgley notes that this taboo, supposedly extinct, has actually had a far more pronounced influence on the mind-sciences than is often supposed. She claims that current scientific concepts are not well adapted to focusing on subjectivity. She characterizes the methodological argument that underlay the theories of Watson, Skinner and others in the following terms;

Only what science studies is real.
Science cannot study consciousness.
So: consciousness is not real.

She asserts that although the conclusion has been officially abandoned (we now have a *Journal of Consciousness Studies*, and an ever-increasing number of popular and technical works on the subject), both the premises still seem widely — if often tacitly — accepted.[15]

This sort of denial was given explicit form by the philosopher Gilbert Ryle in his book, *The Concept of Mind* (1949). In this, he refuted the idea of 'the ghost in the machine', which he wished to show was 'entirely false, and false not in detail but in principle'.[16] Ryle was attempting to destroy what he saw as a deep-rooted cultural myth — that there exists a mind separate from the function it displays. Ryle's main claim was that the popular

---

13 Tatchell, 13 September 1997, Obituary, Professor Hans Eysenck: http://www.petertatchell.net/psychiatry/aversion.htm accessed on 19/09/09.
14 Koestler, 1967, p. 5.
15 Midgley, 2001, p. 117.
16 Ryle, 1949, p. 16. Quoted in Gardner, 1985, p. 67.

idea that the mind exists as a discrete entity represented a 'category mistake', and hence was really a misunderstanding of the use of ordinary language. To Ryle, there was no such place as 'the mind' as a separate realm with its own location, events, and so on. This might be compared to a university, which has no existence apart from its buildings, staff, students, etc.

Ryle claimed that when we talk about people having volitional states like *will*, we are saying that a person is predisposed to behave in certain ways and will probably continue to do so. Ryle was not interested in any possible mechanisms underlying such behaviour.[17]

Whether Ryle succeeded in exorcizing his 'ghost' remains a matter of opinion. Arthur Koestler dubbed Ryle's views 'verbal acrobatics', and it's hard to entirely dismiss this criticism; Ryle's stance would be far more convincing if we didn't have our own subjective experiences. Nonetheless, Ryle's work remained a significant influence on the next generation of post-behaviourist thinkers.

A final negative hand-me-down from behaviourism was that the mind-sciences became more or less permanently entangled with a form of Scientism. The evangelical way in which behaviourism was spread and subsequently policed[18] set a precedent that subsequent generations of neuroscientists have unfortunately adopted.

Contrary to the impression given above, the influence of behaviourism was not entirely negative. Behaviourist data remains useful in understanding some animal and human behaviour; Pavlov's original insights, for example, have hardly been negated. Behaviourist techniques also offered insights with some therapeutic value, especially in the areas like addiction and phobia management. But these positive insights seem minor compared to the behaviourists' initial promise and its negative consequences.

Technocracy and the Cognitive Revolution

Behaviourism's dominance could not end until a new framing theory emerged to replace it. This alternative was the Computational Theory of Mind, or CTM for short, which equated human thinking or 'cognition' with what happens inside digital computers. But the CTM was really part of a wider vision that arose after the end of World War II as a technocratic society came of age and human beings came to be reconceptualized as components in a social machine.

The years after World War II in America belonged to Big Science. In 1945, the Manhattan Project had culminated in the dropping of atom

---

17 Gardner, 1985.
18 Midgley, 2001.

bombs on Hiroshima and Nagasaki.[19] During the subsequent Cold War with the Russians, the Manhattan Project was taken as the model of how to do science. Science became centralized, and subject to levels of government funding that were previously unknown. In 1950, the US National Science Foundation was opened to oversee the apportioning of federal science funds.[20] Science, with a big S, had come of age.

Along with Big Science came a new vision that tightened the association between machines and human beings. One of the architects of this vision was Norbert Wiener (1894–1964), who developed the new science of *cybernetics*, which dealt with self-regulating, self-correcting machine systems. This is derived from the Greek, *kivernitis*, which means 'governor'.[21] Cybernetics concepts were later applied to living systems, including nervous systems.[22] This concept helped to increase the understanding of how, for example, mammals retained a stable body temperature, or how organisms took in and reacted to environmental information.

Wiener conceptualized the nervous system as 'fundamentally like' an automatic machine 'in that they are devices which make decisions on the basis of decisions they have made in the past'.[23] Wiener thought that this view of the nervous system was comparable to machines that consist of a sequence of switching devices 'in which the opening of a later switch depends on the action of precise combinations of earlier switches leading into it, which open at the same time. This all-or-none machine is called a digital machine'.[24] Humans were thus, in some fundamental ways, comparable to new control technology that also relied upon cybernetic principles, examples being the automated guidance systems of missiles and aeroplanes.

Wiener's ideas about *information* were also crucial in the development of the computational model of mind. In *Cybernetics*, he stated that 'information is information not matter or energy. No materialism which does not admit this can survive to the present day'.[25] Information was reconceptualized as distinguishable from its physical substrate, and having its own properties and attributes. Along with fellow MIT researchers Claude Shannon and Warren Weaver, Wiener refined a very technical, mathematical definition of *information* that is rather different from the use of the word in conventional language.

---

19 Rhodes, 1986.
20 'The NSF is an independent federal agency created by Congress in 1950 "to promote the progress of science; to advance the national health, prosperity, and welfare; to secure the national defense..."' From their website www.nsf.gov/about accessed on 09/11/10.
21 Wiener, 1961.
22 Wiener, 1961.
23 Wiener, 1950, p. 116.
24 *Op. cit.*, p. 116.
25 Wiener, 1961, p. 132. Quoted in Gardner, 1985, p. 21.

Digital computers were a primary technology providing the impetus for these new ideas. The first electronic computers had been built during World War II for code-breaking. One of the chief architects of these machines, Alan Turing, had authored a paper in 1950 that suggested that it might be possible to design a computer that thought in a manner indistinguishable from a man.[26]

The digital computer emerged from theoretical work in about 1936. A *Turing machine* is a mathematically idealized computer that carries out procedures in a step by step manner. Each step is completely specified by a mark on the 'tape' that runs through the machine, moment by moment, and by the machine's internal 'state'.[27] It is known as a *finite* state machine because the internal, discrete states are finite in number, although the tape can be of any length. Instructions can be fed on the tape in the form of noughts or ones, and the machine moves the tape according the instructions on the tape. Complex, step-by-step instructions are known as *algorithms*. A *Universal* Turing machine is capable of carrying out any set of instructions that can be encoded in an algorithm, and modern computers are effectively Universal Turing machines.[28]

It was not long before the actions of the computer and the mind were compared. In a paper published in 1950, Turing asked whether a computer could think. He devised a theoretical test whereby an investigator has to judge whether one of two hidden people is a man or a woman. The investigator sits in an isolated room and is allowed to type questions via a teletype machine (today, an electronic messenger system would be a comparable means of communication). Both the hidden subjects, one of whom would be a man, would try to answer questions how a woman would, so the investigator would try to outwit them by asking the right questions.

Now suppose that we replace one of the humans with a computer. The trick changes to guessing which of the subjects is human, and which a machine. Turing guessed that by the year 2000 a computer might be able to play this game so well that an average interrogator would not have a 70 percent chance of making the right identification after five minutes of questioning.[29] He optimistically stated that '[w]e may hope that machines will eventually compete with men in all purely intellectual fields'.[30] Although we have computer programs that can fool people for a short time in specialized situations — say in internet chatrooms or in psychiatric

---

26 Turing, 1950.
27 Explained in detail in Penrose, 1989; 1994.
28 Penrose, 1994, p. 66.
29 Turing, 1950. Quoted in Blackmore, 2003.
30 Turing, 1950, p. 460.

interviews—we still do not have a program that can perform as Turing predicted.[31]

The advocates of Artificial Intelligence eagerly adopted Turing's ideas. To this day, there remain two major schools of the Artificial Intelligensia. One school, that of 'strong AI', holds that a computer at or exceeding a human level of intelligence can be built. The other, the 'weak' view, is significantly more modest, and sees computer programs as a convenient way of modelling human cognition.[32]

Like the behaviourists, the advocates of strong AI have a long history of overly-optimistic claims. In 1965, Herbert Simon, one of the field's founders, claimed on a number of occasions that there was nothing a human could do that could not be done by a machine.[33] In 1988, Hans Moravec was claiming that it would only take twenty years before machines began to *exceed* human intelligence.[34] And in 1995, Marvin Minsky asked, 'Will robots inherit the earth? Yes, but they will be our children'.[35]

AI has certainly clocked some amazing successes. AI systems work on the internet, in aeroplanes, and in the computer-generated characters at the cinema. Face and language recognition have become standard in mobile phones and on the web. And yet, we are still a long way from AI systems being capable of doing *any* work a person can do.

The traditional response to this objection is that whatever AI cannot do now, it could in principle and one day probably will. Hofstadter defined AI as whatever had not been done yet.[36] This means that some human attribute is held to be mysterious until it can be reproduced in a computer, at which point it becomes 'just computation'. This has happened in the past, and is presumed to be extendable to the point where every task can indeed be reduced to computation.

Although human chauvinism is a part of the resistance to the idea that machines might be able to *think*, this should not blind us to the metaphorical nature of the CTM. For now, it is sufficient to note that one's position on Artificial Intelligence depends in part on how literally one wishes to take the identification of the computer with the mind.

Chess Machines, Minds and Functions

The idea that computers and minds were somehow interchangeable became reinforced by the invention of a doctrine named *functionalism* by Hilary Putnam in 1967. This doctrine reconceptualized 'mental states' in

---

31 Blackmore, 2003.
32 Gardner, 1985.
33 Weizenbaum, 1984.
34 Moravec, 1988.
35 Quoted in Kurzweil, 2005, p. 260.
36 Hofstadter, 1979.

terms of what they did or how they functioned. Just as cutting tools could be implemented using rock or metal or a laser beam, so mental states could be realizable in any kind of system, so long as they did the same job.[37]

Daniel Dennett, a student of Gilbert Ryle's, built upon these ideas with his theory of the intentional stance.[38] In developing this, Dennett considered both human beings and a programmed computer as 'agents' whose actions an outside observer tries to explain. He claimed that *intentionality* is the distinguishing feature of mental states, and that one can attribute such intentionality as validly to a computer as to a human being. This notion was suppose to form a conceptual bridge between the intentional world of humans and the non-intentional world of the physical sciences.[39]

The difference between inanimate and animate systems is, according to Dennett, complexity. A complex system is built up of smaller, simpler subsystems that are also 'intentional', in Dennett's sense. These systems in turn are broken down into even simpler systems until one reaches systems that are simple enough to 'discharge' the intentional stance.

To Dennett, 'intention' was only a label that we attach to a system from the outside to describe behaviour. In this respect, the theory is directly comparable to Gilbert's Ryle's idea that mental states like will are just labels for observed behaviour. But unlike his mentor, Dennett was interested in the underlying mechanisms of such behaviour, which he saw in computational terms.

Dennett's idea certainly has broad appeal in the cognitive sciences. However, it is not without its problems. It is unclear, for example, whether the intentional stance illuminates the similarities between living systems and computers or conceals important differences. If one completely buys the idea that a computer playing chess is in essence no different than a human playing chess, one is in danger of obscuring what might be very different approaches to the same problem.[40] To Dennett, these differences are in a sense immaterial if the outcome is the same. But there is no guarantee that the computer and the human use even remotely comparable capacities even if completing comparable tasks.

Similar problems also occur with functionalism as a whole. Block observed that functionalist theories were both too chauvinistic and too liberal. They were chauvinistic in that they deny for insufficient reasons mental attributes to systems that may have them, and conversely they attribute mental properties to systems in which they may be absent.[41] The denial of qualia might be said to be an example of functionalism's chauvinistic side,

---

37   Putnum,1967. Quoted in Kelly *et al.*, 2007.
38   Dennett, 1978. Quoted in Gardner, 1985.
39   Gardner, 1985.
40   See also Bennett & Hacker, 2003.
41   Block, 1991. Quoted in Rao, 2002.

and ascribing a chess machine intentions might be said to be an example of its overly liberal side.

Jerry Fodor and the Language of the CTM

These issues did not stop the emergent 'cognitive psychology' adopting the language of computing and assuming a functional parity between brains and artificial information-processors. Brains suddenly acquired inputs, outputs, memory stores and representational structures and maybe even a 'language' of their own.

Jerry Fodor wrote in 1972: 'It is tempting (perhaps it is mandatory) to explain such interactions [between the senses] by assuming that sensory channels transduce stimulus data into a central computing language rich enough to represent visual, tactile, auditory, gustatory and olfactory information as well as whatever abstract conceptual apparatus is involved in thought.'[42] With statements like this, the assimilation of humans into the technological sphere must have seemed complete. It also justifies Hayes' assertion that '[the cognitive psychologists] eventually took the [computational] metaphor... to be the be-all and end-all of understanding what people do'.[43] She also notes, with some justification, that an over-enthusiastic embracing of their own metaphors is precisely where the behaviourists went astray.

Lashley and his Holistic Rats

As computers were coming to dominate the psychology scene, some odd discoveries were being made in the neurosciences. The first half of the twentieth century witnessed some extraordinary advances in surgical techniques and was (unfortunately for the animals) a heyday of vivisection. One of the pioneers was Karl Lashley (1890–1958), who conducted some of his early work with J.B. Watson. His main influence, however, was Shepard Ivory Franz who had discovered that a lesion in the frontal lobes of mammals did not abolish learned behaviour unless the destruction of the tissue was massive.[44]

Lashley built on this discovery by developing the technique of ablation, where specific sections of the nervous system are destroyed by surgery. The goal of this technique is to determine which behaviour is impaired or destroyed following such surgery. In Lashley's case he taught rats to run down a maze and then observed how ablation impaired the rat's ability to perform this task.

---

42 Fodor, 1972. Quoted in Tallis, 2004.
43 Hayes, 1995, p. 111.
44 Gardner, 1985.

In 1929, he concluded that 'the ability to learn the maze is dependent upon the amount of functional cortical tissue and not upon its anatomical specialization...'[45] Lashley's results were a clear challenge to theorists who favoured the idea of brain *localization*, which is the belief that specific behaviour resides in specific locations.

The believers in localization, however, had a significant body of evidence in their favour. We have already encountered the nineteenth-century work of Broca and Wernicke, which seemed to pinpoint language comprehension and production in a very specific part of the cerebral cortex. David Ferrier (1843–1928) discovered that he was able to localize motor and sensory functions in animal brains. This work was followed up by Wilder Penfield (1891–1976), who found that the representation of the different body parts in the motor cortex was proportional to their function rather than their body mass.[46]

Both the 'localizers' and the 'holists' could advance evidence to support their cause. As Gardner puts it:

> we have here what looks like a scientifically untenable situation... From [the localizers'] perspective, it was only a matter of time before every behavioural function could be adequately mapped in the brain of the organism. The rival school of investigators... considered the localizationist approach to be bankrupt...[47]

The problem with mapping functions according to lesions or brain damage was that the localization of symptoms did not necessarily signify localization of function. For example, just because the cognitive function of 'naming' breaks down following a lesion in the angular gyrus, it does not follow that 'naming' takes place in this specific brain region.[48] Similar dilemmas exist for twenty-first century fMRI studies (see chapter eleven).

The 'localizers'' surgical programme began to run into insurmountable conceptual and logical difficulties.[49] More complex cognitive functions were ill-defined, non-discrete and often continuous with other 'functions'. Secondly, the very nature of the brain as a highly complex, heavily interconnected system precluded its simple analysis into independent functional units.

Donald Hebb attempted to find a synthesis between the 'holist' and 'localizer' points of view in his book *The Organization of Behaviour* (1949). In this, he suggested that behavioural patterns like visual perception were built up over periods of time through connections to specific sets of cells. In this scheme, some functions were localizable, and others depended

---

45 Lashley, 1929, p. 3. Quoted in Gardner, 1985, p. 261.
46 Hothersall, 2004.
47 Gardner, 1985, p. 270.
48 Gardner, 1985.
49 Uttal, 2001.

upon larger sets of cells distributed over the whole nervous system. He thought that this scheme might in principle be able to accommodate both sets of data.

Conclusion

In a sense, this chapter is a story of two seductions. The first is how psychology came to be overwhelmed by ideas of behavioural atomism and ideas of a 'blank slate'. The second is how, in the context of a Cold-War technocracy, humans and machines came to be seen as literally interchangeable.

There is now sufficient historical distance for us to see how deceptive the first seduction was, but culturally speaking, we are still very much in the throes of the second. The idea of human-like machines, and indeed, machine-like people has become very widely accepted in both popular and the elite scientific culture. However, the one thing that history teaches us is that these overarching visions tend to be transient; the idea that the mind 'is' like a machine might prove overly partial or simply wrong.

The historical overview presented in the previous four chapters has thrown up some significant issues. The first is that human beings have a strong need for, and significant ability to, construct framing mythologies to help explain their reality and purpose within it. The second is that these mythologies are not constructed *ex nihilo* but involve a mix of empirical observations and overarching metaphors drawn from experience. In the case of our own culture, these metaphors are frequently drawn from current technology.

There often seems to be an arbitrary element to these mythologies or world-pictures, because empirical observation is never sufficiently exhaustive to complete them. It is also true that different orientations to the world tend to result in the selection and emphasis of different features of the world. This effect can be seen in the different psychologies, where very different pictures of the human emerged depending upon different views of what science and/or the person should or could be. As a result, when compared, these contrasting world-pictures can appear quite idiosyncratic.

Humans also seem very prone to forget just how creative they are and to treat these explanatory frames, myths or world-views *as* reality. Thus anything that is forbidden by a world-view will be seen as literally *impossible*. We have seen how Descartes' arbitrarily excluded purpose and meaning from his mechanical universe, which forced his successors either to see humans as clockwork-type mechanisms only or as mechanisms plus a wholly different, substantial mind.

But the positive side of these world-pictures is that they are not wholly opaque to change. If a certain way of looking at things creates a conceptual problem, then historically either the world-view has been modified or supplanted.

Which brings us to our final point, which is the migration of ideas from the fringe or frontier of science to its heartland (or vice versa). A number of pre-twentieth century examples show that the line between science and what is often dubbed 'pseudoscience' is less substantial than is often claimed: Newton's gravity was inspired by occultism; phrenology drew attention to specific parts of the brain earlier than might otherwise have happened; Myers created an eclectic and inclusive psychology in opposition to the predominant materialism.

By the twentieth century the mainstream had become increasingly good at screening out ideas that were considered *a priori* nonsense. This narrowing might have allowed an increased focus on narrow and technical areas, but it had the cost of an impoverishment of vision. Despite the fall of behaviourism, this trend worsened over the twentieth century as science became more of a corporate enterprise, and shows little signs of reversing in the twenty-first.

This narrowing seems to me to be a mistake if we want to work towards more comprehensive pictures of reality, because history has also shown that we cannot know in advance which approach will prove fruitful and which will not. Many approaches will turn out to be dead ends, but this is at least as true in conventional science as it is on the fringe (for example, one could compare the cures achieved via the mainstream fad of behaviourism with those achieved by the fringe fad of Mesmerism). Kuhn observed nearly fifty years ago that the greater the conceptual change needed, the more fiercely the old guard will resist it, but we have also seen that the avenues of change are such that they cannot be predicted reliably in advance.[50]

---

50 Kuhn, 1996/1962.

Part Two

Philosophical Considerations

Chapter Five

Ontology

What sort of world do you live in? Are there 'nothing but' atoms and the void? Do or could immaterial or even disembodied minds exist? Is, by contrast, the world you inhabit one big mind, and our lives figments in a cosmic dream?

Ontology

These sorts of questions are ontological. *Ontology* is the study of being or existence, dealing with what really exists in contrast with what only seems to exist, and with what permanently exists in contrast with what has a temporary existence.[1] It also deals with that which exists independently and unconditionally in contrast with what which exists dependently and conditionally.

In a sense, an ontology is a theory of everything. A materialist ontology, for example, tries to reduce everything to 'matter' or its derivatives. By contrast, an idealist (mind-only) ontology does the opposite and reduces everything to mind. But these possibilities form only two limited kinds of ontology. Frege and Penrose, for example, split the universe into three 'worlds'; the mental, the physical and the mathematical, and Karl Popper did something similar.[2]

In ontology, one does not even have to restrict oneself to the visible, accessible world. One can posit any number of unseen, hidden or inaccessible alternate 'worlds' about us. These might be theological or pre-scientific in nature (a posited 'heaven' or 'hell') or otherwise supernatural. These worlds might be inhabited by unseen entities, like angels, demons or spirits. Other sorts of alternate worlds are supposed in philosophy and science. The philosopher David Lewis speculated about an infinite plurality of unseen, inaccessible worlds where the rules were different from our own, and the 'many worlds' interpretation of quantum theory invokes

---

1 *Encyclopedia Brittanica*, 1973 ed.
2 Penrose, 2004; Popper & Eccles, 1977.

unseen worlds splitting every time a certain kind of measurement is made.³

The crucial point, for our purposes, is that ontology is a *metaphysical* and theoretical exercise rather than a primarily empirical one. *Metaphysics* is the theoretical philosophy of being and knowing, and is often employed, overtly or covertly, in the philosophy of mind and neuroscience. Midgley has gone as far as to claim that most arguments in the *Journal of Consciousness Studies* arise because of metaphysical differences.⁴ This is because ontology is about more than the existence or otherwise of unseen worlds; it also deals with potential divisions or unities in the world in which we live.

The World

On the face of it, we live in one, inclusive world.⁵ The philosopher David Lewis, who argued for a plurality of isolated and causally diverse 'other' worlds, put it this way:

> The world we live in is a very inclusive thing. Every stick and stone you have ever seen is part of it. And so are you or I. And so are the planet Earth, the solar system, the entire Milky Way, the remote galaxies we see through telescopes… There is nothing so far away from us as not to be part of our world… Likewise the world is inclusive in time. No long-gone ancient Romans, no long-gone pterodactyls… are too far in the past… [not] to be part of this same world. Maybe, as I myself think, the world is a big physical object; or maybe some parts of it are entelechies or spirits or auras or deities or other things unknown to physics.⁶

The majority of scientists probably concur with Lewis, and agree that the world in which we inhabit is a unified, physical entity. Walter and Heckman comment that physicalism has 'outrun its dualistic (and idealistic) competitors and has reached nearly unanimous consensus'. They comment that 'The world we live in, it is quite reasonable to believe, is a physical world, not only at its most fundamental level, but through and through…'⁷ This might, to someone raised in Western society, seem thor-

---

3   Lewis, 1986; Gribbin, 1984.
4   Midgley, 2001.
5   Although this assertion is also metaphysical and can, and has, been challenged. Feyerabend stated that the objects different cultural traditions perceive can only be said to exist in the 'same' world if they are unified via some underlying universal theory, but that since this does not really exist, even in science, then we cannot claim that said objects really belong in the same 'world'. Whilst I have not the space here to unpack the world/worlds debate, I will say that it becomes relevant, even pressing, when one moves from assuming that knowledge can be objective to assuming it to be intersubjective. I touch on this issue in chapter eleven and the book's conclusion; some features of pluralism also suggest it. See also Feyerabend, 1987. Here, I accept the 'one world' idea for temporary convenience.
6   Lewis, 1986, p. 1.
7   Walter & Heckmann, 2003, p. 3.

oughly reasonable, but it remains a metaphysical statement rather than an empirical or factual one.

One reason is that it is very difficult or even impossible to define 'physical' in a comprehensive or definitive way, and there remain philosophers who claim that there is no evidence for physicalism.[8] The second is that the definitions of 'physical' or 'material' have radically changed from their initial definition in early modern times. What twenty-first century physicists mean by 'physical' is very different from what Descartes or Newton meant.

Truth by Declaration

The claim that physicalism must or is likely to be the 'correct' ontology for the world that we live in is very common, and is often justified on empirical grounds. For example, Searle claims that we know too much for, say, an idealist, or mind-only, view to be correct. 'It is hard to send men to the Moon and bring them back and then take seriously the problem, for example, of whether the external world really exists.'[9] Searle's claim is that modern empirical science has advanced in such directions, achieved so much in terms of the manipulation of the physical world, that this is enough to exclude an idealistic alternative. In other words, he is attempting to resolve a metaphysical dispute by using observational data.

But even in experimental science, empirical attempts to resolve differences in theoretical perspectives often have significant limits.[10] It is even less likely that such an esoteric exercise as deciding a 'correct' ontology can be resolved in this way. An idealist might argue, for example, that the reason why we have so much knowledge about apparently physical things is because our minds 'fill in the gaps' as we go along, and the mind-world subtly moulds itself to our general expectations. In this interpretation, we got to the Moon because a collective belief and a mass movement of thought caused us to create the machines we thought we needed to get there (even a physicalist might accept this as *metaphorically* true).

So a committed idealist would probably be able to come up with arguments that were plausible to them and logically consistent within their framework of thought.

We should also note that Searle is *already* committed to his perspective, and the numerous facts of science and technology just reinforce a view already firmly held. Searle also ignores the idealistic bent of a number of theoretical physicists, some of whom speculate about participatory universes and that consciousness might underlie everything.[11] Whether or

---

8   See Koons & Bealer, 2010, for some philosophical critiques of physicalism.
9   Searle, 2007, p. 28.
10 See discussion in Collins & Pinch, 1982.
11 Gribbin, 1984; Henry, 2005; Rosenblum & Kuttner, 2006.

not these speculations are valid,[12] they seem a long way from the sort of objectivism—derived from classical physics—that underlies most of current work in the philosophy of mind.[13]

The primary problem with ontological debates is that many of the combatants of different stripes decide on an 'ism' to follow *a priori* and end up defending it to the hilt whilst ignoring often valid arguments from their opponents. Bolender observed that 'Nature's imagination is richer than the imaginations of the older, less informed philosophers who invented the isms which we are now... so slavishly following'.[14] He quotes Freeman Dyson, who suggests that it is more desirable to makes use of one's unfettered imagination than follow an ism. Dyson went on to say that allying oneself with a school of thought as the basis of one's theory construction is a sure way to fall from brilliance to sterility. We need to heed this caution.

A Variety of Ontologies

I shall now make a brief survey of some ontological alternatives, including variants of physicalism. An initial point is that it is possible to construct many different ontologies and, if we include non-Western ones, that there may be thousands or more in current existence. If we truly and deeply appreciate the sheer variety of ontologies, then it begins to seem a little conceited—not to mention unlikely—to assume that there must be just one 'correct' one. It is rather more likely that different ones might be useful in different social, scientific, and existential contexts. For brevity, I will focus upon Western, post-Cartesian ontologies.

Monistic Ontologies

These ontologies typically assume that everything can be reduced to one 'stuff', essence, or principle. As we saw in the introduction, monism can also be defined as '[t]he metaphysical position that all is the manifestation of a single underlying reality, principle, essence, or substance, and is governed by a universal set of laws...'[15] Rucker[16] points out that there has long been a very strong urge to reduce the world's diverse phenomena to one kind of essence or stuff, and that the candidates have included mind, matter, sensation, and form.

---

12 See Midgley, 1992, and Penrose, 1994, for critiques of these sorts of positions.
13 Stapp, 2007.
14 Bolender, 2003, p. 126.
15 From the Glossary pages of Koch's website: http://www.klab.caltech.edu/~koch/ accessed on 29/09/09.
16 Rucker, 1997.

Ontology	Substance(s)	Closure principle?	Features
Monistic Materialism	Matter	Conserved	Everything reduces to 'matter' (see also Popper's subclassifications, Table 2)
Monistic Idealism	Mind	Conserved	Everything reduces to 'mind'
'Simulation' Models	No substance specification required	Depends on ontology of the simulator's universe	We are living in a post-human simulation of the past
Neutral Monism	Neutral single substance	Conserved	Mind and matter are derived from a single, ultimate substance
Cartesian Dualism	Mind, Matter	Violated	Mind and matter are distinct but interacting substances
Bergson's 'Filter' Dualism	Mind, Matter	Violated	The brain acts as a filter through which a 'Mind-at-Large' flows
Jamesian 'Permission' Dualism	No substance specification required	Violated	The brain releases or permits mental events
Popperian Property Dualism	No substance specification required	Violated?	Mind is a distinct, emergent property of the human organism
Koestler's Dualism	No substance specification required	Violated?	Mind is a distinct, emergent property/quality of the human organism. Multiple sorts of emergent properties possible
Stapp's Dual-Process Theory	No substance specification required	Violated	Consciousness can be seen as a distinct non-deterministic system that 'interrogates' deterministic brain systems

Table 1. Some Western Post-Cartesian Mind-Matter Ontologies.

This move is termed a *monism of kinds*, and was initially mystically motivated. This drive to so reduce reality is very strong in the West, and represents a persistent theme in science.[17] For example, seventeenth-century chemistry was dominated by the search for a universal principle known as 'quintessence', a kind of universal agent or solvent responsible for all chemical reactions.[18] More recently, we have seen a search for a 'theory of everything', or Unified Field Theory, which seeks theoretically to unify all the major forces in the universe. Wertheim suggests that the drive to do this is inherited from the theological principle of relating all of creation back to a single God. Monistic, Western ontologies often try to reduce the world that we experience either to 'mind' or to 'matter'. We shall consider the idealist, or mind-only, option first.

Monistic Idealism

The proposal that the universe in which we live is nothing but mind was most famously voiced by Bishop Berkeley (1685–1753). Berkeley's version contends that we can only know the ideas and sensations of objects, and not abstractions like 'matter'.[19] Berkeley thought it impossible to talk about an object's being, and that we should instead only talk of an object's being perceived by someone.[20]

He went further, however, because he supposed that nothing that appears to be 'out there' in the world has any inherent existence at all. This creates a problem of stability, which is well illustrated by a short story of Borges about a land with an idealist philosophy. In this land, books are supposed to be the product of one anonymous author; lost objects are refabricated, and it is supposed that forgotten items eventually disappear. There are no nouns because nothing is supposed to exist; instead, verbs describe objects. The world is supposed to be unstable in the manner of the mind.[21] Berkeley's solution to this sort of objection is to suppose that objects that are currently not being perceived by humans were kept going by the omniscient mind of God.

Marshall advocates a form of Berkeleyan metaphysics 'suitably modified in the light of mystical experience and modern science'.[22] His study of extroversive mystical experiences, such as those described in our introduction (statements 3 & 5), suggests to him that the universe we see, including physical objects like trees, stones and galaxies, should be considered 'mental' in nature. Like Berkeley's, Marshall's proposition requires a 'great mind' to work.

17 Wertheim, 1997.
18 Taton, 1964.
19 http://en.wikipedia.org/wiki/George_Berkeley accessed on 13/03/10.
20 *Op. cit.*
21 Borges, 1964. The story is titled 'Tlön, Uqbar, Orbis Tertius'.
22 Marshall, 2005, p. 261.

More recent, rationalist-physicalist versions of this sort of theory have eschewed God's all-seeing eye in favour of post-humans in the remote future setting up a computer simulation of the past. Nick Bostrom argues that there is a significant chance that we are living in such a simulation.[23] This theory, however, is not idealistic in the Berkeleyan sense because the ultimate, non-simulated reality of the post-humans is also presumably materialistic.

Idealistic philosophies have been more influential than might at first sight be supposed. An anti-real or instrumentalist approach to the theories of science owes much to Berkeleyan idealism (see chapter six). Recent and problematic interpretations of quantum theory are also idealistic in spirit, although the issue of the mind of God is generally ignored.[24] The problem with idealism is that it often has low pragmatics in many practical contexts, as illustrated by Berkeley's rejection of a physical theory of sound.[25] *In extremis*, if everything is one big thought, then one does not have to find workable physical-type explanations for anything.

Monistic Physicalism

As noted, this is considered by many to be the only viable contender. 'Matter' or 'physical' processes are primary, and so mind and consciousness must be secondary derivations. This becomes explicit when we consider evolutionary theory. According to the dominant, cosmological and Darwinian accounts, the universe began with only simple matter and energy, which gradually evolved into more complex forms (stars, galaxies, planets, then life) over time. A significant body of evidence suggests that minds are only possessed by relatively advanced animals, and consciousness by a subset of these animals. This world-picture strongly suggests that mind and consciousness are the secondary products of complex arrangements of matter. Indeed, some extreme versions suggest that minds and consciousness are (1) reducible to matter, and (2) must therefore be linguistic or neurological 'illusions'.

Karl Popper subdivided this general, materialistic approach into four subclassifications (Table 2). It might seem odd to include *panpsychism*, a stance that holds that all matter has an inside or 'interior' quality, as a materialist theory,[26] but Popper classified a theory as materialist by whether or not it violated the closure principle. His aim was to critique all four of these positions.

---

23 Bostrom, 2003.
24 For example, Henry, 2005; Barrow & Tipler, 1986; but see Midgley, 1992, for a critical discussion of these theories.
25 Discussed in Blackmore, 2005.
26 Chalmers, 1996, proposes a form of substance-dualistic pansychism that is not really materialistic, although it seems causally inert.

Ontology	Features	Proponent(s)
Radical or eliminative materialism	Mind, consciousnesss, subjective experiences do not exist	Dennett, the Churchlands, Rorty, Ryle, J.B. Watson
Panpsychism	All matter has an 'inside' or mental quality	Chalmers, Spinoza, Leibniz
Epiphenomenalism	'Inside' qualities limited to higher animals and not causally effective	T.H. Huxley, Wegner, Carter
Identity theory	Mental events and consciousness 'are' brain or neural events	Damasio, Crick, Koch, Baars

Table 2. Popper's Classification of Materialisms.

Another shared feature of these theories is *ontological reductionism*.[27] This is the idea that one kind of entity can be reduced to a structure of other kinds of entity. It is asserted that subjective states, selves, behaviours, consciousness can be reduced to neural structures. Bennett and Hacker define such reductionism as 'a commitment to the complete explanation of nature and behaviour of entities of a given type in terms of the nature and behaviour of their constituents'.[28] So subjective experiences, for example, can be wholly explained in terms of patterns of 'neural activation'.

Radical or eliminative materialism
According to this view, conscious and mental processes are non-existent or are not scientifically analysable and so in effect non-existent. This was the behaviourist position. Today's eliminative materialists argue slightly differently. Instead of the mind being a 'black box', they tend to characterize it as a vast assembly of functional mechanisms, each specialized for a sub-task.[29] Eliminativists argue that once we have a specific architecture for this machine, then we will not need anything extra (*qualia*, consciousness, subjectivity) to account for its operations.

Paul Feyerabend is credited as one of the creators of the eliminativist position. In two articles written in 1963, he claimed that mental events were incommensurable with the physical models of science and that the successes of science indicated that one should be able to construct a worldview where the mind/body question was irrelevant, in the same way that many of the dilemmas created by Aristotelian physics became irrelevant with the advent of Galilean physics.[30] He claimed that such a conceptual change would eliminate existing arguments against materialism and end

---

27 Bennett & Hacker, 2003, chapter thirteen.
28 Bennett & Hacker, 2003, p. 357.
29 Dennett, 1991; Churchland, 1995.
30 Feyerabend, 1963a; 1963b.

the philosophical mind/body problem.[31] I will discuss this particular claim in chapter eleven, in the context of Feyerabend's later ideas concerning subjectivity and epistemological pluralism.

Panpsychism

This is the belief that all matter has an 'interior' aspect, and is not always associated with a materialist viewpoint. The belief was current amongst the Ancient Greeks, and the Vendanta schools today hold a comparable view.[32] Early modern thinkers who advocated panpsychist views were Leibniz and Spinoza. More recently, transpersonal thinkers like Tielhard de Chardin and Ken Wilber have built entire cosmologies upon the notion that the universe has an 'interior' as well as an exterior aspect.[33]

Popper's primary objection to panpsychism was that the assumption that there must be some sort of precursor of psychical processes was both trivial and vague. He claimed that 'to insist that this [something in evolutionary history] must be mind-like and that it can be attributed to atoms is a misleading way of arguing'.[34] Panpsychism also sidesteps the very deep problem of the emergence of novelty in the universe.[35]

Popper argued that we already know examples of processes in nature that are emergent in the sense that they lead to properties that were not present before. The solidity of crystals emerges effectively from nowhere, as does the capacity for memory or, for that matter, information. In a similar manner, we should not assume that anything that could be termed 'mental' or 'psychic' is present in the precursors to organisms with minds. It is easier to accept that just as there is a step from non-life to life, there is a comparable step from non-minds to minds.

We might also claim that the attribution of a human trait to the whole universe is both anthropomorphic and unparsimonious. Those of us raised in the Western scientific tradition are accustomed to thinking of most of the universe as non-living, and panpsychism seems closer to an animistic way of thinking, where life is projected onto everything. A number of writers have, however, advanced arguments for a teleological or even living universe, arguing that it is just as anthropomorphic to project *mechanism* onto the universe, as many in conventional science often do.[36] But the crux in the current context is whether consciousness is such a novel problem that it requires us to posit panpsychism.

---

31 Feyerabend, 1975, chapter thirteen.
32 Popper & Eccles, 1977; Daniels, 2005.
33 See Barrow & Tipler, 1986, pp. 195–205, for an overview of de Chardin's thoughts; Wilber, 2000.
34 Popper & Eccles, 1977, p. 69.
35 See also the discussion in chapter twelve.
36 See the summary of teleological arguments in Barrow & Tipler, 1986; Sheldrake, 1988; Sahtouris, 1999.

Epiphenomenalism

Epiphenomenalists assert that conscious thoughts are produced by brain function but do not have any causal effect on the brain. The original analogy, given by Thomas Huxley, was that of a steam-whistle. Just as the steam-whistle constitutes a side-effect of an engine's operations without any causal influence, so in epiphenomenalism mental events are causally ineffective side-effects of neurophysiological mechanisms. Pains, for example, do not cause us to wince but are instead caused by the same neurophysiological events that cause the wince.[37]

Epiphenomenalism is a surprisingly popular position in the cognitive sciences, and will be discussed in greater length in later chapters. One champion of this approach is Wegner, who sees conscious will as an illusion, cognitive emotion, or after-effect of neural processes.[38] Carter, too, advances the theory that consciousness itself might be a causally ineffective property that emerges from the architecture of a whole, working brain.[39] Experimental evidence of various kinds is often invoked to justify this epiphenomenal approach. Specifically, there are experiments that record neurological activity that occurs before awareness of an event or personal volition of which we are conscious.[40] The conclusion drawn from this is that since neural firing occurs before conscious awareness, then the underlying neurological mechanisms must be efficacious and not the conscious thoughts.

These experiments will be discussed in later chapters, but it needs to be conceded that at the very least they suggest that antecedent neural activity is a necessary, if not sufficient, corollary of decision-making and volition. They also suggest that volition is not a unitary process but part of a wider causal process. However, we need to bear in mind that many of the observers are for various reasons strongly predisposed towards epiphenomenalism, and that experimental results are often ambiguous and can be interpreted in a number of different ways.

Popper saw epiphenomenalism as incompatible with Darwinism. He held that the theory of natural selection is currently the only theory that explains the emergence of novelty in the world. Secondly, natural selection is concerned with physical survival, or the selection of features that favour the survival of the organism. However, this clashes with epiphenomenalism because the theory supposes that mental events have no causal efficacy. If mental events have no causal efficacy, then they cannot contribute to the survival of the organism. Therefore, according to Popper, consciousness cannot have emerged through natural selection.

---

37 Pauen, Staudacher & Walter, 2006, p. 8.
38 Wegner, 2002.
39 Carter, 2002.
40 Libet, 2004.

This argument seems in some ways compelling. If conscious will, for example, can be reduced to a 'cognitive emotion' or after-effect, then it is hard to see why it needed to evolve in the first place. If human beings can get along in survival terms as mechanisms, and this additional cognitive emotion makes no difference to that function, then it is unclear why or how that emotion could evolve in the first place.

One way of getting round this might be to classify conscious experience as a 'spandrel'.[41] This is a term invented by the evolutionary biologists Gould and Lewontin to describe a feature that is a by-product of evolution rather than a result of adaptive selection.[42] An evolutionary spandrel is supposed to be a by-product of a structural requirement and thus could be causally inert.

Despite this, epiphenomenalism seems in many ways an unsatisfactory ontology. The main reason is that it posits a causal system that only goes one way, which, as Midgley points out, is unheard of in nature.[43] Secondly, it remains a hangover from attempts to create a universal theory of the universe in purely mechanistic terms, with consciousness tacked on as an afterthought. There are surely better ways than this.

Identity theory

Identity theory, or 'central-state' theory or, in some versions, non-reductive physicalism,[44] does not deny subjective states but asserts that they simply 'are' neural activity. For example, in interview, Pat Churchland expressed the hope that one day we will be able to say 'Aha, this is it. This pattern of [neural] activation in this context when the brain stem is doing such and such, that just *is* a sensation of red'.[45] This is not the sort of statement that one can take at face value, and is an expression of ontological reductionism, or the reducing on one kind of entity to another. It is again a *philosophical* rather than a purely *empirical* wish.

Although (with epiphenomenalism) identity theory is held to be the most plausible theory, it boils down to the assertion that subjective states and neural states 'are' somehow the same. However plausibly formulated, this remains an expression of faith.

Identity theory runs into other problems with respect to causal redundancy.[46] In logical form, the argument goes something like this;[47] Suppose mental states must supervene or are dependent upon physical states. So every time there is a mental change, there must be a corresponding physi-

---

41 Carter, 2002, suggests this.
42 Gould & Lewontin, 1979.
43 Midgley, 2001.
44 Heil, 2004.
45 Pat Churchland in interview with Susan Blackmore. Blackmore, 2005, p. 55.
46 Heil, 2004; Popper & Eccles, 1977.
47 Similar arguments are made by both Heil and Popper (*op. cit.*)

cal change to accompany it. But if this is true, and physical events are considered primary or underlying, then it *implies that we can do without mental states at all*. This is because if physical processes and mental processes are exclusive of one another, then in logical terms, one can be reduced to the other. And in physicalism, this means effectively discarding any notion of mental causation.

This sort of point has been made across the philosophical board. Kim and Heil have both argued that non-reductive physicalism, which is a currently popular form of identity theory, entails the causal irrelevance of the mind to both mental and physical effects.[48] So, in this theory, mental states end up as causally irrelevant as those in the epiphenomenal theory, because they are supposed to be exclusive. In these accounts, we do not need to invoke mental or subjective states to explain behaviour, hence the strong impulse to label feelings of volition as 'illusions'. To the strict materialist, then, it seems most parsimonious to say that mental states do not exist.

These sorts of problems with identity theory should make it clearer why there is a strong tendency to downplay or excise consciousness as anything causal. The varieties of epiphenomenalism or non-reductive physicalism that might as well be epiphenomenal can be seen as a concession to the existence of subjective states whilst simultaneously denying them any causal effect on the universe.[49] So the principle of causal closure is retained but at the cost of apparently contradicting our everyday actions.

Dualist Ontologies

Dualist ontologies hold that there exist not one but two domains, essences or principles. The classic example is the substance dualism of Descartes. In most contemporary books on consciousness, this theory is usually raised to be dismissed. Blackmore states bluntly that:

> The insuperable problem for substance dualism is how the mind interacts with the body when the two are made of different substances... If thoughts can affect brain cells then either they work by magic or they must be using some kind of energy or matter. In this case they are physical stuff and not purely mental.[50]

Blackmore's sentiments are very widely held, but they are not as airtight as they might seem. Popper, whilst not advocating substance dualism, addressed this issue. He pointed out that even if we were to presuppose the idea of an ultimate explanation based on essentialist substances, then the dissimilarity of substances argument would not necessarily create an argument against their possible interaction. Current physics, which does

---

48 Koons & Bealer, 2010; Raymont, 2003; Heil, 2004.
49 I would include the theories of both Chalmers, 1996, and Velmans, 2000, in this observation.
50 Blackmore, 2003, p. 13.

not presuppose the existence of one or more ultimate essences, suggests that the action of bodies upon bodies is mediated by fields (gravitational, electrical). So like does not act upon like here, either.[51] So this objection to substance dualism (or vitalism for that matter)[52] is not necessarily valid.

John Beloff was a recent advocate of Cartesian dualism. The reasons he gave were his belief in free will, his belief in a continuous self or ego, and his belief in the existence of psi or psychic phenomena.[53] It must be said that none of these reasons necessarily leads to a substance dualist position, although the conception of an independent mental realm seems naturally congenial to all three ideas.

Filter and Permission Theories of Mind

These theories suppose that the brain is like a television set that filters or limits the mind, rather as a television receives a signal from elsewhere. The theories can be interpreted in terms of a separate 'stuff', but this is not compulsory. Henri Bergson and William James considered both filter and permission models of consciousness. Myers' theory of the subliminal mind could also be interpreted in such terms, although he was more committed to the idea of an eternal Platonic 'self'.

There are two major issues with filter theories. The first is whether the theory is internally coherent. The second is whether such a theory can be used to gain a more comprehensive understanding of conscious and mental processes.

Firstly, it is not clear that filter theories are very consistent in the way that, for all its faults, physicalism can be. This can be clarified with a look at the filter theory of memory. Some have speculated that brains, instead of storing memories, access them from a sort of 'global memory bank' outside. Both Gauld and Blackmore, writers with very different philosophical views, reject such a theory, for similar reasons.[54] In such a system, memories would have to be stored as specific traces. This would allow any brain to 'sort' through memories it needed at any one time. But this relies upon a naïve view of categorization or how, in a memory system, objects are classed as similar to one another or recognized as distinct. As Blackmore points out, my notion of a house might be quite different from yours. The Platonic idea that there is a simple representation of a 'house' floating out there seems very unlikely.

Similar sorts of problems also dog 'holographic' models of the mind. This sort of theory proposes that nature is structured like a hologram, and the brain as an instrument by which this holographic reality is analysed.

---

51 Popper & Eccles, 1977.
52 Braude, 1987.
53 Beloff, 2002.
54 Blackmore, 1993; Gauld, 1982.

This theory has been embraced by some as potentially explaining parapsychological phenomena like telepathy and clairvoyance. Unfortunately, it is also a somewhat incoherent theory, and Stephen Braude objects to it on several grounds.

Firstly, he objects to the reduction of the world into interference patterns. He also highlights its atomistic thrust, because such patterns are held to be the building blocks of familiar perceptual and experiential reality. The theory is, therefore, committed to the parsing of reality into elements of the frequency domain and that the 'objects, events or states of affairs of our familiar reality are simply ordered arrangements or structures'.[55]

Braude correctly observed that no such preferred parsing exists in nature. The classification of objects in everyday life and in science can be seen as to an extent arbitrary. To illustrate this he invites us to try and count the number of 'things' in one's room, which of course depends upon how one classifies a 'thing'. Likewise, there is not a preferred parsing to a person's subjective states; a person's memories of a specific event, say their thirtieth birthday, may be subdivided in any number of ways.

As Braude points out, the elements of a mental state only exist relative to some context in which they will be appropriate. This issue is linked to the wider problem of what — if anything — might be meant by a thought 'structure', which will be examined in more detail later on. For now, it is sufficient to note that the holographic theory depends upon positing certain types of preferred but implausible sorts of structures, and in its current form at least seems deeply incoherent.

If the theoretical underpinnings of filter theory are really so shaky, what can we make of the evidence cited in support of such theories? There has been a recent, and in many ways impressive, attempt to marshal evidence that falsifies biological naturalism and points in the direction of some sort of filter or dualist theory.[56] The cited evidence is that which is typically dismissed by most cognitive scientists in part because of its perceived unlikelihood but also because of its rarity and difficulty to reproduce. It includes; psi phenomena (ESP, telepathy, clairvoyance, psychokinesis), extreme psychophysical influences (placebo effects, voodoo death, stigmata), and evidence of the survival of personality beyond bodily death (memories/birthmarks from previous lives, mediumship, Near-Death Experiences).

A full consideration of the place of 'rogue phenomena' in the mind-sciences must wait for a later chapter, but one observation should be made here. One can immediately see why such evidence would be dismissed by most scientists. The reason is that many of these phenomena seem characteristic of a pre-scientific or animistic world-view, and belief in such things

---

55 Braude, 1981, p. 54.
56 Kelly *et al.*, 2007.

can be seen as atavistic or even anti-Enlightenment. To admit the validity of the evidence of parapsychology, say, would be to some a step backwards. This makes an impartial consideration of 'rogue phenomena', especially the more extreme forms, terribly difficult in a modern setting.

Despite this, such phenomena are worthy of attention because they are hard to dismiss completely. Sagan, a career sceptic, grudgingly admitted to the persistence of three parapsychological anomalies that bore further investigation.[57] If only a small portion of these phenomena are valid, then they might have the potential to allow us to modify or expand our views of consciousness and mental causation. However, we must also remember the earlier observation that empirical data in isolation cannot allow us to definitively decide between differences in ontology. There are simply too many ambiguities and too many potential differences in interpretation, and what looks like a compelling case to one might not to another.

Trialist Worlds

We are not committed to parsing the world into just one or two bits. Karl Popper divided the world into three sub-worlds. World 1 is the physical world of processes, forces, fields and material bodies. World 2 is the world of mental states. World 3 consisted of the products of the human mind, such as stories, explanatory myths, tools and scientific theories.[58] World 3 objects, like books or sculptures, can exist simultaneously as physical and mental (World 1 and 2 objects) but Popper argued that the content, which remains invariant in copies and editions, belongs in World 3. So this book might be instantiated electronically or physically, but its content remains the same (in a sense, Popper was talking about information of a particular form).

Popper also argued that World 3 objects could be unembodied. This is an issue as old as Plato, and hinges upon whether, for example, mathematical concepts really exist before they are discovered or invented by a mathematician. Popper claimed that with the invention or discovery of natural numbers there came into existence odd and even numbers before anyone noticed the fact. This issue of independent existence, in Popper's mind, constituted an entity's separation into a world of its own. So in a sense the existence of odd and even numbers does not fully 'supervene' upon the physical world, and might indeed be thought to exist in an independent, or semi-independent, Platonic 'world'. This conceptual world is not strictly physical, but it is not strictly mental either because it is not fully

---

[57] Sagan, 1995. The phenomena were; the ganzfeld telepathy experiments, the micro-psychokinesis experiments, and the evidence that some young children have apparent memories and birthmarks from previous lives.
[58] Popper & Eccles, 1977.

dependent upon either for an 'existence'. Hence the need for three worlds rather than two.

Frege and Penrose also split the world into three, but more along the lines of Plato; they hold that there is a mental world, a physical world, and a mathematical world. Penrose's arguments for an independent mathematical world are similar to Popper's, in that he argues that if, for example, a mathematical assertion can be settled one way or another by 'some appropriate form of mathematical reasoning' then it cannot be considered a subjective opinion but constitutes some form of objective truth.[59] Penrose states that the mathematical assertions that belong to Plato's world are those that are objectively true, independent of subjective opinion. He suggests that this abstract Platonic 'world' is also where we build our models in physics.

'Trialism' of either the Popper-Eccles or the Penrose-Frege sort is rejected by John Searle, who regards it as worse than dualism. He suggests that it is a kind of mystification to suppose that just because we invent scientific theories or write poems that these somehow inhabit a separate realm 'and not part of the one real world we all live in'.[60] Searle concedes that properties, numbers and universals do exist but calls this observation 'trivial' as they remain human creations. He does not believe that the Penrose-Frege view can be given a coherent formulation. The Popper-Eccles version of trialism is said to fail because 'the world of culture is a part of the one real world that we all inhabit and indeed contains applications of biological capacities for consciousness and intentionality'.[61]

Searle's objections seem to me to miss the point somewhat. The issue is not whether culture or mathematics exist within the 'real world that we all inhabit', but whether it is useful to parse the world in particular ways. In a sense, ontological disputes that concern the accessible world that Lewis described so eloquently can be characterized as a dispute between splitters and lumpers, splitters being those who see it as desirable to divide the totality of reality in different ways and lumpers who prefer to see it as an undifferentiated whole. Some, all, or none of the disputants might be correct.

Penrose could be seen as a splitter; but he emphasizes that his view of Platonic existence is 'simply a matter of objectivity' and 'should certainly not be viewed as "mystical" or "unscientific"'.[62] And as we have seen, those who insist that our world should only be viewed as one seamless reality are hardly immune from accusations of mysticism. And there seems little mystical about considering whether mathematical or cultural

---

59 Penrose, 2004, p. 15.
60 Searle, 2007, p. 23.
61 Searle, 2007, p. 23.
62 Penrose, 2004, p. 15.

Mind and Matter as Metaphors

If nothing else, this brief survey has shown that there seem to be many possible ways of parsing the world in which we live, and that it is by no means obvious that there is one true ontology to which we must or should adhere. This might seem surprising in a culture where these questions are often held to have been definitively settled in favour of physicalism.

I would, in this spirit, challenge attempts to definitively split or lump the world into its 'true' components. To do so is to ignore the metaphorical nature of these parsings.[63] There has long been considerable doubt as to whether this is desirable or even necessary in science. For example, Bertrand Russell was unconvinced that *any* meaning could be attached to either a substantial 'mind' or 'matter'. He noted that '[e]veryone knows that "mind" is what an idealist thinks there is nothing else but, and "matter" is what a materialist thinks the same about'.[64] (This objection also applies to neutral monism, which posits a singular 'stuff' that is neither mind nor matter.)[65]

Instead, Russell defined 'matter' as *what satisfies the equations of physics*. This definition is a logical construction rather than an appeal to a 'stuff'. *Mind* can similarly be defined as 'some group or structure of events'. Russell theorized that 'the grouping must be effected by some relation which is characteristic of the sort of phenomena we wish to call "mental"'.[66] He used the example of memory, and suggested that we might define a mental event as one that remembers or is remembered. 'Then the "mind" to which a given mental event belongs is the group of events connected with the given event by memory-chains, backwards or forwards.'[67]

This conclusion was echoed by Popper, who pointed out that:

> ...with Newton and... with Maxwell... the idea that there must be intuitively self-evident ultimate principles (such as, allegedly, those of a clockwork mechanism) behind explanation, had been exploded. Successive 'self-evident' intuitions as to the 'true nature' of matter had been shattered... What there was of value in essentialism — the desire to discover *structures behind appearances,* and the search for *simple* theories — was fully accommodated by the method of conjectural explanation.[68]

---

63 See Jones, 1982, for a discussion along these lines.
64 Russell, 1946/2004, p. 598.
65 Marshall, 2005.
66 Russell, 1946/2004, p. 598.
67 *Op. cit.*, p. 598.
68 Popper & Eccles, 1977, p. 193.

If we accept that it is science's job to offer conjectural explanations rather than in terms of 'stuffs', then the insistence on physicalism so prevalent in the mind-sciences begins to seem a little dogmatic.

The first step, I propose, should be a relaxation of the insistence that we decide upon a particular ontology, and in particular monistic physicalism. Once this is done, the problem shifts to developing models that can enrich our understanding of the world in which we find ourselves, rather than worrying about ultimate principles that we can probably never directly know. This might sound overly positivistic; but I am not insisting that we should stop thinking about said principles or hidden entities, or even making use of them, just that we need not be enslaved by a certain view of how the world 'must' be.

A second potential advantage is that the problem of the causal redundancy of mental states can be either set aside or perhaps even abandoned. If we accept that the problem is not how an abstract, metaphorical 'mental' reduces or relates to an abstract and metaphorical 'physical', but rather how separate maps can be logically related, then the issue of causal redundancy seems to me to be reduced in importance. This is simply because we cannot always — or even often — reduce very general observations about the world (in this case, the bits we label 'physical' and 'mental') to simple logical equations.[69]

Whatever the neuroscience seems to say (and I will deal with this subsequently), it seems to me reasonable to accept that we have subjective experiences of a particular kind which includes apparent causal efficacy in the world, and that the task is or should not be to 'reduce' these experiences to a theoretical model but to understand better how they might relate to our abstract maps of the 'physical', which includes maps of our bodies and biology. But we should remember how partial and fragmentary these maps will be, even if they seem locally sophisticated and data-rich. If we acknowledge this, then the problem becomes how one might develop better and more inclusive maps than we have currently; but that is a task for epistemology.

---

69 This implies that thought experiments like the 'Mary' colour scientist are rather less useful in determining whether physicalism 'is' true than has been previously assumed. These sorts of arguments, although clever, strike me as akin to the esoteric debates in medieval scholasticism. I do not think they really resolve anything, simply because they assume a specificity in the terms like 'physical' and 'mental' that doesn't really exist. See Beaton, 2005, for a summary of said arguments.

Chapter Six

Epistemology

Epistemology is the part of philosophy that deals with problems concerning the validity, nature, and limits of knowledge. It differs from ontology, which, as we have seen, attempts to tackle the nature of reality directly. Epistemology, by contrast, looks at *theories* of knowledge and of how we know what we know.[1] Also valid for my purposes is Elsasser's definition of epistemology as the 'thinking and reinterpretation of general concepts, primarily about space, time and causality [and, I will add, of "mind" and "consciousness"]'.[2] In this chapter, we will consider a range of concepts that will be helpful in our subsequent explorations of consciousness.

I will also argue, in different ways, for *epistemological pluralism*. This is the view that many different epistemological methodologies are necessary to attain a full description of the world. I oppose the reductionism and fundamentalism of many parts of science, encouraging multiple approaches, and acknowledging that different explanatory levels often cannot be reduced to one another.[3]

Epistemological questions themselves are often terribly difficult and convoluted, and frequently lead to dead ends. Salient examples include the mid-twentieth century disputes over perception, memory, 'sense-data', and language.[4] Such impasses were what led to the rejection of the idea that one *could* ever build a model or 'mirror' of reality, and in part to Feyerabend's form of epistemological anarchism where he claimed that 'anything goes' when it came to constructing theories about the universe.[5]

Entangled with the problems concerning theories of knowledge are problems with realism in science. Most twentieth-century epistemologies were realist in that they assumed that our perceptions were of a 'real' world, and, for practical purposes, I uphold this metaphysical assump-

1   *Encyclopedia Britannica*, 1973 ed.
2   Elsasser, 1998, p. 6.
3   en.wikipedia.org/wiki/Epistemological_pluralism accessed on 16/06/10.
4   See discussion in *Encyclopedia Britannia*, 1973 ed.
5   Rorty, 1979/2009; Feyerabend, 1975.

tion. The real/anti-real debate in the philosophy of science, however, refers to a different debate which is whether scientific theories accurately reflect an unseen reality or whether the theories are just useful tools that allow us to understand observational data better but have no other basis in reality.

We also need to ask whether or not such models offer universal and exhaustive descriptions of reality. In the pluralistic spirit, I will argue against the idea of universal 'laws' of nature and a unified hierarchy of science and in favour of a patchwork view, where specific theories cover limited domains.[6]

These threads form part of a wider argument that will move our thoughts on the mind, consciousness and human nature away from the fundamentalist and absolutist, and towards more pluralistic and open-ended views. A primary concern, therefore, is to question the many imagined restraints on the universe that 'force' us to conceive of human nature — as part of that universe — in a particular way.

To quote Paul Feyerabend, '...the world which we want to explore is a largely unknown entity. We must, therefore, keep our options open and... not restrict ourselves in advance'.[7] Our world-pictures, too, are inevitably partial and local to our own observations, no matter how wide-ranging we attempt to be.[8] If we accept this partiality, then I think we are led in the direction of pluralism and local, rather than 'universal', realism.

Modelling the Real

In the twentieth century, philosophers generally took the 'real' world for granted and tried to attempt piecemeal or local solutions to problems of forming reliable knowledge about it. Of primary importance in the early to mid-twentieth century disputes was the issue of how objects in the world could be related to perceptual knowledge about them.[9] Sight was a prime example, because the claim that seeing was a direct experience of an external object (say a tree or car) did not seem compatible with the complex physiological processes of vision. A gap exists between our knowledge of what happens in the eye and brain and our mental awareness of a tree or car. This, of course, is closely related to our primary problem of conscious experience.

The problem is compounded by illusions and hallucinations. We know that our perceptions can fool us and that we can sometimes see things that are not there at all. We might under some circumstances see a tree or car as double. We assume that this is wrong, but how can we know whether dou-

---

6   Cartwright, 1999; Dupré, 1993.
7   Feyerabend, 1975, p. 20.
8   James, 1909.
9   *Encyclopedia Brittanica*, 1973 ed.

ble or single vision is a more accurate depiction of the real object? There are a number of possible solutions to this sort of dilemma, but none are entirely satisfactory.

One problem is that it is very easy to lapse into a representational view of perception, or the idea that one's mind stores a discrete 'representation' of, say, a tree or car and reacts to the representation rather than the 'real' car. But this sort of argument often leads to infinite regress, because if one cannot interact with the external world and only representations, then how can one be said to be interacting with the external world at all? It becomes apparent that even superficially 'simple' questions like the relation of our perceptions to reality seem fraught with possibly unresolvable difficulties.

Cracking the Cartesian Mirror

Such problematic representational views of perception and thought, according to some, underlay early modern science.[10] According to the revisionist histories of Richard Rorty, Descartes had held the view that science should be the 'mirror of nature', or a direct and unmediated 'representation' of the material world revealed by our senses. In order to make this work, Descartes split the mind off from nature in order to have a realm in which this representational form of science could be built. Rorty saw such a 'mind', in the sense of an interior 'place' or theatre, as a cultural construction with no other reality.[11]

Immanuel Kant (1724–1804) thought that there were or could be privileged representations of reality, which built upon Descartes' naïve belief that one could discern the 'truth' if one thought clearly enough. Kant acknowledged that we experience nothing directly, and that everything was filtered through our senses, but he still thought that appropriate representational structures could reflect the 'real' world.

So, again according to Rorty, the particular philosophical programme developed by Kant relied upon two assumptions:

(1) It required the mind to be conceived as a 'mirror', reflective glass or separate space, and
(2) It assumed a correspondence theory of truth, or that one could build a true and accurate representation of the world that 'mirrored' reality.

Rorty, following Wittgenstein, disputed whether any philosophy or logical structure could actually do this, and criticized a number of twentieth-century philosophers who, albeit implicitly, retained the hope of finding such privileged representations of reality.

10 Rorty, 1979/2009.
11 Rorty, 1979/2009.

In contrast, Rorty observed, by the end of the nineteenth century, such philosophical schemes seemed untenable. He observed that '...the "naturalization" of epistemology by psychology suggested that a simple and relaxed physicalism might be the only sort of ontological view needed'.[12] In a situation like this, he thought, the idea that one *needs* privileged representations of the world might fall into eclipse. This didn't happen, according to Rorty, because thinkers like Russell and Husserl were still committed to untenable 'hidden' truths. Both of these latter thinkers rejected the idea that psychology could simply take over philosophy; Russell favoured logic as the essence of philosophy and Husserl focused upon private experiences.

Rorty, by contrast, embraced what he termed as 'epistemological behaviourism'. This involved a rejection of ontology, or the idea that we need an underlying philosophical way of describing human beings. It also involves the rejection of inner entities. As Rorty says; 'What we cannot do is take knowledge of "inner" or "abstract" entities as premises from which our knowledge of other entities is normally inferred...'[13] Hidden or unobservable entities like minds cannot, Rorty claimed, be used as a foundation for knowledge as external, eternal standards. In the absence of these external standards, philosophers had little left to do but discuss the world as they saw it personally.

Rorty's critiques have some strong points, such as his deconstruction of the specifics of Descartes' mirror of nature, but in other places, they are very much of their time. His rejection of private experience is inspired by behaviourism, and the elimination of hidden entities is based upon the philosophy of the positivists. His assertion that a 'relaxed physicalism' is desirable because, by implication, it *doesn't* require hidden entities seems to me fallacious. As argued in the previous chapter, at least *some* versions of materialism or physicalism *do* seem to imply a particular hidden entity named 'matter', and even those that do not require the reduction of mental states to physical processes, which are often described in terms of hidden entities (see below).

Rorty's view that psychology (or, currently, neuroscience) should 'take over' from philosophy has become remarkably widespread. Tallis notes that philosophers of mind have developed what he terms 'science-cringe', which effectively means the tacit acceptance of the demotion of philosophy to a branch of natural science.[14] So we have writers like Metzinger claiming that epistemological problems will be 'solved' by advances in

---

12 Rorty, 1979/2009, p. 165.
13 Rorty, 1979/2009, p. 177.
14 Tallis, 2004.

neuroscience, and claims that neuroscience can or should 'shoulder the burden' of the conceptual nature of knowledge.[15]

The move to naturalize philosophy seems to me one that should be resisted. This is in part because, as others have pointed out, philosophy and neuroscience actually do very different jobs. Philosophy is about the analysis of concepts, and neuroscience is about the empirical investigation of the brain and its processes. Of course, one might philosophize about the findings of neuroscience, or come to understand how humans think or act better via neuroscience, but this does not seem to me to justify collapsing one discipline into the other.

The most valuable part of Rorty's work is the demolition of the idea that a system of knowledge can 'mirror' nature. But if we acknowledge this, then it seems to weaken the claim of *any* system of thought, *including* naturalized science, to provide a coherent or comprehensive picture of the world. A naturalized physicalist ontology, even a 'relaxed' one, still constitutes a system of thought and a particular orientation to the world. The insistence that it is or should be the only view needed would constitute an ideological claim that can be rejected, because there may well be cases where different orientations towards the world can provide us with insights that Rorty's favoured philosophy cannot. This point can be clarified by further consideration of 'hidden entities'.

Surface versus Depth: An Implicit Epistemic Conflict

There is a split in philosophy between those who advocate the use of 'hidden' or unseen realities to enhance our understanding of phenomena in the natural world, and those who reject such attempts as incoherent and/or linguistic phantoms.[16] I am going to suggest that despite various notable demolition efforts, *both* viewpoints have some merit and both are alive and well in different contexts.

The notion of a hidden reality that is, under some interpretations, as or more 'real' than that revealed by our senses goes right back to Pythagoras and Plato. Plato, we will recall, supposed an ideal world of form and number of which the visible world was a shadow. Such a notion still underpins physics, which routinely relies upon mathematically required but 'hidden' entities (inertia, space, gravitation, dark matter and energy, super-

---

15 Metzinger, 2009; Zeki, 1999; see also critical comments in Bennett & Hacker, 2003.
16 Although Rorty classes private or subjective experiences as 'hidden', I am leaving this issue for a later chapter. This is because I see the question of whether subjective, conscious experiences can be termed as private as distinct from whether, for example, human behaviour requires the presence of a hidden or Platonic 'mind'. In the first case, we are trying to determine how best to understand, accommodate or classify direct personal experience and in the second, we are asking whether a distinct entity that no one can see or directly observe is necessary to explain said subjective experiences.

strings, etc.) to 'explain' the workings of the world. This seems, as Penrose notes, thoroughly Platonic.[17]

At the other extreme lies the rejection of all such hidden entities. It is often forgotten that David Hume's (1711-1776) critiques included a rejection of, for example, Newtonian notions of causation in favour of phenomenology. This was partly because Hume saw Newton's laws as supposing unseen elements that could not be reduced to experience.

The concern about hidden entities became acute when philosophers began to question what nouns actually stand for — and so how to define clearly any hidden or abstract entities. When I say dog, tree, house, black, white, we commonly assume that I am talking about something readily identifiable in the 'real' world. But the problem is actually far from straightforward, especially when we discuss abstract nouns like 'beauty', 'love', 'mind' and 'consciousness', because it is actually very unclear what these words stand for in concrete terms.

Difficulties like this are in part what led philosophers like Wittgenstein and later Rorty to doubt that philosophical or logical structures could form schemes by which we could coherently mirror the world. In *Philosophical Investigations*, Wittgenstein rejected the idea that there *was* an essential core of meaning in a word.[18] The best we could hope for, he thought, was a family resemblance between the word and what it signified. Biletzi notes that:

> Family resemblance also serves to exhibit the lack of boundaries and the distance from exactness that characterize different uses of the same concept. Such boundaries and exactness are the definitive traits of form — be it Platonic form, Aristotelian form, or the general form of a proposition adumbrated in [Wittgenstein's earlier work]. It is from such forms that applications of concepts can be deduced, but this is precisely what Wittgenstein now eschews in favor of appeal to similarity of a kind with family resemblance.[19]

Wittgenstein claimed that words do not stand for a specific, Platonic 'token' object (say an archetypal, perfect tree) but instead could only stand for *families* of specific objects (trees in general). This issue with generalizable categories gets more complicated when one considers more abstract 'objects' like minds and consciousness, and led thinkers like Rorty and Ryle to suppose that minds had no inherent existence at all.

Even today, there are conflicts between those who invoke a hidden or discrete 'mind' or 'consciousness' *as a theoretical entity* and those who regard either or both as some form of linguistic or, latterly, neurological

---

17 Penrose, 2004.
18 Wittgenstein, 1953.
19 Biletzki & Matar, 2010. Web page.

'illusion'.[20] But these views represent two poles on a continuum. On the one hand, it seems possible to demolish or severely critique many philosophies that rest upon hidden or unobservable entities, especially if they are held to be discrete. On the other, those unobservable entities have proved very useful in science in innumerable ways in the past. In the end, it seems better to judge the success or otherwise of invoking a hidden entity in pragmatic terms, or by whether the invocation of an entity is *useful*. This accords well with Karl Popper's idea of 'conjectural explanations' that postulate entities as part of scientific hypotheses but do not regard them as ultimate truths.[21]

Real and Anti-Real Currents in Science

The next question is, given that we cannot as easily eliminate hidden entities as the positivists hoped, whether said entities can be considered real or accurate descriptions of unseen or unobservable portions of the cosmos. There are two conflicting schools here. *Realism* assumes that science tells us the true and literal nature of the universe and its contents, about atoms and molecules, the nature of light, about cells and the furthest galaxies, about the distant past and maybe a little about the cosmos's future. In a realist interpretation, scientific knowledge about the natural world, even hidden portions, can be taken as more-or-less literally true. Many — but certainly not all — scientists lean heavily in the literalist, realist direction.

Anti-realists, by contrast, assert that the theoretical, unobservable parts of science are not literally real, but only useful models by which we can understand our actual observations better.[22] Anti-realists argue that theories like relativity and quantum mechanics are useful models that may not correspond at all with the unobservable aspects of reality, and think that only direct observations can be thought of as 'real'.

Anti-realists tend to appeal to a pragmatic definition of truth, which means that one can call a theory true because it is useful as opposed to useful because it is true. The practical utility of a scientific theory is often used as evidence for its superiority. For example, the 'aeroplane defence' holds that extreme relativism (or the idea that all ideas about the world are equal) cannot be true because scientific theories have provided us with the means for building working aeroplanes, whereas idealist or religious theories about the world, for example, have not given us this power.[23] Whilst these sorts of arguments seem to me reasonable counters to extreme philo-

---

20 Although it would be fair to say that, as far as minds go, the Ryleans have the upper hand, because in cognitive science, 'mind' is supposed to be decomposable to function. The jury is still out on consciousness.
21 Popper, 1959.
22 Chalmers, 1999. Chapter fifteen contains a summary of the realist and anti-realist debate.
23 See, for example, Dawkins, 2004.

sophical relativism, I would also note that they do not really resolve the real/anti-real debate, and on their own rely upon a pragmatic definition of truth. This is because utility does not necessarily follow from underlying or inherent 'truth' (however it may be defined).

This is a problem for some. Midgley complains that such pragmatic approaches only go half way because there are many facts in science that only really make sense if we suppose that they are meant more or less literally. So continental drift or the theory that dinosaurs are descended from birds need to be taken somehow literally. She also worries that pragmatism might lead us to take obviously absurd ideas as true if they are useful, giving the example that if it is expedient to believe there is a ferocious demon in electricity wires to prevent electrocution, then a pragmatist approach would compel us to say this is 'true'.[24] Midgley makes a valid point, and yet surely we are not forced into either a real, anti-real or pragmatic straitjacket. It seems to me entirely reasonable to treat some scientific theories as more literal than others, and often one ends up making a personal judgment on a case by case basis about these issues.

Hidden Structures?

Chalmers makes the case that science is realist 'in the sense that it attempts to characterise the structure of reality, and has made steady progress insofar as it has succeeded in doing so to an increasingly accurate degree'.[25] Broadly speaking, and in at least some circumstances, this seems a reasonable approximation of scientific theory, but I would suggest that this claim has significant limitations, especially in the field of human behaviour.

Chalmers' claim for realism in science hinges upon the definition and applicability of the word 'structure'. The word implies something that is more-or-less stable, regular and identifiable apart from the general background of the universe. Examples might be the division of the human brain into left and right hemispheres, or the heart into four chambers.

But this definition is less useful when considering other kinds of phenomena. Many things have unstable and temporary 'structures', whirlpools and cyclones being examples. Whilst the equations of fluid dynamics might allow us to predict or simulate a generalized whirlpool, they cannot predict the precise form that whirlpools or cyclones might take in the real world; any structure is loose. This is in contrast to the movements of the planets, which can be predicted with accuracy centuries in advance.

The exact behaviour of many dynamic and complex systems cannot be predicted, because there are too many variables and because even minor variations can have dramatic and unpredictable effects on the outcome.

---

24 Midgley, 1992, p. 131.
25 Chalmers, 1999, p. 245.

The 'Butterfly Effect' is the classic example of this: the idea that a butterfly flapping its wings in Tokyo can cause a storm in New York, making long-term weather prediction impossible.[26] This has significant implications for the study of the very complex human mind. Noam Chomsky has gone so far as to suggest that most explanations for human behaviour amount to opinions, because the exact sciences can only really answer questions about very simple systems.[27]

In addition, I would assert that many psychological phenomena that are taken to be derived from definite, definable and more or less permanent 'structures' (specifically, neural or 'information-processing' modules) are probably not reducible in this way. This view contrasts with a significant wing of contemporary psychology that tries to explain human nature almost entirely in terms of very specific behavioural 'modules' within the brain.[28]

Others, like Stephen Braude, go further, suggesting that mental states cannot really be called structured in *any* meaningful way.[29] He points out that mental *content* and *meaning* (a mental image, or what a thought is about) are not reducible to *structure* (neural events in the brain, biochemistry). For example, a memory of a person could be of almost anything (appearance, quirks, anecdotes, significant works) which do not have any underlying, intrinsic link or structure to which they can be reduced. If this is correct, then Chalmers' view of science cannot apply to psychology.

A more moderate stance may be to acknowledge that Chalmers' kind of realism, based upon a concept of structure, might only be of limited use in psychology. Sometimes it may be appropriate to try and identify the 'structures' associated with human cognition, behaviour or perception; sometimes it might not. But if Chalmers is correct that science equals locating structure, and Braude is correct that many mental states lack structure, then this hints at severe limits for a science of psychology.

However, we are not necessarily bound to define science in this way. The problem with Chalmers' view is that it restricts the practice of science to the structural (or, as we will discover below, law-generating systems only), which may be too severe a limit, especially in the social sciences. It is perfectly possible, for example, to observe and record idiosyncratic, unstructured behaviour in a systematic and 'scientific' way, although the fact of its idiosyncrasy may prevent one formulating systematic theories in the way favoured by natural science.

26 Gleik, 1987.
27 Chomsky, 2003.
28 Pinker, 1998; 2002; Fodor, 1983.
29 Braude, 2002.

No Grand Schemes: A Nomological Alternative

But even if we accept that some form of realism seems applicable for at least some of the theories of science, we are not compelled to suppose that these models can be grouped into a universal scheme of explanation.[30] Nancy Cartwright observes that facts can be roughly categorized into either those that are ordered into theoretical schemes, often reflecting behaviour in controlled environments (i.e. in laboratory conditions), and those that are not so ordered. She notes a widespread tendency to privilege the first kind of fact as exemplars of the way in which nature *should* work, and to assume that the facts that are *not* so ordered should conform to them.

Cartwright questions this sort of fundamentalist thinking, challenging the idea that one can 'downwards reduce' everything to the laws of physics, and also the idea that similar physical systems that are not observed in the laboratory might be 'reduced' to the models developed to account for strictly controlled lab experiments. She asks:

> Can our refugee (or unordered) facts always, with sufficient effort and attention, be remoulded into proper members of the physics community, behaving tidily in accord with the fundamental code? Or must— and should—they be admitted into the body of knowledge on their own merit?[31]

What is at stake here is the sort of picture that suggests that scientific knowledge can be considered a kind of pyramid, with the fundamental laws of physics on the bottom tier, then chemistry, then biology, then psychology, etc. (Figure 1a). The reductionist programme suggests that everything should, or could in principle, be reducible to the 'laws' of physics on the bottom tier, as psychology 'should' be reducible to biology which should be reducible to chemistry which should be reducible to physics. This picture is commonly accepted without question in science, and is I suspect the source of the insistence that any theory of consciousness *must* conform to known laws of physics and chemistry.

Cartwright rejects this picture of science, including the notion that there is a universal cover of law, instead adopting Neurath's picture of a patchwork of appropriate domains (Figure 1b). According to Neurath, explanations are 'tied', like balloons, to different parts of the world, but there is no system beyond this. 'Balloons' can sometimes be tied together to co-operate in different ways when solving problems, and the boundaries that 'balloons' cover are not fixed, and can expand, contract and overlap. But specific laws do not operate outside these boundaries.[32] This accords with

---

30   Cartwright, 1999.
31   Cartwright, 1999, p. 25.
32   Cartwright, 1999.

Feyerabend's view of science as a patchwork of partly overlapping, factually adequate but often mutually inconsistent theories.[33]

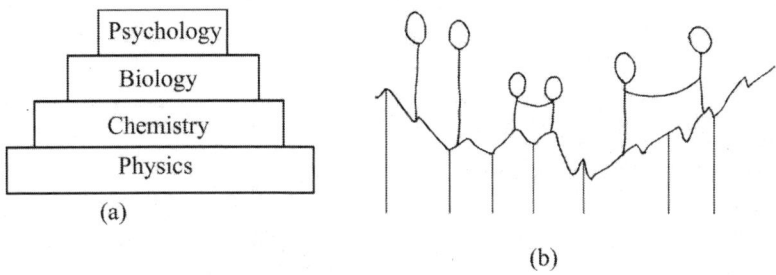

(a)

(b)

Figure 1. Pyramids versus Balloons. Scientific knowledge is usually pictured as a hierarchy, (a) with fundamental and universal laws at the bottom. Neurath and Cartwright suggest instead that theories can be pictured as balloons (b), pinned to bits of reality and with limited domains. In the latter picture, there are no truly 'universal' laws, although different knowledge domains can overlap or be 'tied' together via theoretical structures.

Cartwright expands upon this 'patchwork' notion by introducing the nomological machine. *Nomological* means 'expressing basic physical laws or rules of reasoning',[34] and stands for the various models in physics and other sciences by which we understand processes in the universe. These rule-expressing machines are only applicable in restricted circumstances, or *ceteris paribus*. This is Latin phrase meaning 'all other things being equal or held constant'.[35] Outside limited circumstances, specific nomological machines do not work, so they cannot be regarded as generating universal laws.

Cartwright illustrates this via the laws of planetary motion. Newton invented a model that established the magnitude of force needed to keep a planet in elliptical orbit by an application of the inverse-square kind of attraction in gravitational pull.[36] Newton's laws of gravitation did not seem to apply quite correctly to the orbit of Uranus, which did not move as expected. The irregularities in Uranus's orbit were eventually explained by the existence of a new planet, Neptune, whose gravitational pull perturbed Uranus's motion.

---

33 Feyerabend, 1975.
34 Merriam-Webster online dictionary, www.merriam-webster.com/dictionary/nomological accessed on 22/06/10.
35 en.wikipedia.org/wiki/Ceteris_paribus.
36 Cartwright, 1999, discussing Newton's *Principia*.

Cartwright interprets the failure of Uranus to conform to Newton's law in the following terms:

> The observed irregularity points… to a failure of description of the specific circumstances that characterise the Newtonian planetary machine. The discovery of Neptune results from a revision of the shielding conditions that are necessary to ensure the stability of the original Newtonian machine.[37]

Instead of universal laws, Cartwright argues for an understanding of *capacities*. Laws, she claims, need nomological machines to generate them, and hold only under the limited conditions in which these machines work. *Capacities*, by contrast, signify abilities, tendencies and propensities to do. So we might expect a simple object, like a billiard ball, to behave, or to have the capacity to behave, in a restricted set of ways in different circumstances. By contrast, a far more complex object, like a human being, would have a vastly expanded range of capacities that would be expressed differently according to different circumstances. Capacities are defined in very generic terms and stand for tendencies rather than highly specifiable and deterministic functions.[38] Nomological machines mark (the limited) places where general capacities can be narrowed into highly specific and determinate systems.[39]

One example might be learning. One can learn in a million different ways, via probably millions of different biological 'structures', and one can only loosely define what learning might be. Cognitive science, however, has developed a number of different theoretical models that can tell us something about some of the parameters of some forms of learning—say, learning facts, or how to distinguish oranges from apples. These latter models can be defined as nomological machines, because they apply only in restricted circumstances and concern restricted and specifiable subjects. Machine learning, even with neural nets or genetic algorithms, is also rule-restricted.

So Cartwright's work is of significance for those wishing to gain a better understanding of organisms in general and conscious beings in particular. Specifically it is relevant to subsequent discussions that will assess the validity of those who claim that the high complexity and organization of organisms makes current models of physics inadequate for biology. In this interpretation, such complexity signifies a boundary condition beyond which the nomological machines of current physics and chemistry do not give us wholly satisfactory answers.

The 'dappled world' notion has wider implications, because it suggests that many commonly expressed notions like, for example, universal or

---

37 Cartwright, 1999, pp. 52–3.
38 Ryle, 1949.
39 Cartwright, 1999.

strong determinism might be wrong. This particular belief underlies many of the claims that free will or consciously-determined actions 'must' be illusory.[40] But as Cartwright notes, we have no particular reason to suppose that everything operates under strict, causal laws, and every reason to suspect great causal diversity and even causal 'gaps'.[41] Cartwright:

> ...even our best theories are limited in scope. For, to all appearances, not many of the situations that occur naturally in our world fall under the concepts of these theories. That is why physics, though a powerful tool for predicting and changing the world, is a tool of limited utility.[42]

Implications for Cognitive Science

As indicated above, nomological machines are commonly used in cognitive science and most explicitly in Artificial Intelligence. A common hope in this field — especially amongst the pioneers — was that all human behaviour might be reducible to rule-based systems. This was Turing's basis for assuming that machine intelligence was possible.[43]

Cartwright's re-formulation forces us to look at these rule-generating systems in a different way. One of the objections to classical AI, which based its simulations upon strictly rule-based systems, was that human beings often do not seem to behave in ways that are restrained by formal rules.[44] However, systems with general capacities constrained and/or expressed by local variations in structure might serve as a more useful picture than simply assuming that humans 'are' rule generating systems.

Cartwright's other point, about unordered facts and the tendency to force them to conform to tidy models, seems to me especially salient in the human sciences. This is because a lot of human behaviour (and thought, if we accept Braude's arguments) seems unpatterned or idiosyncratic. Bauer notes a tension in the social sciences between those who wish to reduce human behaviour to models akin to those in the natural sciences and those who seek 'interpretive' approaches that respect the autonomy of human beings and acknowledge the impossibility of accurately predicting that behaviour.[45] But today the latter sorts of investigation have been eclipsed by reductive neuroscience.

Much of experimental psychology seems hell-bent upon reducing all 'real' human behaviours to that which are reproducible under specific conditions and, increasingly, associated with specific neural structures. Mimicking physicists, the aim seems to be to produce evidence of rule-based or structured behaviour that can be wholly described in terms

---

40 Wegner, 2002.
41 See also Dupré, 2001.
42 Cartwright, 1999, p. 9.
43 Turing, 1950.
44 Gardner, 1985.
45 Bauer, 2001.

of nomological machines. *But what if most human capacities are not expressed in reducible, structured ways at all?*

For it is quite possible for a wide range of human capacities to be expressed in idiosyncratic or singular ways. This would suggest that the attempt to restrict 'scientific' descriptions of human behaviour to the easily reproducible or law-generated might be in error. Like Cartwright, I think that facts and observations that cannot be fit into tidy schemes need to be respected, and that this is especially important in the human sciences because of the dangers of dehumanization.

Are Scientific Models Exhaustive?

Related to this concern is the probability that scientific models do not and probably cannot provide exhaustive descriptions of the portions of the cosmos that they describe. This seems especially true for human beings. And yet, we often encounter statements that seem to imply that exhaustive descriptions *can* be obtained from such models. Weizenbaum noted the tendency of AI researchers to assume, without any strong evidence, that computers could in principle do anything a human could.[46] More recently, we have claims like human minds are 'nothing more than a creation of genes and memes in a unique environment',[47] or that 'there is nothing more [than brain function] no magic, no additional components to account for every thought, each perception and emotion, all our memories, our personality, fears, loves and curiosities'.[48] These sorts of statements can only be taken seriously if we accept that scientific models present exhaustive accounts of reality, but there are reasons to doubt this.

As long ago as 1947, Aldous Huxley cautioned that:

> Confronted with the data of experience, men of science [sic] begin by leaving out of account all those aspects of the facts which do not lend themselves to measurement and to explanation in terms of antecedent causes rather than purpose, intention and values... some scientists, many technicians and most consumers of gadgets... tend to accept the world picture implicit in the theories of science as a complete and exhaustive account of reality; they tend to regard those aspects of experience which scientists leave out of the account, because they are incompetent to deal with them, as being somehow less real than the aspects which science has arbitrarily chosen to abstract from the infinitely rich totality of given facts.[49]

Huxley termed this 'nothing but' thinking, which is unfortunately present in much popular science writing today, as the preceding quotes demonstrate. Paul Feyerabend saw this dogmatic slide as common in science and

---

46   Weizenbaum, 1984.
47   Blackmore, 1997, p. 40.
48   O'Shea, 2008, p. 12.
49   Huxley, 1947, pp. 28–9.

ultimately pernicious to it.[50] Assume, he suggested, that scientists have adopted a particular theory, working exclusively upon it and excluding the consideration of alternatives. This pursuit might lead to certain empirical success and the theory may explain some observations that were previously mysterious. Such success will reinforce the commitment to the theory. But, Feyerabend observed, often alternative facts only come about by the consideration of alternative theories under differing methodological rules; the history of science is replete with revolutions that only occurred because conventional approaches were ignored and novel approaches adopted.

If, however, our successful scientists justify their refusal to consider alternative theories because of the reputed success of their theory, then this refusal, Feyerabend claimed, *'will result in the elimination of potentially refuting facts as well'*.[51] This, too, is a situation that is common in science; inconvenient facts that do not conform to established theories are often sidelined or ignored. Kuhn[52] saw these inconvenient facts as potentially revolutionary, but Feyerabend was concerned about the dogmatic potential of ignoring them. For if one is resolute in creating conditions that are favourable for orthodox theories and unfavourable to unorthodoxy, two things will happen. Inconvenient facts will become inaccessible simply because they are not pursued. Secondly, it will appear that 'all' the [selected] evidence will point with 'merciless' definiteness that all processes in a theory's domain will be consistent with the given theory.

Feyerabend went further, claiming that the 'appearance of *success cannot in the least be regarded as a sign of truth and correspondence with nature*' (his italics). He suspected that such appearance or the absence of major difficulties might be the result of a decrease in empirical content brought about the elimination of alternatives. If one refuses to consider alternative theories, and focuses only upon the evidence that suits your particular theory, then *of course* it will seem that your approach is comprehensive and exhaustive. But this is, to coin a phrase, an 'illusion'.

Consider this observation in the context of a cognitive science that insists upon reducing the human personality to rule-based, structured systems only and rejects any aspect of human personality that doesn't fit into these systems. This will result in a picture of the human being as, essentially, an automaton, because rule-based systems (nomological machines) are by their nature strongly deterministic (indeed, according to some this is the only 'scientific' way of thinking).[53] I question the desirabil-

---

50 Feyerabend, 1975; 1978.
51 Feyerabend, 1975, p. 42.
52 Kuhn, 1996/1962.
53 Wegner, 2002; Metzinger, 2009.

ity of reducing human beings in this way, especially if we accept Feyerabend's point as valid.

Feyerabend also thought that these tendencies should and must be resisted because they block progress in science and can lead to oppressive attitudes. His solution of 'anything goes' was far too radical for many, and has been fairly criticized in some of its aspects,[54] but his basic point remains sound. Assuming that one's (scientific) models reveal some aspect of the universe comprehensively and exhaustively is actually rather pernicious, and this seems doubly true for claims about human nature.

Conclusion

> No philosophy can ever be anything but a summary sketch, a picture of the world in abridgment, a foreshortened bird's-eye view of the perspective of events. And the first thing to notice is this, that the only material we have at our disposal for making a picture of the whole world is supplied by the various portions of that world of which we have already had experience. We can invent no new forms of conception, applicable to the whole exclusively, and not suggested originally by the parts. All philosophers, accordingly, have conceived of the whole world after the analogy of some particular feature of it which has particularly captivated their attention.[55]

Thus William James outlines a strong reason for epistemological pluralism and for resisting calls to settle upon one particular philosophy, approach or metaphysic to 'explain' the world. We end this chapter where we began: with the conclusion that our theories about the world are rather more restricted than they are often imagined to be. They are partial, applicable to restricted circumstances, and even if they reflect reality in some sense, they reflect local rather than universal truths. The preceding, brief, survey has shown that:

1. The general trend of epistemology in the twentieth century was away from the universal and towards particular and localized forms of explanation.
2. That despite resolute efforts to demolish hidden entities, they remain useful in some contexts.
3. That laws that were previously supposed to be universal are fact applicable only in *ceteris paribus* conditions, rendering local forms of realism more plausible than universal.
4. That we have *no* good reason to suppose that all phenomena in the universe are generated by nomological or fully deterministic systems. Human behaviour in particular seems partially or even poorly understandable in these terms.

---

54 Chalmers, 1999.
55 James, 1909, ebook on Project Gutenberg, http://www.gutenberg.org/cache/epub/11984/pg11984.html accessed on 23/06/10.

5. We have no reason to think that scientific models are anything like exhaustive descriptions, and if we want to make progress, we have every reason to pursue alternative methodologies and theories to those currently available.

All this might seem tangential to questions of consciousness and the mind, but we have seen that the assumption that any theory of the mind and consciousness *must* fit within 'universal' physical laws remains a widely-expressed sentiment, even amongst those non-reductive physicalists; see the quotation from Searle in the introduction. The thrust of his statement is that since 'science' has most of the universe sewn up, why can't we get consciousness to fit?

But if we assume that even our best theories are *not* universal and exhaustive, but are restricted and parochial, then the contradictions noted by Searle between a 'fields and forces' universe, and intentional, conscious human beings becomes far less troubling. It is simply that even our most general theories about the universe are far more fragmentary and limited than is generally appreciated. In short, the cosmos is quite wide enough for both fields and forces *and* conscious beings, and an immense number of other things, besides. To progress, we must be bold in our thinking and resistant to epistemological dogmatism.

Chapter Seven

The Problem of Biological Causation

Before we can approach the mystery of consciousness, we need to explore the problem of biological, causal capacities. This is because any theory of consciousness may have to contain a causal element. Broadly, I think that causal powers linked to the mind or consciousness would probably arise from or be related to the wider causal abilities of organisms, and we will see that there are reasons for thinking that these probably cannot be fully reduced to mechanism. This is in contrast to consciousness researchers who take current biology as a necessary and sufficient starting point (or constraint) on their theories, but if we are to take a pluralistic view, we cannot. If we acknowledge that even our best physical theories are limited in scope, then there seems a good probability that highly complex biological systems will need new sets of concepts and principles.

A number of researchers have suggested that the complexity and organization of living systems mean that classical physical models have limited application in the biological domain. Robert Rosen, a mathematician and theoretical biologist, noted that current physics absolutely does not encompass many life processes. He wrote that '…with respect to biological phenomena, contemporary physics is in exactly the same situation that nineteenth century physics faced in the atomic or cosmological realms: it either stands mute or it gives the wrong answers'.[1] Rosen's major claim was that purely mechanistic concepts are only suitable for dealing with relatively simple systems, and that the high degrees of complexity and organization we find in living systems represent a situation in which these models are not fully applicable.

Following Rosen, this chapter will focus on the issue of complexity and biological causation, although I am mindful of a faction within both biology and consciousness studies that claims that quantum effects might be important. 'Quantum biology' gathers evidence for quantum mechanical

---

1 Rosen, 1991, p. 37.

or non-classical processes in living systems, although there is considerable debate as to whether such processes are peripheral or of central importance in biology.[2] As such, the quantum challenge to classical biology forms a *leitmotif* as opposed to a main theme in this chapter, although I will examine a quantum model of consciousness in chapter ten. Here, our primary focus is on complexity.

The Capacities of Biological Organisms

In reacting to mechanistic views, Harré and Madden suggested that we regard even inanimate objects as possessing what they termed 'powerful particulars' that give them the capacity to behave in particular ways in particular circumstances.[3] So even a marble could be said to be predisposed to act in certain ways in any given situation. This contrasts with the mechanical view of a marble pushed about by external sources, and represents a partial return to an Aristotelian view of objects as possessors of causal capacities of their own.

A central question is whether organisms possess a wider or different kind of causal agency than do inanimate objects. It might seem obvious that human beings behave very differently from marbles, but a reductionist might argue that, at base, we are governed by the same physical laws as inanimate objects and so in effect are highly complex 'marbles'. Is this correct, or can we find significant causal capacities that distinguish living things?

Goodwin suggested that the two related causal capacities of *regeneration* and *autonomy* might fit the bill. Regeneration is a common feature of organisms, and is expressed in a multitude of different ways, from a salamander regrowing a foot, to a healing wound, to a new plant growing from a cutting. Goodwin describes these phenomena as 'expressions of the property of self-completion of individuation that is distinctive to the living state'.[4]

This active self-maintenance and completion was described by Maturana and Varela as *autopoiesis*. *Autopoiesis* describes a machine that is 'organized... as a network of processes of production... of components which... through their interactions and transformations continuously regenerate and realize the network of processes... that produced them...'[5] A living cell consists of various components bound together in various structures like the nucleus, organelles and cell membrane. These structures produce more 'components' (nucleic acids, proteins) which in turn maintain the structures, so autopoietic systems maintain themselves.

---

2   Abbott *et al.*, 2008.
3   Harré & Madden, 1975. Discussed in Goodwin, 1994.
4   Goodwin, 1994, p. 162.
5   Maturana & Varela, 1980, p. 78.

Machines, by contrast, are *allopoietic* systems. These are not self-producing or autonomous but are built from individual components. A computer does not build itself, but needs to be designed and its components built in a factory using machines different from its own internal structures. Autonomy and regeneration indicate significant differences in the causal features of living things and machines, which has implications for natural and artificial intelligence.

Expanded Epistemologies

We are now ready to consider the ideas of those who suggest we need to expand our epistemologies to better understand biological systems. The following approaches, which focus on the problems of causation in complex systems, might seem too radical to some, and too conservative to others. They might seem too radical to those who think that biology can be conceived in terms of purely conventional physics and chemistry, and too conservative for those who wish to re-introduce a vitalist aspect to biology. To the first, I would recall Feyerabend's observation that 'anything goes' has proved very fruitful for science in the past. Even if novel approaches prove unhelpful, we can at least learn what *doesn't* work. To the latter, I would say that whilst I am not at this point explicitly rejecting vitalistic or alternative approaches, it seems prudent to begin more conservatively from what we know before leaping to entirely new principles.

Elsasser

Elsasser's primary contribution was to lay out a holist alternative in biology that rejected both mechanistic reductionism and vitalism. He defined *reductionism* as a purely mechanistic interpretation of life that began with Descartes, who compared organisms to machines. This view was reinforced by the discovery that living things are made up of the same substances as non-living matter, including genes and molecules. More recently some, like DNA pioneer James Watson, have been even more ambitious and think that biology can or should be reduced to only atoms.[6]

Elsasser defined vitalism as the idea that the laws of nature needed to be modified in organisms as compared to inanimate nature. This he rejected because he accepted that the laws of quantum mechanics were correct and did not need to be modified when applied to organisms.[7] However, he did not think that a rejection of vitalism inevitably led to reductionism.

---

6   See Rose, 1997, chapters four and ten, for further discussions of reductionism.
7   We might dispute this in the light of Cartwright's ideas of limited domains. Firstly, we do not have to prove the 'laws' of quantum mechanics wrong in terms of organisms, just that the nomological models of quantum theory might not be applicable or fully applicable in the domain of large-scale organisms; but see Cartwright, 1999, chapter eight, for a discussion of how the quantum and classical world might interact.

His holistic alternative began with complexity. Elsasser claimed that 'an organism is a source (or sometimes a sink) of causal chains which cannot be traced beyond a terminal point because they are lost in the *unfathomable complexity* of the organism'.[8] The sort of complexity to which Elsasser refers implies that there is a limit to how much we could understand an organism by the sum of its parts, which is a key difference between holistic and reductionistic biology.

The consequence of unfathomable complexity can better be understood with reference to the concepts of quantum physicist Neils Bohr. Bohr developed the idea of complementarity, which is a point of view that was developed in an attempt to reconcile the fact that light seemed to be well described in terms of waves in some experiments and in terms of particles or *photons* in others. These observations were greatly troubling for classically-trained physicists who assumed that matter could only be divided in limited ways, and then understood in terms of straightforward cause and effect. During the 1920s, there was a gradual realization that accommodating the apparently contradictory data would entail a permanent departure from such ideals.

Bohr's response to the problems of wave-particles was complimentarity. Firstly, he asserted that the account of all evidence must be expressed classically, or in straightforward terms. However, he emphasized that at the quantum level it was impossible to make

> ...any sharp separation between the behaviour of atomic objects and the interaction with the measuring instruments which serve to define the conditions under which the phenomena appear. In fact, the individuality of the typical quantum effects finds its proper expression in the circumstance that any attempt of subdividing the phenomena will demand a change in the experimental arrangement introducing new possibilities of interaction between objects and measuring instruments which in principle cannot be controlled. *Consequently, evidence obtained under different experimental conditions cannot be comprehended within a single picture, but must be regarded as complementary in the sense that only the totality of the phenomena exhausts the possible information about the objects.*[9]

Bohr thought that we can only speak of quantum effects or subatomic processes within the context of the measuring instruments that we use, and that such restrictions meant that one could not simply sum these results to gain a comprehensive picture of causation at the quantum level. He believed that these objects or phenomena were so strange that any attempt to build up a picture beyond this could not work and would incur costs, so complimentarity states that the more specific knowledge that we are able

---

8   Elsasser, 1998, p. 37.
9   Bohr, 1949, my italics: see www.marxists.org/reference/subject/philosophy/works/dk/bohr.htm accessed on 07/07/10. See also Wheeler & Zurek, 1983, for an introduction to the philosophy of the Einstein-Bohr dispute.

to extract from a given experimental situation using one of these models, the less knowledge we can extract using the other, or complimentary, model.[10] This principle remains part of orthodox quantum theory, despite some experimental attempts to refute it, and despite complaints that it avoids questions concerning the nature of the reality, the observer and consciousness itself.[11]

A more generalized version of this principle would imply that 'the adequate description of these very complex systems [stable dynamical units, *aka* organisms] can only be achieved *at a loss*...'[12] In the extended version of complimentarity, the more we know about the lower-level physical and chemical processes, the less we can know about the higher-level organizational processes, and vice versa. The whole properties of organisms, Bohr suspected, might only really be understood at the expense of a loss of knowledge about their more mechanical, lower-level parts. If this is correct, then it implies that no series of actual or thought experiments could reduce all the properties of organisms to molecular structure or dynamics.

This has implications for the study of organic systems, because complimentarity suggests that the standard or Cartesian method cannot be entirely successful. The Cartesian method holds that to understand a phenomenon in nature, one must break it into pieces, figure out what the pieces do, and put these individual pieces back together in a working model. It supposes that complex phenomena can be understood entirely in terms of smaller, supposedly simpler, components.[13] However, we have seen that this does not fully work for understanding light, because complimentarity means that in any given situation you cannot simply 'sum' the knowledge obtained via a wave or particle model and obtain a comprehensive picture of the situation. Generalized complimentarity strongly implies that for similar reasons the Cartesian method may be only of limited use in studying living systems as a whole.

By contrast, the efficacy of the Cartesian method is standard and mostly unquestioned in both neuroscience and consciousness studies.[14] Conventional attempts to provide 'mechanisms' for consciousness provide an illustration of exactly this sort of logic; hence Seth's assertion that 'a satisfactory scientific theory of consciousness will require the specification of detailed mechanistic models'.[15] Such an attitude is also present in Michie's articles proposing to treat consciousness as an engineering issue.[16] Carter,

10 Elsasser, 1998.
11 Bandyopadhyay, 2000. See Rosenblum & Kuttner, 2006, chapter ten, for a non-technical discussion of the unease with the instrumentalism of the Copenhagen interpretation.
12 Elsasser, 1998, p. 9, italics in original.
13 Elsasser, 1998.
14 See the claims of Carter, 2002, and Koch, 2004.
15 Seth, 2007.
16 Michie, 1994/5.

too, proposes that once we have broken the correct systems up and understood their individual functions, we can put them back together and gain a picture of where consciousness fits.[17]

Elsasser, by contrast, thought that certain properties in organisms cannot be analysed or fully understood in this way. Any formal biological theory would have to begin by acknowledging this limit (a similar kind of which might exist in neuroscience).[18] Having acknowledged unfathomable complexity, Elsasser suggested a number of principles upon which one might build a theory of biology.

The first is the principle of *ordered heterogeneity*. This starts from the observation that the number of possible combinations of atoms, and thus patterns in biological systems, is immense. However, on a large scale, there are observable regularities; Elsasser termed this 'order above regularity'.[19] This kind of order, Elsasser suggested, was not familiar to the traditional chemist and physicist.

Secondly, he proposed the principle of *creative selection*. He saw that a choice was made in nature for a given biological unit (or cell, to use his terminology) amongst an immense number of possible patterns. He thought 'that *the availability of such a choice is the basic and irreplaceable criterion of holistic or nonmechanistic biology*' (his italics). This is a controversial statement because patterns or morphological structures in biology are generally supposed to be 'selected' by either natural selection or constraints in the physics and biology.[20] However, Elsasser saw the existence of such a choice as a 'scientifically justifiable' form of creativity because it did not posit the creation of something *ex nihilo* but from an immense number of possible choices.

The criterion for this creative choice was supplied, at least sketchily, by a third *principle of holistic memory*. This principle was based upon the selection of a pattern from an immense reserve of possible patterns, on the basis of resemblance to some earlier pattern. He proposed that no mechanism for the transmission of information over time could be specified, and that transmission of information over a time interval happened without an intervening device or storage mechanism and 'without spatiotemporal contiguity'.[21]

He fully acknowledged that such a proposal would be considered heretical, but he held it to be necessary because of what he saw as significant failures in mechanistic accounts of both memory and the transfer of information in reproduction. Specifically, he saw the idea of a 'memory trace'

17 Carter, 2002.
18 Uttal, 2001; 2005; see the discussion in chapter ten.
19 Elsasser, 1998, p. 4.
20 Dawkins, 1986; Rose, 1997.
21 Elsasser, 1998, p. 120.

as untenable on theoretical grounds and in the light of the evidence from neuroscience. Similar observations about memory continue to be made,[22] and many of these problems remain, despite attempts to understand memory in terms of dynamic systems that do not use explicit 'traces'.[23]

Elsasser's idea about holistic memory seems very similar in some respects to Rupert Sheldrake's theories of morphic fields.[24] These posit a sort of non-local field that holds information that helps shape the development of embryos, store memories, and allow communication at a distance between organisms. He suggests that 'habits', which he defines as both behaviours and forms in nature, are 'remembered' by such fields, and that each time a given instance of a habit occurs (say, a behaviour), the field 'remembers', making any subsequent repetitions of this habit easier. This theory has been strongly criticized on theoretical grounds[25] and the mostly behavioural experiments to detect predicted effects have been ambiguous or not successful.[26]

All of which might seem, by extension, damning to Elsasser's proposals. Nonetheless, there are a number of mitigating factors. Firstly, Elsasser's ideas are not strictly identical to Sheldrake's and do not explicitly propose that 'habits' *per se* are what is remembered. This is significant because most of the experiments to directly test Sheldrake's theory looked at this aspect of his theory. (It is true that Sheldrake has, more recently, conducted more successful experiments concerning psi phenomena, but these need not be interpreted in terms of his theory: see also the comments of his critics.)[27]

Even if Elsasser was wrong in the specifics, the insight that memory may be linked to the wider capacities of the organism (like reproduction) and not to specific mechanisms is interesting and also suggested in Ho's work (see below).

One also could reformulate Elsasser's principle slightly in terms of Cartwright's general capacities, which are distinguished from, but expressed via, various sorts of specific mechanisms. Memory might prove amenable to this sort of analysis, as it does not seem to rely on specific traces or tokens, and yet can be affected in specific ways by particular sorts of brain damage to localized areas of the brain.[28] This may be because it is a general capacity whose expression is dependent upon various specific brain structures. These capacities do not come from nowhere, but spring from the organism as a whole.

---

22 See Gauld's chapter in Kelly *et al.*, 2007, for a summary.
23 Shannon, 1991; Brooks, 1991; Port & Van Gelder, 1995.
24 Sheldrake, 1981/2009; 1988.
25 Braude, 1983.
26 Ertel, 1997.
27 A useful example of these more recent controversies is found in a special issue of the *Journal of Consciousness Studies*, **12** (6), 2005, edited by A. Freeman.
28 See Gauld's chapter in Kelly *et al.*, 2007.

Elsasser's ideas undoubtedly demand an expansion of conventional epistemologies of biology, but to him such an expansion was suggested by problems like memory, and by the fact that the continuing work of biologists tended to produce blizzards of new information but very little insight into how biological systems work as a whole. We might note a similar situation in neuroscience, where new fMRI studies are conducted with regularity but which seem often to be interpreted in relatively crude theoretical terms.

Rosen

Robert Rosen developed a slightly different picture of complex systems, specifically organisms, which also suggested the need to expand thinking in biology beyond mechanistic metaphors. He was no more a vitalist than Elsasser, seeing organisms as material systems of very special kinds that are both complex and admit a kind of relational description.

Relational biology is essentially a theory of organization. Like Elsasser, Rosen saw the higher organizational properties of organisms as somehow complimentary to the underlying physics and chemistry. He noted that where reductionist analyses might keep the physics and chemistry and throw away the organization, in his analyses one keeps the organization and discards the underlying physics.[29]

The term *relational biology* was coined by a physicist named Rashevsky. Rashevsky thought that the direct application of physical principles in building a theory of life was 'not likely to be fruitful'. We must, he thought, 'look for a principle which connects the different physical phenomena involved and expresses the biological unity of the organism and of the organic world as a whole'.[30] Rashevsky was looking for the principles that govern the organization of biological systems, rather than the phenomena themselves. (We can already see, however, how Rashevsky's notions might be applicable to consciousness; some of the primary problems we face concern how to 'connect different physical phenomena' and 'express biological (perceptual) unity'.)

Like Elsasser, Rosen began with a rejection of the Cartesian idea of organism-as-machine, or a sum of component parts. Or rather, the Cartesian view was too restricted because it entailed a concentration on the components of the organism at the expense of understanding it as a whole. This missing or ignored aspect could be illustrated by the following analogy; give a physicist a clock, and they would concentrate entirely on how it works and never on how it came to be a clock.[31]

---

29 Rosen, 1991.
30 Quoted in Rosen, 1991, p. 113.
31 Rosen, 1991.

This narrow concentration on components at the expense of wholes meant that 'a strange and rather dreary consensus' had developed in biology:

> On the one hand, biologists have convinced themselves that the processes of life do not violate any known physical principles; thus they call themselves 'mechanists' rather than 'vitalists'... but on the other hand biologists are also, most fervently, evolutionists; they believe wholeheartedly that everything about organisms is shaped by essentially historical, accidental factors, which are inherently unpredictable...[32]

Rosen thought that the combination of mechanism and evolution were insufficient to offer a comprehensive picture of the organism. In part this was because he thought that the conception of mechanism in physics did not satisfactorily carry over to the description of organisms or any sufficiently complex system. Mechanisms were, in Rosennean terms, 'simple' systems, and could not adequately describe the behaviours and properties of complex ones.

Rosennean complexity can be outlined as follows:[33] modern physics (and, by extension, fields like Artificial Intelligence) base their understanding of the world on mathematical modelling. Modelling establishes a congruence between a system in the world and a modelled system (say between a model of planetary motion and the observed motion of planets). Rosen thought that complexity arose, intuitively speaking, when the real system behaved in ways that the mathematical model did not predict, so his theory was rooted in a comparison between a real system and our theoretical models of it.

If we have a model that can predict the behaviour of a system perfectly, this system will not have complexity; it will be, in Rosen's terms, a simple system. However, living systems are rarely, if ever, like this. They often require multiple partial dynamical descriptions, no one of which, or combination of which, will be enough to successfully describe the system.

In other words, the reductionist strategy of taking such a system apart and reconstructing it to gain a one hundred percent understanding of it *will fail*. In Rosennean phraseology, this means a complex system will have *non-fractionable* aspects. This is, in some respects, reminiscent of Elsasser's or Bohr's idea of a generalized complementarity, but expressed in a slightly different way. Complex systems have properties that cannot be derived from the parts.

There is an additional consideration, which has a bearing upon whether strong Artificial Intelligence is possible. Simple systems, those which can be fully described by their models, are Turing computable. Complex sys-

---

32 Rosen, 1991, pp. 13–4.
33 Outline after Gwinn, 2006.

tems are not. What this means is that, no matter how powerful a computer you have, it will be unable to fully model the behaviour of a system that is complex in the Rosennean sense.

Aristotelian Analyses

Rosen's ideas went beyond a rejection of mechanism. Another important aspect of his version of complexity was based upon Aristotle's analysis of causation. Aristotle's sought to explain the causes[34] (*tropoi*) of material objects not in one sense but in four. The material cause is the raw material, or heap of matter without form.[35] The order or *logos* is like the 'plan' of the physical structure. The *efficient* cause is that which brings about a change in a thing, and the final cause or *telos* is the striving toward or realization of an end form.

We illustrated this with a house-building metaphor. The raw material is the bricks and mortar. The act of building the house is the efficient cause, the blueprint of the house becomes the *logos* by the act of being consulted during the construction, and thus imparting its order on the construction. The final cause, or *telos*, is the purpose of the dwelling as a place to live.[36]

Rosen thought that one could usefully apply this sort of analysis to organisms. He recognized, however, that final causes had been expelled from biology because they implied design. 'Nowadays', he wrote, 'biologists generally believe they have papered over this issue. In a nutshell, Darwinian evolution through natural selection, with its attendant adaptations, serves precisely to do this. The argument is that the produce of an evolutionary process gives the appearance of design but without any of the finalistic implications of design'.[37]

Rosen was not implying that we have to resort to an Intelligent Designer to account for biological form or function. What he was suggesting was that natural selection alone, or natural selection plus mechanism, were incomplete explanations for why organisms are as they are. But if we adopt instead something like an Aristotelian analysis, where different causes contribute and are complete in themselves but are not the whole story, then we might be able to gain a more comprehensive picture of organisms. Thus, in biology, one might know all about evolution but nothing about physiology, and vice versa. 'In particular', Rosen noted, 'any exclusion of finality from evolution does not thereby exclude it from phys-

---

34 Although one of Rosen's students has urged that the words 'cause' and 'causation' be dropped because they can cause confusion.
35 Gwinn, 2006.
36 Appleyard, 1992.
37 Rosen, 1991, p. 132; see the various works of Richard Dawkins, especially Dawkins, 1986, for arguments in favour of mainstream views.

iology, or conversely'.[38] So whilst factors like final causes might be unhelpful in explaining changes over evolutionary time, they might not when considering, for example, how an organism might grow from an embryo to an adult.[39]

Rosen's approach, which acknowledges that causation, form and function in organisms can be considered in several different ways, each complete in themselves but not the whole story, is congenial to a pluralistic viewpoint. If we can decompose biological causation into not one but four (or more) different modes of explanation, then we have the potential to develop far richer views of the organism than those based upon one mode of explanation (like natural selection alone, or physiology alone). Recognizing a need for plural causal explanations, each with their own distinct and sometimes contradictory criteria can also help mitigate tendencies towards the absolutist or 'nothing-but' thinking.

It is worth saying a little more about final causes in Rosennean complexity, since these seem particularly germane to the issue of mental causation. Rosen's theories were primarily mathematical and topological. As such, Rosen was concerned with ways of describing the general organization of biological systems mathematically, in terms of abstract block diagrams and functions. A key claim he made was that finality is allied to possibility whereas the other three causal categories involved necessity. In other words, whereas the *material, efficient* and *logos* causes are deterministic, the final cause is probabilistic.

Final causes are in part *verboten* because they seem to violate a traditional 'law' of Newtonian science, that causes must precede effects. Yet final causes seem to indicate that the effects precede the cause. Rosen gets around this by means of a formalization where there is no time parameter. This does not mean anything magic, only that he has created a specific way of describing causation in an organism where one can discuss final causes and identify a component in terms of its final cause or purpose. Instead of a time parameter, relational analyses only consider components, organizations and mappings. It is like, for example, analysing the social organization of a university but ignoring the timetable by which meetings are held. So we can, in Rosen's terms, legitimately talk about the function or purpose of part of an organism without invoking either vitalism or intelligent design.

What is Life?

Lurking at the heart of these sometimes abstruse analyses is the question of the nature of life itself. This has relevance because our understanding of life is inevitably linked to our understanding of consciousness. If we

---

38 Rosen, 1991, p. 132.
39 But see chapter twelve for a discussion of teleology in evolutionary theory and cosmology.

believe that consciousness is wholly generated by the organism, then the nature of this generation will be determined by the nature of life itself. But even if we subscribe to 'filter' or mediation theories, *a la* William James and Henri Bergson, or more recently Hameroff and Penrose,[40] then we have to explain how and why biological systems appear to 'filter' consciousness in such unique and complex manifestations that do not seem evident in non-living things.

As we saw in chapter two, historically, the post-Cartesian definition of life swung between mechanists and vitalists, and since then, the traditional assumption has been that if we cannot find a vital force, and organisms are considered to be atoms only, then mechanism is the only way to go. We have seen, however, that our choice is not only between these two historically-conditioned alternatives. We can posit that even if organisms are composed of atoms only, then certain features of their organization and complexity may well make them differ significantly from mechanisms; the *autopoietic* and *allopoietic* distinction being an example of this.

There have been various other attempts to define life in terms of physiology, metabolism, biochemistry, Darwinian genetics and thermodynamics. Each approach has its advantages, but each has drawbacks.[41] Life itself seems to be an example of a heterogeneous, blurry class rather than a Platonic, definite one. The interesting thing is that one's definition of life often conditions how it is perceived. If one sees life as 'nothing but' selfish replicators then one will tend to see individuals as robots in the service of these organisms, perhaps 'infected' with other selfish replicators.[42] On the other hand, if one focuses upon the bioelectrical properties of living tissues and membranes, then one will tend to see life as electrodynamic or electronic 'through and through' (see below).[43] Each of these definitions will often prove partial, containing some truth but not the whole truth. Organisms and life can be defined in myriads of possible ways.

In recent times, definitions of life have favoured particular types of complexity theory, which focus on molecular and other types of organization, and dynamical systems.[44] Another favoured focus has been on the thermodynamic dimension. Finally, a growing awareness of the role of non-classical or quantum-mechanical processes in biological systems is gradually causing a redefinition of organisms away from purely mechanistic conceptions.[45] The general trend has been to move from static and robotic,

---

40 Hameroff, 2010.
41 See the *Encyclopedia Brittanica*, 1973 ed., Vol. 13, 'Life' entry for a useful discussion of these alternatives.
42 Dawkins, 1976; Dennett, 1991; Blackmore, 1999.
43 Ho, 2008; Presman, 1970.
44 Kaufmann, 1993; 1995; Goodwin, 1994. See also Rose, 1997, for a useful summary.
45 Abbott *et al.*, 2008.

state-determined models towards dynamic and holistically functioning models.

A recent, interesting synthesis is provided in Mae-Wan Ho's book *The Rainbow and the Worm*, written in the spirit of Schrödinger's classic *What is Life?*[46] In *Rainbow*, she moves away from conventional accounts by suggesting that life has a number of common features, including sensitivity to specific cues from the environment, the efficient and rapid transduction of energy, the exhibition of dynamic, long range order and co-ordination, and a wholeness and individuality.

Ho explores these various features of living organisms in a number of different ways. She begins by a re-examination of Schrödinger's contention that life might be definable in terms of 'negentropy'. Entropy, disorder or waste heat, in thermodynamics, is a quantity that increases in real processes and never decreases.[47] This can be illustrated by the cup of coffee becoming cold or a drop of ink in water that diffuses to fill the whole vessel. These processes illustrate a tendency to return to *thermodynamic equilibrium*.

Living things, when alive, appear to sidestep this and to remain in a state that is far from equilibrium, always having energy available for necessary tasks. This is what Schrödinger meant by 'negentropy'. They achieve this in a number of ways. Firstly, they are open, not closed, systems (the laws of thermodynamics only count in closed systems like steam engines, where the theories were first explored). Morowitz suggests that living things might be defined as far-from-equilibrium 'engines' and dissipative structures.[48] The latter are structures that maintain themselves by a continuous flow and dissipation of energy.

Energy in living things is distributed throughout the system in a series of organized, heterogeneous and dynamic loops.[49] This organization has a number of consequences in terms of sensitivity and signal sensitivity. Firstly, it means that organisms can enormously amplify even faint signals from the environment; an example would be the ability of some species' nerves to fire as a result of one photon falling on their retina. This is possible because such tight couplings allow 'molecular cascades' throughout the whole system.

Ho also suggests that memory might be understood in terms of such tightly coupled, multiple dynamic processes. Organisms when alive do not have discrete 'states', but instead consist of multiple constantly moving or changing states. In Kaufmann's words, life exists at the 'edge of

---

46 Schrödinger, 1944.
47 See discussion in Ho, 2008, pp. 14–20.
48 Morowitz, 1978. Quoted in Ho, 2008.
49 Ho, 2008, p. 25.

chaos'.[50] These signals are maintained by constant pulses of chemical and energy flow, and if maintained such signals propagate over larger and larger areas over increasing time-periods.

A typical example is the muscle growth familiar to bodybuilders. The sustained use of a muscle 'boosts' the tissues to a different condition to that in which they originally existed and facilitates growth. Ho suggests that this process 'tunes' the system so that in future a muscle will be ready for anticipated additional use. She generalizes this sort of effect to suggest that memory is ubiquitous throughout the organism, a product of such dynamic coupling, and a response to recent and current activity.

Another set of features explored by Ho are the electrodynamic, which also includes quantum effects. She compares living structures, and in particular connective tissues, with liquid crystals. Liquid crystal, which should be familiar to anyone who owns a digital watch, is a state or phase of matter between the solid and liquid which has some of the properties of both, and which is sensitive to electromagnetic fields. Ho notes that Nuclear Magnetic Response (NMR) studies have shown that muscles have a liquid crystalline structure.[51] However, she acknowledges that few have yet concluded, as she has, that organisms *are* liquid crystalline.

This idea has important consequences for Ho's conceptions of consciousness. She believes consciousness to occur throughout the whole organism. It is not, in her conception, just a product of the nervous system and brain, but of the more general properties previously described, in particular that of liquid crystals. She asserts that:

> ...our consciousness is delocalised throughout the liquid crystalline continuum of the body (including the brain), rather than being just localised to our brain, or to our heart. By consciousness, I include, at minimum, the faculties of sentience (responsiveness), intercommunication, as well as memory.[52]

As far as the brain is concerned, this approach leads her to favour one particular version of the 'global workspace' theories,[53] which holds that consciousness (or, specifically, conscious awareness) consists of temporal patterns of synchonized firing among multiple brain regions (I will examine such theories in part three).

Ho's theories have considerable merit, especially since they place consciousness—or a particular conception of it—in the wider context of the capabilities of the organism. The emphasis on awareness being a whole-body, as opposed to 'brain', phenomenon is also significant. However, in my view, her theories do not solve the problems associated with

---

50 Kaufmann, 1995.
51 Ho, 2008.
52 Ho, 2008, p. 229.
53 John, 2005.

'consciousness', 'sentience', and 'memory'; terms which are never more than cursorily defined. In addition, some of her claims, as for example that her picture of organisms 'solves' the binding problem, are almost certainly premature.[54]

I would also note that Ho's definition of consciousness can be seen as, in its way, as reductionist as more conventional accounts. Although she rejects any *'a priori* dualism', she does not seem to realize that the implied, preferred monism is just as *a priori*. Secondly, I do not think that consciousness can or should be reduced to simple 'awareness', as I will make plain subsequently. At the same time, Ho has provided a far richer picture of organisms than that propagated by those concerned with selfish replicators only, and this should be applauded.

Conclusion

These conclusions might be drawn:

1. Something like Elsasser's holism may be applicable to the study of organisms in general, and when studying minds and consciousness in particular. This is because consciousness, especially, seems to be better understood as the property or quality of whole organisms rather than its parts.
2. Elsasser's conception of memory *sans* intervening storage is more contentious and has points for and against its further consideration. Points against are the incoherence of conceptual formulations of past versions, and the relative experimental failure of one version (Sheldrake's morphic fields). Points for its consideration are the failings of conventional mechanistic and 'trace' theories, and that it remains a relatively unexplored concept. There may be conceptions out there that address past failings.
3. That causal accounts, especially of organisms, can be complete in themselves but not the whole story. Life does not have to be conceived as just a product of 'chance and necessity', but is a rich and multicausal phenomenon that exhibits features (autonomy and regeneration) that are not found (or expressed to nearly the same degree) in inanimate things.
4. That, because of point 3, *telos* or final causes may considered as a cause *within* organisms without implying intelligent design and contradicting the role of chance in evolutionary history (although see my discussion of evolution and consciousness in chapter twelve).
5. That these expanded ways of looking at life have a significant impact on our conceptions of mind, memory and consciousness, even though these implications have not yet been worked out. Specifically, they move our thoughts away from purely mechanistic neo-Darwin-

[54] Ho, 2008.

ian models and towards the idea that many features previously taken to be just features of the nervous system are (i) distributed through the organism, and (ii) aligned with wider capacities of the organisms like reproduction and the creation and maintenance of form. They also hint that the classical physics-only approach may not be appropriate for comprehensively understanding organisms and, by extension, consciousness.

In summary, the biological *milieu* is rapidly evolving in a way that impacts the study of consciousness. Of particular importance is the growing awareness that concepts of causation need not be restricted to mechanical, reductive causation only. In addition, newer pictures of the organism provide a context in which theories concerning neural correlates of awareness can be placed, even implying, as in Ho's work, that such awareness need not be a 'brain only' phenomenon. Thirdly, we have hints that quantum effects may not be as peripheral in biology as they were previously supposed. This biological background, including the heterodoxies of Elsasser and Rosen, will prove important when we consider the cognitive science research programmes developed under the predominant philosophy of Western science, which is, of course, physicalism.

Part Three

Physicalism and its Limits

Chapter Eight

The Computational Model of Mind

There is a deep-rooted cultural myth that humans and machines are interchangeable.[1] The machine metaphor has always been relatively loose, and has continually changed as technology has advanced, but remains pervasive partly because it is seen as the *only* viable alternative to some form of animism or dualism. But how far can the human-as-machine metaphor actually take us in understanding mind and consciousness? Specifically, can currently predominant metaphors based upon our information-processing technology supply a comprehensive picture of a human being?

Additionally, as should become evident, other constraining assumptions operate within the overarching framework of organism equals machine. Rao suggests that Western theories, by assuming a sharp division between mind and matter and by emphasizing the intentionality of consciousness, also entail *representational* views of thought and mental knowledge, or 'that there is a pre-given world of which our cognitions are representations'.[2] Conscious, subjective experiences, when they are not denied, also tend to get equated with representations of an 'outer world'. In fact, debates within the Artificial Intelligence community tend to oscillate between 'representational' views and behaviourist or, more recently, 'dynamical systems' views that deny any 'inner' kind of experience at all.

In this chapter, I examine the general logic of the computational and/or information-processing approach, some of its facets and some of its limitations. I should note at the outset that it seems difficult or even impossible to *disprove* the proposition that the brain 'is' an information-processor akin to a computer. This was illustrated by the difficulties Penrose faced in trying to disprove that the mind works algorithmically or computationally, an approach which a sympathetic commentator admitted was 'very much

---

[1] I am using *myth* in the sense of an organizing story and not something that is necessarily completely false.
[2] Rao, 2002, p. 135.

disputed'.[3] The computational model of mind, then, does not seem to adhere to strict Popperian falsificationism.[4]

We need also to bear in mind the deeply metaphorical nature of these approaches, which is sometimes admitted even by proponents of strong Artificial Intelligence. At the end of *Consciousness Explained*, Dennett admits that all he had done 'is to replace one family of metaphors and images with another', but he stated that 'It's just a war of metaphors... but metaphors... are the tools of thought...'[5] This admission, in my view, sheds some light on why it's so difficult to falsify these approaches, simply because it seems virtually impossible to demonstrate that a metaphor is entirely *in*appropriate.

The Outcome of 60 Years of AI Research

This is not the place to detail exhaustively the pros and cons of the AI approach. However, we should note that the field underwent a certain cycle of events which seems common in post-war science. There was an initial phase of overconfidence, where many overconfident and overblown predictions were made, a period of sobering up, where difficulties were faced, and then a slow consolidation of work that was in some ways impressive but which failed quite to match expectations.[6]

The initial overconfidence should be highlighted. Dreyfus noted that the early champions of AI behaved as if they had made the previous 2000 years of philosophizing about perception and memory obsolete.[7] Many of the strong AI advocates still talk in these terms; in a recent interview, one of the pioneers, Marvin Minsky, commented that '[m]ost words we use to describe our minds (like "consciousness", "learning", or "memory") are suitcase-like jumbles of different ideas. Those old ideas were formed long ago, before "computer science" appeared. It was not until the 1950s that we began to develop better ways to help think about complex processes'.[8] These older ideas are characterized as mostly worthless. This seems like an example of 'presentism' to me, which is the assumption/prejudice that only modern ideas and concepts count.[9]

However, it is difficult to ignore the gap between the claims of early AI champions and the subsequent realities. The archetypal example of an area where success has been limited is the Turing Test (see chapter four). In his 1950 paper, Turing predicted that by the year 2000 computers would

---

3   Penrose, 1989; 1994; comment from Stapp, 2007, p. 52.
4   Although this is not necessarily a problem; see Chalmers, 1999, for a discussion of the limitations of falsificationism.
5   Dennett, 1991, p. 455.
6   See the outline in Horgan, 1999.
7   Horgan, 1999; see also Dreyfus, 1992.
8   Minsky, 1998.
9   Crabtree, 1993.

be generally accepted as thinking.[10] However, in 2010, and despite some impressive developments in related areas like speech recognition and in expert systems, no computer seems close to passing this test.[11] Similarly, AI Holy Grails like investing computers with 'common sense' remain elusive.

Advocates of AI will have none of this. Whitby calls the failure of AI a 'myth' and provides a number of reasons for supposing that a great deal of progress has indeed been made. He calls AI 'a remarkably successful research programme which has delivered not only scientific insight but a great deal of useful technology'.[12] Whitby claims that AI was never intended to reproduce human intelligence, and that Turing's paper was misread. To justify this, he distinguishes AI as technology and AI as science. He claims that the fact that the technology has failed to reproduce human intelligence does not imply the comprehensive failure of AI. He counters this by suggesting that technological AI has goals other than reproducing such intelligence, and that scientific AI is aimed at gaining insights into intelligence via technology.

Whitby illustrates this last point by comparing the history of aviation with AI. He points out that that the same laws of aerodynamics that allowed aeroplanes to be built also constrained the forms of birds and other flying animals. Because the same laws that constrain the flight of aeroplanes also constrain the form and function of flying animals, one can learn a lot about how organisms fly via technology.

However, it seems very unclear whether human 'intelligence' is governed by laws that are comparable with those found in aerodynamics. One problem is that, whilst we can define a problem domain relatively clearly in aviation (e.g. how do you get heavier-than-air vehicles to fly, or how do birds fly?), this does not seem so easy for a very general concept like 'intelligence'. We tend to recognize intelligence when we see it in human beings, but actually nailing it down is another matter. In AI, tasks of a certain complexity that would be taken as the outcome of intelligence in human beings (a chess game, driving a car, painting a picture) may also be called 'intelligent' if reproduced by a computer. Herbert Simon asserted that the goal of AI was to 'construct intelligent programs... that exhibited intelligence by using processes like those used by humans in the same tasks'.[13] But such definitions must *assume* some sort of close parity between human and machine 'intelligence' to be viable. But since 'intelligence' is a highly heterogeneous or blurry category, the definitions offered

---

10   Turing, 1950.
11   See Halpern, 2006, for a critical commentary.
12   Whitby, 2003, p. 1.
13   Simon, 1995, p. 96.

seem loose enough for apparently 'intelligent' behaviour in organisms and machines to overlap without being easily contradicted.

Secondly, it seems unlikely that intelligence is governed by 'laws' of a type comparable to those of, say, aerodynamics, and we have little reason to think that any 'laws' of intelligence would be identical to the sorts of constraints and regularities that govern the operation of computers. I have already examined reasons to suppose that complex systems like organisms cannot be fully simulated on computers, as this was one of the defining characteristics of Rosennean complexity.[14] It may be that the sort of 'intelligence' exhibited by computational devices will only partially overlap with the sorts of intelligence exhibited by organisms. There are things that Turing computers can do better than humans; but there are also aspects of 'intelligence' that will probably remain outside the reach of Turing machines.

AI and Consciousness

There have been a number of attempts by AI researchers to tackle consciousness itself.[15] Here, I will focus on a specific programme to create 'artificial consciousness', initiated by Igor Aleksander, which is representative of the sorts of approach that AI techniques allow. In his book, Aleksander puts forwards five axioms that he thinks non-exhaustively demarcate consciousness. These are:

- A conscious being feels that it is part of but separate from a world 'out there'.[16]
- She will feel that her perception mingles with feelings of past experience.
- Her experience of the world will be purposeful and selective.
- She will be thinking ahead all the time in trying to decide what to do next.
- Her actions will be directed by moods and emotions.

In itself, this constitutes a perfectly reasonable list, and descriptive of some of the attributes of ordinary, waking consciousness. Aleksander's goal is to reproduce or mimic these attributes artificially, and to do this he makes certain assumptions about the nature of consciousness.

The first assumption is that consciousness will be comprehensible via the Cartesian method, e.g. consciousness can be 'broken up' into more easily understood sub-mechanisms. This is a standard assumption in AI, and conventional science, but we have seen that there are reasons for questioning it in the context of organisms. The second assumption Aleksander

---

14 Rosen, 1991.
15 See Chrisley, 2009, for an introduction to these issues.
16 Listed in Aleksander, 2005, pp. 34–5.

makes is the unproblematic identity of consciousness with its neural substrate or 'representation': he gives the example of looking at an empty glass and states that 'every scrap of what I sense must be in this neural representation'.[17] He sees 'sensation' (S) and 'neural activity' (NA) as identical, and as Popper also pointed out, if S and NA both imply each other then, in mathematics, they cancel out. Any alternative, he thinks is tantamount to believing in ghosts. He does, however, accept that consciousness involves an 'introspective faculty' and something like private experience, but the foregoing assumptions constrain him to interpret this in representational terms.

These assumptions are necessary for his programme of 'artificial consciousness' to work. This involves building simulations of functional parts of the brain that mimic certain aspects of neural correlates that have been associated with waking consciousness. Specifically, he seeks to simulate the neural substrate of the 'global workspace' of Baars and others,[18] as a structured neural network.[19]

This sort of simulation, which has also been used in robots, expresses Aleksander's five axioms in particular, functional, ways. The first is covered by internal mechanisms that represent the world. The second, which he terms 'imagination', refers to state trajectories of the neural network that operate when sense inputs are not present. *Attention*, which is equated with purposefulness, refers to the mechanisms that guide external sensors of the organism during perceptual acts and also guide the internal neural state trajectories or 'imagination'. The 'thinking ahead' axiom is equated with planning or simulating acts in the 'imagination', which emotions evaluate.[20]

In 1996, Aleksander built a robot, named Magnus, which replicated some of the neural mechanisms of the human brain. In an interview, Aleksander claimed that 'the robot has a sense of what it is like to be [a] robot. But his sense is a long way down on some gradation scale from my fully blown consciousness... it is still just a robot'.[21] In his book, he denies that Magnus was conscious at all.[22]

Aleksander's work is interesting, and his simulations may well afford us new insights into the nature of neural functioning and the neural substrates of consciousness itself. However, because his is basically a representational and functional view that strongly identifies 'sensation' or first-person experience with neural activity, then his approach is subject to the

17 Aleksander, 2005, p. 33.
18 Baars, 1988.
19 See Aleksander, 2005, pp. 177–85.
20 Aleksander, 2005.
21 Interview in Carter, 2002. Quote on p. 180.
22 Aleksander, 2005.

limitations that come along with the constraining assumptions. Specifically, in embracing an identity between a conscious experience and a neural state, but in rejecting eliminativism, he is forced to adopt a representational theory of consciousness. In addition, to dub certain functions 'conscious' or 'imagination' or even 'attention' does not really establish *any* kind of parity between them and their supposed counterparts in human beings. In sum, we only have an assertion that such a system can be called conscious in any way at all.

Computation and the Nervous System

Aleksander's work does, however, raise important questions about the applicability of such models to the human nervous system. Why did cognitive scientists assume that such a comparison was valid in the first place? In cognitive science, it is assumed that 'mentality' or 'thinking' is a formal activity. Some even claim that if one reproduces this formal activity in a computer, then one actually reproduces 'mentality' in a computer, because the formality underlying such thoughts 'is' thought itself.[23] Thus, contrary to Dennett's admission, at least some cognitive scientists accept some sort of a *literal* parity between computer simulations and mental states; this is the basis of functionalism.

The basis for such a literal parity emerged in part from comparative studies of the nervous system and the emerging technology of the 1940s and 1950s. It began to look as if the nervous system was structured in a way that was directly comparable to both digital computers and artificial cybernetic systems. As we saw in chapter four, in the 1950s cyberneticist Norbert Wiener characterized the nervous system as a sequence of switching devices in which the opening of a later switch depended on the action of precise combinations of earlier switches leading into it, which open at the same time. He termed this a *digital machine*.[24]

The nervous system was characterized in this way because of its basic structure. It is composed of cells called *neurons*. Figure 1a shows the structure of these cells. These are said to carry 'information' via electrochemical pulses, and to simplify the discussion I will adopt the language of information-processing. Bear in mind the metaphorical nature of words like 'information', 'input', 'represent' in the following description.

A neuron consists of a body, or *soma*, and an *axon*, which can be compared to a wire carrying electric current, except that the 'current' is electrochemical in nature. An impulse arrives in the cell body, travels along the axon and through branching sections called *dendrites* at the axon's end. The dendrites terminate in a synaptic knob (Figure 1b), which is separated from the body of another neuron by a microscopic gap called the *synaptic*

---

23 Chrisley, 2009, p. 64.
24 Wiener, 1950.

The Computational Model of Mind

cleft. When the impulse reaches this cleft, it triggers the release of a chemical called a *neurotransmitter* from the transmitter vesicles. The neurotransmitter diffuses across the synaptic cleft, and triggers the impulse in the cell body of the next neuron.

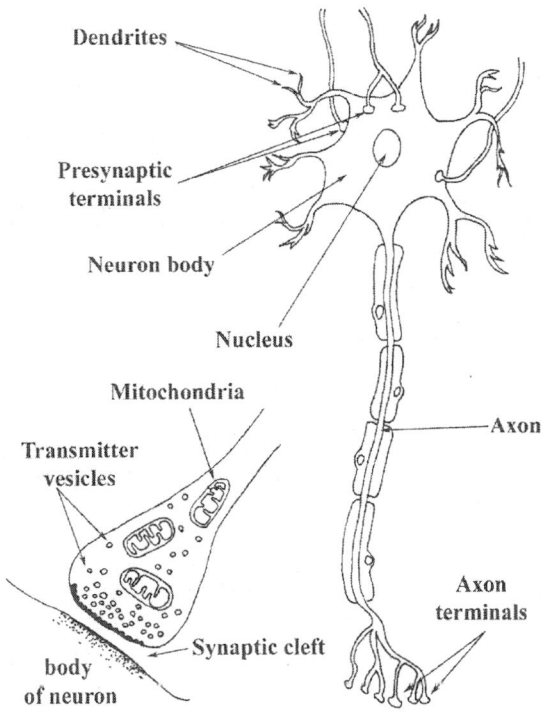

Figure 1a. A Vertebrate Spinal Motor Neuron (after Eckert et al., 1997); 1b. Synaptic Knob (after Guyton, 1981).

Figure 2 shows how the nervous system 'processes information' using neurons. A sensory 'input' is received via the sensory organs (e.g. the eyes, nose, tongue, skin), journeys through the central nervous system (brain and spinal cord) and out to the motor neurons, which initiate muscle and other actions. This highly simplified sketch shows that Wiener's depiction of the nervous system as a 'collection of switches' is not entirely inappropriate.

This collection of switches is also organized in a way which makes something comparable to 'information-processing' possible. This is especially evident in the case of, say, vision, where the cells of the retina and visual cortex are organized in very specific, functional ways for certain tasks. In the visual cortex, for example, there are specialized areas that 'process' lines, movement and colours via cell arrangements that can be readily simulated in a computer.[25] This example is important because, as Eckert *et al.* note, 'the principles that have emerged from the study of

---

25 See Bruce, Green & Georgeson, 2003, for a summary.

vision apply to other sensory systems as well'.[26] They also speculate that the visual system might have settled on universal solutions to common problems faced by working networks of neurons. In short, computational and cybernetic models have proved very useful in helping to understand some of the basic features of the functional nervous system.

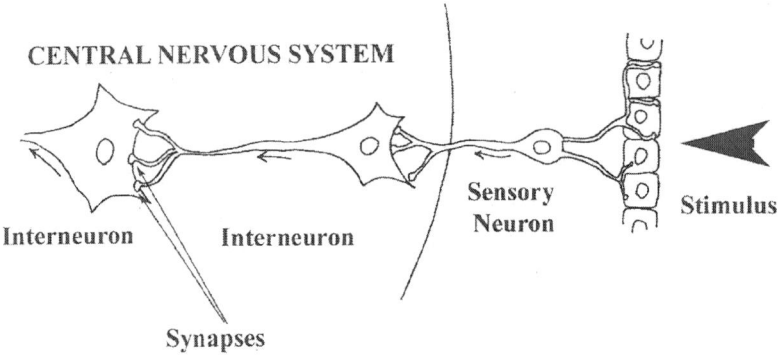

Figure 2. How Signals are Carried Via Neural Circuits. Arrows indicate direction of signal flow, which is triggered when a stimulus triggers a response in sensory cells. These signals are propagated into the central nervous system (after Eckert et al., 1997).

These basic features can also be modelled, to an extent, on a computer. Artificial neural networks are mathematical models of simple, interconnected units that were inspired by the interconnected nature of the nervous system. These neural networks are capable of 'learning' and pattern-recognition, and were significant in the second wave of the cognitive revolution in the 1980s and 1990s. They have been used to try and model 'cognitive systems' in human and animal learning.

We should remember, however, that the extremely high complexity of the human body makes the sorts of conception outlined above superficial at best, and one should not forget the dizzying complexity with which one is faced. In the 1990s, for example, it was discovered that even a single neuron was capable of some highly complex and dynamic forms of 'information-processing'. As Koch noted '…one has the distinct feeling that we have not yet revealed every layer of the onion'.[27] Nonetheless, the general structure and function of the nervous system, and its parity with computational devices, has led many to conclude that we *are* information-processing devices.

---

26 Eckert *et al.*, 1997, p. 438.
27 Koch, 1997, p. 207.

Humans as Information-Processors

This parity, however, should not blind us to the *metaphorical* nature of the computational model of minds. As Hayes points out, analogy is not homology, and in some respects the comparison is appropriate but in others it is not. Hayes is also critical of the unconditional embrace of such a metaphor as the be-all and end-all of understanding what people do.[28] This is falling into the same trap as behaviourism:

> In the case of the behaviorists, it was the... idea of the atom and the molecule: the S-R link as the 'atom,' which could be combined, through increasingly complex learning, until it could eventually account for all human behaviour. In the case of the cognitive psychologists, it is the computer metaphor—the idea that the human being is essentially 'just' a highly complicated processor of information, and that when we have understood fully how that information is processed, we will know all that is necessary about human thought processes.[29]

Such a view is evident in the works of, for example, Steven Pinker, who does not hesitate to equate information-processing with thought. This dovetails with his view of the mind as a system of tightly connected, highly specialized sub-components, justified by the 'wiring' diagrams of the brain's neurons, and by his view of the mind as a sort of evolved 'Swiss Army knife'.[30] Such an approach cannot be completely understood in terms of the 'hardware' of the nervous system, and Pinker claims that many of these 'behavioural modules' would be virtual, or a little like functional 'software' in the brain. Sloman, similarly, talks of the mind in terms of a 'virtual machine' running on the brain.[31]

But this raises problems. If the mind is somehow, *literally* the software of the brain, then it is not too much of a leap to imagine that software being transferred. This leads to the concept of uploading the mind, the idea that one could, at least in principle and maybe in practice, transfer one's mind onto a computer and by doing so, live forever.[32] This would be done either by exotic brain surgery or by very advanced brain scanning, the presumption being that if one could record enough information about the brain and reproduce it in a virtual environment, then one could carry on in such an environment pretty much as before. Ray Kurzweil even suggests that, in the not-too-distant future, we might *prefer* to spend most of our time as uploads rather than physical beings.[33]

---

28 Hayes, 1995.
29 Hayes, 1995, p. 111.
30 Pinker, 1998; 2002.
31 Sloman, 2009.
32 Moravec, 1988; Kurzweil, 2005.
33 Kurzweil, 2005.

Such thinking makes explicit the dualistic undertones of some information-processing metaphors. Moravec admits that his view that the consciousness of the person would somehow 'carry over' to the simulation amounts to information dualism.[34] Wertheim goes further, pointing out that it amounts to the reinvention of the Pythagorean soul.[35] And yet, in its way, such thinking is logical if you are prepared to take the information-processing metaphor as literal and definitive. Such dualistic thinking, however, is one reason why a movement within cognitive science questions whether the brain information-processes at all.

Thought as Dynamical System

The dynamical systems approach arose partly because of conceptual problems with the computer metaphor of mind, and partly because of the dualistic connotations of seeing the mind as 'software' run on the brain. Since the 1990s, this school of cognitive science has been represented not by the computer model by the *dynamical systems* approach to cognition. A dynamical system is a mathematical model that describes such phenomena as the swinging of a clock pendulum, the flow of water in a pipe, and the number of fish each spring in a lake,[36] or a self-regulating steam-engine.

Cognitive scientists like Tim Van Gelder have championed this sort of approach, writing: '[The] usefulness of dynamics in offering the best scientific explanations of phenomena throughout the natural world has been proved again and again. It would hardly be a surprise if dynamics turned out to be the framework within which the most powerful descriptions of cognitive processes were also forthcoming.'[37]

According to the dynamicist account, the brain is not doing computation at all. Harvey's view is that 'cognition', for animals or machines, 'is something that can only be attributed to the behaviour that arises from the conjunction of an organism and the world that it inhabits'.[38] Additionally, dynamic systems, like brain-states, unfold in real time. By contrast, computer programs proceed in a step-by-step manner, and the speed by which they perform is determined by whether they have been fed into a fast or slow machine. According to dynamicists, the behaviour of the organism emerges from the dynamics of its internal states and its interactions with the world.

These changed assumptions have birthed a subfield of cognitive science which not only simulates robots but also an environment for them to inter-

---

34 Moravec, 1988.
35 Wertheim, 1999.
36 Wikipedia entry of dynamical systems at en.wikipedia.org/wiki/Dynamical_system accessed on 20/11/09.
37 Port & Van Gelder, 1995, p. 18. See also Van Gelder, 1998.
38 Harvey, 1997.

act with. The actions of artificial neural networks are only part of a dynamical system rather than just a different sort of computer network. Similarly, human minds are seen, not as an isolated entity, but an interactive part of a body, social and environmental system.[39]

Whilst the dynamical systems approach in some respects improves upon the purely computational approach, it is not as revolutionary as its proponents suggest. Current cognitive science originated from two distinct but intermingled streams, digital computation and cybernetics, the latter of which originated as a study of *analogue* (non-digital) systems. In some respects, the dynamical systems approach represents a swing away from the digital computational approach, back to the cybernetic analogue approach. The dynamical approach seems far closer to that of 1950s cybernetics than is often admitted. The *exempla* of a dynamical system in Port and Van Gelder is a Watt Governor, which automatically regulates pressure in a steam engine, which is also an early cybernetic system.

It is also unclear whether dynamical systems can offer any new insights into phenomenological consciousness. As far as private experiences go, these tend to be explained away in exactly the same way as by the older approach: they are 'illusions'. Harvey's definition of cognition as 'something that can only be attributed to the behaviour that arises from the conjunction of an organism and the world that it inhabits' seems almost identical to the behaviourist definition of mind, with the slight modification that instead of a black box modulating behaviour we have complex neural networks. Harvey uses the same Ryle-Wittgenstein type arguments to dispose of the hard problem, dismissing it as a linguistic phantom.[40] But this seems to be mainly because dynamical approaches seem unsuitable for approaching consciousness. In fact, the dynamical systems approach seems even more hostile to private experiences than that of information-processing because they repudiate representational approaches. This is seen as a good thing, and Port and Van Gelder see the jettisoning of the computational model as the last step in the abolition of the Cartesian mind.

Limitations of Current Approaches

It is time to examine briefly some specific areas where it is unclear whether the computational model of mind is appropriate. To begin, it seems that nothing like phenomenological, first-person experiences are predicted or probably predictable from information-processing theory on its own.[41] In a discussion of AI, Chrisley admits that 'naturalistic, non-phenomenal properties of a system do not explain, or at least do not imply, the phenom-

---

39   Beer, 2000; Varela, Thomson & Rosch, 1991; Froese, 2007.
40   Harvey, 2002.
41   Horgan, 1999.

enal properties of that system'.[42] This is an important point, to which we will return in future chapters.

We have seen that there have been attempts to accommodate phenomenological consciousness within a representational framework, but these seem to me not to match the character of these experiences. And as we discussed, the only other options within the currently discussed framework are to eliminate the 'inner' altogether, or attempt some form or amalgam of the two via attenuated 'representations' in neural networks. So for now, phenomenological accounts stand as one area that cannot be very satisfactorily accounted for within the computational framework. This is, however, not the only area where it seems unclear whether the discussed approaches are adequate.

The Binding Problem

It is known that specialized cells in the visual cortex handle different aspects of the visual scene—movement, colour, shapes, etc.—but it is not understood how or even whether the different 'segments' of a scene come together.[43] This conflicts with our phenomenological experiences; a car moving along a road will be experienced as a moving object of a particular shape and colour. If the sun glints on the window, then I will be able to tell which window and approximately when this happens. We experience the visual world as a coherent whole.

This is a mystery as far as brain function is concerned because at present we only understand how the different bits of the visual cortex process parts of this experience of a moving image, not how it comes together in a whole. Some parts of the cortex handle edges, lines and other basic features, but entirely different parts of the cortex handle movement and colour. The mystery is how all of these attributes of an image 'come together' to form our coherent, subjective experiences. Steven Rose suggests that this might be the number one problem in neuroscience in the twenty-first century.[44]

There are a large number of different solutions to the binding problem, ranging from computational to dynamical systems views. There are also suggestions that quantum effects may be required to explain it. The currently predominant assumption is that binding is related to neurons signalling to each other in concert across the brain. There is an 'emerging consensus'[45] that focuses upon the group actions of neurons firing in the gamma range (about 30–70 Hz),[46] the general idea being that the binding problem can be solved by understanding the function of these families of

---

42 Chrisley, 2009, p. 65.
43 Blackmore, 2003.
44 Rose, 2006.
45 Seth, 2007.
46 Kelly *et al.*, 2007.

neurons. Binding, in this interpretation, can be understood functionally as information-processing.

At this stage, however, alternative views remain viable. Rado and Scott propose a model which is a combination of neural representations and attractor-spaces from complexity theory.[47] They claim that if one accepts the assertion that there are about a billion stable attractors in the brain, identified with Hebb's complex cell assemblies with these attractors, the binding problem is solved in a 'simple and satisfying way'. Their theory falls far short of an explanation for the binding problem, firstly because of their reliance upon representations and secondly because they assume a highly metaphorical and schematic account will map adequately onto the data. Similar criticisms can be made of, for example, Damasio's framework for understanding the binding problem.[48]

It may well be that researchers will be forced to consider more 'exotic' solutions, such as a reframing within Ho's picture of a coherent organism (see chapter seven). Some, however, see it as a false problem, lined to wider misconceptions about information or information-processing within the nervous system. One of the most closely argued and influential approaches is Dennett's *Consciousness Explained*, where he seems to argue that there *is* no binding problem. A large part of this book is a reasonably successful attempt to demolish the 'Cartesian theatre'. This is the metaphor for a place in the brain where all of the sensory processing 'comes together' to form a coherent picture, in a way analogous to a cinema screen or stage. Instead, Dennett suggests, there are a large number of specialized sub-units of the brain that each handle part of the sensory information.

He calls this alternative to the Cartesian theatre the multiple drafts model, in which 'all varieties of perception — indeed, all varieties of thought or mental activity — are accomplished in the brain by parallel, multitrack processes of interpretation and elaboration of sensory inputs. Information entering the nervous system is under continuous "editorial revision"'.[49] This sort of thinking is a central assumption of the 'Grand Illusion' school of consciousness, a group of 'hyper-sceptics' who attempt to demonstrate via experiment that our experience of a flow of coherent subjective experiences is illusory.[50]

Dennett's model refutes the idea that perceptual signals *need* to be 'passed up to' a master control or dominating program in the brain. Actions of the cells in the visual cortex, for example, do not need to be 'passed on' to a higher and more abstract processing part in the brain; as Dennett notes 'feature detections or discriminations only have to be made

---

47   Rado & Scott, 1996.
48   Damasio, 1999.
49   Dennett, 1991, p. 111.
50   Noë, 2002.

once'.[51] To Dennett, it is senseless to ask when this detection becomes consciousness, writing that 'these distributed content-discriminations yield, over the course of time, something *rather like* a narrative stream or sequence',[52] but this stream is only approximate because the brain is constantly editing and re-editing. Dennett's solution to the 'binding problem' is that there *is* no problem and any impression we have of sensory coherence is illusory.

Bennett and Hacker also offer a number of significant remarks about the notion of information 'coming together' in the nervous system. They point out that 'The sense in which neural pathways carry information about colour, shape, movement, etc., is not semantic, but, at best, information-theoretic. In neither sense of "information" can information be organized into "cohesive perceptions"'.[53] This is because, semantically, information is a set of true propositions, and propositions as such cannot be so organized. In engineering terms, information is a measure of freedom of choice in signal transmission, measured by a logarithm to the base 2 of the number of available choices, and they point out that this sort of information cannot be so combined, either.[54] The question of 'information association' in the nervous system is therefore distinct from the binding problem.

Currently, all options are open, and we cannot say precisely how, what form, or whether the binding problem will be solved. It is even possible that it will be redefined out of existence. It is instructive, however, because it marks a boundary point that reveals some of the limitations of *both* information-processing and dynamical models.

Autonomy

In the previous chapter, I noted that organisms had a number of features that seem not to be shared by our current technology. One of these is autonomy. Somehow, humans and other organisms have the capacity to act far more independently and creatively than their mechanical analogues suggest.

Unlike machines, organisms do not need a designer to help them get on with their lives. They exist freely in an environment, eating, reproducing and evolving without any help from 'outside'. By contrast, machines are designed by human beings for a purpose and need their presence to operate. It is true that some forms of quasi-autonomy have been developed (autonomous systems on space probes, or the 'independent' behaviour of simulations on computers being examples), but no machine can yet reproduce itself or independently survive in a physical environment. There

---

51 Dennett, 1991, p. 113.
52 Dennett, 1991, p. 113.
53 Bennett & Hacker, 2003, p. 141.
54 Bennett & Hacker, 2003.

have been various attempts to define formally these differences between living systems and human-made machines, as with the distinction between *autopoietic* and *allopoietic* systems, also discussed in chapter seven.

Current computers and robots are *allopoietic* because they do not build themselves, but need to be designed and built in a factory using specialized machines. The difference has led some authors to claim that truly autonomous machines are impossible.[55]

There have been attempts to model autopoiesis in a computer. The 'artificial life' community has tried to simulate the living cell, but a recent review concluded that 'there has been relatively little progress on the problem of... autonomy...'[56] This review also highlights claims that '[e]volved artificial systems can thus never achieve (full) constructive closure because the inertness of their building blocks entails that the required external degree of design complexity must always be greater than the internal one'.[57]

It is difficult to see how one might dispense entirely with an external designer for a simulation. A simulation exists on a computer that needs a human to turn it on, and the simulation itself requires a programmer. Despite such limitations, the authors claim that it might be possible to model some kinds of autonomy. They attempted to simulate one small aspect of this, but admitted that 'autonomy, as the defining quality of all living beings, turned out to be more difficult to tackle than originally expected...'[58] This reflects a general finding of Artificial Intelligence, and strongly suggests that the nature of such autonomy has not yet been fathomed.

The autonomy problem is just one of the several reasons to be suspicious of 'complete' explanations of human beings in terms of *either* computation *or* dynamical systems. Whilst simulations and robots have been and will continue to be useful to test models of some aspects of human perception and behaviour, they often fall far short of total explanations.

This is to be expected; over twenty-five years ago, Weizenbaum wrote that

> the power of the computer is merely an extreme version of a power that is inherent in all self-validating systems of thought. Perhaps we are beginning to understand that the abstract systems—the games computer people can generate in their infinite freedom from the constraints that delimit the dreams of workers in the real world—may fail catastrophically when their rules are applied in earnest.[59]

55 Sahtouris, 1999.
56 Froese & Di Paolo, 2008, p. 5.
57 *Op. cit.*, p. 7.
58 Froese & Di Paolo, 2008, p. 16.
59 Weizenbaum, 1984, pp. 130-1.

In this case, the 'catastrophic failure' can be extended to the simulations themselves, and it is currently hard to know whether such a failure is a temporary, technical hitch or a permanent barrier.

But as far as theories of the organism are concerned, it is difficult to discard the feeling that a significant part of the equation is missing. For now, we might agree with Koestler when he suggested that whilst it was possible for a person to become like a robot, a robot could not become like a person.[60]

Conclusion

The information-processing metaphor and dynamical systems metaphors are both the predominant and, indeed, often perceived as the *only* viable approaches to the mind and consciousness within mainstream cognitive science. It also seems true that any alternative is not yet sufficiently developed to become the basis of a viable and diverse research programme. This is significant because, as Kuhn long ago observed, scientists will not tend to abandon an existing research programme until such an alternative has arisen.[61] To abandon a research programme without an alternative would be tantamount to abandoning science. So Dennett seems partially justified in asserting that 'the campaign against strong AI, whilst equally well intentioned, can offer only the most threadbare alternative models of mind'.[62]

Having said this, I would note a persistent lack of compromise in the defenders of current orthodoxies. Halpern notes that many AI researchers seem to think that if we reject these metaphors as comprehensive or complete, then we are rejecting Enlightenment values. Said researchers, as Halpern puts it, see themselves as 'defending rationality itself'.[63] This attitude seems to me unnecessarily extreme. First of all, we can acknowledge that the cognitive revolution brought with it a number of new techniques and ways of looking that have aided us significantly in understanding the actions of the nervous system and some aspects of the mind. However, acknowledging areas of weakness or even failure is hardly obscurantism. Neither is acknowledging that there are limits to science, or what scientific knowledge can tell us currently and perhaps in the future. This is especially significant in the case of consciousness, where it is admitted that naturalistic approaches stumble.

The main problem, as Hayes noted, is the assumption that the current approaches *must* be the ultimate explanatory frame for *any* aspect of human nature, and that they are necessarily comprehensive. The history

---

60 Koestler, 1967.
61 Kuhn, 1996/1962.
62 Dennett, 1991, p. 454.
63 Halpern, 2006, p. 63.

of science shows that general conceptual schemes tend to come and go, and the robust data from the previous scheme will be re-interpreted in a new way once this transformation has occurred. This is already happening within conventional cognitive science, as processes previously interpreted in information-processing terms are interpreted as dynamical systems. So according to one interpretation, the nervous system 'processes information', whilst according to another, it doesn't. In such a situation and despite claims to the contrary, I cannot take the computational model of mind literally.

With AI in particular, it seems most appropriate to reject the ideological component of the discussions and remain neutral about the ultimate level of intelligence that machines might express. Maybe we will see the advent of truly intelligent and/or conscious machines, and maybe we won't. As far as consciousness goes, considerable obscurities persist despite aggressive rhetoric to the contrary. With these points in mind, we now turn to some current theories of consciousness, most of which are couched within this general explanatory framework.

Chapter Nine

Some Theories of Consciousness

Here we will examine a selection of current, Western, theories of consciousness, all but one of which is propounded within conventional science. The consensus in mainstream cognitive science is that novel science is not needed to explain conscious experiences, and that what we do not understand now will eventually be understood in physical terms. This conclusion is supported by significant amounts of evidence linking waking awareness to activity in the thalamocortical system (Figure 1), which constitutes most of the mammalian brain.[1] This justifies Koch and Mormonn's definition of consciousness as 'a puzzling, state-dependent property of certain types of complex, biological, adaptive, and highly interconnected systems'.[2] In Kuhn's terms, the hunt for consciousness is seen as part of a 'mopping up' operation that can be handled by conventional science.[3]

But Kuhn also spoke of the 'essential tension' between explanatory frames within conventional science, and those without.[4] In cursory surveys of mainstream literature, these alternative accounts are generally conspicuous by their absence; one looks in vain for extended discussions of quantum theories of consciousness in *Nature* or *Science*. Where such theories are mentioned, they tend to be raised to be dismissed.[5] The only alternative account I have seen widely discussed within cognitive science is the quantum gravity theory proposed by Penrose and Hammeroff, and this is probably because of the high academic status of the former author.

This is potentially a problem because, despite claims that general theoretical approaches can be disproved by significant internal problems or

1   Mormonn & Koch, 2007; see Granger & Hearn, 2007, for a description of the thalamocortical system.
2   Mormonn & Koch, 2007. Web article.
3   Kuhn, 1996/1962.
4   Kuhn, 1996/1962.
5   See Koch & Hepp, 2006, and also a discussion in Hofstadter & Dennett, 1981.

novel empirical findings, this is often not enough. Both Kuhn and Polyani observed how good adherents of established theories often become at ignoring or explaining away problems or anomalous observations via *ad hoc* hypotheses, and we have already encountered Feyerabend's warnings about the consequences of sticking to a theory no matter what.[6] The problem is that such a slavish adherence can result in a theoretical system becoming self-confirmatory, rather as in astrology. In addition, one often needs alternative traditions as comparisons with dominant ones; Feyerabend notes numerous instances where the comparison, contrast and clashes of these rival systems can reveal the strengths and weaknesses of both. In the current chapter, therefore, I will examine the 'quantum' theory of consciousness of Henry Stapp.

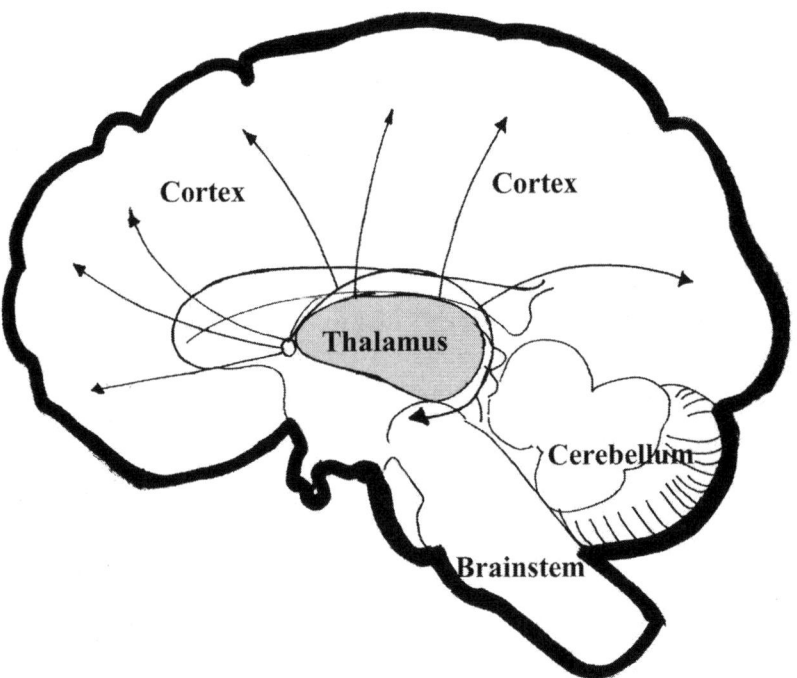

Figure 1. Highly Simplified Section of the Brain Showing Thalamocortical Connections. Conscious awareness seems closely linked to the thalamus and the cortex, which are closely interlinked via looping neuronal pathways. The cerebellum is not thought to support consciousness. Simplified from Mormonn & Koch, 2007.

First, I will give an overview of some conventional theories. The purpose here is not an exhaustive examination, but a search for general patterns and themes within these theories, which are generally framed within the information-processing and neurobiological paradigms. 'Consciousness'

---

6   Kuhn, 1996/1962; Polyani, 1964; Feyerabend, 1975.

here tends to be defined as either the contents of consciousness or as synonymous with 'conscious awareness', or arousal;[7] see Damasio's definition of consciousness as 'an organism's awareness of its own self and surroundings'.[8] *Attention* tends to be seen as closely linked but distinct from consciousness; Koch and Tsuchiya speculate that the two have separate mechanisms.[9] Consciousness is perceived as basically mechanistic or functional and segmentable into sub-components, in line with the Cartesian method.

The work of Christof Koch exemplifies this approach. Koch is confident that the way forward for studying consciousness is to proceed with established experimental approaches and to stop worrying about philosophical problems.[10] This view is shared by at least one reviewer of his work, who comments that Koch has already 'ascended to Base Camp 2 on his quest to the summit'.[11] Since his approach is almost exclusively neurobiological and reductionist, both Koch and his reviewer can be regarded as having a *positivist* outlook, or a view that knowledge should be based only upon direct sensory appearance and experimentation.[12] A common accompaniment to this outlook is a high level of confidence that metaphysical and theoretical worries about the universe will eventually fall to empirical research.

Koch is by no means alone, as much of conventional cognitive science is committed to mechanistic, specifically Cartesian, explanations. For example, in his survey of the 'mosaic unity' of neuroscience, Craver embraces a form of pluralism but formulates this in terms of multiple levels of mechanisms, invoking a 'causal-mechanical model of constitutive explanation'.[13] He does this to offer an alternative to classical reductionism, which still predominates in much of neuroscience, and to revise the approach that attempts to analyse sections of the nervous system in terms of specific functions. The result is a considerably more liberal and pluralistic approach to causation within the brain, which includes discussion of the boundary conditions of causative models. However, even this liberal approach remains committed to a more general form of Cartesian reductionism, as are the conventional approaches outlined below. Therefore, *mechanism* marks a boundary condition of conventional science within which, it is assumed, any theory of consciousness *must* fit.

---

7   Mormonn & Koch, 2007.
8   Damasio, 1999. Although he does acknowledge the importance of subjective experiences, and accepts that a theory of consciousness must accommodate them.
9   Tsuchiya & Koch, 2009.
10 Koch, 2004.
11 Martinez-Conde, 2004.
12 Daniels, 2005.
13 Craver, 2007, p. 107.

Underlying Mechanisms: Consciousness Within Conventional Science

The following is a brief survey of *some* proposed mechanisms underlying conscious states. As noted above, many of them focus primarily on conscious awareness, although *qualia* and conscious contents may also be considered. The theories described here presuppose that neural mechanisms, of various degrees of specificity, underlie subjective experiences. Most, but not all, of these theories are routed in the overarching paradigms of information-processing, computation and/or dynamical systems and cybernetics. These theories attempt to describe the specific brain-functions by which conscious experiences arise. They share some common features, but can also differ significantly in terms of emphasis. This is partly because of the lack of a clear definition of consciousness.

Seth makes some important general observations about these theories. Firstly, he observes, *models* of consciousness should be distinguished from *neural correlates* of consciousness. Neural correlates of consciousness discovered during the examination of the brain do not by themselves provide *causal* theories about consciousness. Just because a part of the brain is active when one thinks about apples, one is not entitled to conclude that the active part is an 'apples centre'. There could be any number of reasons why the said correlation between subjective thoughts and the activation of a brain region has occurred.

A theory of consciousness, ideally, would give us a good idea of why the phenomenological awareness of an 'apple' arises when a given brain region is activated. What those within conventional science are after is a theory that will allow us to explain exactly how a conscious event of this sort can be produced by a neural event. An identity is conventionally assumed between said event and phenomenological experience. U.T. Place made this clear by comparing the case where we say that lightning is a motion of electric charges. He pointed out that no matter how much we scrutinize the lightning, we will never be able to observe the electric charges. Place:

> ...just as the operations for determining the nature of one's state of consciousness are radically different from those involved in determining the nature of one's brain processes, so the operations for determining the occurrence of lightning are radically different from those involved in determining the occurrence of a motion of electric charges.[14]

In the case of lightning, scientific theory is detailed and predictive enough to tell us with some confidence that lightning can be described in terms of electric charges. Place assumed the same to be true of consciousness and

---

14 U.T. Place extract in Flew, 1964. Quote on p. 282; similar sentiments are voiced by the Churchlands, interview in Blackmore, 2005.

neural states; but in fact, a detailed and widely-accepted theory of just how the one 'is' or becomes the other must wait for a theory of consciousness. I would note in this context that a theory of conscious *attention* would by itself be insufficient for this purpose because it would not really tackle how physical states are related to conscious mental states. All it would tell us was why we happen to be aware of some events and not others, not why we experience them in the way that we at least seem to.

Conventional models of consciousness attempt to provide an understanding of the causal relationship between neural correlates and consciousness and how we come to have phenomenological experience in the first place. Neural correlates of consciousness have become commonplace in recent years, due to the advent of neuroimaging. A large number of observations have been made that suggest a close relation between patterns of blood flow and metabolism observed in the brain and many conscious experiences. For example, an area of the extrastriate cortex, the fusiform face area, reacts at least twice as strongly to faces as other classes of non-face stimuli such as objects, hands and houses whilst another region, the parahippocampal place area (PPA), responds strongly to images of places including houses but only weakly when the subjects are presented with images of faces.[15] Kanwisher concludes that '...these findings show impressive correlations between the ability to identify an object, letter, or word, and the strength of the neural signal in the relevant cortical area'.[16] An ideal theory might, for example, be able to *predict* what we were thinking about if we observed a particular pattern of activity in the brain; hence the dreams of a 'mind-reading' machine or *cerebroscope*, to which we will return in the next chapter.

The second important observation that Seth makes is that 'no single model of consciousness appears sufficient to account fully for the multidimensional properties of conscious experience'.[17] From the pluralist's viewpoint, one can make the case that no single model ever will, and this suspicion grows if we survey the models in a little more detail. The following brief and superficial survey is also based upon Seth's review article.

Global Workspace Theories

'Global workspace' theories attempt to reconcile the apparent unity of conscious experience with the lack of unifying mechanisms in the brain

---

[15] Kanwisher, 2001; original work in Allison *et al.*, 1999; Ishai *et al.*, 1999; Kanwisher, McDermott & Chun, 1997; McCarthy *et al.*, 1997.

[16] Kanwisher, 2001, p. 95. Although Harpaz, after surveying the data, claims that the '...FFA [fusiform face area] is not reproducible across individuals, but you can find face-sensitive patches in each individual and call them "the FFA"' — see Harpaz, 2009, Misunderstanding in Cognitive Brain Imaging: http://human-brain.org/imaging.html accessed on 08/06/11.

[17] Seth, 2007.

(and hence the binding problem). In his theory, Baars[18] introduced the idea of a 'theatre of consciousness'. In Baars' view, consciousness/attention is like a bright spot on the stage of a darkened theatre. The actors in the bright spot get all the attention, whilst we might be only vaguely conscious of those on the periphery (William James called this the 'fringe').[19] This can be related to observations in psychology that our attention or 'working memory' is limited to a select number of items. This view is virtually identical to Freud and Jung's theory that consciousness could be viewed as a searchlight,[20] where experiences or 'mental events' move into or out of the searchlight.

The mechanisms underlying this 'workspace' have been described in various ways, but the general idea is that patterns of neurons are activated by sensory information and work in concert, simultaneously inhibiting weaker patterns of input. Thus attention and decision-making are associated with a global pattern of neural excitation arising and inhibiting competing patterns in the cerebral cortex.[21] Neurons are thought to be synchronized by oscillatory electrical activity in the 'gamma' range of 30–70 Hz.

Crick and Koch, who utilize a similar idea, emphasize the role of coalitions of interconnected neurons acting together to increase the activity of their fellow members.[22] The proposal is that different coalitions compete with each other, and the 'winning' set constitutes that of which we are the most conscious. Koch & Crick:

> Coalitions can vary both in size and character. For example, a coalition produced by visual imagination (with one's eyes closed) may be less widespread than a coalition produced by a vivid and sustained visual input from the environment... Coalitions in dreams may be somewhat different from waking ones.[23]

One interesting feature of the analogies Koch and Crick use to describe this process is that they tend to palm off intentional language (in this case, a democratic analogy) onto parts of the brain. So, for example, they liken attention to the efforts of journalists and pollsters to get the system as a whole to focus on certain issues. This, of course, is meant metaphorically, but it does highlight the problem of reducing intentional phenomena to mechanistic explanations. The general idea, *a la* the intentional stance, is that apparently intentional phenomena can be at some level discharged into the mechanical, but one often ends up using intentional metaphors when discussing supposedly mechanical or purely functional phenom-

---

18 Baars, 1988.
19 Varela & Shear, 1999.
20 Gauld, 1968.
21 Dehaene, Sergent & Changeux, 2003.
22 Crick & Koch, 2003.
23 Crick & Koch, 2003, p. 121.

ena. Calling genes 'selfish' is probably the classic example of this, but here it is extended to the brain.[24]

Crick and Koch's framework has another significant element that should be mentioned. Firstly, they cite the extensive evidence for the existence of what they term 'explicit representations' in various parts of the cortex. This refers to sets of neurons that respond as 'detectors' for visual features, for which there is plenty of evidence. They also cite cases in which damage to those parts of the brain prevents subjects from being consciously aware of the perceptual feature to which the detectors were attuned. Two clinical examples are *achromatopsia*, or loss of colour perception, and *akinetopsia*, or loss of motion perception, both of which are associated with damage to the visual cortex.[25] This constitutes clear evidence that certain kinds of neural structure are needed to support certain kinds of conscious experience.

As I will show in the next chapter, this sort of approach is proving fruitful in uncovering the specific sorts of neural mechanisms that are closely associated with various specific aspects of sensory experience. In particular, they reveal that early, purely sensory experiences are tied with more-or-less specifiable neural structures. This is not really surprising; just as one needs eyes to see, so one probably needs a specific piece of intact neural 'machinery' at the other end to be able to experience seeing anything.

However, because Crick and Koch share a low opinion of philosophy, their approaches tend to paper over the significant issue of phenomenology. In denying metaphysics, one often ends up using a covert form of naturalism by default, and assuming that identity theory must be true; one saw a similar situation in the previous chapter, in Aleksander's work. The thrust of Koch's work implies that once specific mechanisms have been resolved, many of these problems will disappear or become irrelevant, and if one defines consciousness as conscious awareness only, then the goal of such a theory can only really be a long list of neural wiring diagrams and functional maps that describe when this awareness is present and when it is absent. But this leaves awkward questions unanswered. Searle, criticizing an earlier book of Francis Crick's, put it this way; 'How, to put it naïvely, does the brain get us over the hump from electrochemistry to feeling?'[26] I find it hard to call this a non-problem.

Dynamic Core

'Dynamic core' theories also utilize the idea of neural competition, and are based upon Gerald Edelman's concept of 'Neural Darwinism'. This is the

---

24 Dawkins, 1976.
25 Crick & Koch, 2003.
26 Searle, 1997, p. 28, commenting on Crick, 1994.

theory that brain development and function can be understood in Darwinian terms, with groups of neurons competing amongst each other for supremacy. When we experience any particular conscious scene, Edelman argues, we make a highly 'informative' discrimination, because conscious scenes are both integrated and experienced as a whole. *Qualia* are supposed to correspond to these unique scenes, and come about via functional clusters in the *thalamocortical* system, where neural processes result in a series of different but individually stable states.[27] This theory is no doubt helpful in suggesting lines of research that may enrich our view of the neuroscience of everyday experience, but as with Crick and Koch's theory, the basic philosophical problems also get underemphasized.

Information Integration

By contrast, 'information integration' theories propose that consciousness 'is' the ability of the brain to integrate information. Like the dynamic core, these models also suggest that the appearance of one scene in consciousness also means that a potentially vast number of other scenes/neural patterns have not been selected. This has echoes of Elsasser's proposals that whole living systems are capable of selecting a pattern out of a vast range of possible alternatives, based upon past selections. It is also reasonably compatible with Ho's depiction of the organism, and even has echoes of Myers' latent or unexpressed potentials, except that the prevailing assumption is that this can be achieved mechanistically.

'Thalamocortical rhythms' theory proposes that synchronous rhythms, in thalamocortical loops in the gamma-band of frequencies 'creates' the conscious state.[28] It is also theorized that the brainstem plays some role in modulating the 'thalamocortical resonance'. The content of consciousness is provided by sensory input during waking and by intrinsic inputs during dreaming. The model has been proposed to account for the binding problem, and also has relevance to James's observation of 'pulses of consciousness'.[29] As stated above, the currently predominant view, backed up by a significant amount of evidence, links waking awareness to activation in the thalamocortical areas.

Field Theories

A variant on the 'workspace' models are those based upon field theory. John, for example, theorizes that a resonating electrical field allows unified experience to occur.[30] John theorizes that the content of consciousness becomes dominated by apperception, or the integration of momentary perception of the internal and external environment with episodic and

---

27 Seth, 2007; Edelman & Tononi, 2000.
28 Llinàs, Ribary, Contreras & Pedroarena, 1998; Seth, 2007.
29 See discussion in Kelly *et al.*, 2007, p. 626.
30 John, 2001; 2005.

working memories. This is activated by associative reactions to a given perception, so the present gets interpreted in terms of the recent and distant past.[31] Like Baars and others, he assumes that 'information' gets 'encoded' via temporal patterns of synchronized firing. His theory is thus a variant on the workspace theories, and, as we saw, also congruent with Mae-Wan Ho's theory that supposes conscious awareness to arise from more general capacities of the organism, and to be distributed throughout the body. This is because these neural patterns are related to other kinds of phase correlations that regulate more general biological processes.[32]

Consciousness as Virtual Machine

Finally, we come to a group of theories most directly inspired by computer science. This school sees consciousness as a sort of 'virtual machine', along the lines of simulator software, and the brain as a place for self-modelling and self-simulation.[33] Revonsuo sees the world we experience as a virtual-reality simulation in the brain. He suggests that dreaming might be a time for 'risk-free simulation' of dangerous scenarios.[34] The 'self', too, is thought to be part of the simulation, representing the body. This sort of theory is also popular with those studying Out of Body Experiences, an 'altered state' where the experiencer appears to stand or float outside of their body. According to these theories, during periods of sensory deprivation or accident the brain tries to reconstruct this 'virtual-reality' image of the world, placing 'self' outside where it is normally located.[35] I will discuss Thomas Metzinger's variant of this sort of theory in chapter fourteen, in the context of the 'self'.

Some Limitations of Conventional Models

Because the above models operate within the 'game-rules' of conventional science, they tend to share a number of limitations:

- They paper over, ignore, or treat as unproblematic the 'gap' between phenomenological accounts or *qualia* and the corresponding neural mechanisms.
- They tend to assume, implicitly or explicitly, that consciousness is a passive product of the underlying mechanisms.
- As previously stated, they often assume that specifiable mechanisms of consciousness exist and can be understood comprehensively by the Cartesian method of breaking them into subsystems.

---

31 John, 2005.
32 Ho, 2008.
33 Sloman, 2009.
34 Revonsuo, 2005.
35 Blackmore, 1993; Metzinger, 2009.

- They tend to focus primarily on waking states and awareness. Although some consideration is given to dreams, comas and some altered states, the rational-analytical, everyday Western state of consciousness is implicitly the gold standard.
- They ignore completely or else dismiss parapsychological data that *prima facie* refutes some underlying assumptions.

Altered states tend to be accommodated only when a particular theory provides an obvious means for 'explaining' them. For example, 'virtual-reality' metaphors lend themselves to phenomena like lucid dreaming and Out of Body Experiences, in which a person experiences an unusual hallucinatory or illusory environment in which they travel (setting aside for the moment apparently veridical data from Out of Body Experiences). In the metaphor, the brain acts as a kind of simulation generator of this environment.

Parapsychological data is rarely considered during theory formulation, or where considered, dismissed.[36] There are both good and bad reasons for this, and I will discuss the difficult problem of the inclusion or otherwise of parapsychological and other controversial phenomena in a later chapter. I would note that parapsychological phenomena often seem associated with various forms of dissociation, extreme states of consciousness and sleep onset, and *not* with everyday conscious awareness.[37] It is sociologically curious, to say the least, that taboo phenomena and taboo states of mind seem to go hand in hand.

I think it is fair to say that, often for reasons of convenience, most experiments on consciousness occur in a waking state. Although other states of consciousness — like dreaming, comas, meditation and hypnosis — have certainly not been ignored, the primary discussions often centre on consciousness as experienced every day.[38] In my view, this implies that said theories of consciousness that are based mostly upon observations in this state can strictly speaking only be said to apply within this state. So waking consciousness could be said to be a boundary condition, in Cartwright's terms, *beyond which the theory may not be wholly valid or even be invalid*.

This demarcation seems to me important, because without it we might lapse into what Tart terms 'normocentric' thinking, or that the 'normal', rational-analytical state of consciousness is the only one for a sensible understanding of the universe, or consciousness itself.[39] This is both preju-

---

36 For example, Metzinger, 2009, ignores apparent examples of ESP perception in OBEs, and Blackmore, 1982; 1993, finds various ways of dismissing — admittedly fairly rare but not non-existent — such examples in the OBE/Near-Death Experiences literature. See Kelly *et al.*, 2007, for a critique of this dismissal.
37 Myers noted this long ago, and the investigation of dissociative and hypnotic phenomena was a major preoccupation of the early SPR. See Myers, 1903; Gauld, 1968; Crabtree, 1993.
38 Warren, 2008.
39 Tart, 1972.

dicial against other states of consciousness and other cultures, because humans are capable of experiencing a huge variety of very different and often very strange states of consciousness, not all of which may be accessible within the confines of our culture. It also mostly ignores the abilities of exceptional people, and those with exceptional levels of training. And even within our boundaries, we should not forget that there is a great variation in conscious states over the course of a day.[40]

Limits to Mechanistic Reductionism

In order to work, mechanistic theories have to redefine consciousness in quantitative and/or narrow ways that end up privileging the proposed 'neural mechanisms' over qualitative states. This is often done in quite subtle ways. For example, in Thomas Metzinger's theory, qualia gets reduced to a *maximally determinate value* (i.e. the specific shade of a colour like green), and Metzinger quotes with approval Dennett's dismissal of qualia, although he admits that the 'Ineffability Problem is a serious challenge for a scientific theory of consciousness'.[41] This reduction allows him to discuss consciousness in mechanistic terms, but in my view, such a move erases the very phenomenon that these theories aim to explain. This may be inevitable; as Levine puts it, 'if one attempts to understand life, including human life, in terms of pure quantities, one must eliminate the human soul'.[42]

This may well be a fatal stumbling block in the development of any theory of consciousness. The prevailing assumption seems to be that one can easily separate quantifiable causal powers and unquantifiable 'qualitative aspects', and comprehensively explain human behaviour in terms of quantifiable effects only.[43] This is the justification for thinking zombies are possible. Zombies are things that look and behave just like human beings, but lack the 'inner light' of consciousness.[44] The main reason why they are considered plausible even by those who acknowledge subjective consciousness is the tacit assumption that all causes are quantifiable and in principle at least separable from the qualitative aspects of consciousness. The qualitative aspects, in this view, either do not really exist or float off as acausal epiphenomena. I personally strongly doubt this, but if I am correct, this creates a significant dilemma, *because currently predominant approaches are simply not geared towards the qualitative, and depends upon the quantifiable only.*

---

40   See Warren, 2008, for an overview.
41   Metzinger, 2009, p. 51.
42   Levine, 2001, p. 263. This is a figurative rather than a literal statement.
43   Heil, 2004.
44   Blackmore, 2003.

There may also be significant theoretical limits by which the *contents of consciousness* can be resolved into localized, underlying 'mechanisms'. Stephen Braude suggests that an underlying assumption of both cognitive science and physiology, that the structures of the brain display their function, may be false. He begins with the observation that we tend to assume that learning and memorizing always result in specific structural modifications in the brain. As a result, memory recall occurs because of an activation of this modification, or memory trace, in our brain.[45] Braude argues that this assumption, dubbed the *Principle of the Internal Mechanism*, is wrong.

He believes it is mistaken to assume the existence of a set of necessary and sufficient conditions for a given thought to arise. One reason is that any given brain structure is functionally ambiguous; it might display an identical state for a range of different mental states. But the potential power of the Internal Mechanism theory rests upon the supposed mechanism being unambiguously linked to a specific mental state (e.g. mental state M and only M is linked to brain state b and only b). However, if the brain state is potentially tied to many mental states, then the idea of a specific trace has no explanatory function.

Secondly, even memories about specific events or people come in such variety that it is often a problem to assign a specific type label to them. A thought of a certain 'kind' may have any number of forms. 'Christmas' might be identified with turkeys, Christmas trees, the smell of pine, Santa, food poisoning, or the fact that last Boxing Day the cat had a bladder infection and it was hard to find a vet during holiday time. There is no reason to suppose any specific 'token' linking any of these memories, as there is no one form for a 'Christmas' mental state and no general feature or set of features that remembering Christmas *must* have.

Braude argues that if we *do* posit the existence of an underlying physical trace for a specific memory, then we need to invoke a Platonic 'token' to link the mental state and the underlying brain mechanism. Some contemporary theories invoke just such a 'Platonic token', except that it is rationalized as a 'stored representation'; for example, in discussing memory, Kosslyn acknowledges that much of our stored knowledge is 'non-modality specific' and that we can access it by multiple routes. Recognition is supposed to occur because of a 'stored unimodal representation',[46] which is effectively evoking a Platonic token to 'tie' the memories together. But, Braude observes, this sort of theory means a return to the assumption that given classes of memories have some 'token' or 'essence' that makes them what they are.

---

45 Braude, 2002.
46 Kosslyn, 1999, p. 1284. See Kosslyn, 1994, for his theory of memory and visual processing.

This problem persists even if we assume that there are different kinds of memory traces for remembering kinds of a specific class of memory. Braude argues that this leads to an endless regress, because subsets of remembering are no more linked by a relevant common property than single instances. Again, we would need these memories to be 'tagged' with some Platonic token to be usefully linked to a specific brain state; but we have no reason to suppose that memories *are* so tagged.

Braude's arguments seem to me quite extreme, because he suggests that such theoretical difficulties are sufficient to dismiss most of cognitive science. But theoretical arguments cannot by themselves be enough, and seem at least partly contradicted by the neural correlates that *do* suggest a close association between features of the nervous system and subjective experience, and also that reasonably discrete, albeit distributed, 'representations' *do* seem to occur in the brain.[47] (In fairness, Braude does exclude basic sensory experiences from his discussion — and this is quite often where the closest correlates are found.) Braude could be seen as sitting at the opposite pole to Koch, who expects to bury theory under empirical data. Both positions have some validity, but in my view, both are overstated.

Beyond the Mainstream:
A Quantum Model of Consciousness

A number of different individuals, dissatisfied with purely neurobiological theories of consciousness, have proposed theories of consciousness that involve quantum mechanics. The highest profile of such theories was the one proposed by Roger Penrose and Stuart Hameroff.[48] Their theory has problems because it relies upon a property called 'quantum coherence' extending over large parts of the brain, which looks difficult to achieve in such a wet, warm environment. Although the debates over this have proved interesting and instructive, the problems are sufficiently acute that I propose to examine another theory that seems in some respects more viable.

Stapp's Theory of Process Dualism
Henry Stapp begins by arguing that one needs quantum theory to understand brain functions properly, rejecting the common notion that classical determinism holds in the brain. Classical physics specifies bottom-up causation only, and so one should be able to predict the behaviour of the brain as a whole from its microscopic constituents. But there are limits to this approach, partly because of the unfathomable complexity of the brain, which can be revealed by some basic statistics. The total number of glial cells and neurons in the neocortex is around 49.3 billion in females and

---

47 See discussions in Carter, 2002; Kanwisher, 2001; Ishai *et al.*, 1999; Crick & Koch, 2003.
48 Penrose, 1989; 1994; Hameroff, 2010.

65.2 billion in males.[49] Each one of the 10^{11} (one hundred billion) neurons has on average 7,000 synaptic connections to other neurons, making 10^{14} connections.[50] This problem is compounded, says Stapp, by a feature of quantum theory known as the uncertainty principle, which limits knowledge of microscopic events. He concludes that we cannot justify the claim that deterministic behaviour actually holds at either the microscopic or macroscopic level. As a result classical physics can, at best, help us build an approximation of brain-states.

Another problem is the interaction between quantum descriptions, which involve smears of probabilities produced by the uncertainty principle, and the description of a single, classically-described, macroscopic brain-state. In the latter case, and theoretically speaking, the quantum mechanical 'smear' of possibilities needs to be reduced to the single, classical, macroscopic state. To answer the question of how such a reduction might occur, Stapp focuses upon the nerve terminals (see Figure 1, chapter eight).[51]

Every time a neuron fires, an electrochemical impulse travels up the length of the nerve fibre to a nerve terminal. When the impulse reaches the nerve terminal it opens tiny ion channels, where calcium ions flow to trigger the release of neurotransmitters from the vesicles. The released neurotransmitters diffuse across the gap and influence the next nerve to fire. The ion channels are small enough for a kind of quantum effect to occur, causing a 'probability cloud' to fan out over a small area of about 50 nanometres.

This effect happens many times, over many channels all over the brain and it means that the actions at nerve terminals, and for various reasons the whole brain, cannot be understood entirely in classical terms. Stapp: 'According to quantum theory, the state of the brain can become a cloudlike quantum mixture of many classically describable brain states.'[52]

This has significant consequences for those who hope to describe brain-states in terms of classical physics. Stapp points out that since the brain is a highly complex, nonlinear system with a very sensitive dependence on unstable elements it is neither reasonable to suppose nor possible to demonstrate that this sort of situation will lead to a nearly classically describable brain-state. The end result is, rather, a mixture of several alternative classically describable brain-states.

Stapp then brings in a formalism from orthodox quantum theory, invented by John von Neumann. This is an extension of the Copenhagen interpretation that formalizes what are termed the 'probing actions' of sci-

---

49   Pelvig et al., 2008.
50   Drachman, 2005.
51   This explanation is based upon the discussion in Stapp, 2007, chapter four.
52   Stapp, 2007, p. 31.

entists as a *separate process* from the classically-describable world. For example, a scientist might take a measurement of radioactivity at a given site. In this formalism, the system being measured can be described in deterministic terms, but the act of measuring cannot. Stapp observes that probing actions of this kind are performed not only by scientists but by people all the time. Such actions are composed of conscious intentions and linked physical actions. Von Neumann called this probing action 'process 1' and the mechanical process being probed he called 'process 2'.[53]

This formalization can be interpreted as a violation of the closure principle, which assumes that such interventions cannot occur in mechanical (physical) systems. If we accept this interpretation, it would mean that Stapp's theory lies outside the 'game-rules' accepted by most cognitive scientists. And yet the theory itself is within orthodox or conventional physics, and as Stapp has observed on several occasions, cognitive scientists are building models inside a world-picture that is thoroughly dated.

Stapp applies this process formalism onto the brain, because he sees the reduction of the 'smeared out' quantum mixture of states as being achieved via a process 1 intervention, which selects from a smear of potential states generated by a mechanical process 2 evolution. 'The choice involved in such an intervention seems to us to be influenced by consciously felt evaluations...'[54] Stapp sees this approach as offering a way of rescuing free will from the clockwork, mechanical universe. He also suggests that a form of mental causation may be possible via something termed the 'quantum Zeno' effect.

The quantum Zeno effect is a consequence of the dynamical rules of quantum theory. If the process 1 enquiry leads to a 'yes', it is followed by a sequence of process 1 queries for which the answer is also 'yes'. In this case, the dynamical rules of quantum theory will entail that the sequence of outcomes will with a high probability also be 'yes', even despite strong physical forces that would otherwise cause a state to evolve differently. According to Stapp, the timings of these process 1 actions would be controlled by the agent's 'free choice'. This would imply, via the basic dynamical laws of quantum mechanics, 'a potentially powerful effect of mental effort on the brain of the agent!'[55] Applying mental effort increases the rapidity of a sequence of mostly identical acts of intentionality, which goes on to produce intended feedback. This sort of holding in place effect is the quantum Zeno effect.

The outcome of Stapp's theory is very similar to William James's idea of attention and pulses of thought.[56] Stapp also re-interprets a number of

---

53   Von Neumann, 1955/1932.
54   Stapp, 2007, p. 32.
55   Stapp, 2007, p. 36.
56   James, 1890.

findings from psychology and neuropsychology in terms of this theory. This bridging is important, because it helps place the new theory in a conventional context.

On the whole, cognitive scientists have been far from impressed by this sort of approach, in part because Stapp's theory amounts to a form of dualism. In a widely cited paper, Koch and Hepp gave a number of reasons why they believed that there was 'little reason to appeal to quantum mechanics to explain higher brain functions, including consciousness'.[57] (1) In quantum formalisms, consciousness has only been a 'place holder', and has little relevance to the study of neural circuits; (2) large quantum systems are very difficult to analyse rigorously, except in highly idealized models; (3) brains obey quantum mechanics, but they do not seem to exploit any of its special features; (4) chemical transmission across the synaptic cleft and the generation of action potentials involve many thousands of ions and neurotransmitter molecules coupled by diffusion of the membrane potential that extends across tens of micrometres. Both processes will destroy any coherent quantum states; (5) massive parallel computation is adequate to account for consciousness. They conclude that '[i]t is far more likely that a material basis of consciousness can be understood within a purely neurobiological framework'.[58]

Of these points, (3) should bother us least. Paradigm-led conventional science often misses novel phenomena that is not geared to its specific forms of research. Kuhn noted that 'Initially, only the anticipated and usual are experienced even under circumstances where anomaly is later to be observed'.[59] The chaotic oscillations of a simple pendulum went unnoticed for centuries before the arrival of chaos theory.[60] Novel approaches often take new research techniques, equipment and observational criteria. The issues often cannot be settled by a simple, single experiment, as Koch and Hepp also suggest.

Stapp's reply to Koch and Hepp, which *Nature* declined to publish, was that the arguments of Koch and Hepp missed the point. He pointed out that the von Neumann formalism explicitly brings consciousness into the dynamics and that 'a conscious experience occurs and the state of the observed system is reduced to the part of itself that corresponds to that experience'.[61] He also claimed that although superpositions were mostly eliminated in the brain, that this did not eliminate the need for process 1. Stapp suggests that by focusing on the elimination of macroscopic superpositions which would disrupt both Penrose-Hammeroff models

---

57 Koch & Hepp, 2006, p. 612.
58 Koch & Hepp, 2006, p. 612.
59 Kuhn, 1996/1962, p. 64.
60 Gleik, 1987.
61 Stapp, 2009, p. 1.

and quantum computation, they did not address the core issue which is the process 1 free choice.

Stapp's response covers some but not all of Hepp and Koch's objections. A key issue is probably point (2), the problem of rigorously analysing large-scale quantum states. Also problematic is the mapping of the interaction between classical and quantum models, which tends to be idiosyncratic even in far simpler, controlled experiments.[62] Stapp's theory will also probably not be taken seriously until the wider issue of the role of quantum mechanics in biological systems generally is better understood.

Having said this, I think that Stapp's application of von Neumann's formulation to these problems is important. The main reason is that, even if he has the details wrong, he has shown that it is possible to violate the closure principle in a way that does not invoke anything like the *verboten* substance dualism. His dualism is epistemological and formal rather than ontological and substantial, and even if his specific application is inappropriate it indicates that it is at least *possible* to talk about the world in a formal way that is not wholly deterministic, and inclusive of an active agent. The importance of this development cannot be understated.

Conclusion

Some of the conventional theories above form the basis of reasonably coherent research programmes of neurobiological research, but *none* really address the deeper philosophical problems of consciousness. The conventional theories tend to cluster close to the 'representational' rather than 'behaviourist' pole of conventional thinking, mainly because they acknowledge consciousness as a problem. This is significant because it shows that the only way of accommodating consciousness in conventional terms is with some sort of representational approach.

The 'quantum' theories, which tend to be inadequately discussed in the mainstream, face similar problems although they do offer ways out of some of the strictures of conventional thinking; Stapp's theory, which challenges strict determinism, being a salient example. But it is far from clear whether bringing quantum mechanics deepens our understanding of why we have subjective experiences in the first place.

Despite these problems, the confidence that wholly conventional theories will prove adequate is considerable. Resolution is seen as merely a matter of time, research money and new techniques. This positivistic approach is justified by the growth of new technologies that allow us to peer into the brain and find correlates of conscious experience that are sometimes very striking indeed.

---

62 See Cartwright, 1999, chapter nine.

Chapter Ten

Neuroimaging and its Limits

We live in an era of reductionist neuroscience, where virtually any aspect of human experience is held to be based upon specific forms of brain activity. This notion has been reinforced significantly by emerging technologies that allow us non-invasively to 'listen in' to the living brain. In light of this advance, there has even been a highly questionable trend to rebrand areas traditionally not considered science with a 'neuro' prefix — as for example 'neurophilosophy', 'neuroethics' and even, apparently, 'neuroarthistory'.[1]

In the current chapter, I will examine the practical and statistical limitations of brain-scanning and problems with the underlying theories. Neuroimaging technology has transformed cognitive science within the last two decades, seeming to confirm a picture of the brain that is a highly compartmentalized agglomeration of semi-autonomous 'modules', each of which has its own aims, talents and influences.[2] The nature of much of this material can be quite technical, but I think it is necessary to examine this closely to gain an understanding of the technology and its implications.

Some neuroscientists even hope that one day we might be able to build a *cerebroscope*; a machine that translates brain activity into a report about the subjective state of the participant.[3] According to some, this would entail unlocking the neural code of the brain, just as geneticists unlocked DNA in the 1950s,[4] and a number of developments suggest this possibility. Carter noted that it is already possible to identify, from a large set of completely novel natural images, which specific image was seen by an observer via neural patterns and that 'it may soon be possible to reconstruct a picture of a person's visual experience from measurements of brain activity alone'.[5] To this we might add striking developments, such as the 'decoding' of

---

1   Scruton, 2009.
2   Carter, 2008a, commenting on Minsky, 1986.
3   Rose, 2006.
4   The Churchlands, in Blackmore, 2005.
5   Carter, 2008b.

neural patterns of severely paralysed people via microelectrodes, which allows brain signals to be translated into words.[6] As Carter notes, 'whenever someone says of brain scanning "it'll never be able to do that," it goes and does it'.[7]

Neuroimaging experiments often rely upon a range of implicit *a priori* assumptions to work, including a commitment to some form of neurological reductionism and the idea that the mind/brain is modular in nature and consists of basically stable elements. It is also often assumed that the underlying 'cognitive architecture' is robust and uniform between humans, or at least comparable. But the central assumption seems to be that mental states can be considered purely a result of specific structures and functions of the brain and could, at least in principle, be read off in various ways. Collectively, these sorts of assumptions narrow the field of enquiry and make a research programme possible and practical. Whilst there is nothing wrong with this narrowing in terms of a research programme, it is important to understand that this work is predicated strongly upon them, and will necessarily produce a partial picture of human beings.

How to Map the Brain

There are a number of ways to map brain activity. *Electroencephalograms* (EEG) measure changes in electrical potential using scalp electrodes, a technique first used in 1929 by Hans Berger.[8] *Positron Emission Tomography* (PET) scans rely on the administration of a radioactive substance, which becomes incorporated into blood glucose, and emits positrons. These are detected by rings of radiation detectors that build up a picture of slices of the brain. fMRI (*functional Nuclear Magnetic Resonance Imaging*) measures radio signals emitted by hydrogen atoms when they are placed in a magnetic field. Hydrogen atoms are common in the brain's water molecules. In a magnetic field, these atoms emit measurable energy. This signal effect is finite, and decays over time, resulting in decreased image intensity,[9] so there is only a limited time window in which to acquire images. Oxygenated and deoxygenated blood have different magnetic properties, and an increase in deoxygenated blood in the brain also affects image intensity, whereas a decrease has the opposite effect. fMRI can produce very detailed pictures of the human brain, especially with the use of the BOLD (Blood Oxygen Level Dependent) contrast, which lets researchers measure local brain metabolism.[10]

---

6   Kellis *et al.*, 2010.
7   Carter, 2008b.
8   Blackmore, 2003, p. 228.
9   Heeger & Ress, 2002.
10 Blackmore, 2003, p. 229.

An fMRI study is performed as follows.[11] Experiments produce two kinds of 3D pictures, one of which shows an anatomical scan, the other a functional scan. Functional scans show the BOLD signal, which is represented by roughly cube shaped areas called voxels or 'volumetric pixels'. The total number of these voxels is between 40,000 and 500,000, depending upon the scanner settings. A new image is produced every two to three seconds in a scan.

This data is then pre-processed for the reduction of noise and to allow comparison between different brains. For statistical reasons, voxels are then often mapped onto a model 'average brain'. In experiments that involve behavioural tests, participants are often told to move back and forth between different tasks, and then differences in the BOLD signals between different tasks are analysed. This will provide two different data sets for the researcher to analyse. Voxel sets are analysed statistically as matrices, and investigators often end up selecting between subsets of voxels and measure averages across them. Voxels are often selected on the basis of their anatomy and functionality in a scan.

Sometimes, such an analysis reveals extraordinary correlations. For example, in early 2009, a team at the University College London found that they could accurately predict the position of subjects within a virtual environment solely from the pattern of activity in a part of the brain called the hippocampus.[12] They concluded that the results showed 'that highly abstracted representations of space are expressed in the human hippocampus'.[13] Whether or not the 'memory trace' interpretation is correct,[14] this finding demonstrates a very close match between 'thinking' of a particular spatial location and a particular neural activity.

The picture muddies somewhat with more complex cognitive functions, where persistent correlations seem harder to find and the evidence more contradictory. In a systematic literature review and meta-analysis, Cabeza and Nyberg compared regions that were activated during similar tasks. They found that regions associated with sensory and motor activities, such as the perceptual studies mentioned above, do seem to show localization, but for higher cognitive processes (problem solving or 'working mem-

---

11 Based upon a summary in Vul *et al.*, 2009.
12 Hassabis *et al.*, 2009.
13 Hassabis *et al.*, 2009, p. 549.
14 I would note that the 'engram' interpretations of such findings, tempting though they may be, still fall foul of two of Gauld's (in Kelly *et al.*, 2007) objections to trace theories, namely (1) that representations require interpreters who are already knowledgeable enough to comprehend them, and (2) that to understand membership of a category one must possess a network of further concepts, and that it is not clear where such would be stored (see Kelly *et al.*, 2007, p. 269). See also my discussion later in the chapter.

ory'), the data is far more diffuse. In the latter, the peaks of brain activity spread to from a quarter to a half of the brain.[15]

Issues with Statistics and Data Selection

A number of different imaging and statistical methods are used for sorting through the data. A central assumption is that the fMRI signal is proportional to a measure of local neural activity, averaged over a few millimetres in the brain and a time of several seconds. This is known as the linear transform model, and is claimed to allow for a complex relationship between an outside stimulus (say a word or picture) and the activity of the brain. The model is acknowledged to be 'at best an approximation of the complex interactions between neuronal activity, metabolic demand and blood flow and oxygenation'.[16] This model assumes a more-or-less straightforward relationship between what the neurons do, the energy they need and different levels of bloodflow.

There is some question whether this model is realistic. Heeger and Ress admit that 'these measurements... would be worthless if the linear transform were not a valid approximation'.[17] Some of the mechanics of blood flow challenge this view. Signals can derive from larger veins, smaller vessels and capillaries, and different techniques can emphasize these different signal sources differently.

A new technique, multivariate pattern analysis (MVPA), uses a form of Artificial Intelligence to analyse differences between brain-scans. When a person thinks about tennis, for example, the program can detect a corresponding signal in the pattern of activity among motor area voxels.[18] From this data, it can make predictions about how the data relates to a person's mental state. MVPA can also make distinctions between large numbers of brain states and mental states; a new pattern-recognition program can guess which of 1,000 pictures a person just viewed from scans alone.[19]

Many of the specific neural patterns detected by MVPA are context-dependent. Bor, who is generally enthusiastic about the potential of mind-reading admits that 'studies that demonstrate that the technique makes accurate predictions are statistically significant, but that often means that the computer's guess is a hair's breadth above chance'. He admits that many studies that rely on MVPA to pick between two alternatives score around 60 percent accuracy, where a blind guess would give 50 percent.[20] He also points out that subjects could easily break the rules, and think about other targets, without the experimenter's knowing.

15 Cabeza & Nyberg, 2000. See also Uttal, 2005.
16 Heeger & Ress, 2002, p. 143.
17 Heeger & Ress, 2002, p. 143.
18 Bor, 2010.
19 Bor, 2010.
20 Bor, 2010, p. 57.

There are other, more serious problems with data selection and circular analysis. Kriegeskorte *et al.* noted that '…the more we search a noisy data set for active locations, the more likely we are to find spurious effects by chance'.[21] They cast doubt on the efficacy of widely-used statistical techniques to meet the goals of identifying voxels containing particular effects and to estimate the size of the effect. They concluded that slight distortions were common in the literature, although severe errors were less common, and that there was a lack of consensus on statistical methods, such as the definition of a large effect size.

More severe problems have been observed. There have been myriad claims that particular brain regions are involved in some very specific areas of social cognition like social distress (associated with the anterior cingulate cortex or ACC), 'empathy-related manipulation' (the ACC), or anxiety proneness (right cuneus). In 2009, Vul *et al.* caused a storm of controversy by claiming that the 'impossibly' strong effect sizes claimed in 55 articles were probably the result of analysis problems. They concluded that the investigators were using statistical techniques that guaranteed to offer greatly inflated correlation estimations. They added that, 'The underlying problems… appear to be common in fMRI research of many kinds—not just in studies of emotion, personality and social cognition'.[22] The bottom line seems to be that much of this work is exploratory and the meaning of the results less clear cut than is often claimed.

Experimental Limits

Another issue is the relationship between fMRI scan results and experimental protocols that investigate correlates of behaviour. Nichols and Newsome report that, '[e]quipped with sound conceptual frameworks originating in behaviour, neurophysiologists can then study underlying brain function at several levels'.[23] But this assumes that firstly a behaviour has been or *can* be defined in a 'sound' way, and that said behaviour has a specific underlying brain function that *can* be reliably discriminated.

There is no doubt that, in some cases, some useful results can be obtained. Kosslyn, for example, wished to see whether mental images of strongly emotive subjects affected the *autonomic* part of the nervous system. The autonomic system controls involuntary bodily functions, like heart rate and breathing, the blush response, and erections in males. They asked subjects to visualize babies with tumours over their eyes or bodies whilst undergoing a PET scan.[24] The *control* or comparison group had to visualize neutral images like trucks or lamps. When the 'aversive' brain

21 Kriegeskorte *et al.*, 2010.
22 Vul *et al.*, 2009, p. 274.
23 Nichols & Newsome, 1999, p. 36.
24 Kosslyn, 1999.

scans were compared to the 'neutral' controls, it was found that, as predicted, the *anterior insula*, a major component of the autonomic system, was activated. So theories can be successfully tested using this equipment.

Limitations Due to the Function and Structure of the Brain

In a review article, Logothetis pointed out a number of limitations that have less to do with the technological or statistical limitations of the technology, and more to do with the brain itself.[25] The modular organization of different brain systems he accepted as an established fact. A module was defined as 'the classical neuronal circuits repeated iteratively within a structure (for example, the columns or swirling, slab-like tangential arrangements of the neocortex), as well as entities within which modules might be grouped by sets of dominating external connections'.[26] Even given distinguishable modularity, the issue is how far fMRI can go in revealing the 'neuronal mechanisms' of behaviour. Logothetis observed that the limitations of fMRI are mainly due to that it reflects mass action, and less to do with technological limits. Logothetis:

> ...only in certain special cases can [fMRI] be really useful for unambiguously selecting [a particular hypothesis], or for explaining the detailed neural mechanisms underlying the studied cognitive capacities.[27]

Logothetis then highlighted the widely-held assumption that brain structures can, in principle, be thought of as 'information-processing' entities with an input, a local processing capacity, and an output. He disputed this interpretation for areas of the cerebral cortex, calling the input-elaboration-output model an oversimplification. The reason is that input to the cortex from the subcortical regions is weak and there are a massive number of feedback connections. Quite often, too, BOLD outputs reflect not just rises in cortical activity, but changes in the balance between excitatory and inhibitory circuits. fMRI cannot be used to easily distinguish between the two, and Logothetis pointed out that

> the [thalamo-cortical] organization... evidently complicates both the precise definition of the conditions that would justify the assignment of a functional role of an 'active' area, and the interpretation of fMRI maps.[28]

He concluded that the ultimate limitations of fMRI had more to do with the circuitry and functional organization of the brain, as well as with experimental protocols that ignore this.

---

25 Logothetis, 2008.
26 Logothetis, 2008, p. 869.
27 Logothetis, 2008, p. 870.
28 Logothetis, 2008, p. 873.

Logothetis's thoughts in some respects echo those of William Uttal, perhaps the most ardent critic of neuroimaging. Uttal observes that the fMRI studies represent the latest incarnation of a long search for localized regions of the brain that represent or control specific cognitive functions.[29] Uttal accepts that some processes are more or less localized, such as the sensory, motor, emotional and appetitive regions, but claims that assumption may not hold for higher-level cognitive processes. One problem is the difficulty in defining specific 'cognitive functions', another was the

> surprising lack of appreciation that the brain was a highly complex, heavily interconnected system displaying nonlinear properties that precluded its simple analysis into independent functional units.[30]

These observations demonstrate the limits of any given methodology that restricts itself to a narrow set of assumptions. Clearly, some sometimes striking results have been obtained — but only at a cost of an adherence to a model that only has limited application within its problem domain.

Some Philosophical Assumptions

The Mind/Brain is Modular in Nature and 'Mental Functions' can be Localized

It is worth examining this issue a little further. Donaldson points out, in his apologia for fMRI studies; 'the best neuroimaging studies always aim to go beyond asking "where," and try to answer questions about "what" the activity reflects — why the activity is occuring.'[31] He asserts that fMRI is for parsing and not just mapping the brain, and that mixed designs can do this:

> The basic idea is that fMRI can be used to 'parse' rather than simply 'map' the brain. In linguistics, 'parsing' refers to the assignment of constituent structure to a sentence. Without adequate organization, a sentence is potentially ambiguous or even meaningless. An analogous task is required if neuroimaging is to provide psychologically meaningful data.[32]

In mixed designs, the idea is to measure the temporal profile of activity in the brain. This, according to Donaldson, allows the separation of transient and sustained activity. He suggests these two patterns of change in signals allow us to deduce functional differences in

> what kind of role a region plays in supporting behaviour. Specifically, the distinction between transient and sustained signal changes maps onto a functional distinction between item (trial) related and state

---

29 Uttal, 2005.
30 Uttal, 2005, p. 3.
31 Donaldson, 2004, p. 442.
32 Donaldson, 2004, p. 442.

(task)-related processing, and provides one clear way of characterizing brain regions in functional terms...[33]

Essentially, whichever regions light up at specific times are deemed to be functionally necessary for a specific task.

Uttal, however, provides a number of reasons why this sort of programme may be limited.[34] It is difficult to know whether an active area is responsible for all processing of a task, or whether it is a critical line of communication between other areas. This sort of problem is recognized, even in the popular literature. Mariette di Christina, the editor-in-chief of *Scientific American Mind*, noted that 'The more researchers may attempt to look at a single processing question, the more it turns out to be interrelated with many other things going on in the brain'.[35]

With higher level cognitive processes like decision-making or problem solving, it is more likely that each region of the brain mediates many cognitive processes and that 'each cognitive process is encoded by activity in widely distributed brain regions'.[36] Uttal's is not an argument for functional homogeneity, as some of the holists proposed, but for some kind of compromise between those who believe the 'mind' can be decomposed into modular units and those who think we have to look at the system as a whole. The 'workspace' theory may also be regarded as a working towards such a compromise.[37]

Conscious awareness also poses problems for localizers. Kanwisher, whilst claiming a strong causal relationship between awareness and the activation of local brain regions during sensory experiences, acknowledges that the activation of, say, the fusiform face area by itself is not enough to 'explain' awareness of a face. To illustrate this, she provides a thought experiment by which we imagine said specific neural system to be dissected out and isolated from the rest of the organism and still able to perform its function.[38] Intuitively, it seems unlikely that such an isolated system would be aware in any sense of the word. Kanwisher concludes that to be aware, even localized functions would need to be able to receive 'information' from the rest of the brain and nervous system.

There is also the difficulty of localizing consciousness in a specific brain area, although parts of the brain, like the cerebellum, are hypothesized not to be conscious at all.[39] As we saw previously, human-type conscious awareness is currently supposed to be generally localizable in the cerebral cortex and thalamocortical loops. One of the reasons for supposing this is

---

33 Donaldson, 2004, p. 442.
34 Uttal, 2001; 2005.
35 Editorial in *Scientific American Mind*, July/August 2010, p. 1.
36 Uttal, 2005, p. 5.
37 Kelly et al., 2007.
38 Kanwisher, 2001.
39 Mormann & Koch, 2007.

that various kinds of injuries that impair the function of these brain areas also disrupt consciousness.

Disorders that disrupt consciousness, like epilepsy, are associated with widespread disruption in the cortex and also thalamic areas.[40] Comas and 'persistent vegetative states' can also be defined as global disorders of consciousness. However, a recent experiment demonstrated that a patient in a vegetative state following severe brain injury showed the same pattern of brain activity as non-damaged people when asked to imagine playing tennis or to imagine visiting all rooms in her house.[41] The fact that a patient could so respond would suggest that they are still aware in some sense.

Certain kinds of brain injury also cause a loss of consciousness. These can include damage to the cortex and also discrete injuries to midline subcortical structures. The reason for this is that such structures are associated with brain arousal, an example being the Reticular Activating System, which regulates waking and sleep. Damage to the nuclei in this area can cause coma.[42] So we have a fair idea about the gross areas of the brain that are necessary to support waking awareness. The next question is: to what extent can the contents of consciousness, *aka* mental contents, be 'translated' into 'neural language'?

The Mind as Neural Code

There is currently a massive effort in neuroscience to unlock the neural code, that is, to translate the mind—which is conceived as a kind of software—to the functional neural language in which it is written. One neuroscientist, John Chapin, even stated that 'if you're a real neuroscientist, that's the game you want to play'.[43] The idea that the mind can be understood in this way harks back to the computational and cybernetic models developed in the 1950s (chapter eight), and we have already seen that much data from neuroscience gets interpreted as 'processing information' and 'representing' data. Neuronal functions, too, lend themselves to interpretations in terms of information theory, as the constituents of perception (colours, edges, movements, etc.) are thought to be 'represented' as neural patterns. For example, visual objects have been theorized to be 'represented' via synchronized neurons in the visual cortex which detect specific features of visual objects that are encoded by temporal correlations.[44]

This sort of idea has been applied to many functions within the brain, the aim being to find a sort of 'Rosetta stone' that can match 'mind lan-

---

40 Mormonn & Koch, 2007.
41 Owen *et al.*, 2006; in Mormann & Koch, 2007.
42 Mormonn & Koch, 2007.
43 Interviewed by Horgan, 2004.
44 Engel *et al.*, 1997.

guage' and 'brain language'.[45] Ideally, one should be able to put mind language – mental states – parallel to brain states, and learn the translation rules between the two. To do this, as described above, one performs experiments, looks at the difference in the brain between tasks, and tries to determine what has changed in structure or function to glean the 'neural' counterpart of the subjective state.

The writings of Steven Rose are interesting in this regard, because whilst sympathetic to this idea – he coined the 'Rosetta stone' analogy – he is also honest about its limits. In his discussion of memory – a prime constituent of mental states – he notes a number of problems and unknowns that are not always apparent from reading other popular works.[46] He observes:[47]

- Problems with defining what constitutes a memory.
- Unknowns concerning the persistence of memory even after apparent forgetting or extinction.
- Problems with the separation between a 'memory' and retrieving it, and the 'mental scanning' for a memory.
- Some temporal recovery of memory after brain injuries despite heavy kinds of amnesia.
- Problems with mapping temporal scales and regional distribution studies of memory onto molecular and cellular studies.
- Problems with the idea that memory is encoded via synaptic change, as in the theories of Donald Hebb, despite evidence for the truth of some of this theory.[48]

He concludes by admitting that

> ...we don't know how memories are made, how and in what form they are stored in the brain (if 'storage' as in a filing cabinet or computer memory is even an appropriate way of speaking) or the processes by which they are retrieved.[49]

Many of these blanks will, no doubt, be filled in as neuroscience progresses, yet Rose observes deeper conceptual problems. Neuroimaging, he says, serves as a *description* rather than an explanation of brain function, so can provide us with correlations but not explanations on its own. He also sees disarray between theoretical concepts at multiple levels, as psychological models of memory often seem to map poorly onto both neuroimaging and cellular/molecular studies. This, of course, is an indication of

---

45   Rose, 2006.
46   For example, reading Carter, 2002, one gets the impression that virtually all of these problems are solved, or will be soon.
47   Rose, 2006, chapter eight.
48   'Memories do not seem to be encoded within these specific changes in connectivity, but rather, over time, other brain regions and connections become involved. The imaging studies add to these problems of interpretation by revealing the dynamic nature of the cortical processes involved in both learning and recalling...' (Rose, 2006, p. 211).
49   Rose, 2006, p. 212.

the necessary methodological pluralism of neuroscience, and one can argue for a 'patchwork unity' of methods,[50] but Rose seems to be saying that deeper conceptual revisions are needed:

> Empiricism is not enough. Simply, we currently lack a theoretical framework within which such mountains of data can be accommodated. We are, it seems to me, still trapped within the mechanistic reductionist mind-set within which our science has been formed.[51]

Rose's favoured alternative seems to be a form of dialectical materialism, such as that favoured by the Marxists, where different explanatory levels exist, even though everything is ultimately composed of matter. He also seems unwilling to break away from standard accounts of determinism, and is scornful of 'holistic' accounts. In my view, however, at least *some* of the problems of memory may require a holistic and non-mechanistic approach of some kind, but I do not know what form this revised theory of memory might take to be viable and to produce workable experimental results.

Representations, the Brain and the Missing Person

Many neuroscientists seem to take it for granted that minds can be conceptualized at least partly as a system of representations running on the brain. For example, Kosslyn writes that 'information processing systems are organized in neural tissue' and accepts that representation occurs in the brain: '…A "representation" is a physical state that serves as a repository of information, and a "buffer" stores representations.'[52] Logothetis also accepts that there is an 'underlying neural representation' of a stimulus.[53]

Kanwisher makes an argument for a type-token hypothesis, arguing that

> awareness of a particular perceptual event requires not only activation of a representation of that attribute, but also individuation of that perceptual information as a distinct event.[54]

She observes that perceptual experience is made up of discrete objects that appear in particular spatial locations and at specific times. Because of this, she claims that activated perceptual attributes must become associated with 'representations of specific objects and/or events in order to be experienced as fully conscious percepts'.[55] Kosslyn also invokes a very similar type-token theory.[56]

---

50 Craver, 2007.
51 Rose, 2006, p. 215.
52 Kosslyn, 1999, p. 1283.
53 Logothetis, 2008, p. 871.
54 Kanwisher, 2001, p. 107. See Kanwisher, 1987; 1991, for a fuller exposition of this theory.
55 Kanwisher, 2001, p. 107.
56 Kosslyn, 1999.

The main problem is that representations, like 'illusions', generally need an observer. If there are representations in the brain, then to what or to whom do they 'represent' the world? Representations presuppose consciousness. But mechanistic views like those espoused above attempt to speak of representations in the *absence* of consciousness which, as Tallis observes, seems deeply illogical.[57]

The reason for this may well be ideological. I have already noted that researchers often redefine subjective experience in narrow, mechanistic and reductionistic terms to accommodate it within the current frames of neuroscientific explanation. Wallace even suggests that various cognitive terms, like 'information' and 'representations' became purged of their subjective content so they could be viewed as objective and mechanical processes in line with the ideology of the cognitive revolution of the 1950s.[58]

At first glance, these objections may seem to contradict reams of data from neuroscience that do seem to suggest that both 'information-processing' and 'representations' occur there. However, this is, I suggest, an example of the power of paradigm-led thinking.[59] Bennett and Hacker observe that the brain does not process symbols, information or representations. What happens is that researchers perform, say, fMRI experiments, and *derive* information from the results. But this, they observe, is not information the brain has or evidence for a brain language 'any more than dendrochronological information about the severity of winters in the 1930s is written in the tree trunk in arboreal patois'.[60] In this view, 'representations', 'information' and 'symbols' constitute theoretical concepts or metaphors that theoretically frame the information derived from neuroimaging and other experiments. To ascribe them to the brain seems to me an exercise in literalism. In short, we are looking at manufactured knowledge and mistaking it for nature.

Mind-Readers, Bill Clinton and Metaphysics

Some of the limitations of the current approaches can be better understood by a thought experiment which imagines what would happen if the aspirations of the neural decoders become fulfilled. In doing so, I am deliberately ignoring a range of significant problems and limitations with the 'decoding' exercise.[61]

Let us suppose that they succeed in building a mind-reader that can, for example, stimulate a grandmother neuron and translate the pulses from

---

57 Tallis, 2004, p. 91.
58 Wallace, 2000.
59 Griffin, 1998.
60 Bennett & Hacker, 2003, p. 153.
61 See Horgan, 2004; Rose, 2006, chapter eight, for a discussion of these problems and limitations.

this and the patterns in the visual cortex into an image of Bill Clinton.[62] Surely, this would prove that physicalism, the machine-code metaphor and representationalism were 'true'? In what follows, I am going to be perverse and suggest that even if we accomplished such a feat, that *on its own* this still would not resolve the argument in favour of these propositions. First of all, we should acknowledge what it *would* achieve.

(1) It would demonstrate the highly impressive pragmatic utility of neural coding theory, including the efficacy of representational metaphors *when considered in the context of the enabling technology itself*.

(2) It would demonstrate an *extremely* close relationship between at least some mental states and the 'neural code'.

(3) It would strongly imply that we can understand the storage/retrieval (*if* those are the correct terms) of at least some memories in representational terms, and in terms of something like machine code, and would constitute powerful evidence that these particular memories are not stored outside unless by some form of duplication.[63]

(4) It would constitute a powerful *emotional* argument for information physicalism being 'true'.

Surely, such an achievement would mean that the mind/body problem had finally been solved, and that physicalism was an objective fact, rather in the way that the Earth 'is' really round, and it really does orbit the sun? Surely, it would mean that our minds 'are' nothing but machine code that use representations that run on biological machines?

Whilst I am willing to concede that such an achievement would at the very least invite a revision of certain metaphysics, I would assert that looking to such a development as either proof of physicalism or a 'solution' to the mind/body problem misconstrues the nature of the debate. To deal with the representational issue first: I have stated, along with Tallis, Bennett and Hacker, and others that 'representations' can be seen as derived concepts and not things or processes that can be said to be inherent in neural tissue. But if we accept this, and the invention of such a machine, then how might we explain the picture of Bill Clinton on the TV screen? A potential answer to this can be found by recalling the constructed nature of light, and by taking a basically instrumentalist view of these occurrences (which is suggested by the strongly metaphorical nature of the 'representation' issue).

---

62 This particular suggestion is prompted by the discovery by Fried and Koch of a neuron in a patient's brain that only fired when he was shown pictures of Bill Clinton! Described in Horgan, 2004.

63 So it would constitute, in my view, persuasive evidence that this *particular* memory was *not* stored in a sort of 'cosmic reservoir' *a la* William James and/or Henri Bergson, unless one supposes—somewhat redundantly—that a duplicate were made. But see chapter five for theoretical problems with this.

The physicist David Bohm, amongst others, observed that facts can be said to be manufactured. This is suggested by the Latin root of 'fact', *facere*, which means that which has been made. Bohm goes on to say that:

> ...in a certain sense we 'make' the fact. That is to say, beginning with immediate perception of an actual situation, we develop the fact by giving it further order, form and structure... In classical physics, the fact was 'made' in terms of the order of planetary orbits... In quantum theory, the fact was 'made' in terms of the order of energy levels, quantum numbers, symmetry groups, etc.[64]

And in the current case, the fact is 'made' in terms of information-processing systems, representations, information-processing, etc. So each way of 'making' a fact involves weaving observations into a conceptual matrix that cannot really be said to be 'real', but is more a creative expression of the observing minds.

In addition, facts can only continue to be made if nature remains cooperative to the theoretical approach that is adopted. This was one of Feyerabend's key criticisms against the adoption of any rigid methodology in science. Certain given approaches—such as the assertion that minds can be understood in terms of a 'code'—only make sense if they are structured in a way that allows us to come up with usable results.[65] Now, it may be that nature will prove sufficiently cooperative to allow us to produce that image of Bill Clinton on the screen; but equally, the metaphor of the Rosetta stone might already be seen to have certain limits.

Today, such facts (neural correlates of subjective states) are 'made' by comparing subject reports with brain-scans, but the neural decoders would like to bypass this by producing a lexicon and grammar that allows us to 'read' neural states *without* having to ask subjects for their reports. But currently this cannot really be done, as an individual's 'neural code' is often idiosyncratic, varied and can even change according to circumstances. So the facts that are created in neuroscience remain of a correlative nature, even though some correlations can be locally striking.

So in the absence of a neural base-code, the decoders would have to rely on matching the phenomenology of the perception to the neural bursts. Processing and translating this would also, presumably, involve some sort of computer program that could translate the pulses/neural patterns to a picture. Something like this may be possible if/when we develop technology that can decipher the neurological events in the visual cortex, which has specialized cortical cells that react selectively to different visual features. If one were 'translating' these, then one could presumably use a program on a powerful computer to 'stick' the various cellular reactions together and form a picture that way, but in the absence of a detailed bind-

---

64 Bohm, 1983, p. 142.
65 Feyerabend, 1978.

ing theory, one would have to 'cheat' in order to stick this disparate data together. But even if all this could be done, I would still argue that any 'representations' that would result would be (1) manufactured and (2) in the eye of the beholder, namely, the experimenter.

Even more significant problems occur with the argument that this finally 'solves' the mind/body problem. The reason is that the mind/body problem seems better characterized as a *metaphysical* rather than an *empirical* dispute, and interpreting it as something that can be finally resolved empirically constitutes, I think, a category error. To understand why, we need to look again at the nature of scientific explanation and its relationship to technology.

Consider Newton's laws of motion, which, *ceteris paribus*, successfully describe the motion of the planets. Newtonian theory has also proved very successful in technological feats like putting humans on the moon, and sending probes to the planets. There is no disputing that Newton's theory works, and very well. There is also no question that it has predictive power, so, for example, one can predict the movements of the planets centuries hence. However, there is a significant difference between acknowledging predictive power and pragmatic utility and asserting that Newton's theory is the objective truth.

Part of the reason is that Newtonian physics must imagine shibboleths to work, as Mach pointed out in the nineteenth century. In particular, Mach singled out Newton's notion of absolute space and inertia because they were purely 'thought thing[s] that cannot be pointed to in experience'.[66] Secondly, Mach opposed the idea that Newton's laws could be applied universally, attacking 'the conceptual monstrosity of absolute space'. And, as history demonstrated, it's possible to reformulate ideas of space and time via relativity in a way that allowed anomalies that were previously unexplained, like the movements of Mercury, to be accommodated by the new theory.

The usual story here is that Newtonian physics were accommodated as a special case of relativity, which could potentially explain more, but it is possible to interpret what happened in a different way. Feyerabend argued strongly that the idea that new physical theories could explain more than the older constitutes a sort of epistemological illusion. This is because new theories, ideologies and traditions (which is how Feyerabend characterized science) tend to create entirely new problem domains and are often not directly concerned with 'solving' the problems of the older ideology. Where older theories are accommodated, they occur in an *ad hoc* way or even simply via assertion.

So, in the case of the neural decoders, we have a programme that is predicated upon an assumption that it is appropriate to think of the 'mind' in

---

66 Quoted in Burke, 1985, p. 295.

terms of a sort of natural machine code running on wetware. The problem, then, is to 'decode' this natural neural 'language'. A different sort of theory—say, for example, Myers' subliminal mind—would have little or nothing to say about this, and rightly so, because *they deal with different problem domains*. Myers theory, by contrast, was concerned with co-ordinating a wide range of what today seem rather peculiar phenomena, and has little or nothing to say about neural codes. To be sure, there is a domain overlap, as today we have some people trying to explain, for example, Out of Body Experiences in representational and computational terms, but on the whole the theories do not cover the same ground *and moreover have clashing metaphysics*.

What I am trying to say is that it remains possible to conceptualize both the mind and consciousness in a number of possible ways, and the fact that one approach has produced even amazing pragmatic fruit does not necessarily negate alternative approaches, even, maybe, ones that at least appear to contradict the favoured approaches. Very often the issue is not who is right and who is wrong, but whether, how and why a theory is formulated in the first place, and for what purpose. This latter point is very difficult to see mainly because of the scientism implicit in much of cognitive science, which insists that to be viable, a theory *must* ape physics or reductive biology. As a result, theories of human nature that do not pass this supposed gold standard get written off as 'unscientific'.

Finally, and most importantly, and despite a considerable emotional pull, such a development would not necessarily negate alternative interpretations of the mind/body link, simply because of the gap between direct experience and whatever neural pattern would be decoded. Zapping a grandmother neuron and producing an image of Bill Clinton on a TV screen would involve a number of things, but mainly it would be a translation of a pattern written in neural 'language'. This would mean that, even if a fairly accurate reproduction of an experience *were* possible, it would still be derived from the neural pattern or code and not the experience itself. This is why it would be misleading to actually term this machine a 'mind-reader'; a more accurate term would be brain decoder.

And the interpretation of the relationship between this code and subjective experiences would *still* be up for grabs. This point was recently made clear by Edward Kelly, who observed that even if we were able to divide the streams of conscious experience into a sequence of states and pair them with the corresponding physiological processes in the brain and find the perfect 1:1 correspondence, then we still would not have solved the mind/body problem. For a start, even perfect correlation would not necessarily entail identity, and he asserts that 'it remains at least conceptually possible that minds and brains are distinct'.[67] Fantasies of a mind-reader or cerebroscope, I suggest, posit just such a 1:1 correspondence, and are useful because they demonstrate the limitations as well as the strengths of the technology.

The conclusion I draw from this is that (1) the mind/brain problem and consciousness probably cannot be solved by empirical means alone, and (2) that the emergence of such technology would not necessarily preclude alternative views of the mind and consciousness, any more than the success of Newtonian mechanics precluded alternative ways of conceiving space and time. The danger is that we become so enamoured of our amazing technologies that alternatives get trampled in an ideological stampede.

Conclusion

Reviewing the neuroimaging work, and neuroscience in general, is a strange business. Superficially, the literature gives one the impression that most problems are or will be solved via standard, mechanistic science; that sometime in this century the 'neural code' will be cracked and that we will understand everything — including consciousness — in terms of models that are more-or-less current. Then one comes across a little tear in the tapestry's apparently seamless fabric — an empirical unknown here, or a conceptual difficulty there — which can soon widen into a gaping hole, if one persists in poking it.

The primary issue remains an unwavering commitment to reductionistic neurobiology and the Cartesian method, and the proposed alternatives within conventional science may be said to constitute extensions and elaborations of this basic metaphysics rather than a substantial revision. Additionally, we have the assumption that these gaps will somehow get solved by additional knowledge and more results. But knowledge is not understanding, and whilst we have unprecedented levels of the former, we have a surfeit of the latter. And whilst holistic biology can take us a little further, it provides no obvious way of reconciling subjective experiences, even with this expanded knowledge, if it means a reduction to the flatland holism of science. It is time to look at subjective views, actual and whole.

---

67 Kelly *et al.*, 2007, p. 27.

Part Four

Controversies and Speculations

Chapter Eleven

Pluralism and the Mind

The previous three chapters have been concerned with physicalism and its limits. We have examined claims that minds and consciousness can be understood in terms of 'information-processing', 'virtual machines', dynamical systems, neural structures, and functions. These sorts of approaches are widely considered to be the *only* viable ones, and rest upon basically physicalist presumptions. We have seen, however, that each of these approaches has limits and none seem to be able to handle the basic problem of subjective experiences, or *qualia*. In my view, this inability strongly suggests that we need to look at some alternatives.

The primary problem is that physicalism, *per se*, constitutes a theory of objects or the 'objective', whereas a theory of consciousness needs to be a theory of *subjects*. Even an expanded, holistic, biology of the kind I advocate in chapter seven still exists within the realm of 'flatland holism', as Ken Wilber put it[1] — which means that subjective elements get left out.[2]

We have also seen that Western theories of consciousness tend to be representational ones, or assume 'that there is a pre-given world of which our cognitions are representations'.[3] This representational view follows, Rao says, from a sharp split between subject and object and the assumption that the physical world out there is separate from and 'realer' than the 'inner' world, which 'is' a 'representation'. So the choice one faces, if *working within the game-rules and prevailing biases of Western thought*, is *either* the elimination of consciousness *or* a clearly flawed representational view of conscious/mental experiences.

There are three primary aims of this chapter: (1) to defend the subjective aspect of human beings (i.e. raw *experience*) as primary, (2) to advocate relational views of consciousness that accommodate the observation that

---

1   Wilber, 2000.
2   Although some aspects of organicism may allow some kind of understanding of the relation between subjective states and physical states to be developed — see my comments on generalized complimentarity, below.
3   Rao, 2002, p. 135.

we exist as *both* subject and object in the world (from the perspective of a science of objects, this move may entail some form of property pluralism, anti-materialism, or at least holism). Finally, (3) I utilize a relational view from Buddhism to expose the limits of Western theories and cast doubt on *all* of our concepts of a world that we can only know via our own, primary experiences.

The Mystery of Subjective Experiences

Despite claims to the contrary, there seems to be little or no deep understanding of private, first-person conscious experiences (*qualia*) within the scientific domain.[4] We have seen that most current neuroscientific approaches to consciousness tend to reduce conscious experience to simple awareness, as in Damasio's definition of consciousness as 'an organism's awareness of its own self and surroundings'.[5] Nagel's question, 'what is it like to *be* something?', does capture something of the quality of experience,[6] but the Buddhist descriptions of consciousness as 'that which is clear and knowing'[7] or 'that which thinks of its object'[8] seem in some ways preferable.

Consciousness can be considered primary in the sense that experience comes *first*, before language and before abstract knowledge. This means that anything we posit about the world — including knowledge about the brain, information-processing, evolution, cosmology, etc. — forms part of the matrix of that experience. As William James observed, this means that such knowledge will always be secondary to said experience where it is not merely interpreted but *re-created* within this matrix.

This point can be clarified by the words of William James, who wrote that

> Individuality is founded in feeling; and the recesses of feeling, the darker, blinder strata of character are the only places in the world in which we catch real fact in the making, and directly perceive how events happen, and how work is actually done. Compared with this world of individualized feelings, the world of generalized objects which the intellect contemplates is without solidity or life...[9]

James was emphasizing the centrality of the individual mind in the creation and re-shaping of not just intellectual ideas but emotional responses towards the world. James found the impersonality suggested by fashionable intellectual or scientific views shallow because '...so long as we deal with the cosmic and the general, we deal only with the symbols of reality,

---

4   See Baars, 1999.
5   Damasio, 1999.
6   Nagel, 1974.
7   Rinbochay, 1980; consciousness described in these terms on pp. 43–8.
8   Buddhaghosa, 1920, p. 148. Quoted in Rao, 2002, p. 235.
9   James, 1902/1985, pp. 501–2.

but *as soon as we deal with private and personal phenomena as such, we deal with realities in the completest sense of the term'*.[10]

The primacy of experience is, for me, the strongest reason for doubting the arguments of those who would eliminate or completely identify said experience with brain function. This is not, of course, to suggest that neurological knowledge reflects nothing, but that we all *begin* with a flow of conscious experiences and that any explanation we develop for how these experiences relate to the world, including intricate neurological or physiological studies, is secondary to that flow.

One problem with the explosion of neurological and cognitive studies is that the flood of new knowledge has obscured this basic point. When reading about consciousness today, one is typically bombarded with a thousand and one fMRI or other studies that demonstrate this or that piece of functional detail. This new knowledge has had a price, which is a downgrading or devaluing of the primary experience in favour of the functional data; the person, and with it subjectivity, tends to vanish in a welter of technical detail. Subjectivity, in this picture, is naturally reduced to precisely measurable data only, and along the way, much of the richness of experience tends to be lost or discarded as irrelevant. In such a situation, it seems very easy to conclude that subjective or private experiences do not exist at all.

Subjective Experiences — Yes or No?

Feyerabend's Eliminativism

As mentioned in chapter five, Paul Feyerabend claimed that it was possible to eliminate the philosophical mind/body problem by formulating a world-view in which the dilemmas posed by a dualistic point of view do not exist.[11] Dualistic conceptions of the mind/body, Feyerabend thought, constitute a possible ideology or 'way of life' that separates and polarizes mental attributes from physical, and that since such a polarization was a construct, it would be possible to constitute an alternative ideology or conceptual structure where such polarization is not a feature. He also claimed that concepts of the mental were *incommensurable* with the concepts Western science has developed for describing and understanding physical objects.

To some, this means that conscious mental events, subjective experiences, etc. should be jettisoned, rather as the concept of phlogiston was jettisoned to account for combustion.[12] Feyerabend's own writing therefore follows a similar philosophical vein to Wittgenstein, Ryle and Rorty in that

---

10 James, 1902/1985, p. 498, his italics.
11 Feyerabend 1963a; 1963b; 1975.
12 Churchland, 1986.

he thought that 'minds' and 'selves' were not concrete entities but abstractions or particular conceptions that were local to a particular set of ideologies.

He retained such views late into his career, criticizing, for example, the idea that creativity is akin to a special, inner ability possessed by an individual self. He compared this view against the Homeric conception of persons, where

> there is no spiritual centre, no 'soul' that might initiate or 'create' special causal chains... the modern conception separates the human being from the world in a manner that turns interaction into an unsolvable problem (such as the mind-body problem), a Homeric warrior or poet is no stranger in the world but shares many elements in it.[13]

Feyerabend was asserting, correctly in my view, that many of the terms that we use to denote human abilities, or alleged abilities, like creativity and free will, are not inherently 'real' but local to our culture. The local nature of our concepts for describing subjective attributes or abilities needs to be conceded, and becomes obvious when we consider how other cultures define, delineate, and divide human beings.[14]

However, this view must also be seen in the context of Feyerabend's epistemological relativism. Just because it is *possible* to formulate a world-view where folk psychology is irrelevant does not mean that those pushing such a world-view have the right to drive out other ideologies. Secondly, just because conceptions like individual creativity, free will, etc. are local and culturally conditioned does not mean that they are without pragmatic value. Notions like love, hate, compassion, creativity, etc. may arguably be useless within, say, neuroscience, but they can be of immense use in everyday life. Feyerabend was also strongly against the idea of formulating one ideology, approach, tradition to rule over all others; so, for example, the argument that we should replace 'folk psychology' with neuroscientific language can be seen as a form of ideological imperialism.

Finally, Feyerabend also advanced arguments for the primacy of everyday experience over scientific concepts, and held that it was possible to dissent from a scientific view if one felt that it diverged significantly from one's own personal experiences of the world. This may be necessary, for example, if one finds the 'objective' world promulgated in the name of science dehumanizing. And as we shall see below, at times he seemed to support a Protagorean viewpoint, which held that the subjective worlds

---

13 Feyerabend, 1987, p. 138. Although gods and daemons often took the place of an autonomous mind, creativity, etc. in Greek explanations.
14 See Edge, 2002, for an argument against the supposed universality of beliefs in (substance) dualism or essential selves, and Daniels, 2005, chapter seven, for a survey of the myriad ways in which differing cultures divide human personality, self, soul. It becomes apparent, when surveying the historical and transcultural material, just how parochial the blunt mind/body split actually is.

which individuals and cultures inhabit may be seen to be a primary reality that changes as concepts and experiences change. In sum, I think that these later responses at least dilute his earlier eliminativism.

Private Experiences as Linguistic/Conceptual Phantoms

Bennett and Hacker are dismissive of private experiences on the grounds that the metaphors often used to describe them ('inner', 'outer', 'public', 'private') seem incoherent. In doing so, whilst making some valid points, they throw the baby out with the bathwater. They deconstruct what they see as four 'misconceptions':

Misconception 1: that of privacy or the private ownership of experience.
Their critique: they assert that it is possible for different people to have the 'same' pain, belief, or experience. The 'inner', they claim, is metaphorical and a misnomer. For example, in toothache, it is the tooth that hurts, and not the mind. There is no such thing as mental toothache.[15]
Response: Of course 'inner' and 'outer' are metaphorical and as such may be unhelpful or misleading if taken too literally. But it is also problematic to conflate the *observation* of an experience with the experience itself, and to deny that any aspect of such an experience can be attended to or participated in by the observer. For example, they claim that '…if a person groans in pain, says what he sees or expresses his opinions, then he has revealed *what in our metaphor* of "inner" or "outer", is the inner'.[16] This ignores the fact that many aspects of an experience such as toothache will be only roughly communicable and sometimes incommunicable, whether we use the inner/outer metaphors or not. Finally, toothache need not be 'mental' to be part of subjective, conscious experience.

Misconception 2: introspection as a form of inner perception.
Their critique: introspection is not a form of inner vision or internal sense because it involves no perceptual organ or observational skills. There is no mind's eye except metaphorically; and we speak of seeing *in* and not *with* it.[17] Introspection is better understood as a form of reflexive thought, a route to self-knowledge and self-understanding. But to attend to one's feelings is not to *perceive* one's feelings.
Response: this is a stronger critique, especially for those who claim that the 'mind's eye' is a literal space within the brain.[18] However, what Bennett and Hacker have done is to substitute spatial metaphors for attentional ones. It is that we *can* attend upon a habit or thought or behaviour and use this to affect changes that is the problem.

---

15   Bennett & Hacker, 2003, p. 88.
16   Bennett & Hacker, 2003, p. 89, their italics.
17   Bennett & Hacker, 2003, p. 91.
18   Kosslyn, 1994.

Misconception 3: that someone can have privileged access to their thoughts, feelings and experiences.
Their critique: the subject does not have access to anything 'inner' at all. Feeling a headache is the same as having one. One cannot feel a pain in the same way one feels a penny; one is a form of perception, the other is not.
Response: this critique turns on the conflation of different people's pain. For example, they claim that if two people 'have a throbbing pain in the left temple, then [they] *do* have the same pain'.[19] Firstly, even in observational terms, this is an oversimplification, because it is unlikely that the two pains are precisely identical. Secondly, it is very unlikely that two people will *experience* such pain in an identical way. It is the unique character of experience, and the incommunicability of every aspect of that experience, that denotes privacy.

Misconception 4: that psychological predicates stand for 'inner entities'.
Their critique: psychological terms do not denote inner entities, but attributes of the whole person.
Response: I agree that psychological attributes should be seen as attributes of the whole person or subject, but differ in my interpretation of this because I think this conclusion leads to property pluralism and not Hacker's preferred psychophysical unitarianism (see below).[20]

Bennett and Hacker's critiques are important because they force us to become far more careful about using terms which, taken too literally, may cause us to attribute, say, brain-parts abilities or dispositions which only make sense for the whole person. This is what they mean by the *mereological fallacy*, which is the attribution of whole-person or system capacities to that of a part (e.g. in neuroscience we constantly find researchers attributing intentional states to parts of the brain). However, their critique of private experience seems to me unconvincing overall.

Reductionist Objections to Subjective Experiences

Reductionist materialists believe that conscious, first-person experiences either do not exist, or can be unproblematically reduced to neural patterns. Their arguments are made on several grounds, but there is a common conviction that everything can and should be reduced to physical processes only, or that the underlying physical processes have a privileged status over high-level descriptions. Often, as in the example that follows, arguments against private experiences are conflated with arguments against any kind of dualism.

---

19 Bennett & Hacker, 2003, p. 95.
20 Meixner, 2010, notes that Hacker's stance is neither monistic nor dualistic. It is not monistic because it does not seek to reduce subjective attributes to the material. It is not dualistic because it denies non-physical entities.

Churchland begins by labelling the 'argument from introspection' (i.e. the existence of subjective states or *qualia*) 'deeply suspect'.[21] He writes that the argument

> assumes that our faculty of inner observation... reveals things as they really are in their innermost nature. This assumption is suspect because we already know that our other forms of observation — sight, hearing, touch and so on — do no such thing. The sound of a flute does not sound like a sinusoidal compression wave train in the atmosphere, but that is what it is. The warmth of the summer air does not feel like the mean kinetic energy of millions of tiny molecules, but that is what it is. If one's pain and hopes and beliefs do not introspectively seem like electrochemical states in a neural network, that may be because our faculty of introspection... is not sufficiently penetrating to reveal such hidden details.[22]

This argument seems itself deeply suspect. The first questionable point is Churchland's assumption that introspection (or any other kind of observation) *must* 'reveal things as they really are in their innermost nature'. This implies that the things we observe, whether inside or outside our minds, *have* an 'innermost nature' that they 'really are'. As we have seen, physics long ago abandoned this position.[23]

Similarly, the claim that the sound of a flute 'is' a sinusoidal pressure wave, or the warmth of a summer breeze 'is' the 'mean kinetic energy of millions of tiny molecules' seems problematic. Both sorts of description appear secondary to primary phenomenological experience, and there seems little reason to privilege one over the other. Why *should* the description of the 'warmth of a summer breeze' be less apt than a description of the 'mean kinetic energy of millions of tiny molecules'? One is a sensory description, the other is an abstract physical description; one is not less 'true' than another, and *both* are derivations from different kinds of phenomenological observation. The only reason we have for privileging the technical description over the tactile is the metaphysical assumption of strict reductionism, which assumes that lower-level descriptions are inherently more 'real' or valid than higher-level descriptions.

Churchland's position becomes even more problematic when we move away from raw sensory perceptions. It seems *very* unclear whether pain, or joy, or compassion, or humour can be fully described as 'electrochemical states in a neural network' because the experiences are so much more than that. It is rather like saying that a play at a theatre is 'nothing but' actors in makeup reading lines in front of painted sets, which is in some sense true but seems an excessively narrow way of looking at things.[24] Asserting that

---

21 Churchland, 1984/1994, p. 15.
22 Churchland, 1984/1994, p. 125.
23 See chapter five.
24 Bennett & Hacker, 2003.

a neural-level explanation of subjective experience is complete and correct also runs afoul of the mereological fallacy; neural patterns alone do not have feelings, any more than feet alone have sensations.

Churchland's position, although extreme, reflects a deep suspicion of subjective experiences commonly found in cognitive science.[25] In another example, philosopher Ned Block criticizes the idea that reports of conscious experiences should be the 'gold standard' in neuroscience. He points out that (1) observed electrons can provide evidence about electrons that cannot be observed, (2) it is not true that our theory of consciousness should be determined by subjective reports, because no piece of data can be privileged and we should use parsimony to distinguish the best theories, and (3) any neuroscientific approach that bases everything on reports about a subject's own experience will only find the neural basis of higher-order (conscious) thought which might leave out cases where subjects have experiences without such thought. 'Higher-order thought' is defined by him as the 'thought to the effect that I myself have an experience'.[26]

To the first point, we might respond that the electron analogy is of limited use because, even if hidden, we suppose unobservable electrons to be of more-or-less the same character as electrons we can observe (although strictly speaking one cannot observe, i.e. see, electrons). Comparing subjective reports with neurological data seems like a different kind of problem, more like comparing two different kinds of 'maps'.[27] To the second point, I should acknowledge that no piece of data should be privileged, but would also emphasize that this also includes 'objective' neuroscientific data. I would add also that without subjective reports, or experiences, there wouldn't *be* a phenomenon to explain! The third point also has some validity, but I would question, again, the expectation that neuroscience can provide exhaustive accounts of experience. Without subjective reports, it is hard to see how the existence of a good number of 'lower-order' phenomena could be suspected, if they are not indirectly deducible from psychophysical data.

Dennett's Arguments Against Qualia

Dennett has argued repeatedly that 'there simply are no qualia at all',[28] and attempts to prove this via a number of ingenious thought experiments. He claims that the only way qualia would make sense was if there was a Cartesian theatre (or mirror!), but that since there isn't,

---

25 Wallace, 2000; Varela & Shear, 1999.
26 Block, 2005, p. 50.
27 Midgley, 2001; see discussion below.
28 Dennett, 1997, p. 620.

there is no way to isolate the properties presented in consciousness from the brain's multiple reactions to discriminations, because there is no such additional presentation process.[29]

Dennett also tries to demonstrate the inadequacy of *qualia* via a thought experiment involving beer drinkers. He points out that beer is often an acquired taste, and that one often takes time to learn to like it. So a beer drinker might claim that, for an individual who grows to like beer, the taste gradually changes as they continue to imbibe. But other beer drinkers would claim that the beer always tasted as it did when they first started, only they now like the same taste. Of these two different interpretations, Dennett states 'in the first sort of beer drinker the "training" has changed the "shape" of the quality space for tasting, while in the second sort the quality space remains roughly the same, but the "evaluation function" over that space has been revised'.[30] Or it could be, Dennett thinks, that both sets of drinkers are fooling themselves, and we have to go to the 'actual happenings' in the beer drinker's heads to 'see whether there is a truth-preserving [if "strained"] interpretation of the beer drinkers claims' which will only be a 'complex of reactive dispositions...' Dennett concludes that in the latter case, we have to '"destroy" qualia in order to save them'.[31]

This objection seems to amount to a 'demolition' of a type-token interpretation of subjective experiences. Dennett's experiment seems most convincing if we assume that said subjective experiences are meant to consist of groupings of discrete, identifiable tokens (e.g. qualities, in Dennett's account, can only be said to exist if they have a discernible 'shape'). But this is not necessarily so, and brings us back to disputes over whether words actually stand for discrete categorical objects or heterogeneous families. I do not think that private experiences, or portions thereof, need to be defined in this way to be valid. (Note also the privileging of the 'actual' [i.e. neural] events in the speaker's head over his experiences.)

Dennett's argument seems to me to be the converse of Stephen Braude's arguments about the impossibility of reducing mental states to a neural 'token'. The only difference is that, in Braude's case, he argues against the likelihood of an underlying, specific or Platonic 'token' linking a given mental state and neural substrate, whereas Dennett argues that one cannot reduce a 'quale' to a Platonic token. The interesting thing is that both writers draw radically different conclusions from similar arguments; Braude argues that this supports a level-of-explanation dualism, and for Dennett it implies brain-function only.

---

29 Dennett, 1991, p. 392.
30 Dennett, 1991, p. 396.
31 Dennett, 1991, p. 396.

My own view is that the totality of conscious experiences probably cannot be reduced fully to verbal or logical constructions, and that the problems with defining or nailing *qualia* may reflect this limitation. This makes sense when we remember that conscious experience precedes language which precedes science. We should remember that what is being demanded in a theory of consciousness is some way to squeeze the totality of experience into a small abstracted portion of itself. There may be some fundamental limitation to our ability to do this, as Gödel's incompleteness theorem puts limits to mathematical reasoning.[32]

Funnily enough, mystics have intuited this for millennia; for example, the Middle Way teachings of Tibetan Buddhism (see below) claim that experiential reality can never be accurately described because words can only point to partial aspects of experience.[33] This, too, recalls Korzybski's principle of non-identity, that whatever we say something is, it isn't. My own view is that *qualia* or private experience remains elusive for precisely this reason; that words at best can point the way or form rough descriptions, they cannot *be experience itself*. All this might sound defeatist, but I believe it perfectly legitimate to posit limitations to language, reasoning and logic, especially with regards to the totality of experience. And if we accept the arguments against philosophical systems being 'mirrors' of nature, then why do we expect to be able to reduce everything to said systems?

Relational Views of Consciousness

My assertion that subjective experience can be considered a primary reality could be interpreted in a number of ways. One can interpret this assertion in idealistic terms and conclude, as some quantum physicists have done, that everything 'is' mind.[34] However, this seems too extreme a move, despite the various shortcomings of physicalism. A better strategy, in my view, is to try and understand ourselves better as subjects, but in doing so we need to find a way of looking that accommodates our immediate experience and does not try to shoehorn it into a preconceived, one-dimensional explanatory frame.

Some variety of phenomenalism seems to me to be a necessary first step in accommodating subjective experience. *Phenomenology* was developed by philosopher Husserl in the early twentieth century, and uses various

---

32 Rucker, 1997.
33 Madhyamika teachings actually go much further. Trungpa, 1973, p. 191: 'Words or concepts only *point* to partial aspects of experience. In fact, it is dubious that one can even speak of "experiencing" reality, since this would imply a separation between experiencer and experience. And finally, it is questionable whether one can even speak of "reality" because this would imply the existence of some objective knower outside and separate from it, as though reality were a nameable thing with set limits and boundaries.'
34 Henry, 2005.

techniques to investigate and describe subjective experience without theoretical commitment. An updated version, which relates phenomenology to neuroscience, was proposed by Francisco Varela.[35] However, this updated version, known as neurophenomenology, ultimately rests upon similar assumptions to other physicalistic theories: it posits that subjective consciousness *must* be fit into schemes consisting of functional, physical objects and processes. Feyerabend was critical of such holistic views because they retained many of the deeper problems of more reductive approaches. He complained that '[t]his is the old objectivism all over again, only wrapped in revolutionary and pseudo-humanitarian language'.[36] He thought that the conceptual edifices advocated by more holistic thinkers like Varela were as irrelevant to the problems of everyday experience as older, reductionist views.

Feyerabend's suggested alternative was that we should abandon the search for grand schemes, even holistic ones, and seek a more humanitarian approach that can somehow do justice to the full variety of human experience. Something close to such an approach had been suggested by the Ancient Greek Protagoras. Protagoras (c.490–420 BC) can be seen as an early phenomenalist who rejected the Platonic notion that a hidden, theoretical reality was more real than that of our everyday experience.[37] His most famous statement, that 'man is the measure of all things', is ambiguous, but probably refers to the notion that many of the things we project onto the world — properties, feelings, ideas, and judgments, etc. — have no inherent existence apart from our minds. Plato saw Protagoras as a relativist who opposed his (Plato's) vision of an objective reality, and in his *Theaetetus* explains but tries to discredit Protagoras's stance (in fact, the *Theaetetus* is still worth reading for its presentation of Platonic versus Protagorean ideas of what constitutes the 'real').

Protagoras asserted that perception and opinion were infallible and that the 'worlds projected by different individuals, groups, nations as they perceive them are all equally real'.[38] This assertion might sound horrific, especially to those cognitive psychologists who have spent a career researching just how fallible common perceptions and judgments can be. *But however fallible, our perceptions, concepts and dispositions still form the only direct reality we can know.* The properties, conceptual schemes and imaginative worlds that help explain our existence further are *necessarily* secondary and derivative, no matter how plausible they might seem.[39]

---

35 Definition from the glossary in Blackmore, 2005. See also Varela & Shear, 1999.
36 Feyerabend, 1987, p. 6.
37 http://en.wikipedia.org/wiki/Protagoras accessed on 17/12/10.
38 Feyerabend, 1987, p. 51.
39 Sahtouris, 2008, also makes this observation.

So 'reality' can only be really judged on individual, direct terms by people and groups living particular kinds of life. And these lives are necessarily idiosyncratic, fluid, and adapted to local conditions. Different people and different cultures live in different subjective worlds, some of which might allow personal growth and development, others of which might not. And as our concepts, ideas, experiences and viewpoints change and develop, so do our personal realities.

Consciousness as Mapping Problem: Mary Midgley

The problem remains, however, how we could relate abstract — and specifically neurological — knowledge to our subjective experiences. The philosopher, Mary Midgley, tries to accommodate the subjective and the physical by favouring something like a dual-aspect approach, and asserting that we have to come to terms with the fact that we are both subjects and objects in 'the' world. Consciousness, she asserts, cannot or should not be reduced to a 'stuff', or something magical or 'extra'. Instead, it can be thought of as our condition of being a subject, 'someone for whom all... objects are objects. The questions [consciousness] raises are therefore primarily about the nature of a person as a whole, a person who is both subject or object'.[40] As a result, the problems associated with consciousness are not how to reduce the 'mental' to the 'physical'. Rather, they are how to relate subjective maps — which include everyday ways of talking about thinking, feeling, and human behaviour — to the maps we have constructed about 'objects'. The dilemma relates to our dual nature as both subject and object.

Midgley also sees consciousness as having a primary causal role. Indeed, following Hume, she suggests that our models of causation may well be *derived* from our observations of our own, personal actions. For this reason, she categorically rejects epiphenomenalism — observing that science itself requires conscious, active agents to work. Midgley claims that we need to reposition ourselves as active, subjective agents and redefine consciousness adverbally 'as a mere matter of our acting consciously'[41] rather than as a noun or a passive quality floating separate from the 'doing' portions of the organism.

Midgley is also keen to reposition consciousness in the context of evolution. She believes that the separation of consciousness as a magical property *'is what stops it being accepted as a normal aspect of mental activity, an emergent capacity acquired naturally by social creatures during the regular course of evolution'*.[42]

---

40 Midgley, 2001, p. 114.
41 Midgley, 2001, p. 153.
42 Midgley, 2001, p. 153, her italics.

Midgley's approach can be seen as a compromise between physicalism and idealism, or mentalism, and has significant merit. However, I would suggest that our current concepts of emergent properties still end up 'converting' subjective consciousness into quasi-'objective' (physical) processes, which seems wrong to me. I think that any theory of consciousness needs to begin by acknowledging how *alien* subjects are within the conceptual worlds of current science.

Non-Physical Emergent Properties?

This point becomes apparent when we consider the problems of emergentism. Wallace, for example, criticizes it on the grounds that consciousness seems so radically different from other examples of emergent properties. Emergent properties, he claims, are just functions of complex configurations of inorganic chemical processes, emerging from the action or complex configurations of atoms and elementary particles. Consciousness, by contrast, seems utterly unlike all other known emergent properties so cannot, in Wallace's view, be classified as emergent. Searle makes similar observations, but unlike Wallace is convinced that somehow consciousness *can* be naturalized (i.e. conceptually converted into an object, function, or complex physical feature).[43]

My own view is that we need to accept that our models of the physical form part of a conceptual matrix within which consciousness and subjectivity are currently incommensurable, as Feyerabend suggested. But these physical models are very partial. On the other hand, our 'folk conceptions' of psychology, which accommodate consciousness, represent a different 'take' on the world where subjectivity fits quite happily, but are not really theoretical or scientific.[44] If one insists upon trying to fit consciousness inside the object-worlds developed by science, then something like property dualism or pluralism seems to me the best bet, where it is admitted that humans and probably animals have non-physical[45] properties (i.e. consciousness, intentional states) apart from physical ones.[46] But the fit will probably seem a little awkward, because this sort of conception is in effect a marrying of two incommensurable kinds of world-picture.

The generalized complementarity suggested by Bohr and Elsasser may be of some help here. In the extended version of complimentarity, the more we know about the lower-level physical and chemical processes, the less we can know about the higher-level organizational processes, and vice versa, so the whole properties of organisms might only really be understood at the expense of a loss of knowledge of their more mechani-

---

43 Searle, 1997.
44 Bennett & Hacker, 2003.
45 Or, debatably, 'holistic' or at least whole-person properties.
46 BonJour, 2010, argues along these lines.

cal, lower-level parts. This sort of approach may be applicable to accommodating qualitative consciousness and subjective states, but at the cost of compromising physicalism. This is because we can no longer really assert that these holistic states 'supervene' upon lower-level physical states, just as we cannot assert that the particle model of light can be 'reduced' to the wave model, or vice versa.[47] What we are left with are local models that describe either qualitative, non-physical or holistic states, or more quantitative, reductionist sub-systems, but one can no longer 'sum' the latter to arrive at the former.

This conclusion again forces us to question the insistence upon the metaphysical stance of monistic physicalism in our accounts of consciousness. Are there any good reasons, apart from historical habit, cultural inertia, and/or religious phobia for insisting upon such a position? In this context, it is worth looking at how a non-Western, relational view of consciousness that is *not* burdened by the sharp, Cartesian split between subject and objects deals with raw experience.

Relational Approaches in Buddhist Traditions

Buddhism is of interest because it contains a relational view of consciousness. The early teachings of Buddhism do not have a favoured ontology or metaphysic,[48] because the Buddha thought that such speculations detracted from his primary goal, which was the relief of suffering (*duhkha*) and the attainment of mental balance and enlightenment.[49] His approach must therefore be seen as primarily ethical, pragmatic, and empirical in the introspective sense.

The only permanence in Buddhist thought is change, and this extends to the stream of experience possessed by each individual. Like Hume, the Buddha discerned no permanent or discrete self, but only a flow of ever-changing experiences. These could be decomposed into *skandhas*, which are aggregations or groupings of bodily or mental states. The five kinds of skandhas are: (1) *rupa*, (2) *vendana*, (3) *sanna*, (4) *sankhara*, (5) *vinanna*.[50] *Rupa* corresponds roughly to what we would term 'matter' and 'sensory data' (but Rao reminds us that Buddhism does not make a sharp distinction between *physical* and *mental*; or, I would argue, that the categories 'physical' and 'mental' are not fully commensurable with Buddhist

---

47 The same goes for attempts to resolve supervenience in terms of whole-part relations (see, e.g. Murphy & Brown, 2007) as I show in chapter fourteen, such holistic physicalist views retain many of the limitations of assuming that 'higher' mental states somehow supervene on 'lower' physical processes. *Viz.* they do not really seem to handle subjective states in a significantly different way to older reductionist or 'information-processing' accounts.
48 Although many of the subsequent schools *did* adopt various metaphysical positions and various different ontological interpretations of the earlier teachings.
49 Most of the account of Buddhist thought is taken from Rao, 2002, chapter ten.
50 Rao, 2002, p. 236.

thought). *Vendana* corresponds with feeling, *sanna* with perception and sensation, *sankhara* volition, and *vinanna* with consciousness.

Consciousness in Buddhism can be defined as a relation between subject and object. As Rao observes, both subject and object need to be understood as relative and mutually dependent. What does not occur is the sharp division between the 'objective' (or 'physical') world and the 'mental', 'inner' world. The phenomenological world, in Buddhism, is seen and divided differently.

The Madhyamika School

The Madhyamika philosophy is particularly relevant to the discussion of consciousness, and the concepts used to explain it.[51] This 'Middle Way' is a radical approach that suggests the only reality we can really know is the present. Perceptions tend to be momentary, and are constantly changing. The 'efficacy', or mental impact of perceived objects ensures their reality. This is the only measure of reality we have. Some harmony or lawful consistency does exist between a momentary reality and the apparent permanence of an object but, as in Hume's writing, this does not mean that we can assume a causal link between moments.

To the followers of the Middle Way, reality *is* appearance. The Really Real cannot be touched or grasped, but only apprehended via momentary sensory perceptions and via our concepts. Conditioned realities, which are what we typically perceive, are perceptions tinged or 'bundled' with concepts. So our experience of a table, chair or pot plant will be a combination of momentary perception plus our conception of these objects. The strength of experience or efficacy of sensory impressions is that which suggests existence.

Concepts, by contrast, are inevitably fictions, and this judgment includes generalities and ideas about Platonic, persistent realities (*including* the physical). The Madhyamika philosophy, by contrast, seems closer to the Aristotelian and Protagorean school by equating efficacy with the particular, or direct experience, which follows from the idea that only percepts that significantly impact can be considered 'Real'. So the teachings show in part the self-contradiction inherent in any fixed concept of the nature of reality, and anticipate the writings of Wittgenstein and anti-real movements in science.[52] The aim in Middle Way practice is to leave concepts behind and experience *sunyata*, or 'emptiness', which is percept without concept.

This sort of view diverges significantly from physicalism. We have seen that the two choices one has within physicalism concerning the subjective mind are *either* that it does not exist *or* that it is some kind of illusion (or

---

51 Pandeya, 1964.
52 Hope & Van Loon, 1994.

secondary representation). From a Middle Way perspective, as Wallace argues, it is a mistake to view the brain as substantially, inherently real and the mind as an illusion, he observes that '[a]ccording to [the Middle Way], the 'hard problem' [of subjectivity] is really an insoluble problem as long as you view either the brain or the mind as inherently real'.[53] If one regards electrochemical processes as more 'real' than subjective experiences, then, suggests Wallace, this privileging *creates* the apparently unbridgeable gap between them, and forces one to either reduce to illusion or eliminate the subjective.

If one stops privileging the physical side in this way, then it can be re-designated as part of a conceptual system that includes consciousness:

> Therefore... the physical brain is not an absolute. It exists as something conceptually designated upon its parts and functions. On the other hand, the mind is not a pure illusion or nothing. Although that which is designated as 'the mind' is conventional and therefore dependent upon its attributes (thought, images, feelings and so on), this concept, 'the mind', does appear to our consciousness.[54]

So to devotees of the Middle Way, physicalism is insufficiently radical in designating the mind only as illusory, because physicalism reifies and makes concrete one aspect of the flow of experience that, according to Buddhism, has no more inherent reality than the mind. This is because the totality of the flow of experience, including perceived physical objects, is part of the ever-changing world of *Samsara*, or the circular chain of existence. 'Mind', 'Self', 'Matter' can be said to be illusory because they lack an inherent, independent existence and can only be defined in relational terms.

The Buddhist approach, and in particular the Middle Way, is of interest for several reasons. Firstly, we have noted currents of similarity between this and relational views previously discussed. Some aspects of these differing relational theories overlap. However, there are also significant areas of divergence. A key point of difference is that Buddhist thought arose in a culture that was animistic, whilst Westerners live in a culture whose mainstream has been largely purged of such elements. For example, the interrelatedness of subject and object implies psychic phenomena, and in Tibetan Buddhism the apprehending mind has an active and magical role in the world (such abilities are said to arise in training, but are held to be distractions on the way to enlightenment).[55] There is also a widespread belief in reincarnation.

A common strategy, in Western forms of Buddhism, is to reject said views as 'superstition' and accept only those portions that appear to coin-

---

53   Wallace & Hodel, 2008, p. 161.
54   Wallace & Hodel, 2008, pp. 161-2.
55   Roney-Dougal, 2006.

cide with Western views.[56] For example, the doctrine of no-self has been claimed to be compatible with cognitive science's view of the person as an aggregation of biological structure and function.[57] There have also been lengthy attempts to relate the various states of meditative consciousness to neuroscience.[58] In this sort of view, Buddhist thought can only be accommodated by cutting it down to fit within current Western models.

But this sort of approach seems quite ethnocentric to me. It seems quite conceited to assume that other cultural ideas and practices like meditation can *only* be acceptable if they can be shoehorned or otherwise assimilated into our dominant culture. In doing so, the original ideas get stripped out of context and become transformed to a degree that does not seem to be necessarily desirable. The problem with this is that we risk losing many of the insights about the world provided by an alternative take on things. In this case, we risk losing the insight that *all* of our concepts, including our most venerated scientific theories, can ultimately be seen to be *fictions*, of a sort.[59] At the very least, it should invite a little humility about promoting some concepts at the expense of other people's, or other cultures'.

Conclusion

The least unsatisfactory position on phenomenological consciousness is, in my opinion, suggested by relational views such as those outlined above. These views seem to me to hold the seeds from which more satisfactory accounts of subjective consciousness might be developed. Relational views that place subjectivity first at least potentially accommodate the viewpoints of myriad individuals and cultures without trying to assimilate them into one big monocultural system, and help counter the significantly dehumanizing effects of trying to reduce human beings to objects, mechanisms and functions. What they do not do is settle the issue of whether consciousness arises as an emergent property/capacity/quality or whether it can be considered somehow inherent in the universe, and I will examine this issue next.

---

56 This would accord with the *opportunistic* response to cultural relativism; one picks handy concepts from another culture one encounters (Feyerabend, 1987).
57 Blackmore, 2003.
58 Austin, 1998.
59 The Middle Way can also be quite effective in exposing dogmatism; for example, during a discussion between neuroscientists and the Dalai Lama on the issue of mental causation, it is quite often the *neuroscientists* rather than the Tibetans who come across as inflexible. For most experts, it seems, it's physicalism or nothing. See Goleman, 2003, chapter nine.

Chapter Twelve

Consciousness, Teleology and Evolution

Having created a world of 'objects', and in doing so the mind/body problem, it becomes very difficult, theoretically speaking, to work out how to fit subjects back into the cosmos. The problem is how to account for how insensate objects somehow become capable of subjective experience, which seems incompatible with purely 'physical' or material processes. This chapter deals with how different Western traditions attempt to resolve this difficulty.

One predominant view is that Darwinism has somehow 'solved' this problem. Before Darwin, the story goes, there was a need to posit the pre-existence of minds, specifically a Great Mind (*aka* God) to explain the appearance of complex, apparently 'designed' forms in the world — specifically, life, people and their own souls. With the advent of natural selection, such a need vanished because we were able for the first time to understand how minds evolved from insensate matter.[1]

However, others claim that consciousness cannot be fully explained in this way. They hypothesize instead that some latent form of consciousness is inherent in the 'stuff' of the universe, and that the emergence of complex life merely allowed for its expression. Theories like this are often labelled panpsychism. In this chapter, I will focus on a specific from of this sort of theory, *panexperientialism*, which posits that all individuals have some form of experience (the problem of defining an individual I will leave for later).

A third option acknowledges the radical novelty of consciousness, but claims that the issue is to understand better how and why the universe exhibits such radical creativity. A number of studies of emergence move in this direction,[2] because studies of complexity are continually revealing that such systems often exhibit radically novel behaviour that cannot be

---

1 Dennett, 1995; Richards, 2000.
2 Murphy & Brown, 2007.

predicted from the sum of the parts. Opponents of this, however claim that this option is not radical enough to account for consciousness, which seems to them *sui generis* and not classifiable as an emergent property at all.[3] Each of these positions will be examined.

One significant problem is that theories that posit that mind or consciousness came first in any form tend to have teleological features. *Teleology* is defined in the Oxford Dictionary as the 'doctrine of final causes' or the 'view that developments are due to purpose or design that is served by them'. So any theory that posits that consciousness somehow exists prior to its evident manifestations (say, in animals or humans) seems to me to be teleological by definition, because positing a necessary precursor 'seed' of consciousness implies that such a seed was supposed eventually to sprout. In addition, many of the theories that posit some form of panpsychism are often explicitly teleological.

Why Consider Teleology at All?

The addition of teleology to a theory is often enough to guarantee its rejection within conventional science. Like it or not, teleological accounts of evolution have been, historically speaking, associated with theological arguments for design,[4] a classic example being the arguments of William Paley (1743-1805), who compared living organisms to a watch found on a heath. Paley reasoned that such an object, containing working parts made for a purpose, was clearly designed by someone. According to Paley, this argument could be applied to the design of living things. Such 'design' arguments were strongly challenged by Darwin's theory of natural selection,[5] which showed how successive adaptations could account for the *appearance* of design, and this is one reason why natural selection was resisted as a theory.

By the twentieth century, the status of teleology had declined to the point that writers like Jacques Monod denied that it could have any place in scientific theories at all.[6] In part, this was because teleological theories are perceived to have a weak explanatory power compared to more mechanistic ones, especially in an evolutionary context, although we have already seen that the usefulness of teleological (or at least *teleonomic*) ideas in biology may have been underrated (chapter seven). A continuing association with theological ideas has not helped, especially amongst atheistic scientists, and it is true that even theories that cannot be classed as either

---

3 Griffin, 1998; Wallace, 2000.
4 See Barrow & Tipler, 1986, chapter two, for a discussion of the overlap between teleological and pre-twentieth century 'design' arguments.
5 Dawkins, 1986.
6 Monod, 1972; see Barrow & Tipler, 1986, chapter three, for teleological theories in the twentieth century.

Creationism or 'Intelligent Design' have often, but not invariably, involved a deity; see the works of Tielhard de Chardin and Samuel Alexander.[7]

Despite this, there are a number of reasons for considering evolutionary and cosmological teleological arguments in the context of the consciousness debates. The first general reason is that, whilst teleology might be reviled within mainstream evolutionary thought, it has to an extent enjoyed a revival in cosmology. In particular, I refer to the anthropic principle, which posits the necessity of (conscious) observers in the universe, and brings in arguments involving certain cosmological observations and those in quantum mechanics.[8] This includes speculations that the universe is in some sense 'created' or 'completed' by participatory, conscious observers.

A second reason is that teleological assumptions have proved far more difficult to uproot than was first thought, and may be impossible to eliminate entirely.[9] For example, a common strategy amongst the sceptical is to contrast earlier, teleological or specifically supernatural cosmologies with those that involve 'chance and necessity' alone. Yet on close inspection, those favouring the latter kind of universe tend to posit *mechanism* to be universal, and 'mechanisms' imply design. This is so whether one posits a universe of clockwork or the universe as some sort of 'information-processing' device. Simply lopping off an external 'designer' does not eliminate the design implications of such metaphors.

We should not read too much into this, because, in my view, it says more about the metaphorical and imaginative nature of our theories than the existence or otherwise of a designer. Theories that posit that everything 'is' mechanism illustrate how extensively human fingerprints appear on even our best and most 'objective' theories; in this respect, scientific theories resemble works of art as opposed to revealing directly 'objective reality'.[10] Yet we will see that some writers do not seem to appreciate this, and continue to insist that mechanisms exist 'in' the natural world.

Thirdly, and most relevantly, we come to the aforementioned panpsychic theories of consciousness. Chalmers' theory is one such, but his conscious aspect is effectively epiphenomenal, and as such could not play an active role in the organism's life. We know this because he thinks that 'zombies' are possible.[11] Philosophical zombies are beings that behave just like us but are without consciousness, and if one accepts them, one tacitly accepts that the subjective aspect of human life has no causal effect what-

---

7   Barrow & Tipler, 1986.
8   Barrow & Tipler, 1986; see Davies, 2007, for a popular account of the more recent debates.
9   Midgley, 1992.
10 Feyerabend, 1975; 1987.
11 Chalmers, 1996.

soever. This is a serious problem when considering the possible emergence of various forms of consciousness in evolution; for example, if epiphenomenalism is an accurate way of describing consciousness, then it seems pointless trying to observe its effects in animals, because there would be none.[12]

Given the controversial nature of any form of teleology in biology, I should stress that both teleological and non-teleological theorists agree upon much of the commonly settled general picture of cosmogony and development of the cosmos and life.[13] It is generally agreed that the universe began 13.7 billion years ago with the Big Bang, that galaxies formed from protogalaxies, stars from nebula, and finally planets from protoplanetary disks. It is also agreed that the Earth was formed about 4.5 billion years ago, with life appearing early in its history. The human line of descent via evolutionary processes from common ancestors with apes is also not disputed. Nor do they propose that an intervening deity 'tinkers' with biological forms at set points of said evolution. Teleologists, in short, agree with the basic scientific understanding of the universe as built up through numerous observations, so it is unfair indiscriminately to lump these theories with Creationism and 'Intelligent Design'. What *is* disputed is the interpretation of these observations, especially because of the problems of how consciousness in particular might have emerged.

Since I am undecided about these issues, I propose to 'compare and contrast' conventional evolutionary theories with teleological ones, expose their different problems and see whether there is any justification for departing from conventional science. Many within conventional cognitive science might consider this a futile exercise, but such is the state of our understanding that we cannot say with any *a priori* certainty that conventional evolutionary theories are adequate. In this situation, I feel that an exploration of alternatives is warranted. First, however, we need to know how far conventional theory can give us a comprehensive account of the appearance of consciousness in evolution.

Conventional Evolutionary Explanations

Although there are a number of theoretical variations within conventional evolutionary science, a number of core features are accepted. These include most of the game-rules discussed in previous chapters, including the assumption of atoms and derivatives only, physicalism and that consciousness is generated by or wholly dependent upon the brain. This *a priori* rules out any form of panpsychism. The corollary of this is that minds and consciousness *must* be a ('physical') emergent property of, or even fully reducible to, constituent atoms or their combinations. Even more lib-

---

12 Griffin, 2001.
13 Or whatever the prevailing view was at the time of their writing.

eral variants of conventional evolutionary theory accept these basic restraints.

Despite a number of criticisms, modifications, and additions, Darwinian natural selection remains at the centre of conventional evolutionary theory. This theory posits that a good portion (or in some interpretations, all) of the variety that we see in the natural world can be explained by the following basic process:[14]

(1) With variations, like breeds like.
(2) Some variations favour the survival of the individual who possess them.
(3) All organisms breed more offspring than can be supported by the resources available.
(4) Variations that are favoured are more likely to survive long enough to reproduce.
(5) This means that there will be more of the favoured variety in the subsequent generation.
(6) So species will evolve over time.

This simple, but very powerful idea was not quite enough to ensure the ascendancy of Darwinism as three significant problems remained: (1) the mechanism of transmission of variations and similarities remained unknown, (2) no one understood how gradual change could result in perfectly adapted structures like the eye, and (3) Darwin did not explain how new species could emerge via his mechanism.[15] Although the first problem has been at least partly solved (the transmission mechanism of genes), the second and the third, despite very significant progress, still pose major theoretical problems.

Neo-Darwinism is the result of a fusion and refinement of Darwin's idea of natural selection coupled with modern genetics. This fusion became the foundation of much of modern biology, supporting such diverse fields as molecular biology, genetics, anatomy and physiology, psychology, and cognitive science. The far-reaching, technical and complex nature of the scientific evolutionary programme, as opposed to popular writings on evolution, should be stressed. The theory penetrates to the core of biology and a dozen other fields.

The central claim of neo-Darwinism is that all biological phenomena, including minds and consciousness, can be understood to have evolved from insensate matter via natural selection in a series of progressive steps. Specifically, complexity can emerge from simplicity by purely physical processes without there being any intentions or designs at all.[16] Many of

---

14 Summary paraphrased from Rose, 1997, p. 181.
15 Problems paraphrased from Rose, 1997, p. 182.
16 Richards, 2000; Dennett, 1995.

the so-called 'Darwin Wars', fought within and without academia, concern just how far Darwinism, or more specifically neo-Darwinism, can be applied beyond biology.[17]

The many subtleties within these arguments are frequently lost on those who adopt neo-Darwinism. This issue is pressing because a particularly vocal neo-Darwinian school is often perceived to speak for the whole of evolutionary theory. This school has a high profile, with representatives (i.e. Richard Dawkins, Daniel Dennett, Matt Ridley and Steven Pinker) who are often in public eye. These writers are also significantly influential inside academic cognitive science and psychology.

This school interprets Darwinism in a very particular way, to which it is impossible to do full justice in a short summary. Firstly, there is the emphasis on genes as 'selfish replicators' and organisms as their robotic carriers.[18] Secondary replicators called 'memes' are also invoked. These are elements of cultures that may be passed on by non-genetic means, by imitation. These memes can be copied across brains and in other storage devices like books or computers. Examples include songs, crazes, clothes, the skill of riding a bike.[19] Memes are regarded by some as a major component of the human mind, allowing consciousness and forming the 'self'. They are regarded by others as incoherent and non-existent.[20]

The emphasis on 'memes' and 'genes' as information carriers is partly because the 'school' is rooted in an interpretation of neo-Darwinism that leans heavily on information-theory and computer science. Steven Pinker and Dennett both characterize the brain as composed of discrete information-processing modules, and Richard Dawkins argues for an information-processing or computational interpretation of evolution and reproduction, even denying that this is metaphorical.[21] Dennett is a strong proponent of AI, and characterizes evolution as 'engineering'.[22] These writers have a strong tendency to interpret any biological phenomenon or behaviour as the result of a specific Darwinian adaptation. This has led some to label them 'Ultra-Darwinists'.[23]

All of these writers, but especially Dennett, tend to see the application of their version of Darwinism to pretty much everything as desirable. Darwin's idea, Dennett writes, is a 'universal acid' that 'eats through just about every concept, and leaves in its wake a revolutionized world-view, with most of the old landmarks still recognizable, but transformed in fun-

17 Richards, 2000; Brown, 1997.
18 Dawkins, 1976.
19 Blackmore, 2003; 1999; Dawkins, 1976; Dennett, 1991.
20 Midgley, 2001.
21 See discussion in Rose, 1997.
22 Dennett, 1995.
23 Rose, 1997.

damental ways'.[24] Those promoting the school have frequently acted in ways to promulgate their ideas at the expense of those they feel are undesirable. Pinker deplores the 'blank-slate' idea of mind that he thinks the social sciences hold, promoting instead his interpretation of evolutionary psychology.[25] Pinker's interpretation, shared by many evolutionary psychologists, is that the human mind can be characterized as a 'Swiss army knife' of specifiable modules that was evolved for a natural environment and which has not had time to adapt to modern life. Hence most of our (in principle discrete or decomposable) behaviours can be thought of as frozen relics from the Stone Age.[26] This is not the place to offer extensive critiques of this range of views, but they are not universally held even within the mainstream,[27] and should not be confused with the whole of conventional evolutionary theory. Indeed, these sorts of interpretations are just beginning to be complimented by what are in some respects radically different approaches.

One reason is that the concept of neo-Darwinian natural selection is increasingly supplemented by a number of evolutionary mechanisms that may be equally or even, according to some more radical biologists, *more* important. Alongside genetic mutation are hybridization (still thought to be a minor factor in evolution), the fusion of separate species (thought to be more important than natural selection by some), and Horizontal Gene Transfer.[28] To this we can add extra-genetic evolution, or evo-devo.[29] It is also possible that some from of Lamarckism occurs in the immune system, although this interpretation of retrogenes is disputed.[30] Neo-Darwinian natural selection is no longer a lone player in the evolutionary field.

Conventional Theories and Consciousness

Dennett's writings are of especial note in the context of the evolutionary theories of consciousness. His interpretation of the emergence of consciousness is, naturally enough, tied into his particular interpretation of evolutionary theory. In *Darwin's Dangerous Idea*, he reinterprets Darwin's theory in terms of a 'blind algorithm'. Algorithms are formal processes that can produce a result whenever they are 'run', so following the algorithm, or set of step-by-step instructions, for making a cup of tea will invariably produce a cup of tea. A glance at Darwin's basic formulation, above, will show that it can be interpreted in this way. According to

---

24 Dennett, 1995, p. 63.
25 Pinker, 2002.
26 Pinker, 1998; 2002.
27 Rose & Rose, 2001.
28 Lawton, 2009; see Margulis & Sagan, 2002, for the case for species origin by symbiogenesis.
29 Elsdon-Baker, 2009.
30 Steele, Lindley & Blanden, 1998.

Dennett, algorithms have three advantages: they are neutral as to substrate (or can 'run' wherever a given set of conditions occur); they are mindless or 'simple enough for a dutiful idiot to perform';[31] third, the results are guaranteed, so long as the algorithm is followed to the letter. His thesis, which he claims is a restatement of Darwin, is that 'Life on Earth has been generated over billions of years in a single branching tree — the tree of life — by one algorithmic process or another'.[32]

Dennett explicitly characterizes biology as engineering. By this he means that the evolution of biological systems can be understood in terms functional mechanisms, their design, construction and operation. Small, simple robotic mechanisms accrete into more complex ones and from this process comes the 'concomitant birth of meaning or intentionality'.[33] Throughout the book, and elsewhere, he emphasizes that teleology emerged from non-teleological matter: 'In the beginning, there were no reasons; there were only causes... but after millennia there happened to emerge simple replicators. While they had no inkling of their interests, and perhaps properly speaking had no interests, we... can nonarbitrarily assign them certain interests — generated by their defining "interest" in self-replication.'[34] Whilst they would undoubtedly differ in details, most conventional biologists would agree that any purpose or intentionality could *only* appear from non-purpose and non-intentional matter.

Dennett emphasizes how mind/consciousness (but not *qualia*, which he dismisses as non-existent) emerges gradually by a step-by-step accumulation of mechanisms that allow survival. At the lowest levels are 'impersonal, unreflective, robotic, mindless little scrap[s] of molecular machinery...'[35] whose collective actions somehow produce beings with intentionality (which Dennett defines in terms of third-person observations).[36] He writes: '*of course*[37] our minds are our brains, and hence are ultimately just stupendously complex "machines;" the difference between us and other animals is just one of degree, not metaphysical kind.'[38] Hence *biology* is equated with *mechanism*. He also claims that 'those who deplore Artificial Intelligence are also those who deplore evolutionary accounts of human mentality...'[39] — thus lumping AI critics with his despised anti-evolutionists.

---

31 Dennett, 1995, p. 51.
32 Dennett, 1995, p. 51.
33 Dennett, 1995, p. 228.
34 Dennett, 1991, p. 173.
35 Dennett, 1995, p. 203.
36 Dennett, 1991.
37 Korzybski discouraged 'of course' statements as being of a piece with X 'is' Y statements. Whatever we say something is, it isn't.
38 Dennett, 1995, p. 370.
39 Dennett, 1995, p. 371.

The book is full of polemics like this, and in addition, Dennett distinguishes between what he terms evolutionary 'crane' explanations, in which the emergence of mind is describable in (his) evolutionary terms, and 'skyhooks', which is his pejorative for those ideas that he thinks fall outside this range of explanations. This label is also fairly undiscriminating; people who are said to employ 'skyhooks' range from Creationists to his rivals who do not think that consciousness is fully explicable in terms of conventional science. These include Noam Chomsky, Roger Penrose and John Searle, who is labelled 'another favorite champion of skyhook-seekers'.[40] These sorts of polemics are by no means unusual, and characterize much of the field of popular Darwinism.

Problems

Problems Specific to Dennett's Theory

There are a number of problems specific to Dennett's particular interpretation of Darwinian theory. Firstly, Dennett is apparently unaware that seeking a universal theory to explain *everything* is hardly a new phenomenon. Descartes attempted to explain everything except the (male) mind in terms of clockwork, and seventeenth-century chemists also spent a lot of time searching for the ultimate 'quintessence', out of which all chemicals could supposedly be derived. In fact, Descartes' 'universal clockwork' failed because it proved necessary to introduce the ultimate 'skyhook' (gravity) to create a coherent conceptual scheme to account for the movements of the planets.[41] It is not impossible that one 'skyhook' or another may be needed to better understand consciousness.

Dupré notes that Dennett's 'engineering' stance marks him as a thoroughly pre-Darwinian thinker. A major reason why Darwin's 'dangerous' idea was considered better than the 'design' arguments of Paley was that it used the concept of *adaptation*, not design, to explain the appearance of complex forms.[42] As noted above, the problem with re-introducing design, even in metaphorical terms, is that such a term implies a designer. This is also true of algorithms, which many be mindless, but are generally written or programmed by someone.

The stock reply to the problem of an implied 'designer' is that 'chance' and 'necessity' are sufficient explanations for the spontaneous emergence of the blind algorithms of evolution earlier in cosmic history, but lingering questions remain. The major problem is how the cosmos just 'happened' to occur in such a way that evolution of the sort that we observe could emerge *at all*. This is unsolved in cosmology, where a number of people are

---

40 Dennett, 1995, p. 397. This particular pejorative has also spread; Koch and Hepp, 2006, label those favouring quantum theories of consciousness as looking for 'quantum skyhooks'.
41 Taton, 1964.
42 Dupré, 2001.

unsatisfied with the 'chance and necessity' sort of explanation; hence the invocation of, amongst other solutions, the anthropic principle.[43] Such problems demonstrate just how limited our explanations tend to be.

General Problems of Conventional Theories of Evolutionary Emergence

The central problem for all theories is how conscious experience could ever emerge from non-conscious 'materials', a problem shared by *both* strongly dualistic and materialist views of consciousness.[44] At this point, all we really have is the *assertion* that some of emergentism is sufficient as an explanation, and we have seen that this has problems. This is recognized in Dennett's volume; hence his assertion that the development of strong Artificial Intelligence would demonstrate the accuracy of this theories. But this seems to me another example of 'promissory materialism', or the simple assurance that these problems will some day be solved via conventional science.

On the other hand, the probability that consciousness exists in other animals *could* be considered as evidence in favour of emergence. It seems quite likely that non-human animals possess varying degrees of consciousness. Donald Griffin made a quite strong case that such phylogenic continuity does actually occur, so we can assign a very high probability that, in some cases at least, animals have consciousness. Griffin defined consciousness as meaning both perceptual awareness and maybe, sometimes, memories or anticipations.[45] He distinguished between a basic *perceptual* form of consciousness (awareness of something) and a more complex, reflective form (awareness of one's own thoughts or activities or reflexive introspection).[46]

My own — reasonably wild — guess is that the perceptual form of consciousness is probably very widely distributed throughout the animal kingdom, and is possibly dimly present even in single-cell organisms like amoebae and paramecia. It seems reasonable to assume the presence of reflective consciousness in many mammals at least, almost certainly, in other primates and probably cetaceans. This guess, however, illustrates the problem of drawing the line between sentient life and insentient matter, a line that is always going to be arbitrary because in many cases we cannot empirically test consciousness either way. However, the supposition that *some* form of consciousness may be so widely distributed is important because it emphasizes the evolutionary continuity between ani-

---

43 Davies, 2007.
44 Griffin, 1998.
45 Griffin, 2001.
46 Griffin, 2001.

mals and human beings and highlights that it is not something unique to us.

Another issue is whether consciousness appears gradually or suddenly, at a given point in the evolutionary process.[47] Griffin asserts that that such a jump or 'miracle' is what drives those of a purely physicalist persuasion to adopt the argument that consciousness 'is' somehow illusory. He reinforces this point with a quote from Strawson:

> Insofar as we are committed to naturalistic no-miracles materialism, we seem obliged to hold that the appearance of radical disconnection between experiential properties and nonexperiential properties is a kind of illusion... But it won't go away, and it constitutes a vivid proof of the limitations on our understanding of reality.[48]

Griffin's argument has, however, been criticized for assuming that conscious awareness must be binary, or something one does or does not possess.[49] This ignores the possibility of qualitative or gradual differences in the phylogenic tree; but the issue remains unresolved. In sum, there seem to be enough unknowns and uncertainties within the conventional views to justify the examination of alternatives.

The Radical Novelty Option

This is the option favoured by Karl Popper; and there was also an explicitly teleological version proposed by Henri Bergson (1859–1941). Popper suggested that, no matter what one's position was on the relation between the mind and the body, one could not get away from the strong observation that the universe seemed radically creative. By this he meant that one could not really predict emergent phenomena from its basic constituents; he gave the example of the memory of crystal, an attribute of which was not apparent in the basic atomic structure.[50] He suggested that the evolutionary emergence of mind/consciousness (he conflated the two) could be understood as another example of radical emergence.

In Henri Bergson's theory, *being* was the fundamental metaphysical concept. Bergson saw evolution as fundamentally creative because it engendered something wholly new; like Popper, he thought that these novel entities could not be predicted by what had come before.[51] He also had the notion of nature as an organic whole, driven by an *Elan Vital* or life-force, and in this sense his theory was strongly teleological.

---

47   Griffin, 1998.
48   Strawson, 1994, p. 75. Quoted in Griffin, 1998, p. 66 (fn).
49   Nordberg, 1999. Nordberg also suggests that some variety of hylomorphism would serve Griffin's purpose as well; and this comes close to suggestions made in chapter seven.
50   Popper & Eccles, 1977.
51   See summary in Barrow & Tipler, 1986, pp. 189–95.

Current theories of emergence seem in some respects to be moving in the direction of radical novelty. Deacon describes emergent phenomena as having novel properties not exhibited by their constituents, and we have already examined the potential emergence of 'holistic properties' in chapter seven.[52] It is possible that the development such theories may allow us a better understanding of how one system jumps 'miraculously' from one state to another at a certain level of complexity; but currently, this assertion remains promissory.

Problems

I will deal with some of the key problems with unconstrained teleology later, but here we should note the important distinction between *progress* and *evolution*. Conventional evolutionary theory recognizes that, whilst kinds of progress (in terms of innovations) can occur within evolution, there is arguably *no* overall direction, although because of the nature of the processes we do tend to find more complex life-forms appearing later than more simple ones. This does not, however, imply a linear progression to evolution, and there is much in the fossil record that suggests the opposite.[53]

Secondly, with radical novelty, we are still stuck with the problem that consciousness at least seems *sui generis* and its appearance somewhat miraculous. Griffin, like Wallace, observes that the examples of physical emergence given by writers like Popper seem to be of a different kind than the alleged emergence of consciousness from insensate matter. He suggests that the two examples are so different that such a suggestion constitutes a category error.[54] This impression may, of course, be wrong, but currently we cannot say either way with any certainty.

Panexperientialism

The mathematical physicist Alfred North Whitehead (1861–1947) suggested in *Process and Reality* that the world was built out of actual entities or 'occasions' of experience. This was based upon William James's observations about the atomic or indivisible character of experience. To Whitehead, such entities actively decided things and moved or evolved from 'continuous potentialities' to 'atomic actualities'. These entities 'decided' things or realized potentials. In Barrow and Tipler's terminology, A may change to B in a non-random way, as A somehow actively orients its change to B. Whitehead also suggested that 'external [Platonic] objects' acted as lures for the process of change.[55] To him, such teleological processes underlay and gave rise to the world of efficient, visible causes. But

---

52   Murphy & Brown, 2007.
53   Rose, 1997.
54   Griffin, 1997; 1998.
55   Barrow & Tipler, 1986; Stapp, 2007.

the key here is that experience is written into the basic 'stuff' of the universe from the start, in the form of instances of experience.

For panexperientialists, each individual 'unit' in the cosmos has some kind of experience. So this is true for single-celled animals and whole human beings. What actually constitutes an 'individual' is moot (see below). Griffin suggests several reasons for favouring this theory, including that:[56]

- It allows us to truly naturalize the mind without having to 'explain' experience or consciousness as a side-effect of insensate matter.
- It is truly monistic, and allows us to see experience as equally 'real' as planetary movements.
- It might provide the basis for an ontological unity of science.
- It avoids many of the problems of both dualism and materialistic monism; specifically, in this context, the emergence problem.
- It provides hope of solving the mind/body problem, where experience is not the 'Great Exception' to an otherwise satisfactory physicalist view.

So, in Griffin's revised view, experience did not gradually evolve with the first selfish replicators because, in some sense, 'moments' of experience were already present, and distributed throughout the universe even before the appearance of what we would recognize as life-forms. Griffin also argues that there is a difference in principle between 'aggregational societies' such as billiard balls and computers, and what he terms 'compound individuals' such as rats and human beings.[57] He asserts that only the latter can be said to have experience and freedom (which still suggests that, for example, atoms have experience, as they classify as compounds). In compound individuals, the relation between the whole and its parts is qualitatively different from those in aggregate individuals, which may be said to be truly the sum of their parts.

Problems

There are a number of problems with panexperientialism, most, but not all, of which are tackled by Griffin.[58] There is the charge that it is vitalistic, which Griffin thinks does not apply to panexperientialism because vitalism holds that, prior to the first appearance of living things, all was mechanism, and that it was only with the appearance of living things that such a new life principle emerged. There is the argument from implausibility, because panexperientialism seems so foreign to the way in which those with a scientific training have become accustomed to viewing the universe.

---

[56] See Griffin, 1998, pp. 89–92.
[57] Griffin, 1998, p. 40.
[58] Griffin, 1998, pp. 92–8.

There is the argument that the theory may be unintelligible. The strongest arguments about this revolve around what the 'units' that have experiences might be, and how we might characterize compound individuals. More serious is the implication that things like telephones and rocks have experiences; but Griffin claims that this objection does not count here, because telephones and rocks can be termed aggregate individuals. Finally, there is Popper's objection that panpsychism can be classed as a form of parallelism (see also chapter five), which denies any efficacy to conscious thoughts. Griffin replies that because of the difference between aggregate and compound individuals, we can say that there is a dominant relation between the higher 'experiences' and lower-level experiences.

Another issue is parsimony. Why should we assume that something has 'experience' if we can explain its actions in 'mechanistic' or 'robotic' ways? Related to this is the detection problem. It is difficult enough to decide whether other mammals are conscious, but far harder to test whether a bacterium has awareness. These difficulties highlight the metaphysical nature of the debate, as well as empiricism's limits.

Another big problem is that, in distinguishing aggregate from compound individuals, one is still left with the emergence problem. There was presumably a time, in the early universe, when compound experiences did not exist (unless one counts the whole cosmos as one big compound experience). This would mean that there would be a moment when the first compound individuals, and thus units of experience, appeared. Thus, even with panexperientialism, we still have a 'miracle' to contend with, which is: how and why does experience appear as, in evolutionary terms, aggregate individuals become compounds?

In fact, the problem could be even worse, depending upon how we define emergence. New compound individuals are continually formed via reproduction, so at what point does the 'germ' of compound awareness arise within the embryo? And even if lower-level compounds (say complex cells) retain a level of awareness, said awareness seems transient in more complex individuals. One's waking awareness seems to dissolve every time one goes to sleep. Panexperientialism does not seem to us to offer easy solutions to these dilemmas, so we seem stuck with *some* form of emergence, 'miracles' notwithstanding.

General Problems with Teleological Theories

It is time to examine, briefly, some other problems of teleological theories. The main problem is that unconstrained teleological reasoning can be used to explain anything whatsoever. William James used the example of the ruins of the Lisbon earthquake to demonstrate this: '…the whole of past history had to be planned exactly as it was to bring about in the fullness of time just that particular arrangement of debris of masonry, turniture and once living bodies. No other train of causes would have been sufficient.'[59] The same problem dogs the anthropic principle in cosmology. Just because the universe *seems* uniquely suited to life in general and *Homo sapiens* in particular, this does not necessarily mean that we are entitled to suppose a cosmos made for observers.[60]

The second reason, as observed above, is that teleological theories have, historically speaking, fared very badly against non-teleological ones. Today there are those who argue that the anthropic principle would be negated if ours was just one of a vast number of universes which have 'evolved' life-giving conditions by a sort of natural selection. In this interpretation we are by necessity in a universe with conditions suitable for life, but only because we could not, by definition, exist in a universe that is unsuited to life.[61] One could make a similar sort of 'selection effect' argument for consciousness, which seems similarly spectacularly unlikely; because non-conscious beings would by definition not notice its absence.

A Note on Evolutionary Cosmologies

There is another theme that should be mentioned in passing, which is the conceptual change from universes with static, eternal laws to ones that are evolutionary. Evolutionary universes are not necessarily teleological; a universe that is one of many could be said to evolve from the same 'chance and necessity' that is supposed to occur in biological evolution. Barrow and Tipler highlight three possible ways in which a universe might be held to be teleological; by tying evolution to some form of inevitable progress, by supposing the universe is moving towards a goal, or by supposing some sort of living universe that is teleological by nature.[62]

This third possibility is in many ways the most interesting, and perhaps germane to some form of panpsychism. Both Bergson and Whitehead, echoing the Ancient Greek Anaximander, supposed that the universe was like an organism. Elisabeth Sahtouris has produced one recent formulation that has some merit. She proposes that it is at least as reasonable to project living attributes onto the cosmos as it is mechanism, pointing out that galaxies, stars and planets fit the definition of *autopoiesis*, or self-generation, as well as organisms. She also proposes that the cosmos is somehow 'intelligent throughout'.

Such ideas seem more attractive than a dead universe where form, structure and consciousness have come about through blind chance, and despite entropy. The latter view also fuels claims that the universe 'is'

---

59   James, 1909, p. 438 (fn).
60   See Barrow & Tipler, 1986, for the case for the anthropic principle, and Midgley, 1992, for some objections along Jamesian lines.
61   See Davies, 2007, for a popular treatment of these issues.
62   Barrow & Tipler, 1986.

pointless or 'absurd', and accepted as a given by many in science.[63] But the living-universe metaphor instead implies *self*-generation, which may be a more intellectually satisfying solution than a machine cobbled together by chance and necessity. In the final analysis, however, whilst the cosmos may suggest any and all of these interpretations, it demands none of them.

To me, it *does* seem very strange that we should happen to live in a universe where elaborate structures *just happen* to evolve on multiple levels and produce consciousness. Perhaps the multiverse 'explains' this, but such an explanation still does not seem very satisfactory. The cosmologist Paul Davies favourite solution is some sort of life principle, although he admits that this would allow a form of teleology. One problem is where such a principle might come from, which may be solved by allowing the multiverse idea, but Davies points out that 'invoking [multiverse explanations] merely transfers the problem of where the life principle came from to the problem of where the multiverse came from'.[64] The bottom line is that all explanations have their limits.

Conclusion

Although I reach no firm conclusions about these issues, a few comments are in order. The first is the observation that different writers with very different points of view express an often strong desire for the widespread or even universal adoption of their own ontological and epistemological schemes. For example, Griffin lists ontological unity as a point in favour of his theory, and Dennett repeatedly mocks anyone who does not adopt universal neo-Darwinian thinking. Such a unity may, however, be misplaced, especially given significant problems with *both* conventional and heterodox theories.

A pluralistic option would be to resist the adoption of a 'universal' theory at all, which, given the frequent collapse of such 'Grand Theories' in the past, has some appeal. We have to remember the difference between the cosmos and the ways in which it gets described, and also the dearth of empirical data about many of these problems.

That said, bits and pieces of both mainstream and heterodox theories may well prove useful for deepening our understanding. Evolutionary thinking *has* spread far beyond the context in which it was originally formulated, and our general picture of the universe has changed from something static and clockwork to something dynamic and constantly evolving. It also seems appropriate to regard the forms of consciousness we observe in ourselves and at least some other animals as biological (although if we reformulate the whole cosmos as somehow biological, it

---

63 See especially Monod, 1972; Davies, 2007.
64 Davies, 2007, p. 301.

may be possible to see consciousness as *simultaneously* biological and inherent throughout).

One of the most interesting portions of the panexperientialist theory is the distinction between aggregate and compound individuals, a distinction which those in conventional cognitive science naturally fail to make. In 1949, Gilbert Ryle compared the 'mind' to a university, which suggests that 'mind' refers to the activities and behaviours of an 'aggregate' rather than a compound individual. This idea of aggregation is also central to the programme of Artificial Intelligence, where minds are often supposed to be composed of collections of functional sub-units.[65] Yet if we do distinguish between aggregate and compound individuals, then this implies severe limits upon the success of such programmes. For if Griffin is correct, then our current technology, being composed of aggregates, *cannot generate experience*.

It may, in fact, be possible to formulate a compromise between panexperientialism and radical novelty of emergentism. If we marry the idea of compound individuals with some of the ideas emerging from complexity theory, then we might say that only individuals with a certain range of attributes (for example: unfathomable complexity and a wide range of heterogeneity) could be classed as having experience. This reclassification would imply that atoms were not conscious, or experiential units, as they would be too simple, but it would hint that the cosmos itself and maybe some sub-units (galaxies, stars, the living Earth?) also have experiences. Or it may be that experiences only appear in given sets of circumstances, like biological evolution or in individuals with certain sets of capacities. We simply do not know.

Clearly, much is open to debate. Conventional theories about evolutionary emergence have plenty of holes — but the heterodox theories are far from unassailable, especially those that invoke teleology. It would probably be foolish to jump to conclusions, but we *can* plead for a more comprehensive assessment of such alternatives. The main barrier to such discussions is the often excessive conservatism of the mainstream, and I share Griffin's doubts as to whether the conventional science communities are *capable* of such radical innovation.[66]

---

65 See especially Minsky, 1986.
66 Griffin, 1998.

Chapter Thirteen

Free Will

Free will, in the sense of personal agency and voluntary action, is widely, but by no means universally, held to be incompatible with the 'scientific' picture of the universe. For example, Blackmore makes this claim on the basis that (1) determinism is obviously true, and (2) any kind of personal freedom would need an inner substantial self, which conflicts with science.[1] I leave questions of the self to the next chapter. Here, I survey some of the current claims concerning personal volition and suggest ways in which this debate may be advanced.

Unlike with the previous chapter, this is a topic on which I do not feel neutral. I believe that claims that we are nothing but 'puppets of our neurons' to be seriously flawed. Yet a number of cognitive scientists seem to support such assertions. Chris Frith, for example, sees conscious reasoning as mostly an attempt to justify a choice after subconscious processes have already made a decision.[2] Daniel Wegner's book goes further, asserting strong determinism to be 'true' and conscious will to be therefore wholly illusory. His book was received favourably and the cover includes quotations from a number of leading neuroscientists including Chris Frith, Bernard Baars, Gordon Bower and Michael Gazzaniga. The latter wrote a book in 2005 suggesting legal reform in the light of the 'neuron-puppet theory', largely, as Roger Scruton observed 'to the detriment of our old ideas of responsibility'.[3]

Despite this largely uncritical enthusiasm, there remain strong grounds for questioning the assumptions that (1) scientists *must* believe in strong determinism, and (2) therefore they cannot believe in any form of free will or volition. The first point to make is the general and wide-ranging nature of the phrases 'free will' and 'determinism'. To be sure, each phrase stands for something, but what, exactly? The second is to note that, despite their

---

1   Blackmore, 2007.
2   Frith, 2008.
3   Scruton, 2009, p. 9.

neuroscientific sophistication and secular tone, the current debates derive much of their logical structure from theological precursors.

A Theological Precursor of the Free Will Debate

Early-modern historians would find the current debates over free will very familiar, because they echo quite closely a reformation debate over salvation. In the middle ages, the Catholic church held that human beings had free will, and could choose freely between salvation and damnation, but this was to change with the rise of Protestantism. Protestant theologian and reformer John Calvin (1509–1564) disputed the Catholic interpretation, highlighting God's omniscience. If God is all-knowing and all-seeing, Calvin reasoned, then He will already know the life-stories of every human being in advance, and it follows that God would know whether they are saved or damned in advance. This led to the idea of an 'elect' or 'predestined' elite who would be saved after death.

This doctrine led theologians to believe that God 'begat' faith in the faithful and conversely a *lack* of faith in the reprobate. William Perkins, a radical Calvinist at the University of Cambridge, wrote that in the faithful, God 'prepareth the heart that it maie be capable of faith'. In the damned, however, God 'in his just judgment hardened their hearts, blindeth the eies of their minds, he maketh their heads giddie with a spiritual drunkeness, and by the strength of their inward lusts…'[4] The saved are saved because God puts salvation into their hearts, whereas the damned are damned because He places sin there.

As we will see, Perkins' rationale comes very close to some contemporary arguments against free will, but instead of an omnipotent God 'putting' salvation or damnation into the heart of every person, we have evolution 'placing' mechanisms into people's brains, making them behave as they do. And instead of God knowing and seeing the complete future of the universe and everyone in it, we have the abstract notion of a fully determined universe where everything happens for a 'cause' and there is one future and one future only.

The Debate Within Conventional Science/Philosophy

The players in the free will debate can be divided into the following rough classes.[5] Firstly, there are the strong determinists, who think that determinism is true and so therefore free will must be false. These are often labelled *incompatibilists*, and constitute a significant portion of the cognitive science community. Then there are those who think that some form of

---

4 Quoted in King, 2008, pp. xii–xiii. From William Perkins, *A treatise tending unto a declaration whether a man be in the estate of damnation or in the estate of grace…*, 1590, p. 3.

5 See Blackmore, 2003, chapter nine; Murphy & Brown, 2007, chapter seven, for introductions to the debate.

free will *is* reconcilable with determinism. These are known as compatibilists. 'Libertarians', by contrast, believe that although free will is incompatible with strict determinism, strong or complete determinism can be rejected. Strawson adds a 'pessimist' group who also think that free will is incompatible with *indeterminism*.[6]

This debate has been in a stalemate position for some time, for a number of reasons. For a start, the debates tend to be framed in terms of Aristotelian logic. That is, 'determinism', 'indeterminism' and 'free will' tend to be interpreted as (1) concrete or naïvely realistic concepts, (2) to be comprehensive and exhaustive descriptors, and (3) absolute and polarized categories. But the fact that it is possible to consider free will as incompatible with either determinism or indeterminism demonstrates just how vague all three concepts are, which belies the illusion of precision.

It should also be noted that within this debate the implicit concern seems mostly to reconcile or prohibit 'free will' with *efficient causation* only.[7] What this means is that, even with 'liberal' compatibilists and often libertarians, any free agency or volition tends to be translated into functional terms.[8] Even with compatibilists, then, any freedom of agency tends to be 'translated' into terms that are or could be subsumed within a scientific frame (and often, in practice, within a broadly conventional frame). In some ways, this seems a perfectly reasonable move, and yet we should remember that the terms 'free will' or 'free agency', like consciousness, cover a very broad canvas indeed and, again, none of these models will be anything like comprehensive. Despite the significant problems with even defining terms, a number of researchers have taken reasonably or very strong positions concerning free will.[9]

Determinist Views

Incompatibilists

A relatively recent and voluminous attempt to demonstrate that personal volition is illusory comes from Harvard Professor Daniel Wegner.[10] Wegner claims that a strong form of determinism is the *only* scientifically respectable approach, and that we should aim to understand every aspect of human behaviour deterministically, or as a strictly causal result of prior

---

6   Murphy & Brown, 2007.
7   Griffin, 1998.
8   For examples see Rose, 2005; 2006; Murphy & Brown, 2007.
9   Although Murphy and Brown suggest that 'given the shift to physicalism' a rephrasing in terms of free agency or free choice might be preferable. A change of terminology, however, does not seem to me to automatically narrow the concept to something workable. I would also note the questionable assumption that we are 'all' physicalists now (or should be).
10 Wegner, 2002.

experience and biology.[11] Because of this, we need somehow to reconcile the 'folk psychology' idea that we have freedom of agency.

The problem for Wegner is that most of the time our feeling of voluntary agency seems to coincide with our actions; we choose to do something, and do it. There are, however, cases where people believe that they caused certain behaviours even though they have not. Secondly, there are instances when people can produce behaviours that look purposive even though they deny that they are producing them. Evidence like this may indicate that the feeling of agency and the causal actions themselves may arise from different sources.

Wegner uses a range of evidence to support the idea that the feeling of voluntary action and the causal action themselves are separable. These include:

- Neurological evidence where direct brain stimulation produces actions without the feeling of volition.
- Evidence that conscious experiences are too slow to manage rapid actions.
- Experimental and clinical phenomena where people's sense of 'authorship' or ideas or actions is muted or non-existent.
- Evidence from automatisms like automatic writing and Ouija boards that suggests complex activities or thinking without conscious control.
- Some suggestive evidence that children have to learn to explain their actions in terms of their own conscious behaviour.
- Neurological phenomena like effects from split-brain patients and blindsight.
- Evidence from extreme dissociative phenomena like Dissociative Personality Disorder and apparent spirit possession.

Wegner certainly marshals a wide range of intriguing evidence in support of his thesis, which I cannot examine in full here. Some of the evidence for dissociative phenomena and automatisms will be dealt with more fully in chapter fourteen, but such evidence need not be interpreted as demonstrating that conscious will is wholly illusory. Much of Wegner's evidence is similarly ambiguous; it can be fitted into a framework of strong determinism, but it can also be interpreted in other ways. Strong determinists like Laplace could, and did, interpret the thousands of observations from solar system astronomy as evidence that we lived in a clockwork type universe, but this does not mean that the universe was 'really' a giant mechanism. Observations made outside the straitjacket of strong, classical determinism suggest a very different universe that is unpredictable, com-

---

11 Wegner, 2002, p. 1.

plex, nonlinear, out of equilibrium, and frequently violent.[12] In the case of astronomy, this forces us to look at the planetary movements—precise though they may be in some respects—very differently; and I suspect that much of the above evidence will need to be reframed in a similar way.

I would concur with Kelly's assessment that just because some actions or aspects of actions are not subject to voluntary control does not entail that none are.[13] Kelly also notes, accurately in my view, that 'What begin as suggestions to this effect early in the book undergo by constant repetition a kind of "hardening of the categories," which gradually bestows upon it the status of established fact'.[14] This demonstrates how powerful one's world-view can become, and how one tends to interpret evidence in terms of what one has already decided to be true. Of course, this is true of everyone, the present author included. The issue, however, is whether this is the *only* interpretation congruent with the evidence.

Wegner's thesis is broadly congruent with the schools of thought that see conscious experiences as causally ineffective. In Heil's terms, the 'powers' and the 'qualities' of the person are separated so that one can safely think about consciousness as a passive quality that is caused but has no causal effect on anything.[15] Wegner himself states that 'the subjective experience is one of the indicators we have of the objective system', adding that 'most of the time the subjective feeling is riding along; you might think of it as the mind's compass, that gives a sense of where the body is going, and we're watching the whole process go on'.[16]

This position seems deeply incoherent to me. Firstly, we have the tacit assumption that direct experience ('subjectivity') is somehow less real than an 'objective' system that we cannot directly observe (fMRI scans, etc. do *not* constitute images of such an 'objective' system; they are data that can only be understood in terms of an imaginative framework, which is what Wegner must be referring to). And the place we formulate these imaginative models is within our subjective experience, so Wegner is claiming that an abstracted fragment of our imagination is more 'objective' than direct experience.

Secondly, compasses are generally used for something, which implies that conscious experiences do have a place in the causal scheme after all. If one does not have a compass on a hiking trip, for example, one might get lost. But Wegner's position, which seems indistinguishable from epiphenomenalism, denies any sort of causal efficacy whatsoever. This, however, leads him into contradictions. For example, he concedes that thoughts do

12   Corliss, 1994.
13   Kelly, 2003.
14   Kelly, 2003, p. 169.
15   Heil, 2003. In Walter & Heckmann, 2003.
16   Interviewed in Blackmore, 2005, pp. 245-57. Quote on p. 254.

have a causal effect on actions, but claims that 'consciousness doesn't always know that if a thought has caused an action it should create an experience of will associated with that'.[17] This, again, seems incoherent. First of all, note the attribution of knowledge and the thingification of 'consciousness', which is treated as an observer. Secondly, Wegner's statement suggests that consciousness *does* have a causal role of 'labelling' thoughts with the cognitive emotion of volition. So despite the interesting evidence he marshals, Wegner's approach has significant internal problems.

Some Neurological Evidence Interpreted as Supporting Epiphenomenalism

What about the evidence from neuroscience that is supposed, by some, to demonstrate the inefficacy of consciousness? Benjamin Libet was responsible for a good portion of the pioneering work in the field, building on the robust discovery that there is a 500 millisecond (msec) delay between a stimulus and subjective awareness of this stimulus. So if one touches or taps a tabletop, there is a gap of about half a second before one becomes aware of the feeling of the surface.

There are a number of lines of evidence supporting this assertion, ranging from cerebral stimulation experiments to those involving normal sensory input and visual experiments like retroactive masking.[18] The latter involved giving subjects a weak electrical pulse stimulus to the skin and determining the length, frequency and intensity of the pulses needed for conscious awareness to arise. In these experiments, the Evoked Potentials (EP) in the cerebral cortex were also measured via EEGs. Researchers found that the primary EP produced by a skin stimulus was neither necessary nor sufficient to elicit a conscious sensation. It was not necessary because a conscious sensation could be elicited by a weak stimulus on the cerebral cortex without an EP occurring. It was not sufficient because a single stimulus pulse in any part of the sensory pathway can elicit an EP in the sensory cortex, but this single pulse does not seem to result in a subjective sensation.[19] This discovery dates back to the 1960s.

Libet's team began to experimentally investigate volition in the early 1980s. In a key experiment, they got a participant to report the time the conscious intention to act occurred whilst moving a finger or wrist.[20] To this end, a cathode ray oscilloscope was set to have a spot of light revolve near the other edge of its face, which was marked with clock seconds. The spot of light completed the circle in about 2.56 seconds in order to allow a time difference to be measured in milliseconds.

---

17   In Blackmore, 2005, p. 254.
18   See Libet, 2004, chapter two, for an outline.
19   Libet, 2004, pp. 47-9.
20   Libet *et al.*, 1983; also described in Libet, 2004, chapter four.

The participant was asked to sit in front of this display and to perform a voluntary act (a flex of the wrist) at any time they felt like doing so. They were also asked to note the time the first awareness of this intention or wish to move, as it was supposed to be a free or spontaneous act. The wish was labelled W and they also measured the readiness potential (RP) via scalp electrodes. One subject performed wrist movements 40 times in a session. A control was also run where subjects just reported the time of a skin pulse whilst watching the clock, to check the accuracy of time-reporting of the subjective experience.

The results consistently showed that the readiness potential or activity in the brain began at, on average, about 500 msec *before* the reported urge to move the wrist arose. This finding has since proved robust. Libet concluded, after several variants of the experiment were performed, that 'the process leading to a voluntary act is initiated by the brain unconsciously, well before the conscious will to act appears. This implies that free will, if it exists, would not initiate a voluntary act'.[21]

However, Libet's experiment, in his view, did not rule out the possibility of conscious will or volition having any effect whatsoever. Firstly, he observed that even though the readiness potential arose first, the subjective sensation still occurred 150 msec before the motor act of wrist-flexing.[22] In a later experiment, he set out to test the possibility that the conscious 'vetoing' of an act could occur. In these experiments, the participant was asked to prepare to act at a certain 'clock' time (say 10 sec) but consciously to veto that act when the clock reached 100–200 msec before the preset time. Libet's team found that the RP built up before the veto but flattened afterwards. Libet interpreted this to mean that whilst conscious or voluntary will did not initiate actions, it could control the outcome. He also suggested that 'Conscious will might actively enable the progression of the voluntary process to action; it would not simply be a passive observer…'[23]

Libet's general picture is that voluntary acts begin with unconscious acts arising from the brain, and conscious will acting as a selector of initiatives. He is also critical of Wegner's approach, noting that Wegner's book, whilst accurately describing Libet's initial experiments, completely ignores the veto phenomenon.[24] However, there have been more recent claims that subconscious activity also precedes the veto phenomenon, which is apparently preceded by activity in the anterior medial cortex.[25]

---

21 Libet, 2004, p. 136.
22 Libet, 2004.
23 Libet, 2004, p. 139.
24 Libet, 2004, p. 144.
25 Brass & Haggard, 2007.

Not everyone has been impressed by Libet's experiments. Bennett and Hacker offer some strong criticisms of both Libet's theory and his interpretations of his experimental findings. They suggest that one can perform voluntary actions perfectly well without any 'subjective urge' to do so whatsoever; 'it is neither necessary nor sufficient for an act to be voluntary that it be preceded by a feeling or desiring, wishing, wanting or intending to perform it…'[26] One can perform any number of voluntary acts without any subjective 'urge' to do so whatsoever. But even without the 'urge', it is also possible to say whether an act is voluntary or not.

They also criticize the 'veto' option, claiming that 'Libet's theory would in effect assimilate all human voluntary action to the status of sneezes or sneezes which one did not choose to inhibit'.[27] They observe that just because neurons in the motor cortex (or wherever) began to fire before said feeling was 'allegedly' noticed does not show that the brain 'unconsciously decided' before the agent or whole person did because a voluntary movement is not a movement caused by the felt urge. Bennett and Hacker's critique follows their general stance against what they term 'brain–body' dualism, or the assumption that the brain or part of the brain can act somehow autonomously (like the Cartesian mind) apart from the organism as a whole. They are highly critical of Libet's approach, even suggesting that such experiments are so incoherent that they should be abandoned.

Despite this, Libet's arguments have some merit. The general picture of unconscious portions of the brain 'bubbling up' activity before portions enter conscious awareness fits with a wide set of observations that suggest that much of our activity is pre- or unconscious. Creativity might serve as an example of this, because much music, creative writing, painting and also scientific and mathematical discovery seems to be in part accomplished unconsciously.

Acknowledging this, however, does not establish the causal inefficacy of consciousness, nor for that matter does it establish that *un*conscious processes are necessarily robotic or deterministic. Libet claims that his discoveries, taken as a whole, actually seem to create more problems for the strict determinist than for a non-determinist. He concludes that 'Great care should be taken not to believe allegedly scientific conclusions about our nature that depend on hidden *ad hoc* assumptions'.[28] With this piece of wisdom in mind, we shall now examine the views of those who claim that free will is, after all, compatible with some form of determinism.

---

26 Bennett & Hacker, 2003, p. 229.
27 Bennett & Hacker, 2003, p. 230.
28 Libet, 2004, p. 155.

Compatibilists

Conventional Compatibilism

This is my term for those who assert that some variety of free will can be accommodated with little or no expansion of our views of causation. The term is a loose one; I am not claiming that the said researchers assume all causal laws to be known, only that they generally eschew attempts to expand our ideas of causation to accommodate voluntary action. Two recent exemplars of this position are Daniel Dennett and Steven Rose.

In his book *Freedom Evolves*, Daniel Dennett claims that a form of free choice is possible within a deterministic and reductionist viewpoint.[29] He tries to fit his story of the emergence of free will into his wider picture of an engineering-style evolution (see chapter twelve). In this account, behavioural flexibility and use of information increase with general evolutionary complexity. The evolution of language is also seen as important for the emergence of self and free will. Language is supposed to create the capacity for morality, and via upbringing we develop an ability to monitor the results of our actions and to form intents. Such an evaluation allows us to create 'self-forming' actions and allow us to in effect 'redesign' ourselves.

Dennett's account has a number of significant points with which I agree. He rejects the idea that freedom is all or nothing, and that there is no need to suppose that self-forming actions come *ex nihilo*. He also, correctly in my view, rejects the idea that the key issue is between determinism and indeterminism in science. Despite this, Murphy and Brown argue that his account fails to provide true freedom because he fails to distinguish between the determinism/indeterminism issue and causal reduction.[30]

Dennett only accepts bottom-up causation from the organization of trillions of 'robot teams' of which he conceives organisms to be composed. Murphy and Brown claim that this acceptance of bottom-up causation alone can only allow for the appearance of intentionality and free will. Murphy and Brown, via an analysis of Dennett's use of language, conclude that Dennett's world-picture is strongly mechanistic and Cartesian, a conclusion that I share. Dennett's attempt to provide a reductionist account of free will does not seem to me very convincing.

Steven Rose, similarly, claims that it is possible to reconcile conventional accounts of biological causation with some from of free agency. Rose is not a reductionist, and argues that questions of agency cannot be 'collapsed' into gene or neuron speak despite current or prospective advances in neuroscience. He argues for a view of human beings as radically underdetermined, 'living as we do at the interface of multiple determinisms we become free to construct our own futures, though in

---

29 Dennett, 2003.
30 Murphy & Brown, 2007. See an in-depth discussion of Dennett's book on pp. 291-8.

circumstances not of our own choosing'.[31] He views human beings as '...the result of an autopoietic process—our self-creation from the raw materials of our genes and environment'.[32] On the other hand, Rose rejects any possibility of 'downwards causation' as an unnecessary 'escape route' which he lumps with Cartesian dualism and terms an 'abdication'.[33]

There seems to be a curious paradox at work here. On numerous occasions, Rose has written against the sort of reductionism favoured by Dennett, Dawkins and others, and has written favourably of the expanded picture of biology provided by researchers like Ho.[34] Yet, taking the above statement at face value, it would seem that he favours upwards causation only. The problem is that if one takes a view based upon complexity theory and autopoiesis, etc. as one's founding view of biology, then arguably, one is tacitly accepting at least weak forms of downwards causation. This should become clearer in the review of Murphy and Brown's proposal, below. But by apparently rejecting any kind of downwards causation, Rose's interpretation ends up being as problematic as Dennett's.

Expanded Science Compatibilism/Libertarianism

In contrast to those who think that the 'deterministic' nature of science rules out free will *a priori* are a growing group of thinkers who argue against reductionistic determinism and for the emergence of dramatically new system 'laws' of nature during the course of cosmic history. Accounts of volition or free agency including conventional science views of consciousness are then fitted into this expanded and non-reductionist view of science. I have labelled this group expanded science compatibilism/libertarianism because the nature of their views cannot be strictly called either determinist or libertarian, but a mixture of both.

These thinkers tend to (1) reject atomistic reductionism but embrace ontological physicalism or naturalism, and (2) support versions of the 'radical novelty' or emergence picture of the evolution of organismic capabilities. Both of these assumptions constrain their view of consciousness and its role in causation. Murphy and Brown distinguish between *atomistic* reduction (or the assumption that causation flows in an upwards direction only, and that the only forms of secondary causation can be from atoms-in-combination, or mechanical) and *ontological* reduction.

Murphy and Brown also argue that the appearance of complex systems might lead to new 'laws', which coincides with the opinions of another writer, Hodgson, who also argues that the 'natural' is not as narrow and limited as it sometimes seems. He argues for multiple laws of nature,

---

31 Rose, 2006, p. 301.
32 Rose, 2005, p. 1001.
33 Rose, 2005.
34 In Rose, 1997, he cites Ho, 2008, as a key influence in his thinking.

including laws that constrain outcomes (C-laws), laws that empower systems to select or direct outcomes, and laws that guide systems in such selections.[35] These laws can be associated with the emergence of complex systems, and conform well to Cartwright's idea that within certain boundary conditions one will need new modes of description to conceptualize capacities.[36] It is not so much that new laws spontaneously appear in the universe; rather, systems emerge or evolve that are beyond the descriptive capacity of models of simple systems.

These conceptions can be placed alongside arguments against strong determinism. Dupré observes that strong reductionism implies that there can be one and one only future.[37] If this is so then we cannot, by definition, have any kind of freedom whatsoever. He goes on to state that in fact we only have very limited and disputable evidence that this is so, and that the assumption is so strong that the burden of proof needs to be placed with the strong determinists. As far as deterministic models of reality go, he accepts Cartwright's picture of patchwork explanations, which means that strictly deterministic nomological machines (Newtonian laws, for example), can only be valid within restricted circumstances. Beyond these local situations we do not have a plausible picture of strong, universal determinism. Cartwright adds that human volition and action might be properly conceptualized as species of order rather than simple randomness.

Murphy and Brown present a wide-ranging, coherent and well argued account of many recent developments in complexity theory and cognitive science which they claim significantly diminish the claim of strong determinists to be the only 'scientific' way of looking at things. In doing so, they present a far richer and deeper picture of organismic causation than has been previously suggested, and which is broadly compatible with some of the views discussed in chapter seven.

Murphy and Brown's argument begins by marshalling a number of arguments against atomistic reductionism. These include:

- The question of where the atoms or substantial matter have gone, in the light of quantum and relativity theory.
- Questioning the assumption that explanations at the atomic level have automatic priority over those at other levels.[38] They also examine a variety of ways in which these 'upwards only' causal accounts can be considered incomplete.
- They raise the issue of wholes versus parts, and table newer assumptions that allow 'downwards causation' in biology and cognitive science.

---

35 Hodgson, 2005.
36 Cartwright, 1999.
37 Dupré, 2001.
38 This mirrors Craver's, 2007, arguments against reductive explanations in neuroscience and for a mosaic unity *a la* Cartwright and Dupré.

- They note the failure to define determinism or causation in specific terms and acknowledge that these terms are too wide to allow easy or succinct definition.

They move on to define downwards causation in terms of Alicia Juarerro's whole-part constraint in dynamic systems.[39] This defines a difference between higher- and lower-order systems. A higher-order system is defined by both Murphy and Brown and Juarerro as one that participates in a broader, more complex causal or 'semantic' system than a lower-order system (say a specific subsystem like the metabolic loops Ho describes). They prefer in some ways Juarrero's 'whole-part constraint' to 'downwards causation' because the latter term is in some sense misleading. This is because it implies a 1:1 correlation between a lower state (say a neural state) and a 'higher state' (say a mental state). This latter picture, commonly evoked in the philosophy of mind, ignores that lower-order descriptions tend to be descriptions of parts, not wholes; hence Bennett and Hacker's mereotic fallacy, where a behaviour of the whole is supposed to be comprehensively desirable in terms of a part. Their picture is therefore holistic.

They then begin to develop a picture of how self-directed systems might emerge as evolutionary complexity increases. This can happen in several ways; via feedback and 'information' loops, via cybernetics and increasingly complex systems, and through nonlinearity and chaos. They emphasize just how far these concepts depart from Newtonian and Cartesian pictures of causation.

As far as mental states and consciousness go, they affirm the causal efficacy of both and embrace a generally representational view of cognition. They utilize Deacon's concept of a 'symbolic threshold' (i.e. language), which allows a significant increase in the causal capacities of an organism. They also utilize Metzinger's account which claims that selves can be expressed in terms of symbolic systems, and that 'consciousness' (which is, again, partly conflated with mind) can be conceptualized as embodied in a currently activated symbolic 'world model'.[40] They also attempt, with a limited success in my view, to provide a naturalistic account of both representation and meaning.

As far as conscious awareness goes, they embrace the 'dimmer switch' metaphor and Edelman and Tononi's 'dynamic core model', arguing for a role in behavioural flexibility and adaptability. They reject claims that, for example, blindsight experiments 'prove' that consciousness has no efficacy. Blindsight is the ability of some individuals to reach out and intercept a target moving within the area of visual blindness even though they claim they cannot see this target (this phenomenon is one of those used by

---

39 Juarrero, 1999.
40 I will examine Metzinger's ideas in the next chapter.

Wegner to claim that conscious volition is an illusion). They suggest instead that, whilst some primitive forms of action may be performed without conscious awareness, this does not rule out the probability that more complex actions may require consciousness. They also reject the idea of 'zombies', arguing for a 'primary causal role' of consciousness: 'Consciousness provides flexibility in modulating one's behaviour that is not available to more primitive organisms. It allows for the prioritization of needs and drives.'[41]

Limits of Expanded Science Compatibilism

The sort of expanded causal picture provided by Hodgson, Dupré, and Murphy and Brown is in some respects congruent with my own. However, in my view, they fall short of forming a resolution to both the problem of phenomenological consciousness and its causal role. I would note, also, that these views assume that the closure principle is conserved.

For a start, Murphy and Brown claim that the qualia that make a causal difference can only be a quale that provides 'information'. Qualia *sans* information is supposed to be epiphenomenal. But in making this assertion they do not, in my view, convincingly establish the causal role of qualia, the reason being that the causal split between qualia and causal efficacy remains. This is because, if said 'information' effectively provides the causal difference, then we may still suppose that the same 'information', minus qualia, could potentially have the same effect that qualia plus information would have. In other words, a causally effective state can occur minus subjective states *without making a difference* to the action, so long as the 'information' is preserved. So the problem of the causal efficacy of subjective consciousness remains. Because despite a radically expanded view, Murphy and Brown, and the others to a degree, are still trying to fit phenomenological consciousness within a world-view that assumes that everything (significant) can be reduced to functional or efficient terms only. This is, I would claim, an inevitable result of a monistic, physicalistic approach to the cosmos. Even though the revised picture seems far more desirable than a strongly deterministic or reductive one, I would claim that many of the deep problems of consciousness, including its causal efficacy, remain untouched.

We should also remember that even these expanded views retain a deeper assumption that subjective experiences must be somehow 'translated' into functional objects in order to be 'scientific'. If we accept this assumption, then attributes that are commonly taken as 'subjective' measures can only be dealt with by being concretized and treated in literalistic terms. Put crudely, subjective qualities, in these models, are only considered 'real' if they can be specified in physical or quasi-physical terms or as

---

41 Murphy & Brown, 2007, p. 219.

wiring diagrams. This is especially apparent in the attempts to naturalize meaning, which is reconceptualized as a complex form of function. This seems to me to be a similar step to the narrowing of definitions of 'qualia' to technical terms like hue in order to get them to 'fit', with the similar effect that aspects of meaning that are *not* so explicitly expressible or translatable get jettisoned or considered unimportant.

I think the main problem is the insistence that observed phenomena conform exactly, at all times, to our simplistic models, coupled with the assumption that the conceptual world 'is' realer than immediate everyday experience. So, on a deeper, philosophical level, even scientific liberals like Murphy and Brown are at one with those who think strict determinism prohibits free will. These problems make me wonder whether even a revised physicalism will be able to cope with subjective experiences in a way that is truly different from the older, more reductive views. But maybe the mistake is in expecting scientific models to comprehensively 'mirror' the phenomenological realities we inhabit.

The problem of objectivism, and causal issues thereof, dogs even writers like Velmans, who has produced a non-reductive, 'reflexive' view of consciousness. Velmans claims that first-person and third-person (intersubjective) perspectives of consciousness are complimentary in the sense that from a first-person point of view consciousness seems central to human action, but from a third-person (intersubjective) point of view epiphenomenal renderings are sufficient and consciousness has no causal role.[42] This mismatch between experience and 'third-person' observation leads to what Velmans terms a 'causal paradox' between the efficacy of consciousness in the first-person, and its inefficacy according to intersubjective observations.[43] Velmans argues that consciousness instead seems to be there for essentially aesthetic reasons, to make the entities experienced via our cognitive and perceptual systems subjectively real. He also supposes this acausal quality of consciousness to have been present at the beginning of the universe, and claims that his theory is ontologically monistic but epistemologically dualistic.[44]

Velmans' account seems to me to amount to a restatement of Huxleyan epiphenomenalism, where consciousness is conceived as distinct from brain function but an acausal side-effect. Rao comments that much of Velmans' analysis seems logical and semantic, and as such does not really expand beyond other epiphenomenal models. However, he finds it 'provocative' when Velmans writes about things entering consciousness and about consciousness being dissociable from cerebral functioning. Rao also

---

42 Velmans, 1991. This use of complementarity is distinct from the sort of 'generalized complementarity' referred to in chapters seven and eleven of this book.
43 Velmans, 1991; 2000.
44 Velmans, 2000.

notes that 'it makes [more] sense to think that consciousness is not only different in kind from cerebral processes, but also has primacy of its own and can indeed causally influence other processes'.[45]

Velmans' theory perpetuates the divide between consciousness as an acausal quality and quantifiable causal powers that are supposed to be reducible to neural processing.[46] Whilst this might render consciousness acceptable from a perspective of monistic physicalism, it really makes little sense at all. What Velmans seems to be saying is that there are two 'worlds', the 'physical' and observable and the 'mental' and publically unobservable, each of which contains an apparent pattern of causal actions, but each of which is unrelated to the other. But the whole *point* of conscious choices, including in science, is to produce changes within the worlds in which we live, which often produces changes others can observe. In denying this, one must once again appeal to the 'illusion' argument, in the fashion of Wegner. But this seems unsatisfactory, for it is by conscious actions that we know the world.

Because factoring in the observer has undeniable causal implications, as some mid-twentieth century quantum theorists recognized. Von Neumann's separation of 'process 2' observer queries from 'process 1' deterministic systems, which we met in the context of Stapp's theories, is an example of this. In this, the 'observer' actively asks or interrogates a system to receive answers. This implies that observers are not just passive but *participating, and that they have capacities over and above the system studied*. In fact, this assumption is implicitly and deeply built into the very fabric of science. Descartes' separation of the (manipulating) observer from the (manipulated) mechanical universe is predicated on the assumption that one can manipulate said universe in ways not reducible to mechanism alone.

This renders absurd the epiphenomenal claims of a good number of neuroscientists and philosophers. This is sometimes weakly acknowledged; for example, Nichols and Newsome, after generally supporting claims that (strong) physical determinism in the brain has 'disquieting' implications for volition, add that 'the assumption of a meaningful degree of personal freedom is essential... to science... Scientists require the freedom to evaluate data and to reject false hypotheses'.[47] In my view, this seriously underestimates the issue, which cannot merely be reduced to evaluating data and 'rejecting false hypotheses'. *Every step of the processes of*

---

45 Rao, 2002, p. 169.
46 Heil, 2003, in Walter & Heckmann, 2003. It also throws up problems of over-determination; see Chrisley & Sloman, 1999.
47 Nichols & Newsome, 1999, p. C38.

science relies upon active observations, evaluations and manipulations. Any comprehensive account of the scientific process cannot ignore this.[48]

Conclusion

The person in the street might be forgiven for thinking that very little has changed in the free will debates. Four hundred and fifty years ago, some scholars were assuring us that we lacked freedom because our thoughts and actions were shaped by the hand of God. Today, we are told that we lack freedom because our thoughts and actions are shaped by the laws of physics and biology. Operationally speaking, there seems very little to choose between these two options: both suggest that human beings are controlled from outside and have little power over their fate. And the rejection of religious domination in favour of scientific domination was supposed to be liberating. So what if we know the neuroscience better, if the conclusions are operationally identical?

Having said this, the expanded compatibilist/libertarians provide encouraging evidence for the rejection of neurobiological reductionism even within the conventional physicalist frame. But even the expanded accounts have deficiencies which arise in part from an uncritical acceptance of monistic physicalism and the assumption that science builds pictures of a purely 'objective' universe. In short, I do not believe that current science and physicalism can handle the problem of mental and conscious causation.

The free will debates can be used as evidence against taking the omnicompetence of science as read. One of Paul Feyerabend's main arguments for the separation between science and the state was that science, as an institution, has a domineering side that, if left unchecked, will tend to smother alternative viewpoints.[49] If the legal system was reformed as Gazzaniga and others suggest, this would place a significant amount of power into the hands of the consultant neuroscientists and simultaneously reduce the power of the 'layperson' (who is, after all, effectively an—often malprogrammed—robot in these conceptions). This would be part of the wider trend of the appropriation of mental health management from private individuals to various experts. If we all came to accept the 'free agency = illusion' claims of a certain segment of these experts, then the corollary would be greater reliance upon drugs and other forms of psychiatric intervention in our lives. This is because beings who lack control generally need outside intervention (or 'manipulations', as Wegner puts it) to help them to gain it.

---

48 I also reject claims that science is possible in zombieland because of a 'scientific method' that could in theory allow robots to churn out reliable results simply by its blind application. Science just does not work in this way. See Collins & Pinch, 1998.

49 Feyerabend, 1978.

In my view, people should not be asked to deform their own lives and beliefs to a (current) knowledge system that in effect asks them to surrender abilities that they use on an everyday basis for the benefit of their lives, even in the name of the 'objective truth'. Claims that one can live happily without believing in any form of free will do not dilute this point, because a suitable intellectual position and lifestyle choice for one person may be totally unsuitable or even harming for another person.[50] The first freedom must be a freedom to decide one's own beliefs and test one's own capacities for oneself, no matter what current dogmas say. But to paraphrase William James, any act of free will seems to require belief in some form of free will.

---

50 Blackmore, 2007.

Chapter Fourteen

The Hidden Portion and Our Selves

We need to consider more deeply the consequences of claims that most cognitive or 'mental' activity is carried out unconsciously, especially with regard to conceptions of the 'self'. As part of his argument against volition, Wegner supplied evidence that some very sophisticated and apparently intelligent modes of thought can occur either subconsciously, or with the person who generates these modes of thinking attributing them to some entity other than themselves. These include:

- Evidence from automatisms like automatic writing and Ouija boards that suggests complex activities or thinking without conscious control.
- Evidence from extreme dissociative phenomena like Dissociative Identity Disorder (DID) and apparent spirit possession.
- Hypnotic phenomena where subjects act under the suggestion of the hypnotist and without a will of their own.
- Creative acts like writing or music composition that seem to the authors to come from 'nowhere'.

Different traditions have interpreted these various phenomena in very different ways, and much can be learned by comparing their differing interpretations. For example, Wegner's interpretation clashes with the socio-cognitivists, who argue that hypnotic phenomena and DID are therapeutic artefacts, and can be explained by forms of role playing. And both schools clash with the older theories of Frederic Myers, who used the *same range* of phenomena to argue for a Platonic, unitary self and a wider consciousness existing below the threshold of awareness.[1] This, again, clashes with the

---

1   This situation also occurs in other areas of disputed data. For example, the partisans of differing theories in the twentieth-century continental drift dispute in geology 'appealed to different facts and classes of facts [and] interpreted the same data in different ways...' (Le Grand, 1988, p. 1).

'virtual' self ideas of Thomas Metzinger, who restricts consciousness to an 'ego tunnel' associated with the correlates of conscious awareness.[2]

The aim of this chapter is to present the sociocognitive tradition, Metzinger's conception of the ego tunnel, and Myers' theory of the subliminal mind as competing explanations of both subconscious activity and accounts of the self in order to show respective strengths and weaknesses. In doing so, we will see how very different primary assumptions generate very different ways of looking at the data. At stake is the interpretation of subconscious/pre-conscious aspects of our mind with respect to ideas of both self and consciousness. Subjectively, much of our thinking does seem to bubble up from nowhere, or from a place opaque to our conscious awareness; think of the 'calculating prodigies' who can produce impressive mathematical feats, but cannot say how they do it. Think, too, of the number of creative writers who cannot say where or how their ideas arrive. Ray Bradbury, for example, reported waking up in the morning to find stories that were 'hid asleep behind my *medulla oblongata*' and desperate to be written.[3]

According to theorists like Metzinger, this can be explained in terms that are roughly analogous to the 'hidden processing' that is necessary for a computer screen to display a desktop on a screen — the 'desktop' being a metaphor for the contents of our awareness. In this way, both the self and the pre-conscious are interpreted in terms of 'information-processing'. However, Frederic Myers rejected the idea that such products could be the result of mechanistically explicable 'unconscious cerebration' because of their depth and sophistication, instead proposing that the evidence from automatisms, hypnosis, etc. might be explained in terms of submerged streams of consciousness.[4] In doing so, he redefined consciousness as something far wider and more fundamental to the person than simple conscious awareness that could exist subliminally. This sort of interpretation goes completely against current views of consciousness and the self, but in its own terms seems a logical interpretation of the evidence. The primary problem is that Myers' theory relies heavily upon paranormal phenomena, which runs against the materialistic preconceptions of the other schools.

Differences also arise because of the vague definition of words like 'consciousness', and 'the self'. We will see that each player tends to define these terms in ways that favours their own particular values, agendas, and basic beliefs. Evidence is then sought or interpreted in a way that reinforces these various agendas. So Myers, seeking evidence for a Platonic

---

2 Metzinger, 2009.
3 Bradbury, 1998, p. 258. Bradbury has often written that his stories are written 'blindly', and mostly subconsciously.
4 See Crabtree's chapter in Kelly *et al.*, 2007, chapter five, pp. 301–66.

self that survives death, arranges and interprets the evidence according to this particular aim. This stands in contrast to Wegner, who uses the evidence to back up a deterministic view of human behaviour, or Metzinger, who is interested in 'virtual' selves, or the sociocognitivists, whose primary aim is to debunk what is to them only apparent hypnotic and dissociative behaviour.

These traditions clash because they conceptualize various fundamentals in very different ways. The main conflicts revolve around the following concepts:

(1) The 'self' as a co-ordination versus the self as a unity.
(2) The question of whether subconscious activity can be reduced to mechanistic terms.
(3) Whether consciousness can be defined as somehow omnipresent in the organism and perhaps beyond ('deep' consciousness), or whether consciousness can be equated with conscious awareness only, or a small fragment of the organism, or as a 'user illusion' ('shallow' consciousness).

Note also the blurry line between notions of 'self' and 'consciousness' in both deep and shallow accounts. In 'shallow' accounts, consciousness, the self and cognition (roughly, 'mental' activity) tend to be assumed to be co-ordinations of functional, physical processes and 'information-processing'. In 'deep' accounts, the self and consciousness (but not necessarily 'mind') tends to be conceived as unitary in some way. The difference between 'self' and 'consciousness' in the latter accounts and to a degree in the former tends to be one of emphasis; 'consciousness' stands for passive being and 'self' stands for an active 'doing' or intentional aspect.

We will now examine the different traditions' views on these issues, beginning with the orthodox and moving to the heterodox. First, I look at the claims of the 'sociocognitivists', and second, I will examine a recent theory of Thomas Metzinger, who sees the 'virtual self' as a narrowly focused, emergent phenomenon of our biology, poised between the 'real' world and the cognitive subconscious. Finally, we will briefly re-examine Myers theory in the context of the self.

The Sociocognitivists and the Abolition of the 'Subconscious'

The first school of thought proposes the abolition of any notion of the 'subconscious' whatsoever. Heap declares with some confidence that there is no such **'thing'** as the subconscious mind (his bold type).[5] He justifies this assertion partly by denying that the subconscious could be a substantial 'thing', and partly by a dismissal of hypnotic and other phenomena like

---

5 Heap, 2000.

DID. In doing so, he draws heavily on the social psychological view of hypnosis, automatisms and dissociative phenomena.

The social psychological approach justifies the abolition of a subconscious or submerged consciousness by claiming to explain *all* hypnotic and dissociative phenomena in terms of role playing and involuntary action produced via suggestion.[6] In doing so, they dispute assertions that such phenomena involve special states of consciousness (the view of the so-called 'neodissociationists'). The sociocognitive sort of view was first aired in 1972 when Sarbin and Coe offered a role theory of hypnotic phenomena, where they suggested that an apparently 'hypnotized' person is really attempting to act a part, due to social pressure.[7] Although subjects will differ in their ability to enact such a role due to social settings, imaginative capacity and the ability to show physiological change, they are not really under the control of the hypnotist, but are really acting.

Spanos, amongst others, further developed this line of thought, supposing that both hypnotic and dissociative behaviour can be primarily thought of as social behaviour.[8] A hypnotized person uses various 'cognitive strategies' to fulfil the role of a hypnotic subject in a way that goes beyond fakery. Spanos did not assume that those reporting involuntary responses to suggestions were lying. Rather, he maintained that they managed to convince themselves as thoroughly as they convinced the audience and hypnotist of being 'hypnotized'. Spanos used this general approach to explain, in various ways, the purported behaviour of both hypnosis and 'dissociative' disorders. Most relevant to this chapter are Spanos's thoughts on Dissociative Identity Disorder.

Dissociative Identity Disorder (DID) is better described by its previous label, Multiple Personality Disorder. It is where one individual manifests two or more different personalities or *alters*. DID in a person is characterized by firstly a strong tendency to dissociate and secondly a history of often chronic and severe childhood trauma.[9] (Many sufferers report childhood experiences of incest or sexual abuse.) DID sufferers learn to avoid extreme suffering by turning the experience over to an *alter* or alternate personality. DID sufferers can have two, distinct personalities, or three, or many. Braude reports that more recent cases tend to report more multiples than earlier ones did.[10]

Spanos believed that the various phenomena of DID could be explained mainly in terms of medical iatrogenesis (self-creation) and role playing. According to him, the explosion of DID diagnoses during the 1980s and

6   Spanos, 1996; Crabtree, 2007 (in Kelly *et al.*, 2007); Gauld, 1992.
7   Gauld, 1992.
8   Spanos, 1982.
9   Braude, 1995.
10 Braude, 1995.

1990s could be accounted for by patients learning to enact the social role of a DID sufferer. Psychotherapists themselves help to originate and stimulate the enacting of the role. He concludes that multiple identities 'are both implicitly encouraged and then constantly validated by high-status experts'.[11]

The issue of the medical iatrogenesis of dissociative symptoms is an important one, and there is some evidence that it occurs in the case of hysteria.[12] However, there are a number of deficiencies in the sociocognitive picture. Gauld criticizes the role playing analogy on the grounds that 'being a good hypnotic subject is not something one can do or achieve. It is something one is, and hypnosis with its consequent phenomena is something that happens to one...'[13] Gauld then supplies a number of reasons to support the idea of hypnotizability as trait rather than role.

Having said this, Gauld also criticizes those who claim that hypnosis can be considered a special state, as hypnotic phenomena 'are readily obtainable from persons who are not in a state of sleep-like passivity and have not been put through any form of traditional hypnotic induction procedure'.[14] He proposes instead that one views both hypnosis and dissociative states in terms of enhanced suggestibility. He admits that we are almost totally ignorant of what actually happens when suggestions 'take' (or manifest themselves, as in a subject feeling an arm get heavier when it is suggested), and observes that most of the suggestions, including that of the sociocognitive theorists, 'hover on the margins of testability'.[15]

Crabtree criticizes Spanos's approach in a slightly different manner, noting significant problems with the claim that a subject might feel a behaviour to be involuntary even if it is really, somehow, voluntary. He points out that the only reason we can know whether a subject's action was voluntary or not was via their own subjective report. But Spanos claims that such a report of involuntariness is wrong, and that the subject is 'really' obeying voluntarily some interiorized social command. Crabtree notes the circularity of such an argument: 'If voluntariness—which can only be determined subjectively—is not to be determined by the experience of the subject, but rather by a theory of the experimenter, the term has lost all meaning.'[16] This also implies that an experimenter may, *a priori*, rule out any results that do not fit their theories.

Spanos's approach to the phenomena under discussion also constrains him to adopt a unitary and 'shallow' view of consciousness. This is

---

11 Spanos, Weekes & Bertrand, 1985, p. 365. Quoted in Gauld, 1992, p. 602. See also Spanos, 1996.
12 See Read, 2005, for a range of examples.
13 Gauld, 1992, p. 603.
14 Gauld, 1992, p. 609.
15 Gauld, 1992, p. 615.
16 Crabtree, 2007, p. 343 (in Kelly *et al.*, 2007). We may extend this observation to the 'free will' debates.

because of his assumptions that (1) there can only be one centre of consciousness, and (2) that 'unconscious' behaviours can be explained entirely in terms of involuntary or reflex actions. However, because of its emphasis on voluntary behaviour, the sociocognitivist approach seems incompatible with Wegner's conception of volition as wholly illusory. It also contradicts, for example, Libet's assertion that most of our thinking proceeds *unconsciously*.[17] It does, however, inadvertently affirm Descartes' view of the active conscious mind that sits at the centre of all voluntary activity.

It seems that the sociocognitivists have argued themselves into a corner. Whilst the case for a 'special state' interpretation of hypnosis seems hardly proved, neither is hard-line sociocognitivism. Whilst the idea of social role playing has merit, the case for the abolition of some form of subconsciousness that goes beyond robotic reflexes seems to me quite weak. We now turn to a theory that suggests that, far from being at the centre, the conscious 'self' represents an altogether different role.

Metzinger's Ego Tunnel

A recent formulation of a 'shallow' view of the self can be found in Thomas Metzinger's *Ego Tunnel*. Metzinger's first claim is that whilst there is no such thing as a 'self', humans do have what he terms a Phenomenological Self Model (PSM) which is 'the conscious model of the organism as a whole that is activated by the brain'.[18] The 'ego' is said to be the contents of the PSM: 'Conscious experience is like a tunnel. Modern neuroscience has demonstrated that the content of our conscious experience is not only an internal construct but also an extremely selective way of representing information.'[19] Metzinger conceives of this 'tunnel' arising firstly by the generation of a world-simulation 'so perfect that we do not recognize it as an image in our minds'.[20] Secondly, an inner image of ourselves is generated, termed the conscious-self model or PSM. Metzinger's central claim is that subjective experience emerges via this virtual self model.

Metzinger claims that consciousness emerges from myriad microphysical events in the brain and a 'complex property of the global neural correlate of consciousness'.[21] He also claims that '[a]ll evidence now points to the conclusion that phenomenal content is determined locally, not by the environment at all but by internal properties of the brain only'.[22] What he seems to mean by this is that any phenomenological experience (a par-

---

17 Libet, 2004.
18 Metzinger, 2009, p. 4.
19 Metzinger, 2009, p. 6.
20 Metzinger, 2009, p. 7.
21 Metzinger, 2009, p. 11.
22 Metzinger, 2009, p. 10.

ticular touch, smell, image, etc.) could in principle be created by the direct stimulation of the brain area involved. Consciousness is also said to be a space of attentional agency, and conscious information is that set of information to which we can direct our high-level attention. Qualia is reduced to a *maximally determinate value* (i.e. the specific shade of a colour like green) or else non-existent.[23]

Via a discussion of the neural correlates of phenomena like Out of Body Experiences, Metzinger breaks down the PSM into further 'subcomponents', which includes the 'self as embodied', 'self-identification' and the 'self as localized'. OBEs are interpreted to show how this self-image can break down and significantly change under certain circumstances. OBEs and other phenomena are of interest because they seem to show how these subcomponents may be disrupted, revealing their 'virtual' nature.

Metzinger concludes that the essence of self seems to be location in time and space plus a transparent body image. He equates selfhood with a sense of ownership that is linked to control of the body. He posits that self-consciousness is what makes control possible, explicitly positing the existence of an image of the body and the fact that the organism does not recognize it as an image, which he terms identification. This agency can be extended to other things (the manipulation of the outside world) or the monitoring of one's thoughts.

All of this is posited within a deterministic frame. He asserts that 'the scientific worldview' is that 'the current state of the physical universe always determines the next state of the universe, and your brain is a part of this universe'.[24] Despite this, he still views free will plus determinism as possible, but only in terms of his PSM model. He seems not to realize that his definition of causation in terms of specifiable states strongly implies a one future only, Laplacean cosmology, which precludes free will by definition and further demonstrates how neuroscience is strongly wedded to classical physics.

Metzinger claims that there currently exists a theory that explains how what he terms 'subpersonal brain events' can become the contents of the conscious self:

> When certain processing stages are elevated to the level of conscious experience and bound into the self-model activated in your brain, they become available for all your mental capacities. Now you experience them as your own thoughts, decisions or urges to act—as properties that belong to you, the person as a whole. It is also clear why these events... appear spontaneous and uncaused. They are the first link in the chain to cross the border from unconscious to conscious brain processes...[25]

---

23 Metzinger, 2009, p. 51.
24 Metzinger, 2009, p. 126.
25 Metzinger, 2009, p. 127.

Despite the fact that Metzinger's theory is backed up by a range of data from what he terms 'modern neuroscience', it seems to me to have a number of significant problems. Firstly, we may note the reduction of *qualia* to a maximally determined value, which seems a rather narrow and literalist interpretation that can be classified as strongly functionalist; in the latter part of the book, he writes enthusiastically about the future of Artificial Intelligence, and supports Dennett's view of quales. Despite some reference to dynamical systems approaches, Metzinger's model places him towards the representational pole rather than the behavioural.

In fact, the PSM theory is so strongly representational that it recalls the Cartesian mirror. Descartes claimed that: 'When external objects act on my senses, they print on them an idea, or rather a figure, of themselves; and when the mind attends to these images imprinted on the pineal gland in this way, it is said to have sensory perception.'[26] If one replaces the 'mind' with the brain and 'pineal gland' with an appropriate neural correlate, then one is close to how many neuroscientists view sensory perception today. Metzinger's 'space of attentional agency' simply replaces the Cartesian mirror with a 'virtual space' metaphor. In short, his theory has the underlying logical structure of the representational theories of Locke, Kant and Descartes.

One modification, of course, is that the 'self' is also conceived as a sort of representation (or confluence of representations) within this virtual space. This representation is supposed to allow a form of agency. And yet, I would claim, the observer problem remains because a representation cannot really observe itself (and I would add that I do not find attempts to reduce self-observation to a form of 'strange loop' very convincing either).[27] And if, as we noted, strong determinism 'is' true, then this agency can only be illusory, anyway.

Metzinger's theory also in effect imprisons us within a 'tunnel' or virtual, representational space that cannot directly access either its own cognitive subconscious or the 'real' world. This creates exactly the sort of deep epistemological problems about knowledge that we noted in chapter six. Namely, if we can only experience the world via 'representations', then how can we claim to know anything at all? This also renders scientific knowledge suspect, something Metzinger tries to sidestep with the usual story about how '…scientific communities… design and test theories, constantly criticize one another, and exchange empirical data and new hypotheses'.[28] This, again, implies that abstract knowledge should be considered more 'real' or 'objective' than everyday experience, because only

---

26 Quoted in Bennett & Hacker, 2003, p. 234. Metzinger's theory seems to me to exemplify the 'crypto-Cartesianism' to which Bennett & Hacker strenuously objected.
27 See Hofstadter, 2007.
28 Metzinger, 2009, p. 9.

via the 'scientific method' can we know the 'truth'. But this latter assertion counts as an item of faith, and conceals what should by now be familiar problems with representational theories of mind.

If all that we can know is a 'representation', then the assertion that we can somehow 'glean' the 'real' world via a special method cannot work, because if we can only interact with representations, then we cannot know whether we are interacting with the 'real world' at all. All scientific communities would do in this case is compare 'representations' that, however persistent, may not bear any relation to reality (or, to put it another way: the only reality we experience would be mental or, if one insists, neurological). It is exactly this sort of problem that leads to the adoption of an idealistic ontology.[29]

This problem is exacerbated by Metzinger's claim that *all* phenomenal content 'is' determined locally in the brain. If this is really so, then it is hard to see how one could have science *or indeed any kind of intersubjective knowledge at all*. We could indeed be 'brains in vats', being manipulated by a Cartesian demon. For all these reasons, and despite the evocation of an impressive array of neuroscience, Metzinger's theory seems significantly flawed. It is time to look at a more radical alternative.

Myers' Theory of Personality

We turn now to a conception of the self as, not shallow, epiphenomenal and composite, but deep, fundamental and unitary to the person. As mentioned in chapter three, Myers had a particular vision of human personality. In *Human Personality*, he began by contrasting two different views of the person; one being the idea that the 'self' is a co-ordination and the other being that the self has an underlying unity. He concluded that *both* of these notions were true:

> I regard man as at once profoundly unitary and almost infinitely composite, as inheriting from earthly ancestors a multiplex organism but also as ruling and unifying that organism by a soul or spirit absolutely beyond our present analysis—a soul which has originated in a spiritual environment which even while embodied subsists in that environment; and which will still persist after the body's decay.[30]

Myers' view of consciousness was as something over and above the physical body, as reflected in his belief in a Platonic and unitary 'self' that existed before birth and persisted after death. This latter notion is probably unpalatable to many readers of a rationalist bent, but I would argue that his theory cannot be fairly considered by ignoring it. That said, we have already encountered several senses in which the organism can be thought of as 'at once profoundly unitary and almost infinitely compos-

---

29 See Henry, 2005, for a physicist who reaches such a conclusion via quantum theory.
30 Myers, 1903/2001, p. 14.

ite'. The various holistic, organismic theories we examined earlier may offer escape routes for positing a unitary self that is neither deathless nor strictly Platonic (although such views are of course closer to Aristotle's).[31]

Myers' built his theory of the subliminal mind on the basic notion of a hidden self. Firstly, he invoked the idea of a threshold of consciousness, or 'a level above which sensation or thought must rise before it can enter into our conscious life...'[32] This term he proposed to extend to cover all that took place beneath the ordinary threshold. The portion of consciousness of which we are aware and identify with our selves, he termed the *supraliminal*. 'Submerged' thoughts and emotions he classed as *subliminal*. Myers:

> Perceiving further that this conscious life beneath the threshold or beyond the margin seems to be no discontinuous or intermittent thing; that not only are these isolated subliminal processes comparable with isolated supraliminal processes (as when a problem is solved by some unknown procedure in a dream), but that there also is a continuous subliminal chain of memory (or more chains than one) involving just that kind of individual and persistent revival of old impressions, and response to new ones, which we commonly call a Self...[33]

Myers' defined consciousness not in terms of simple awareness but in terms of memorability, or that which is capable of being comprehended within a given chain of memory. Thus it was possible for consciousness to (1) exist below the threshold of awareness, and (2) for multiple streams of submerged consciousness to exist within a person.[34] Beneath this multiplicity, Myers believed, lay a fundamental unity.

Unlike those who equate consciousness with awareness, Myers accorded no primacy to the ordinary waking self, 'except that among my potential selves this one has shown itself the fittest to meet the needs of common life'.[35] He believed that it was 'perfectly possible that other thoughts, feelings and memories, either isolated or in continuous connection, may now be actively conscious... within me – in some kind of co-ordination with my organism, and forming some part of my total individuality'.[36]

Myers used this general framework to make coherent a wide range of observations, ranging from the commonly observed to the unusual and paranormal. In fact, one of his aims was to show that there were natural

---

31 I view Myers' theory in instrumental terms as an imaginative construct that should probably not be thought literally 'real' without a good reason for doing so. It should be clear that I apply the same criteria to orthodox theories.
32 Myers, 1903/2001, p. 6.
33 Myers, 1903/2001, p. 6.
34 See Emily Kelly's chapter two in Kelly *et al.*, 2007.
35 Myers, 1903, Vol. II, p. 201. Quoted in Gauld, 1968, p. 283.
36 *Op. cit.*

affinities between widely-accepted facts and those dubbed 'paranormal'.[37] The general topics discussed included:

- Disintegrations of personality (e.g. hysteria, DID, and the dissolution of consciousness between waking and sleep).
- Genius and its creative products (Myers spoke of 'subliminal up-rushes' in to consciousness that were 'characteristically different in quality from any element known to our ordinary supraliminal life').[38]
- Hypnotic phenomena (which Myers conceived as the agency by which faculties beyond the reach of the supraliminal self became sporadically available. For an example, see Puységur's hypnotized peasant in chapter three).
- Sensory and motor automatisms. *Sensory automatisms* are where verifiable information unknown to the supraliminal mind manifest in the form of hallucinations or dreams. These included evidence of apparent telepathy and clairvoyance. *Motor automatisms* are where this information is conveyed via movement of limbs or hands, as in the Ouija board or automatic writing.

Human Personality consists in part of a catalogue of evidence for 'paranormal' phenomena, including extensive records of cases where people come to know things that they should not. These undoubtedly strain the credulity of the modern reader, and I can only suggest that the original work be consulted before any definitive judgment is made. I will consider contemporary evidence for the paranormal more fully in the next chapter, but they cannot be ignored because they formed part of Myers' case for a deep, unifying self. He believed that the various kinds of phenomena and lines of evidence led in the direction of his subliminal self. In his view, the products of genius, spasms of insight and enhanced curative abilities of the hypnotized were part of a wider spectrum that reached a higher expression via paranormal phenomena. He wrote that '…in the background… we catch glimpses of still higher facility; or those supernormal powers of telepathy and clairvoyance on whose existence our belief in a unitary self must ultimately be so largely based'.[39]

Whether or not we accept said phenomena into our conceptual lives, Myers' theory, or something like it, offers an interesting alternative approach to the phenomena of DID. Assuming that the sociocognitive approach is inadequate to fully explain DID, we are left with two alternatives. The first assumes that the 'self' is a co-ordination, and that DID represents the fracturing of this co-ordination due to trauma. This approach is favoured by, for example, Daniel Dennett, who, rejecting the idea of a single self, interprets DID as evidence that the self is (1) abstract, (2) a virtual

---

37 Gauld, 1968.
38 Myers, 1903/2001, p. 7.
39 Myers, 1903/2001, p. 127.

construction, and (3) part of a result of lots of subsystems 'doing their own thing'.[40] The functional specificity of some alters might be seen, in this view, as different but in principle isolated subsystems or clusters of subsystems fracturing along predetermined lines according to isolatable function.

Stephen Braude argues that this interpretation of the phenomena of DID is deeply flawed.[41] He observes that human capacities and traits do not, typically, split into easily definable functional units. In fact, many human traits have a number of features that are only broadly definable and considerably overlap. Braude observes, for example, that being gregarious and friendly is not separable from a person's other abilities and traits. One could, of course, argue that even if such high-level traits are not functionally decomposable, then low-level traits (from which high-level traits could conceivably be built) are. Braude see this as irrelevant in the case of alters, which typically exhibit what might be termed high-level traits.

Which brings us to the second possibility, which is that a basically unified self can be fractured or split in any number of ways under the right (or wrong) circumstances. In light of this alternative, Braude suggests that the colonial picture is untenable. A big problem, he claims, is the inability of colonial views to explain the at least partial reintegration of a multiple and also the occasionally observed re-disintegration along novel functional lines. This seems to be better explained by a shared pool of capacities that decompose on the basis of need and *are not initially discrete functions*. He posits that such multiplicity as happens occurs within an overall unity, and that the alters represent 'distinct apperceptive centres'.[42]

He likens the self to a pie that may be cut in any number of directions, but asserts that some form of transcendental ego is needed to explain the basic features of the alters, as well as the adaptational nature of their formation. I personally find Braude's arguments considerably more compelling than those of the 'colonialists'. The idea of a shared pool of capacities can be accommodated into an expanded picture of a compound, as opposed to aggregate, individual and in my view seems better supported by the evidence from biology, which points to a deep level of organismic integration at every level.

This does not, in itself, demonstrate that Myers' broader theory of a Platonic self is a useful way of organizing the data. Many aspects of that theory remain very difficult to test directly; specifically, the idea that we may have submerged streams of consciousness.[43] Since the only way we can know of a stream of consciousness is via introspection, then it is hard to see

---

40 Dennett, 1991.
41 Braude, 1995.
42 Braude, 1995, chapter three.
43 Gauld, 1968.

how one might know of a stream that is absent from one's awareness. fMRI data suggestive of continual underlying neural activity is not in itself enough to demonstrate the theory either; said data could just as easily be interpreted in terms of a cognitive pre-conscious.

Myers' theory, or something like it may, however, offer a better framework for understanding a range of psychological phenomena than do the theories that posit (1) an essentially robotic pre-conscious, and (2) a shallow 'virtual' self only. Human creativity, for example, seems to me to be both very poorly explained in computational terms and to require capacities significantly beyond that of the waking mind.[44] Whether this compels us to posit submerged streams of consciousness and/or a Platonic self is of course open to debate. The main problem, especially for those of a physicalist persuasion, is that this sort of theory requires metaphysics that have been ruled as alien to 'scientific' thought.

Philosophical Implications of 'Deep Self' Theories

It almost goes without saying that any theory involving a substantive, Platonic self would be rejected by the vast majority of cognitive scientists. This rings doubly true for any theory that suggests that such a self somehow survives the dissolution of the body. Less obviously, a theory that proposes submerged streams of consciousness actually has more in common with mystical views of the mind.

Lancaster observes that the idea of an unknown realm that is an active agent in human life has both religious and psychological branches. He compares the depth psychologists use of 'mental' with the spiritual traditions, observing that one cannot classify these views of a deeper level of being as 'rigidly mechanical'.[45] According to both mystical and depth psychology, the contents of this hidden realm may be 'unveiled' via contemplative practice or psychotherapy. Western mysticism was concerned with communing with the divine that lay immanent in everyday reality and in the person's own soul.

Lancaster notes several suggestions that mystics actually learn somehow to access pre-conscious processing. When this occurs, he says, the mystic's conscious is expanded by the amount and intensity of mental content. Mystics, in Lancaster's account, are not contacting the divine, they have just learned to access a 'rich fount' of material from pre-conscious processing. He does, however, later acknowledge some limits of such naturalistic explanations.[46]

Myers' theory was intended as a form of expanded naturalism, but it seems better classified as falling somewhere between supernaturalism

---

44 See chapter seven of Kelly *et al.*, 2007, for a critique of current theories of creativity.
45 Lancaster, 2004, p. 227.
46 Lancaster, 2004, chapter eight.

and naturalism. It also sits uneasily with contemporary versions of theories that posit the brain as a kind of filter, and consciousness a feature of the physical world as a whole (Lancaster terms this holophysicalism). Nonetheless, it is not enough to reject a theory just because it seems incommensurable with current conceptual fashions, or even because of its supernaturalistic taints. In an historical context, we have seen numerous instances where theological or 'pseudoscientific' ideas have sparked fruitful avenues of research and thought.

Is a Compromise Position Possible?

My own feeling is that some form of compromise might be possible, especially within the organismic framework advocated earlier. There seems to be a couple of semi-implicit assumptions common to many discussions that dismiss suggestions of 'deeper' kinds of selves. These are that:

(1) Only substantial (magical, supernatural, Cartesian) selves can be truly causally efficacious.
(2) But no such substantial self exists in the brain.
(3) Therefore, any self we think we have cannot be (a) substantial and (b) causal.

One could argue that Metzinger's model refutes this, because his claim is that the PSM *does* allow the 'brain' to exert higher levels of control over the body. Whilst there is, arguably, some truth in this, Metzinger's position seems to be severely attenuated by his adoption of strong determinism with upwards causation only. Secondly, his view relies upon the model of organism-as-machine, which includes the assumption of self-as-co-ordination and brain activity as reducible to 'information-processing'. These assumptions virtually force one to consider the 'self' in terms of a sort of program.

My own feeling is that we do not have to invoke substantial selves to see organisms in general and humans in particular as autonomously acting individuals. Buddhist views are informative in this respect. Buddhism simultaneously rejects the notion of a substantial ego and acknowledges that conscious beings have an active will or volition (*cetana*).[47] It is this volition that produces karma, which can be good or bad, depending upon the moral choices one makes. We therefore have a system that sees the everyday 'shallow' self as *both* a construction and causal.

If, too, we subscribe to the notions of radical novelty and causal incompleteness, then it is far easier to see how a non-substantial self that is fully autonomous in its own way might evolve. Once an organism is formed, it may well have the capacity to generate novel forms of 'causation' simply

---

47 Wallace, 2009. Wallace suggests that the Buddha rejected both strongly deterministic and strongly indeterministic models because both led to apathy.

by virtue of being compound and complex in the Rosennean sense. My feeling is that any theory of the self must accommodate such a revised view of the organism.

This revised view may well accommodate a number of aspects of Myers' theory, without the need to posit a Platonic self. Braude's idea of human beings as a pool of intermingled capacities seems to me congruent with Cartwright's conception of systems with general capacities, and with the organismic view. As for a subliminal self, perhaps we might allow that capacities surpassing Turing-computability that are somehow active and not decomposable into specific functions could occur in the absence of awareness. Mae-Wan Ho's view of 'consciousness' and distributed control throughout the body may well be a congenial framework within which to develop a view.

However, in view of the serious conceptual problems with even holistic physicalist interpretations, anti-materialist options (perhaps less radical than Myers') seem viable. For example, William Hasker rejects both biological holism and Cartesian dualism but presents arguments for the unity of self and consciousness. He suggests that there is a non-material subject which somehow emerges from complex brain function: 'Normally what is generated by a brain is a single, well unified conscious subject, but under special conditions, as seen in commissurotomy [split-brain operations] and multiple personality, the consciousness can still divide or fragment.'[48] He terms this *emergent substance dualism*. Despite Hasker's rejection of biological holism, I see little reason why this interpretation of personality is incompatible with the versions of organicism advocated in this book.

Such holistic, anti-materialistic views might also provide an alternative account for the delay between neural activation and conscious awareness that avoids epiphenomenalism. These experiments, to me, indicate that we need to look at conscious volition as a capacity of the *whole organism*, and not just a property of an executive, Cartesian 'self' that sits within our awareness. In some respects, this notion is similar to Metzinger's notion that the emergence into consciousness allows a level of control that did not exist before, but I differ because I do not think that selfhood can be reduced to the sort of conscious-only 'representational' models that he seems to favour. The reason I do not think so comes in part from Myers' and Braude's interpretation of phenomena like DID.

The idea of the human personality as a unity which can split along novel lines and then reintegrate itself seems to me to call into question conceptions that reduce said personality to a 'user illusion'. One reason is that it is hard to see how said 'user illusions' can possibly repair themselves. Saying that the 'brain' might initiate a cure is no answer, because the occur-

---

48 Hasker, 2010, p. 184. For example, biological holism might be a necessary but not sufficient condition for the production of an unified self.

rence and persistence of alters was never solely determined by neural activity, but by personal need. It seems easier to assert that the personality, as a whole, can heal itself; but this reinforces my initial point that the self, conscious or unconscious, cannot simply be reduced to a sort of user illusion.

This is not to reject wholly the idea of body images and/or the metaphor of 'virtual reality' with respect to Out of Body Experiences or lucid dreaming. The phenomena seem to fit reasonably well within such metaphors, and recent neuroimaging studies have provided useful insights into some of the processes underlying such experiences. But Metzinger's treatment of these subjects is partial because, unlike Myers, he ignores the reasonably persistent body of evidence that links such altered states to psychic functioning.[49]

The limits of such an organismic, compromise position are also demarcated by the paranormal, especially phenomena that suggest some kind of survival of bodily death. These topics are today strongly heterodox, and tend to be dismissed *a priori*. And yet, we have to remember that Myers and his colleagues at the SPR took such topics seriously, and amassed a body of evidence that, to them at least, suggested the reality of psychic phenomena. Myers theory leant strongly upon such phenomena, and we do these investigators an injustice if we fail to give the evidence due consideration.

---

49 See Tart, 2009, pp. 222-4, for a similar 'simulation' model of consciousness that does take such things into account.

Chapter Fifteen

Limits of the Possible

Science has, by appeal to various bases, included a multitude of data... Science has, by appeal to various bases, excluded a multitude of data. Then, if redness is continuous with yellowness: if every basis of admission is continuous with every basis of exclusion, Science must have excluded some things that are continuous with the accepted.
— Charles Fort[1]

The only way of finding the limits of the possible is by going beyond them into the impossible.
— Arthur C. Clarke's second 'law'[2]

The two quotes above form part of the justification for a serious examination of subject areas that the majority of cognitive scientists would probably judge ludicrous. There are a number of reasons for considering ostensible 'paranormal' phenomena in the context of consciousness. One reason is that if people can, sometimes, read each other's minds at a distance, directly manipulate physical systems without apparent physical action or see the future, then this would constitute evidence that conventional (neural states only) theory is significantly lacking. Evidence suggesting that memories and maybe personalities could, somehow, persist after bodily death would also severely challenge some deeply held beliefs about the nature of the world in which we find ourselves.

If these suggestions sound exotic and even absurd, we should remember that psychic experiences form persistent parts of the full spectrum of human experience. The debates tend to revolve around, not whether people believe themselves to be telepathic, to have seen the future or to have had a previous life, but how such experience might be *interpreted*. Anomalistic psychology, for example, seeks to explain most or all supposedly 'paranormal' phenomena in terms of cognitive quirks, cultural bias, and strongly-held (non-rational) belief systems.[3]

---

1 Fort, 1974, p. 5.
2 Clarke, 1999, p. 2.
3 Reed, 1988.

But science itself contains various belief systems and, as Fort notes, often acts quite arbitrarily to include or exclude data according to currently held standards and *a priori* notions about how the world works. As far as psychology goes, we are talking about a discipline that refused to speak about 'consciousness' and 'minds' for something like half a century. We have also seen how dissociative phenomena like DID have been held in suspicion, simply because they did not accord very well with the particular belief systems of the critics. Yet other claims made within the accepted belief systems tend to get supported, even when the evidence remains ambiguous or even barely existent. For example, many of the predictions of evolutionary psychology have not proved terribly robust or are even testable, and yet the discipline remains predominant.[4]

Much of the reason for this arbitrary inclusion/exclusion lies in what Griffin terms 'paradigmic thinking'.[5] Our world-views tend to lock us into very specific orientations to the phenomenological world, making truly unbiased assessments very difficult. This is especially true with phenomena or theories that are perceived to threaten said world-view. This author is no exception; for example, whilst I have no particular emotional or philosophical objections to allegedly 'psychic phenomena', I do have issues with evidence suggesting some form of survival after death. This is because said evidence conflicts with my general picture of mind and consciousness as primarily biological phenomena, and thus contingent upon the organism. Nonetheless, and in some respects *because* of this personal bias, I will examine, briefly, some of the evidence that suggests that some form of personal survival occurs.

Natural Science, Social Science, Frontier Science and Anomalistics

Bauer notes that when people speak of 'scientific proof' or demonstrating something 'scientifically', that this often translates into 'like the natural sciences'.[6] (The natural sciences consist of physics, chemistry, biology, and subdisciplines therein.) He states that in our (often covertly) scientistic culture, natural science is often deferred to as the 'supreme arbiter of truth'.[7] This means that evidence must be relatively clear-cut, robust and ideally conform closely to the outputs of the various nomological machines that generate the so-called 'laws of nature'.

This, as Bauer also notes, tends to simplify matters. In practice, scientific knowledge, even in the natural sciences, ranges from highly reliable to

---

4   See the discussion in James, 2008, on the problems with replicating studies of alleged gender differences in evolutionary psychology. Rose & Rose, 2001.
5   Griffin, 1997; 1998.
6   Bauer, 2001.
7   Bauer, 2001, p. 5.

highly unreliable. Highly reliable can be generally termed *textbook* knowledge, but much *frontier* science can be classified as unreliable. Bauer observes that the interesting 'knowledge fights' occur in just those areas where convincing disproofs are not possible, and definitive answers are not to be had. Bauer also cautions against forgetting the 'enormous obstacles that the human search for new knowledge faces', reminding us that 'human knowledge-seeking ambitions easily outstrip humankind's knowledge-gaining capabilities'.[8]

Secondly, the study of anomalies like psychic phenomena has far more in common with social sciences (of which consists the majority of cognitive science) than their natural counterpart. Progress in the social sciences is rarely as clear-cut as in the natural sciences. This is partly because, unlike in the natural sciences, the social sciences often deal with entities that are far too complex to be described in terms of simple cause-and-effect relations. Social science can either seek to be naturalistic or interpretive.[9] The naturalistic school, which tends to dominate in cognitive science, seeks to resolve the observed phenomena in terms of naturalistic models; hence the appeal of reductive neuroscience. Interpretive approaches, by contrast, tend to respect the autonomy of human beings. Broad consensus is sought but not often achieved, and different schools tend to form as a result of ideological, methodological, and other differences.

The study of anomalies seems far closer to social science than natural, especially with regards to the levels of evidence. When Collins and Pinch wrote about a discipline that was '...all pedantically stated hypotheses, and endless statistical manipulation of marginal data...'[10] they were writing about experimental psychology and not parapsychology, yet the comment seems equally valid for both fields. I would claim that, whilst the quality of evidence for various kinds of psychical phenomena are not up to the standard of the natural sciences, that they compare, in some respects favourably, with a good portion of the evidence within experimental psychology. Similarly, the lack of perceived progress within parapsychology, commonly observed by critics, seems in many respects to be mirrored by the social sciences.

Another complicating factor is that the study of heterodoxies tends to gain the pejorative label of 'pseudoscience'. Bauer suggests that the term is best understood as a *reaction* from the scientific community, rather than denoting something specific. This is in part because it has proved nearly impossible to define clearly 'real' or 'good' science from 'bad' or 'pseudo' science. Many of the features attributed to so-called pseudoscience can also

---

8   Bauer, 2001, p. 7.
9   Bauer, 2001.
10 Collins & Pinch, 1998, p. 141.

crop up in 'real' science, and vice versa. The study of controversies and heterodoxies within and without science are better termed *anomalistics*.[11]

Scepticism and the Dynamics of the 'Psi' Debates

The debates over parapsychological phenomena mainly occur beyond mainstream attention. There is a small parapsychological community whose members operate either as amateurs or as professional psychologists within psychology departments. There has been, historically, the occasional laboratory or research centre devoted to parapsychology, and these have been often but not always privately funded. Today, in the UK, there are several centres devoted to parapsychology and anomalistic psychology, mostly in the New Universities. Most parapsychological work, again with exceptions, tends to be published in specialist journals and is almost totally ignored by mainstream publications like *Science* and *Nature*. Most cognitive scientists seem mostly unaware that this network exists at all.

Similarly, many of the debates over 'psi' are not handled within science at all, but outside.[12] This tendency has been exacerbated, especially in the US, by the rise of organized scepticism. A survey of sceptical literature tends to reveal scepticism of heterodox claims within and without science and proportionally less criticism of many of the claims made within conventional science itself.[13] The orientation tends to be to defend (robust, conventional) science from what often gets labelled 'pseudoscience'. Truzzi claimed that the outlook of such organizations is often better termed 'rationalist' than truly sceptical, or non-believing.[14]

The role of such organizations in resolving the debates over psychic phenomena has not, in my view, been wholly beneficent. As Collins and Pinch warned 'It is important that these vigilante organizations do not become so powerful that they can stamp out all that is strange in the scientific world. Saving the public from charlatans is their role, but scientists must not use them to fight their battles for them'.[15] To a degree this seems to have already happened, as in popular discourse sceptic seems often equated with 'scientific expert'. Rosenblum and Kuttner, in their book on quantum theory and consciousness, report that 'evidence for the existence of paraphenomena strong enough to convince sceptics does not exist'.[16] But the history of science shows that the 'sceptical' side of any controversy, especially at the extreme end, rarely converts, but will often find ways of

---

11   Bauer, 2001.
12   Hansen, 2001.
13   See the magazines *Skeptical Inquirer* in the UK as well as US *Skeptic* for numerous examples.
14   Truzzi, 1987.
15   Collins & Pinch, 1998, pp. 141–2.
16   Rosenblum & Kuttner, 2006, p. 192.

explaining new data in terms of their current world-view.[17] Having said all this, I should acknowledge that 'sceptic' organizations tend to be composed of both *informed* and *uninformed* members, and that the critical comments of the informed parties have proved useful to parapsychology.

The dynamics of the 'psi' debates make objective assessment especially difficult. Strong claims and counter-claims abound. So, on the one hand, Susan Blackmore concludes that '[t]here probably are no paranormal phenomena',[18] whereas Dean Radin claims combined odds against chance from all the 'psi' experiments of 1.3×10^{104} to 1![19] Both parties have many years of experience working within parapsychology, yet both have come to very different conclusions. So we are in a position where one person or group looks at a spread of evidence and finds it convincing, and another person or group looks at the same spread of evidence and finds it unconvincing. Neither party consists of people who are obviously stupid or gullible, but neither, *in extremis*, seem to agree on anything very much.

I do not plan to follow the ins and outs of these debates exhaustively. After a closer look at some sample 'rogue phenomena', I will survey a recent series of articles from the US *Skeptic* magazine, that give overview assessments of the achievements of parapsychology to date. Two of these articles are by self-labelled 'sceptics', and two are by parapsychologists. These examples should be enough to give a general flavour of the sorts of exchanges that occur. But before we do this, we need to know what these disputes are about.

Disputed Human Abilities

There is a whole spectrum of alleged human abilities that lie on or beyond the borderlands of respectability. This spectrum is far wider than is generally recognized, and battles over whether or not to include phenomenon x or y have been periodically fought within and outside the mainstream.

The term *parapsychology* was adopted from the German in the 1930s by J.B. Rhine, who initiated its experimental phase, intending it to mean the study of a small subset of these alleged abilities. Psychic phenomena can be classified in two broad types. The first is Extra Sensory Perception, or ESP. This can be broken down into three categories; *telepathy* (person to person ESP), *clairvoyance* (detection of information about distant or hidden objects and events by ESP), and *precognition* (information about future events gained via ESP). The second major type is PK or *psychokinesis*. This refers to the alleged ability of people to influence objects, events or other

---

17 Kuhn, 1996/1962.
18 Blackmore, 2003, p. 302.
19 Radin, 2006.

people through an act of will.[20] A general collective term for these abilities is *psi*.

The range of disputed abilities goes far beyond the psi subset, and mingles imperceptibly with other phenomena that one would not class as 'psychic'. To illustrate this, I have included stigmata, below, as one case alongside two more traditional parapsychological examples. Stigmata are one of a wide range of psychophysiological effects suggestive of the action of the mind upon the body, only some of which fit into the above classifications.[21]

Alleged extraordinary human abilities are not all equal in terms of *a priori* likelihood, a subtlety often lost in spats between advocates and counter-advocates. In the examples given below, spontaneous bleeding from the hands seems *a priori* more likely than the idea someone can clairvoyantly 'see' images in a distant room, which in turn seems more likely than the possibility that personalities from deceased individuals can manifest in living children.

Pretty much all of the 'rogue phenomena' under consideration at least appear to violate the closure principle in one way or another. Even the humble placebo effect has been questioned because some formulations of it apparently violate this principle: 'We usually think about mental states as emerging from physiological processes. In placebo, there is a mental state that seems to alter physiological processes.'[22] Under this interpretation, then the placebo effect seems to imply some variety of mental causation, and so 'must' be wrong.

Case Studies

To simplify matters, I will first briefly examine three case studies of rogue phenomena, arranged in descending order of *a priori* likelihood. This should give us some idea of the problems raised.

Case Study 1: Stigmata

In Easter Week, 1974, in Emery High School, Oakland, California, a school girl began to bleed spontaneously from her forehead and from the palms of her hands.[23] Twelve-year-old Cloretta Robertson began to bleed in a maths lesson taught by Rev. Anthony Burrus, who reported that 'Blood was flowing all down her face, all over her eyes. It was as though there was a crown of thorns around her head and she was just smiling and talking'.[24] Her wounds persisted, and she was examined by a paediatrician who

---

20 Definitions from Eysenck & Sargent, 1993, p. 10.
21 See chapter three in Kelly *et al.*, 2007, for numerous examples.
22 Kihlstrom, 1993, p. 215. Quoted in Kelly *et al.*, 2007, p. 140.
23 Fahrley & Welfare, 1985.
24 *Op. cit.*, p. 146.

observed spontaneous bleeding from her hands. The doctor observed no wound, only a pea-sized bluish discolouration. The stigmata were also witnessed by a psychiatrist, but they could find no medical explanation for the phenomenon. In time, Cloretta became the centre of a cult at the New Light Baptist Church.

This report raises many issues typical of a stigmata case. There is the question of the religious background and social motivations. There is the issue of fraud. And there is the difficulty of the psychology of the young girl, along with problems of deception and self-deception. Paradoxically, though, the very reasons to suspect hoaxing — namely, a highly religious atmosphere — are also the same factors in which we might expect such a psychosomatic phenomenon to occur.

The Robertson case is hardly unique; the first stigmatic was Sir Francis of Assisi, 700 years ago. Probably the most famous case of the twentieth century is Padre Pio, born in 1918. There is evidence, however, that Padre Pio 'helped' his stigmata with acid.[25]

It is accepted that stress and other emotions can produce marks on the skin. Sometimes, these marks can even be specific. *The Lancet* reported in December 1946 that a 35-year-old man produced rope marks on his skin which were identical with those that had been caused by being forcibly restrained nine years earlier.[26] In 1967, under hypnosis, four disturbed patients were able to spontaneously produce wounds, and it is known that skin conditions like warts are also responsive to hypnosis.[27] There is also the phenomenon of autoerythrocyte sensitization (AES), where a patient who has suffered trauma spontaneously bleeds or bruises.[28] AES may be an autoimmune disorder, but this has not yet been proved.

Stigmata is certainly a dramatic phenomenon, and poorly understood, but it does not break the 'rules' in quite such a dramatic way as other disputed human abilities. Although the problem of fraud exists, it is well enough documented and fits reasonably well with other, medically observed phenomena. It can be explained, with some handwaving, in more-or-less rationalistic terms. Emily Kelly, however, points out that there remain significant unknowns in terms of specific mechanisms; for example, stigmata are not identical to AES because stigmatics do not typically bruise or inflame.

Case Study 2: The Ganzfeld Debate
Experimental technique: Ganzfeld (whole-field) is a method of putting participants into a state of mild sensory deprivation, based upon data that

---

25 Harrison, 1994.
26 Harrison, 1994.
27 Kelly *et al.*, 2007.
28 *Op. cit.*

suggests that sleep-like states are favourable for the production of psi.[29] The subject relaxes in a reclining sofa, their eyes are covered by bisected ping-pong balls and a red light is shone. They listen to a relaxation exercise over headphones, and during the experiment, white noise or static eliminates outside sounds. In a remote room (which in some set-ups, has been in a different building) a 'sender' looks at a still image or watches a brief film clip and tries to 'send' it mentally to the 'receiver'. In the later, automated versions, the same clip is played over and over again during an experimental session, which typically last half an hour. There is also a 'clairvoyance' mode, where a target plays without a sender. In the early ganzfelds, this meant that a single picture or postcard had been selected from a target set and was hidden in an envelope. During the session, an experimenter is on hand to record any mental impressions or 'mentations' the 'receiver' reports.

After the session, the 'receiver' is played one of four clips (or in earlier static tests, was shown one of four images) and has to choose which one most closely fits the target. According to chance expectations, they would select the target 25% of the time.

Debate: The 'ganzfeld' debate was the major issue in parapsychology in the 1980s and 1990s. It had a number of phases and concerned replicability of the effect over studies, and whether or not methodological flaws could account for any positive effects. Two separate meta-analyses were conducted by advocate Charles Honorton and the counter-advocate Ray Hyman. Overall hit rates for twenty-eight early studies were in the order of ten billion to one, but Hyman thought this might be due to flaws giving false positives. In 1986, Hyman and Honorton wrote a joint communiqué in the hope of ironing out these potential flaws in future experiments.[30] In response, an 'autoganzfeld' system was created to conform to the communiqué. By 1994, Daryl Bem and Honorton had published a paper in the *Psychological Bulletin* showing that in the 364 sessions of the autoganzfeld in which 240 subjects had participated, 122 direct hits had occurred giving a 34% hit rate. Odds were forty-five thousand to one.[31]

However, in 1999, counter-advocates Milton and Wiseman published an update with 30 studies conducted between 1991 and 1996 and found a near-zero effect size. They did concede that no potential methodological flaw could explain away the positive results of the autoganzfeld in 'any immediately compelling way'.[32] They had also left out a number of studies, including a highly significant one. Radin compared the first 44 studies with the last and found that whilst the former had a 34.4% hit rate, the lat-

---

29 Eysenck & Sargent, 1993.
30 Hyman & Honorton, 1986.
31 Bem & Honorton, 1994.
32 Milton & Wiseman, 1999, p. 389.

ter had a 30.3% rate; still significant, but smaller. This 'decline effect' has been noted several times before in the parapsychological literature.[33]

Most recently, Storm, Tressoldi and Di Risio analysed 29 ganzfeld studies from 1997 to 2008. Of the 1,498 trials, 483 produced hits, corresponding to a hit rate of 32.2%. This hit rate is statistically significant.[34] Chris Roe has also reported a positive result from a meta-analysis of 10 further studies performed since the last one.[35] Despite this, critics remain unmoved, pointing to the negative definition of psi and suspecting that, although more obvious errors have been ironed out, the results may prove to be experimental artefacts. In reply to the Storm *et al.* article, Hyman accused the authors of 'manufacturing' a consistent result via data selection, and claimed that parapsychology needed to develop a positive theory in order to explain the alleged effects.[36] In turn, Storm *et al.* accused Hyman of one-sidedness and argued for further research.[37]

Case Study 3: The Past-Life Memories of Children

The Case Studies: These are cases when young children produce often accurate memories of previous lives, and in some cases have birthmarks corresponding to injuries from past lives. They have mostly but not exclusively been collected by a team led by Ian Stevenson, a psychiatrist at the University of Virginia, who has amassed over 2,500 such cases.[38] Most, but not all, of these cases come from regions where there is a belief in reincarnation; India, Thailand, Jordan and amongst the Druses in Lebanon. There have been comparable cases in Europe and the Middle East.

Apparent past-life memories manifest in a number of ways. For example, Suzanne Ghanem of Lebanon claimed she was 'Leila', and she began telling her family of a previous life that ended with a trip to the United States for heart surgery. Her family did not track down her previous personality until she was five, who had died in the US after heart surgery and had a daughter called Leila. Suzanne made forty statements about her previous life that could be verified, including the names of twenty-five former associates.[39]

In another case, Chanai Choomaliaiwong was born in Thailand in 1967 with two birthmarks, one on the back of his head and one above the left eye. When he was three, he began to talk of a previous life in which he had been shot and killed on the way to school. He gave the names of his parents, wife and two children from that life and identified the location of his

---

33 See Colborn, 2007, for a summary.
34 Storm, Tressoldi & Di Risio, 2010a.
35 Roe, 2010.
36 Hyman, 2010a.
37 Storm, Tessoldi & Di Risio, 2010b.
38 Tucker, 2005.
39 Tucker, 2005.

home. The location of his birthmarks also corresponded with the gunshot wounds. These details were confirmed by Stevenson upon investigation.[40]

Debate: Reactions to this data have been varied and mostly dependent upon the reactor's belief system. Stevenson's data has been held by some to be the best supporting survival, but by others as insufficiently controlled and biased. A significant issue is that most of the best cases come from cultures where a belief in reincarnation is strong, so children could in theory confabulate a previous life and be encouraged in this confabulation by their parents. In this view, the details of a previous life might be attained by lucky guesses or maybe by hearsay. Fraud is not impossible in some cases, and Braude notes that survival researchers have often underestimated the psychological needs and complexity of the witnesses in these cases.[41]

Angel has criticized Stevenson and his successors as failing to eliminate the 'null hypothesis'.[42] He has challenged the team to run experiments mixing up true past-life statements with bogus ones to see whether one could tell the difference. Criticisms of this sort are not new, however; Louisa Rhine made a similar point in her review of Stevenson's *20 Cases Suggestive of Reincarnation*. She worried that the parents might have read meaning into the children's memories and built up a fictional story around them, and also worried about biased judgments and the lack of controls.[43] Stevenson replied that he had taken these factors into account and pointed out that if, as Rhine acknowledged, fraud and hidden memories were unlikely, then how could parents build up a 'fictional' personality which included significant numbers of accurate statements about the former personality?[44]

Other criticisms tend to be more generic. In a useful compendium of arguments against reincarnation, Paul Edwards calls the very idea 'ridiculous'.[45] He suggests that the sheer unlikelihood of the concept means that a combination of lies, fallible memories and faulty powers of observation *must* be considered a more likely explanation for all Stevenson's data. Despite these issues, and whatever the cause of these memories, this phenomenon has proved persistent enough to be worthy of further study.

Four Recent Overviews of the Psi Controversy

Having considered these case studies, it is instructive to consider the current state of the field. Recently, the US *Skeptic* magazine asked two coun-

---

40 Stevenson, 1997; Tucker, 2005.
41 Braude, 2003.
42 Angel, 2008.
43 Rhine, 1966.
44 Stevenson, 1967.
45 Edwards, 1996.

ter-advocates and two advocates to offer their views of the progress of parapsychology. The responses are illustrative of the sorts of divisions and perspectives that are fairly typical of the debates.

Ray Hyman, a 'sceptic', charted the demise of parapsychology from 1850 to 2008, claiming that the field 'no longer exists'.[46] He noted that those originating the discipline claimed both the status of a science and that it would meet strict scientific criteria, and that the initial aim was to gather evidence for psi that met these criteria. He then claims that this goal has, in the last decade or so, been recognized as unrealistic by what he terms 'neo-parapsychologists'. These researchers acknowledge that psi tends to be inconsistent, elusive and 'fails to meet scientific criteria'.[47] This admission, Hyman claims, has killed the traditional idea of parapsychology.

He is similarly scathing about claims for replicable psi effects, as in the ganzfeld. He claims that claims for strong replications are 'illusory', criticizing the meta-analysis technique on methodological grounds. He also claimed that, despite claims, a failure to replicate basic effects was still common in parapsychology.

He then moved onto other, familiar criticisms, including the lack of a positive definition of the concept and a criticism of recent theories that attempt to provide a theory to account for the 'elusive' nature of psi. He concluded by saying that '...scientific methods without a lawful, scientific and replicable phenomenon cannot be science'.[48]

Richard Wiseman, another sceptic, agrees with much of what Hyman has to say, and also focuses on the replicability problem. He points out that 'The main problem is that the databases they draw upon [to demonstrate psi effects] are constructed retrospectively, and the alleged effects have a curious habit of not replicating in prospective studies'.[49] When replication fails, Wiseman says, parapsychologists swap procedures and again experience a failure to reproduce replicable effects. He calls this 'ship jumping' and sees it as a constant feature of parapsychological research. He ends by providing three recommendations to avoid this pattern of 'false dawns':

- Parapsychologists should recommend one or two procedures that have already yielded promising results and focus on them instead of trying lots of new ones.
- They should arrange for several labs to carry out methodologically sound and 'psi conducive' replications.
- Problems with retrospective meta-analyses might be avoided by registering key details of studies.

46 Hyman, 2010b, p. 17.
47 Hyman, 2010b, p. 17.
48 Hyman, 2010b, p. 20.
49 Wiseman, 2010, p. 21.

- He claims that if these details were adhered to, parapsychology might finally be able to 'come in from the cold'.[50]

Caroline Watt, a parapsychologist, provided the third piece. Firstly, she agreed with some of the points both Wiseman and Hyman made, especially about the need to focus on the most promising paradigms. However, she noted that a number of features of the field meant that it was difficult to reach closure on the psi question. These included that there were less than 100 researchers worldwide who were actively researching, and of those, many will also spend time on the psychology of paranormal experiences and beliefs. She pointed out that 'purely as a numbers game, it would be surprising if much could be learned about the possible existence and nature of psi under these circumstances'.[51]

She also criticized Hyman's portrayal of 'neoparapsychologists', claiming that it was unfair to portray them as claiming that psi cannot be tested in a 'scientific' manner. She claimed instead that this group were claiming that parapsychological claims could not be made with usual scientific techniques, but that testable predictions can be made.

The final article, by parapsychologist Chris Roe, asked when the evidence might be called sufficient. He responded to Hyman's claim by saying that the death of parapsychology was an exaggeration. Firstly, he questioned the assumption that gaining the recognition of the scientific community and meeting exacting standards were the primary goal of the founders of parapsychology. He claimed instead that the founders of the SPR were committed to 'extend the reach' of the scientific method. Contemporary parapsychology, similarly, seeks to 'make the best sense of an array of phenomena that superficially seem difficult to accommodate in our current worldview…'[52]

Roe then reconsidered some of the claims that replicable evidence for psi effects had been found. He notes that Hyman's criticisms rest on 'vague allusions' to lack of experimental quality and about limitations inherent to meta-analyses (limits that, as Roe notes, are not specific to parapsychology). Roe also points out that Hyman never makes the 'established criteria' to which parapsychology is supposed to adhere especially clear.

As to replication, Roe points out how easy it is to selectively report either positive or negative results if one focuses on specific studies, stating that 'we must accept that individual studies are susceptible to giving outcomes that reflect sampling error and also are affected by idiosyncratic features of the experimental environment'.[53] Whilst admitting that the

---

50 Wiseman, 2010, p. 22.
51 Watt, 2010, p. 23.
52 Roe, 2010, p. 23.
53 Roe, 2010, pp. 24–5.

ganzfeld results were not robust and heterogeneous, he went on to claim that a good case could be made for this being in part due to different experimenters posing different research questions. He then quoted a paper by Bem, Palmer and Broughton which demonstrated a strong correlation between studies that closely replicated Honorton's original approach and a hit rate of 31.2%.[54] Roe states that 'That looks rather like replication to me'.[55]

Finally, Roe criticizes the claim that parapsychologists have had 150 years to try and fail to deliver the scientific goods. He observes that the rhetorical device encourages the reader to assume that this time was filled with intensive activity, whereas in fact, comparatively speaking, very few people have been at work at the problem. Roe also commented upon the tendency of parapsychology to flit from one technique to another like a butterfly. He interprets this because parapsychology contains a disproportionately large number of innovators, rather than 'technicians' who run more routine experiments (even so, he claims, technicians do exist, and some replication of routine experiments occurs). He also agrees with Wiseman and Watt about systematizing a research programme, and focusing on the most promising experiments.

This exchange is instructive because it reveals what Dick terms the 'differing cultures' of science.[56] The counter-advocates tend to invoke the high standards of natural science, and Hyman's comment that a science must include 'lawful, scientific and replicable phenomen[a]...' is telling in this regard.[57] Hyman clearly belongs to the school of social science that wishes to naturalize its chosen area of study, rather than simply note and observe the idiosyncrasies of human behaviour. One suspects that, to Hyman, parapsychology can only be scientific if it is *like the natural sciences*.

On the other hand, the advocates tend to argue for a more liberal approach. Roe argues for an extension of the 'scientific method' and the use of a range of conceptual and methodological tools to make the best sense of an array of phenomena. This suggests a subtly different approach and definition of what constitutes science. His interpretation of replication, too, seems far closer to the sorts of replication found in the social sciences rather than the natural.

I would suggest that the insistence that parapsychology can only be 'scientific' if it adheres to the 'standards' of natural science is unrealistic. The standards to which parapsychology is supposed to adhere can also be modified indefinitely by critics *because there are no such standards*; as

---

54 Bem, Palmer & Broughton, 2001.
55 Roe, 2010, p. 25.
56 Dick, 1996.
57 I would also query the assumption that all 'real' phenomena must behave in a lawful manner. There is no reason to suppose that everything in the natural world follows laws or regularities; see comments in chapter six and the conclusion.

Feyerabend observes, most of the major advances that have occurred in science have been through the modification or abandonment of any such standards that were held to be essential to 'proper' research.[58] And many of the standards that are appealed to ('the scientific method', hypothesis testing, falsifiability, etc.) can be found to have been broken within conventional science, because they are *post hoc* rationalizations as opposed to rigid requirements that one *must* follow to get research — especially on the frontiers — to work.

Recent Philosophical/Theoretical Trends

Recent theoretical trends in parapsychology seek to accommodate the phenomena within physicalism by offering explanations couched in terms of new physics. This often involves using interpretations of metaphors drawn from quantum theory. Radin explicitly draws parallels between the sorts of 'nonlocality' and observer effects seen in quantum experiments with the effects apparently observed in psi experiments. The theories he surveys include signal-transfer theories, theories of goal orientation, field and multidimensional theories. He also outlines five theories inspired by quantum mechanics; observational theory, 'pragmatic information theories', 'weak-quantum theory', Bohm's implicate/explicate order and a Stapp-von Neumann model.[59] (The latter being an extension of the theory discussed in chapter nine.)

The claim tends to be that, while psi phenomena may seem to be incompatible with the assumptions of classical physics, the new physics and especially quantum theory are more congenial. Other writers sympathetic to psi phenomena argue that quantum theory would have to be extended beyond its current form to adequately accommodate such phenomena.[60] It should also be noted that others interpret said theory as specifically forbidding psychic effects.[61] Collins and Pinch, offering a useful if dated survey, found the arguments for and against accommodating psi via quantum physics to be inconclusive.[62]

Other recent researchers have sought to repudiate parapsychology's 'dualist' origins in favour of physicalism. Edge observes that parapsychology 'has been moving in the direction of naturalism',[63] and cites the quantum entanglement theories mentioned in Radin as evidence of this. He sees parapsychologists as more likely to regard psi as a 'natural' rather than 'mind-dependent' phenomenon, as new physics interpretations

---

58 Feyerabend, 1975.
59 Radin, 2006, chapter thirteen.
60 Carr, 2008.
61 See Collins & Pinch, 1982, chapter four.
62 Collins & Pinch, 1982.
63 Edge, 2008.

make this possible. Edge claims that, in light of modern neuroscience and philosophy of mind, there is no mind/body problem in parapsychology. He justifies this by (1) embracing expanded physicalism, including neurobiological reductionism, (2) accepting a naturalistic view of personhood, and (3) adopting the entanglement idea of quantum physics.

However, there is some doubt whether psychic phenomena can be accommodated so easily. Even if we posit that it is the whole person (or even 'brain') that can influence other people's minds, somehow communicate directly to another person, or see the future via some form of entanglement, this still implies a very different sort of universe from the one that most scientists inhabit. Braude points out that whilst the existence of ESP and PK do not really offer support for substance dualism, they *do* imply an animistic universe. This is most obvious in the case of PK. Braude notes that once we admit the existence of any kind of PK,

> ...we will be forced to entertain seriously a world-view associated only with so-called primitive cultures. It is a kind of magical worldview, according to which thoughts can have hostile (and even lethal) consequences, and in which our conscious and subconscious desires can surreptitiously influence the course of our lives...[64]

As Griffin points out, the closure principle was initially constructed specifically to exclude this sort of thinking.[65]

Inconvenient Evidence for Survival

Evidence suggesting survival beyond bodily death is a problem for a discipline that seems eager to subsume itself within a physicalist frame. Edge admits that, 'the philosophical issues become more difficult with a more naturalized understanding of a person'.[66] He observes that it may be difficult to identify which aspects of personhood would need to survive in order to build a concept of survival. He also alludes to the methodological problems that have plagued survival research, claiming that we have not solved the super-psi hypothesis (i.e. that, for example, children claiming reincarnation have gained their knowledge via a very powerful form of telepathy or clairvoyance). Edge concludes by saying 'I do not think that we have been able to designate what would count straight-forwardly as evidence for survival and not be thought of as an example of psi on the part of the living'.[67] A short answer might be that if (1) we cannot delimit the capacities of 'psi', and (2) it is all-pervasive, then it may be impossible to distinguish between the two. All we can do, as some writers have already attempted, is balance probabilities in individual cases; although I

64 Braude, 1987, p. 286.
65 Griffin, 1997.
66 Edge, 2008, p. 457.
67 Edge, 2008, p. 458.

would say that in the case of the reincarnation stories, the quality and quantity of correct facts sometimes seems to outweigh the 'hit' rate in experimental tests of ESP.[68]

This suspicion of survival theories can be seen as an example of how reformulating one's metaphysics recalibrates one's conceptual filters in favour of accepting some data and rejecting others. In my personal experience of the field, I have found that different people tend to find different sub-phenomena acceptable or unacceptable, often according to some quite arbitrary standards. Some people, for example, accept ESP but strain at PK. Others accept PK but reject precognition. When pressed, rationalizations ensue, but anecdotally, beliefs about *a priori* plausibility seem quite idiosyncratic.

As previously mentioned, my own bias is away from survival, in part because of the increasingly torrential amount of neuroscientific data suggesting a close dependence of conscious thoughts on sometimes very specific parts of the brain. Whilst, too, I have had occasional experiences that suggest to me some form of psychic functioning, I have not seen anything that would make me think any part of us survives beyond death (and I have observed quite a lot that suggests the opposite). Having said this, *some* of the so-called survival evidence makes me wonder, a bit.

On the other hand, I am not satisfied by the conventional explanations for some of the survival evidence, including the reincarnation cases. It could be, as Gauld suggests in an overview of Stevenson's work, that the two seemingly contradictory bodies of evidence are reconcilable via some unknown linking factor that we have not yet discovered or thought of. Such contradictions between bodies of knowledge, Gauld observes, have occurred before. In the nineteenth century, Darwin's theory of evolution apparently contradicted physics. This was because calculations suggested that the Sun was not nearly old enough for the length of time needed for evolution to occur. This dilemma was resolved by the discovery of nuclear physics, which extended the Sun's theoretical life by billions of years, giving ample time for evolution.

Gauld concludes that in such cases, it does not follow that, where the evidence produced by either parties seems to contradict, one is 'right' and the other 'wrong'. He suggests that 'perhaps a previously unknown factor may intervene in the reincarnation/brain function case...'[69] The moral seems to be that one should not throw out one set of data just because it appears to contradict another.

---

[68] Gauld, 1982; Braude, 2003.
[69] Gauld, 2008, p. 30.

Conclusion

We return to the theme of the in part arbitrary nature of our individual and collective world-views, and how profoundly this shapes the ways in which we perceive the world. Fort satirically observed that 'Science relates to real knowledge no more than does the growth of a plant, or the organization of a department store…'[70] And any system must exclude as well as include. Perhaps the conceit is that we can fit the whole phenomenal universe inside one belief system.

On the other hand, it does not help that many of the things of which we have doubts seem transient and difficult to reduce to systematic science. Unfortunately for the parapsychologists, the levels of evidence demanded by the critics may be difficult or even impossible to obtain. The evidence from spontaneous cases strongly suggests that, generally speaking, the phenomena tend not to be consciously controllable, which further compounds difficulties. In case after case of alleged psychic experience, we find that people 'know' things they shouldn't, and cannot say why.[71] Our demand for control may be unreasonable in such circumstances. All we can do is continue to watch, and neglect demands that we turn our heads away.

---

70 Fort, 1974, p. 22.
71 See Rhine, 1981, for some examples.

Conclusion

Pluralism, Consciousness and Society

To conclude, I will consider two outstanding problems:
(1) *Could* we construct a one-size-fits-all theory of consciousness?
(2) *Should* we construct such a theory to the exclusion of others?

The short answer to question (1) is probably affirmative, within limits, and provided one is willing to reduce 'consciousness' to functions, objects, 'information-processing', or maybe novel physical processes, and provided one is willing to actively supress or to subsume alternative models and/or modes of knowing. As for question (2), I will argue *against* the *desirability* of constructing a one-size-fits-all theory of consciousness.

This latter argument represents a significant break from prevailing assumptions within the field of consciousness studies, where different factions compete over problems in what is often perceived as a zero-sum game, where the winner takes all. This is why the disputes are often characterized in either martial ('battle of metaphors') or in frontier terms (e.g. the descent of a mountain). In contrast to this, I question whether the supremacy of one faction would be either good for science or good for the populace at large, who, in a science-led society, will also have to live with the ramifications of a predominant theory.

Now this may seem a startling—or even perverse—position, because consensus is often seen as being desirable within science. The whole point of a shared paradigm—as Kuhn ably explained—is that shared assumptions, research techniques, technical language, etc. allows the development of an enterprise where researchers can build upon the work of others and participate in a theoretical and applied research programme. The lack of a consensus, by contrast, could be perceived as bad because it divides resources and makes technical progress more difficult, partly because different scientists have to begin conceptually from scratch each time they start a research project.[1]

---

1 Kuhn, 1996/1962.

Since any given consensus view is also held to represent the best approximation to nature at a given time, it is also held to be desirable because it reflects a truth. It is this factor that makes challenging a given consensus very difficult because one tends to be perceived as advocating falsehood. The situation is complicated when it is claimed that significant, practical, harm may result from deviating from the consensus view, which potentially makes the dissenter foolish as well as wrong. A dissenter from a consensus is often perceived as deviating from *nature* and not from a human social choice.[2]

In social terms, a consensus also means that those originating and supporting ruling paradigms get money and resources. Practically speaking, the more ubiquitous a research paradigm, the more powerful it becomes and the greater its social and political reach. This provides a very strong incentive for promoting one's own favoured approach and for denigrating alternatives.

If this latter point sounds cynical, or at least removed from more ideal depictions, we should remember that science, today, is very different from how it was in the past. Science now constitutes a career and a profession within institutions that are woven into the fabric of our technological society or 'military-industrial-academic complex'. Different factions, or power-interests, vie within institutional structures, as they do in any other bureaucracy.[3] Workers within science, too, are subject to the same economic and social restraints as the rest of us, often serving the various interests that fund them, which include the military and, increasingly, big business. Finally, whilst democratic traditions do exist within science, there also exist various mechanisms by which knowledge gets monopolized by what Bauer terms 'research cartels'.[4]

Unfortunately for the rest of us, and because we live in a society that is profoundly shaped by science and technology, decisions made behind closed doors within these 'knowledge cartels' often have significant ramifications in our own, private lives. This observation is especially true when we consider decisions about human nature, where elite choices can have significant personal, social, medical, legal, and even political impacts. Such significant influences are often justified by assertions like 'experts know best', that experts are disinterested, that the research programmes reveal truths about human nature via a powerful 'scientific method', and that they are working in the interests of humankind as a whole.

The problem with this sort of story is that it presumes (1) the unqualified benevolence (not to mention ideological neutrality) of those working

---

2   It is, of course, very difficult to generalize about the accuracy of this claim to truth, still less about the claim to harm. I suspect that assessments need to be made on a case by case basis.
3   Martin, 1979; 1999.
4   Bauer, 2004.

within science, (2) that these workers *alone* have access to tools to discern 'truth' (e.g. the 'scientific method'), and (3) that non-specialized 'laypeople' should just passively accept whatever decision these supposedly neutral experts arrive at, *even if it conflicts with their own personal values and beliefs*. Each of these assumptions is highly questionable, especially in a world where these often unaccountable experts are developing tools that allow, for example, unprecedented levels of control of the brain—and routinely selling these techniques to the highest bidder.[5] In this situation, the stakes are just too high to take the mostly publicly unaccountable expert's word for it.

Could We Construct a One-Size-Fits-All Theory of Consciousness?

With these considerations aired, we are now ready to return to the question with which we started, concerning the gap between our personal conscious experiences and the models of science. Recall Searle's question of '[h]ow can we square [the] self-conception of ourselves as mindful, meaning-creating, free, rational, etc., agents with a universe that consists entirely of mindless, meaningless, unfree, nonrational, brute physical particles?'[6] There are a range of possible responses to this question, a selection of which have been surveyed in this book, but here I would like to focus upon three broad-brush responses, each of which has conceptual costs:

(1) One can *objectify* consciousness (i.e. reduce 'it' to function, information-processing, representations, neural patterns, quantum effects, etc.) *Cost:* To achieve this, one must narrow the definition of consciousness to fit one's particular, often technical, definition. This approach also seems the most dehumanizing if applied much beyond specific technical problems.

(2) One can admit that subjects are not fully reducible to objects. *Cost:* May imply a form of dualist or anti-materialist stance or at least a break from reductive monism. Some versions may imply 'mysterianism'.

(3) One can accept the limits of (1) and (2) whilst simultaneously accepting that *both* approaches may sometimes be valid within restricted or local situations but not in others. Some versions of (3) entail a rejection of universalism, and/or the idea that one *can* have a 'grand scheme' of consciousness. *Cost:* This would amount to admitting that

---

5   A quick survey of the websites of several top neuroscientists will reveal close ties to commercial and military interests; I invite the reader to do their own research to confirm this. In the US, the Bayh-Dole Act (1980) prompted many academics to develop close commercial ties with industry and to profit from publicly funded research. In the UK, a cash-strapped academe has been encouraged by successive governments to form close links with private interests. The image of the 'neutral' academic voice—if it was ever appropriate—cannot apply in such an atmosphere. The problem is that the *myth* of such neutrality still persists.

6   Searle, 2007, p. 5.

science has limits and also may imply *some form* of cultural/ epistemological relativism.

Option (1) is clearly the option favoured within conventional science, and covers both reductive and non-reductive modes where conscious states supposedly 'supervene' on a material substrate. Whether one thinks consciousness can be fully reduced to neural patterns or whether one favours a non-reductive solution, one is *still* seeking to reduce consciousness to a function or ultimately 'physical' property (or, at most, 'information-processing'). The underlying assumption here is an ontology of monistic physicalism, which is presumed to be non-negotiable.

Even if we stick to option (1), physicalism remains a broad church, or at least broader than many accounts suggest. For example, one is *not* committed to strong determinism, universalism, or other classical assumptions within this church. There are also a number of encouraging trends within biology that suggest a move away from excessively narrow and mechanistic views of life, and towards holistic views that promise to provide richer and broader accounts of biological causation, perception, and maybe consciousness. An expanded biology, as explored in chapter seven, may also point beyond the mechanistic *impasse* in which neuroscience finds itself.

So if one *must* be a physicalist, at least one does not have to be a narrow physicalist. Maybe we can even concede that physicalist assumptions hold well within the restricted circumstances of certain cognitive and neuroscience experiments, and only begin to fall apart when one attempts to place them within a wider context involving whole personalities. But for reasons explored through this book, I am far from convinced that even non-reductive physicalism works very well when considering phenomenal consciousness in the broader sense.

Option (2) tends to get fiercely resisted because of its dualistic implications, and because admitting that the subject may be in some sense 'irreducible' might be seen as giving up. In a way, (2) was Descartes' solution but, being an heir of essentialism even whilst rejecting it, he made his observer a concrete substance and so initiated the 'mind/body' problem in its modern form. I am afraid, however, that we may be stuck with the problem of the irreducible observer, at least in some contexts. As Rosen observed, dualisms (i.e. splits, discriminations) tend to be fundamental to science, the most fundamental being that of the observing scientist and the observed system.

Option (2) also accommodates a wide range of anti- or non-materialist conceptions (dualism, neutral monism, anti-reductionist hylomorphism, idealism, etc.)[7] As previously discussed, my favoured solution, if we feel we *must* marry 'objective' models with subjective, is for a form of property pluralism, where it is admitted that physical descriptions are not exhaus-

---

7   See Koons & Bealer, 2010, for a survey of some anti-materialist stances.

tive, and that alternative takes can furnish us or allow us to see non-physical or perhaps holistic attributes (consciousness, intentionality, etc.) that seem incommensurable with physical or even information-processing models. But I would repeat that in some respects this seems an awkward compromise to me.

Despite their declared allegiance to physicalism, I would class Elsasser and Rosen's work as sitting on the boundary between option (1) and (2), simply because aspects of holism naturally strain the claim that (existing) physical models plus information-processing are sufficient for accounting for biological causation. Rosen's approach seems very close to anti-reductionist hylomorphism to me, and Elsasser admits that his theory of memory resembles 'parapsychology'. These sorts of theories may, however, help to 'bridge the gap' between the holistic, qualitative attributes and reductive, quantitative attributes of organisms.

Even if we reject 'quantum' interpretations of consciousness, I think that we have a lot to learn from physics on the topic of incorporating the observer into our experimental accounts. Consciousness researchers would profit much by referring to the epistemological discussions concerning the transition from classical to relativistic and quantum physics that occurred early last century.[8] Many of these concerned the place of the observer, a revision of the classical notion of the world being made up of discrete 'objects', and a questioning of then sacrosanct notions concerning the laws of nature. The first, and most obvious target in the current context should probably be the mostly unquestioned application of the closure principle.

Currently, much of cognitive science seems to function by simply supressing or ignoring the problem of subjectivity, which has the price of treating the observed system (i.e. human or animal participants) as passive mechanisms. But this strategy is only sustainable if one assumes that the subsystem one is examining is mostly stable and/or an easily defined natural kind that will not be significantly perturbed by observations and manipulations. Many of the neuroimaging experiments seem to assume this by claiming that experimental manipulations simply reveal what is already there—i.e. they presume a sort of naïve naturalism. Sometimes this assumption may be more-or-less sound, as with low-level perceptual phenomena. Other times, however, I suspect that concrete results become called into existence via reification, iatrogenesis, and specific experimental conditions.

---

8   See the introduction of Wheeler & Zurek, 1983, for an outline of the philosophical disputes over measurement. See also Feyerabend, 1987, chapter seven, for Mach's philosophy and its influence on Einstein. Mach's work caused Einstein to question the classical laws of physics, which he had previously regarded as sacrosanct. In my view, a similar questioning is urgently needed today in the philosophy of mind; but unfortunately, institutional science is not an especially easy place to do this.

I suspect that the situation may be far worse in neuroscience than in subatomic physics, again not necessarily because consciousness might be 'quantum' but because human organisms are in some senses the definition of perturbed systems, and exist in social and semantic matrices from which they cannot really be separated, even in experiments. This means that factors like *meaning* and *purpose*, which cannot be easily quantified, may significantly contribute to the outcome of experiments—including the physical patterns observed in neuroimaging. In such a situation, 'experimenter effects' may be the tip of the iceberg.

One problem with accepting this is the expectation that, to be causally efficacious, mental events have to be akin to a sort of 'force' that operates the brain rather as a player operates a piano, to use Sir John Eccles' metaphor.[9] This is often countered, in some respects reasonably, by the observation that no such force is apparent when examining brain function (and by questioning the coherence of the idea of 'mental events').[10] My own suspicion is that, parapsychological data notwithstanding, this 'force' metaphor is too literal and again ends up objectifying subjective concepts in order to make them comprehensible within a certain way of looking. But this still leaves the problem of how meaning and nuance may be causally efficacious in the world.

Whilst I can claim no easy way to reconcile this problem, my own suspicion is that something like an extended version of Rosennean complexity may be needed to resolve it, if indeed it is resolvable. For example, if one can analyse an organism by 'throwing away' the physics and examining the organization, I do not see why one cannot throw away both the physics and organization and examine patterns of meaning and purpose.[11] (The aforementioned cost of this is property pluralism and at least a partial rejection of monistic physicalism.) But if we do this, then we can say that these factors contribute to the overall causal pattern of the organism without being reducible to physics, organization, or function. The main problem with this from the point of view of formal science is that these factors are not easily quantifiable and are frequently idiosyncratic.

This latter issue can be clarified by returning to the writing of Walter Elsasser. Elsasser noted that, whilst science itself must remain 'rational', there was no guarantee that nature herself *could* be comprehensively ordered into a fully rational scheme. A consequence of assuming that nature *can* be so reduced implies that, for example, the Cartesian method can be relied upon, but a consequence of its abandonment is that we widen the scope of philosophical argument significantly beyond rationalistic

---

9 Popper & Eccles, 1977; Eccles, 1994.
10 See for example, Melnyk, 2003.
11 Putnam, 1998/1988, suggests something similar.

concepts.[12] Elsasser's solution to this problem was to reclaim intuition as a legitimate means of filling in the gaps left by a limited rationalism (in practice, this occurs anyway — it just tends to get hidden or denied). He also recognized that, although highly successful within certain bounds, it was important to face up to the limits of our rational knowledge.

To clarify this, Elsasser exchanged the notion of 'rational' for that of repetitiveness, noting that 'repetition of phenomena is the necessary condition for experiments to be always feasible'.[13] But spontaneous and idiosyncratic phenomena rarely repeat in an orderly manner, if at all, and Elsasser suggested that science may have to re-learn its conceptual language so as to come nearer to the 'language of nature' than it does currently. One of the most urgent facets of this is a rejection of homogeneity as a necessary parameter of scientific models, and to embrace the deeply heterogeneous nature of organisms in general and human beings in particular.

Now apply this observation to conscious activity, which has been defined as in some sense the converse of robotic (e.g. repetitive) behaviour.[14] Experiments in neuroscience are subject to just the same restraints that occur in other parts of experimental science — they are geared towards netting repetitive or robotic responses, replicable patterns, stable differences. Instability and idiosyncrasy tend to get jettisoned or de-emphasized. Under such circumstances, it seems unsurprising that human beings tend to be perceived as uniform robots in these circumstances, but this could be said to be an observer artefact. The result, however, is a terribly skewed and partial view of human beings.

The assertion that there may be limits to rational enquiries can lead to accusations of 'mysterianism', or the idea that some aspects of consciousness may forever lie beyond our reach.[15] But let us turn this charge on its head, and ask what those who are *not* mysterians wish to achieve, and I think the answer is pretty clear from their writings: comprehensive and extensive (and ironically, mechanistic) naturalization, which in practice often means that consciousness *must* yield to some form of solution (1) or, at most, and with a grudge, some heavily diluted form of solution (2). If this is achieved, the story goes, then we may finally comprehensively understand our place within a 'fields and forces' world-view.

But the 'universe of mindless, meaningless, brute physical particles' does not exist out there in the phenomenological world, but *only within the models of science*. To understand this, we should recall Protagoras's point about 'man being the measure of all things'. *We* project various qualities

---

12 Elsasser, 1998, chapter twelve.
13 Elsasser, 1997, p. 131.
14 Crick & Koch, 2003.
15 Flanagan, 1992.

and properties out into the world,[16] and as the ancients and medieval thinkers projected life and animation, many scientific rationalists tend to project mechanism and meaninglessness. But the latter is just as much a conceptual, imaginative vision as the former. The main reason it has such force is that it is built into the very fabric of our culture, and reinforced via the practical marvels and achievements of science. But these achievements do not point to such a vision being 'true'; in fact, Einstein was probably right to suggest that they constitute *fictions* by which we make broad sense of the cosmos.[17]

These sorts of considerations weight my own personal inclination towards response (3), which entails a rejection of universalism. As mentioned, this response has a price which means that we admit that the world-views of science have limitations and that we might have to admit some form of epistemological and/or cultural relativism.

Relativistic approaches tend to be rejected in science because of the perception that they render all ideas equal, so, for example, the idea of a flat Earth has parity with the idea of a round Earth. But such extreme philosophical relativism is not the only sort that is possible. It is perfectly feasible to allow for local truths and for the possibility of robust pragmatic utility (e.g. technologies), but to assert that differing traditions may have valid takes on the world they inhabit and to have approached truths that Western science has not or cannot. This is reinforced by the following consideration.

Throughout the course of this book, I have considered a range of arguments for the rejection of universally applicable 'laws', research methods, theoretical stances. In the case of the mind/body problem, we have a wide range of responses ranging from monistic, eliminative materialism to substance pluralism or even strong animism, with a dozen and one potential stances in between. If we take universalism, objectivism and epistemological realism as correct, then, broadly speaking, one and one only of these stances can be true. However, if one comes to see any given approach as, not a potential 'truth', but an *inevitably partial and distorted imaginative vision* of how the world might be, then it becomes far easier to imagine that each of these stances may provide a more-or-less fruitful orientation towards the world.

Some of these stances may, of course, be more pragmatically useful than others, and one reason why mechanistic, monistic physicalism and the Cartesian method have dominated is that they facilitate research programmes

---

16   To put it another way, there exists *no* certain means by which we can formally segregate those properties which we project onto the cosmos and those that might be thought of as separate of us or 'objective'. At best, we can assign greater or lesser 'objectivity' to various properties on a case-by-case basis but we cannot absolutely separate the 'subjective' from the 'objective' because these poles form part of a continuum.

17   Feyerabend, 1987.

and technologies. Alternative methods of viewing the mind and consciousness have, so far, proved less pragmatically useful — from the point of view of science and technology. However, a pragmatic criterion of truth, based on usefulness, can go beyond science and technology. The key question is: useful to whom, and why? There are therapies where an interactive dualist stance, as an approximation, arguably functions better than a physicalist one. A recent example of such a therapy is Jeffrey Schwartz's treatment for OCD sufferers, where patients actively, consciously modify their behaviour, which in turn seems to modify brain function over time.[18] The interesting thing about such a therapy is that it was *not* devised by a physicalist. To this we may add a long list of alternative therapies, a good portion of which have been clinically demonstrated to work, and which also assume a dualist interactionist, or non-physicalist stance.[19]

I should also reiterate that we are hardly restricted to the Cartesian dualist–monist dilemma, which is of course an historically conditioned choice. Edge, for example, rejects both the physicalist and dualist schemes, justifying this by citing the wide variation in folk psychologies and theories of self that exist beyond the Western models.[20] Whilst I would not go as far as eliminating the 'Western spectrum' or folk psychology, I do see the value in repositioning these as a selection of traditions amongst a wide selection of traditions, takes, or formulations of human nature. Again, if we accept that *all* of our models are partial, distorted, and adaptations to local demands, cultures, environments, ways of life, etc. and that these external pressures *themselves* constantly fluctuate, then this pluralistic viewpoint seems preferable to a zero-sum battle for the One True Way.

Some will no doubt reject response (3) as not worth the price of admission. Much of the appeal of science as an institution is the perception that it provides 'objective knowledge' via a sceptical examination of the evidence that allows the rejection of errors and false ideas. In this context, *any* sort of cultural relativism may be seen as unviable because non-scientific approaches, the story goes, do not possess the self-correcting mechanisms of science and often accommodate what are to us very fanciful or implausible views of the cosmos and human beings.

From this it follows, *in extremis*, that the only objective, real, or maybe even useful ideas can come from institutional science. Non-scientific ideas may, of course, be used in lieu of science coming up with a better solution

---

18 Beauregard & O'Leary, 2007.
19 Murphy, 1992. Gauld, 1992, suggests that many cures that rely on hypnotic-type effects may rely upon the general cultural ambiance in which the subject lives. Institutional conceptual frameworks, even what are to us fictitious ones (e.g. Mesmer's conceptions) may be effective in triggering hypnotic suggestions to 'take' or to trigger placebo-type effects. So even if the concept of interactive dualism 'is' 'wrong', or a fiction, there may still be therapeutic contexts in which it is useful.
20 Edge, 2002. Although, more recently, he seems to have embraced physicalism and naturalistic models after all. See discussion in chapter fifteen.

or explanation, but once the elites of science have found a satisfactory solution, then we must surrender all alternatives in favour of the (realer, better?) ones supplied by science. This sort of attitude forces a consideration of one of the most difficult problems in consciousness studies.

Should We Construct Such a Theory to the Exclusion of Others?

Alongside the 'hard' problem and the 'binding' problem in consciousness studies, there is a third problem that tends to be overlooked. This is the 'colonization' problem, which is: if or when the elites of science produce what they feel constitutes a satisfactory solution to the mystery/problem of consciousness, what happens to the competing modes of explanation that already exist, both within and without science? The common assumption seems to be that these alternatives with either wither or else fall before the projected 'explanation' that solves all the important problems. Furthermore, this 'withering' is generally seen as a desirable within a discipline, because it allows the formation of a unified paradigm, desired for reasons outlined above. Consciousness, in this sense, can be seen as virgin territory or an unconquered frontier, ripe for the conquistadors of science. Such a conceptual space is conceived as empty or else in need of occupation.

The main problem with frontiers, however, is what one does with the people already living there. Historically speaking, frontiers have tended to be exciting for explorers and prospectors, but rather less so for those colonized. Ursula Le Guin makes this point beautifully in an essay on geographical frontiers:

> Coming from another world, they take yours from you, changing it, draining it, shrinking it into a property, a commodity. And as your world is meaningless to them until they change it to theirs, so as you live among them and adopt their meanings, you are in danger of losing your own meaning to yourself.[21]

The colonizers, in this analogy, are those within the scientific elite who would seek to impose their ideas upon everyone else. Certainly rational argument and evidence count in this process, but so does rhetoric, active and passive censorship, the denigration of competing views, and social and economic exclusion. Those colonized represent those within the scientific community who do *not* accede to a dominating idea, and also, potentially, every single member of the human race. The assumption is that once the scientific elite have decided upon the 'truth', then everyone else should yield. Within our culture, this is seen as a natural, inevitable, and even desirable process, and to reject scientific ideas is often seen as synonymous with rejecting reality itself. For example, Carl Sagan, reacting to those who find scientific world-views demeaning, asks rhetorically:

---

21 Le Guin, 2004, pp. 28–9.

> But what is the alternative?... To adopt a comforting belief system, no matter how out of kilter with the facts it is?... For practical reasons, we cannot live too much in fantasyland... How can we be sure which of the thousands of human belief systems should become unchallenged, ubiquitous, mandatory?[22]

For Sagan, the choice was simple; live with the 'realities' revealed by science or become 'deluded' within other belief systems.[23] Acceptance is inevitable because science reveals objective truths about the universe, and those who reject x or y theory are simply in flight from this objective reality.

I have come to believe that this tacit acceptance of the inevitability of scientific 'truth' is questionable with respect to the natural sciences and a liability in the social sciences. To be sure, there are many facts within science that seem pretty undisputable, and I am far from suggesting a wholesale rejection of scientific knowledge, theoretical or applied, *per se*. There is no doubt that science has contributed many deep insights into the world. The issue, however, is (1) whether we should uncritically accept the many and varied claims that issue from institutional science, and automatically change our lives or belief systems according to those pronouncements, and (2) whether we should abandon non-scientific ways of knowing that are personally useful just because 'science', or cultural inertia, pressures us to.

Issue (1) has repercussions within and without science. Within institutional science, and especially in a day of research cartels and knowledge monopolies, there is strong pressure upon individuals to conform to whatever the prevailing consensus may be. This trend is exacerbated by the bureaucratic nature of contemporary science, as bureaucracies routinely favour internal cohesion and actively supress internal dissent.[24] This is *not* automatically desirable, either from the individual point of view, or for science itself. There exist a range of arguments for the support of a plurality of views within science, even where the evidence seems robust enough to exclude alternative possibilities. John Stuart Mill supplied four reasons for accepting diverse and dissenting views within science, and Feyerabend a fifth:[25]

---

22 Sagan, 1994, p. 48.
23 Note, too, the assumption of a simple split between the 'objective' world-views of science and all other 'subjective' belief systems, cultures, ways of life. If these different ways of life represent adaptations to local conditions, one would not expect or want any single one to become universal, any more than one would want an alien weed overrunning a particular ecosystem. But then one might also apply the same logic to scientific knowledge, especially concerning human nature; why *should* we allow the elite traditions of science to become unchallenged, ubiquitous, mandatory, especially if the price is mental monoculture, and the death of other ways of knowing?
24 Martin, 1979.
25 Mill, 1859; Feyerabend, 1987, p. 34.

(1) A view one might reject for various reasons or which has problems may still be true.
(2) A view with problems may still contain *some* truth.
(3) A view that is completely true but not disputed may become an unquestioned prejudice.
(4) The meaning of even true (e.g. robustly supported) views can often only be found by contrast with other views.
(5) (Feyerabend) That often strong evidence against an opinion can only be found *via* an articulated alternative.

I hope that the myriad traditions surveyed in this book have demonstrated the utility of these points, especially no. (5). Competition between competing world-views has often served to sharpen the arguments of any given tradition, and to stimulate research that otherwise would not have been done. For example, the consideration of teleological cosmologies alongside more mechanistic ones highlights both the relative strengths and weaknesses of either approach. Likewise, the conflicting views of self discussed in chapter fourteen also demonstrate respective strengths and weaknesses, and highlight that whilst a given view of the 'self' may be useful in some circumstances, they are often less useful in others.

Even discredited traditions like phrenology have in the past served to prompt new questions and research that otherwise might not have been done, and alternative traditions like Mesmerism have anticipated important therapies and provided relief where conventional medicine failed. So there exist a range of reasons for allowing competing alternatives to conventional views to exist, in order to oppose totalist strains within science and provide new avenues that may improve human life. Alternative views do *not* serve as distractions from 'legitimate' research programmes; they serve as ways by which our understanding may be made richer. And even if novel theories/practices prove to be in error in some way, then we stand to learn from these errors. So, even within science, there are strong arguments *against* a blind acceptance of a given ideological point of view and for the support of even radically heterodox ideas.

As for those outside the elite cadre of thinkers, I think that there are strong reasons to resist pressure to change one's own personal views of human nature just because a given view is held to be more 'scientific'. This is simply because different individuals approach and learn to cope with life in very different ways, and often adopt world-views and beliefs in response to local problems and differing personal challenges. If history is anything to go by, those propagating a one-size-fits-all view of human nature often end up ignoring or even denigrating aspects of existence, concepts, and beliefs that may be necessary for individuals and alternative ways of life to function and prosper: behaviourism may serve as an historical example of this.

This issue becomes acute when we are faced with demands that we should drop our favoured beliefs or viewpoints for fear of being deluded or irrational. For example, Susan Blackmore, apparently accepting strong determinism as true, has long assumed that there is no free will, and comments that whilst people may be afraid that they will do bad things without such a facility, that this 'common fear is no excuse to carry on living in delusion'.[26] Meanwhile Dennett, whilst acknowledging that 'a theory that radically assaults the belief environment has a genuine potential for doing harm', suggests that those worried about 'unasked for enlightenment should take a hard look at the costs of the current myths [about human beings, souls, consciousness, etc.]'.[27] For both writers, the choice is again stark; to accept the rational, enlightened, objective view of science or continue to support the probably harmful myths and superstitions of the 'belief environment'.

It seems to me that suggestions like these rest upon the assumption of the automatic superiority of any idea propounded within the rational academe and the automatic inferiority of any idea that occurs outside. The assumption is, again, that 'unenlightened' laypeople who still harbour irrational beliefs about souls, free will, etc. need enlightening, and that their current set of (irrational) beliefs, which probably do more harm than good, should be replaced with 'better' ideas supplied by the educated elite. This is because acceding to expert opinion is, as Feyerabend noted, quite often what being 'rational' means today.[28] It does not mean thinking for oneself, or coming to one's own conclusions; it means compliance to authority.

Secondly, I would question the right of *anyone* to judge the beliefs and way of life of other people as inferior to their own. Ways of life can be regarded as adaptations to local conditions, and will often contain both beneficial and harmful elements (and as Dennett admits, Western scientific rationalism is hardly universally beneficent, either). What matters is for individuals to develop their own ideas, strategies, and beliefs that suit the challenges of their own lives and not try to distort their lives to fit into an imposed set of beliefs about human nature. Science may contribute to this, but it cannot be allowed to dictate terms.

It also remains perfectly possible to dissent from scientific authority. Feyerabend noted that:

> The sciences have now left the qualitative world of our everyday experience far behind. Some scientists claim that this world is a mere appearance and that reality lies elsewhere. They see human beings in terms of this reality and approach them accordingly. But human beings may object to such treatment. They may declare themselves to

---

26 Blackmore, 2007, web version.
27 Dennett, 1991, pp. 453–4.
28 Feyerabend, 1987.

be a reality different from reality as defined by scientists... For example, they may decide to stabilize the qualitative world of our experiences and regard every deviation from it as a step into inhumanity.[29]

This is not to suggest that one rejects an expert or scientific view on a whim, or just because of a personal prejudice. But conversely, one should not just uncritically accept a view simply because it is sanctioned by the experts. It is to assert the right of everyone to engage and assess claims for themselves, and if necessary to reject those claims if they seem to be incompatible with one's own personal experiences or even absurd. This may not be easy, because of the high status of science in our society, and because these issues are often obscured by technical language and concepts. And as stated above, resisting scientific views can also be terribly difficult precisely because they are assumed to derive from nature rather than human authority.

Brian Martin has noted that when experts come to agree unanimously this gives a 'persuasive justification' for a particular view. He goes on to note that this means that anyone opposing a given point of view can then 'be dismissed as uninformed'.[30] However, Martin also notes that this authority is precarious because a few dissidents can undermine any claim made with the authority of science. I would even suggest that, in some cases, the lack of consensus in science can *protect* both scientists and non-scientists from the consequences of adopting a given view whose uncritical adoption has potentially negative repercussions. This makes dissent important both inside and outside science.

Dissent also becomes incredibly important in a culture which seems, in many ways, terribly dehumanizing. Like it or not, the models and ideologies that issue from institutional science form part of a hierarchical and bureaucratic society that, despite lip-service, often favours personal uniformity and internal cohesion over diversity. In this situation, institutions, not individuals, get to define human beings, including which behaviours and beliefs are 'normal' and which are not. A big problem in a mass, consumer culture is not that people feel freer than they actually are, but the opposite: almost every aspect of our lives is strictly regulated, and 'freedom' often gets reduced to consumer choice or putting a cross in a box every five years. It is my perception that, not coincidentally, a good deal of 'modern neuroscience' exacerbates rather than ameliorates these social trends.

In fact, I personally find it very suspicious how well the vision of the human produced by cognitive science fits with the agendas of a consumer society. This observation is not new, and was made in the 1950s by Erich Fromm. Fromm noted that excessive abstractions were pursued far

---

29 Feyerabend, 1987, p. 262.
30 Martin, 1999, web page.

beyond what was necessary so that 'everything, including ourselves, is being abstractified', which meant that real people were replaced by conceptual ghosts who 'embody different quantities, but not different qualities'.[31]

Whilst such a reduction might allow bureaucracies to operate and economies to run efficiently, it often has disastrous consequences for individuals. Fromm traced much alienation and depression as resulting from the abstractification of human beings, an observation also made by Victor Frankl, a psychiatrist and concentration camp survivor whom we met briefly in the introduction. Frankl recognized that nihilism had become a 'collective neurosis' in mass society, and also noted the 'danger inherent in the teaching of man's "nothingbutness"'. Such a view, Frankl wrote, 'makes a neurotic believe what he is prone to believe anyway, namely, that he is a pawn and victim of outer influences and circumstances'.[32]

Implications for Consciousness Studies

> Scientific knowledge is never unique: there is always a large number of ways of explaining any feature of reality. The actual way of explaining reality that is chosen or latched upon by a person or group will be suited more for some purposes and less for others. Because it is somewhat arbitrary, the actual content of scientific knowledge is in one sense socially defined. It is not the *only* way of viewing or understanding reality but *a* way that has been chosen or that has developed on the basis of human needs, desires and purposes.[33]

I think that, in the context of consciousness studies, we need to take the above statement very seriously. Institutional, commercial, military neuroscience today stands approximately where genomics did in the early 1980s. This parallel seems especially appropriate in the wake of announcements that the brain's blueprint is now being sought, rather as the human genome was mapped in the closing years of the twentieth century.[34] And, as in the early 1980s, many hope that this new knowledge will allow us to penetrate nature's secrets, and provide a solution to the mystery of consciousness.

From a certain point of view, the assimilation of consciousness will mean the total and comprehensive success of the monistic, physicalist scientific programme, and will mean that Rorty's hoped for ontology/epistemology of 'relaxed naturalism' no longer has any serious problems. In this

---

31 Fromm, 1955/1991, p. 114.
32 Frankl, 1992, p. 132.
33 Martin, 1979, web edition.
34 *New Scientist* cover story, 7th Feb 2011, no. 2798. The claim is that a map is needed to track down memory, thought, and identity. Very similar grand claims were made for the mapping of DNA in the 1980s; see the preface in Sheldrake, 2009. My suspicion that the mapping of the 'neural code' will, in a similar manner to the human genome project, demonstrate the limitations of such approaches as well as the strengths, and raise as many questions as it answers.

view, scientific knowledge can be viewed as a giant jigsaw puzzle in which there is a gaping hole, for which various factions are fashioning a new piece that they are sure will fit. Many within cognitive science seem to think that it's just a matter of time and research funds before this final piece is fitted and consciousness understood. Sure, there are lots of unknowns about brain function, but these constitute what are essentially puzzles or technical problems rather than unfathomable mysteries.

In contrast to the jigsaw idea, I prefer to conceive of the many sciences as expanding waves of theoretical schemes and possibilities that surge as our experience grows and we encounter novel phenomena that render current models inadequate. New models, visions, techniques, concepts, coming from multiple traditions, will flower and fade as experience changes, fashions wax and wane, and human needs transform. Such growths will of course be restrained by experience: we are not free to create *ex nihilo*. In human terms, this means an acceptance of the basics—that we are born, grow up, grow old and die, that we need food, shelter, and the support of other humans to survive. Science, of course, tries to extend the reach of experience to understand what wider constraints exist in what is termed 'nature' in part to understand how the human condition came about in the first place; but it is hardly the only tradition to do so. In any case, beyond the basic constraints of life there exist considerable grounds for negotiation. And we should be very, very careful that we do not mistake a constraint that we have invented to be a basic constraint forced upon us by existence. In fact, scientifically speaking, *I can think of no better way of testing this than by seeing what happens if we remove or rewrite such a constraint.*

In this book, I have tried to show that many of the supposed restraints within which we construct our theories of consciousness are basically imaginary conveniences which can be discarded or modified when necessary. I have tried to show the extent to which the 'hunt for consciousness' is historically and culturally conditioned. I have tried to show that one is not necessarily committed to one particular metaphysic—monistic physicalism—and that a range of alternatives exist, which for the most part have been ignored by the mainstream. I have tried also to highlight what I feel are the most promising alternatives, in the areas of organicism, property pluralism, and by conceiving consciousness as somehow active rather than passive.

Many questions, of course, remain unanswered. I do not know whether consciousness is wholly emergent, or whether some precursor exists within the 'stuff' of the universe, or even whether these will prove useful ways of looking at the situation. I do not know whether we will ever be able to create conscious machines (although I suspect that the qualitative differences between organisms and current technology may constrain this). I do not know how far the technologies of neuroscience will develop, and to what extent they will resolve these problems. I think that the nature of biological causation has scarcely been fathomed, let alone subjective causation. I do not really understand the nature of the 'self' (or no-self theories, for that matter), and I certainly do not really understand how so-called psi phenomena, if they occur, fit into the wider scheme of things.

Of one thing, however, I have become relatively certain; that within the constraining matrix of experience, many conceptual worlds remain possible. In fact, given that experience has a potentially unlimited reach, and that mainstream culture tends to focus on a relatively narrow subset of experience, this means that individuals *must* engage in some conceptual creativity in order to 'complete' their own personal world-pictures. For this reason, I suspect the amount of variance in individual world-views to be far wider than is often suspected. And this is a positive thing, because the worst thing in my world would be that everyone ends up thinking, and believing, exactly the same thing. Let us learn to love difference.

Bibliography

Abbott, D., Gea-Banacloche, J., Davies, P.C.W., Hameroff, S., Zeilinger, A., Eisert, J., Wiseman, H.M., Bezrukov, S.M. & Frauenfelder, H. (2008) Plenary debate: Quantum effects in biology — trivial or not?, *Fluctuation and Noise Letters*, **8** (1), pp. C5–C26.

Aleksander, I. (2005) *The World in My Mind, My Mind in the World*, Exeter: Imprint Academic.

Allison, T., Puce, A., Spencer, D.D. & McCarthy, G. (1999) Electrophysiological studies of human face perception. I. Potentials generated in occipitotemporal cortex by face and non-face stimuli, *Cerebral Cortex*, **5**, pp. 415–430.

Alvarado, C.S. (2009) Frederic W.H. Myers, psychical research and psychology: An essay review of Trevor Hamilton's *Immortal Longings: FWH Myers and the Victorian Search for Life after Death*, *JSPR*, **896**, pp. 150–170.

Angel, L. (2008) Reincarnation: Overview of the work of Ian Stevenson, *The Skeptic* (UK), **21** (1), pp. 8–14.

Appleyard, B. (1992) *Understanding the Present*, London: Picador.

Austin, J.H. (1998) *Zen and the Brain: Toward an Understanding of Meditation and Consciousness*, Cambridge, MA: MIT Press.

Baars, B.J. (1988) *A Cognitive Theory of Consciousness*, New York: Cambridge University Press.

Baars, B.J. (1999) There is already a field of systematic phenomenology, and it's called psychology, in Varela, F.J. & Shear, J. (eds.) *The View from Within*, pp. 216–218, Exeter: Imprint Academic.

Bandyopadhyay, S. (2000) Welcher Weg experiments and the orthodox Bohr's complementarity principle, [Online], doi:10.1016/S0375-9601(00)00670-8, http://arxiv.org/abs/quant-ph/0003073 accessed on 07/07/10.

Barrow, J.D. (1991) *Theories of Everything*, Oxford: Oxford University Press.

Barrow, J.D. & Tipler, F.J. (1986) *The Anthropic Cosmological Principle*, Oxford: Oxford University Press.

Bauer, H.H. (2001) *Science or Pseudoscience: Magnetic Healing, Psychic Phenomena and Other Heterodoxies*, Urbana and Chicago, IL: University of Illinois Press.

Bauer, H.H. (2004) Science in the 21st century: Knowledge monopolies and research cartels, *Journal of Scientific Exploration*, **18**, pp. 643–660.

Beaton, M. (2005) What RoboDennett still doesn't know, *Journal of Consciousness Studies*, **12** (12), pp. 3–25.

Beauregard, M. & O'Leary, D. (2007) *The Spiritual Brain: A Neuroscientist's Case for the Existence of the Brain*, New York: Harper One.

Beer, R.D. (2000) Dynamical approaches to cognitive science, *Trends in Cognitive Sciences*, **4**, pp. 91–99.
Beloff, J. (1993) *Parapsychology: A Concise History*, London: Athlone.
Beloff, J. (2002) Body & soul: Another look at the mind–body problem, in Steinkamp, F. *Parapsychology, Philosophy and the Mind: Essays Honouring John Beloff*, pp. 9–15, London: McFarland.
Bem, D.J. & Honorton, C. (1994) Does psi exist? Replicable evidence for an anomalous process of information transfer, *Psychological Bulletin*, **115**, pp. 4–18.
Bem, D.J., Palmer, J. & Broughton, R.S. (2001) Updating the ganzfeld database: A victim of its own success?, *Journal of Parapsychology*, **65**, pp. 207–218.
Bennett, M.R. & Hacker, P.M.S. (2003) *Philosophical Foundations of Neuroscience*, Oxford: Blackwell.
Biletzki, A. & Matar, A. (2010) Ludwig Wittgenstein, in Zalta, E.N. (ed.) *The Stanford Encyclopedia of Philosophy*, [Online], http://plato.stanford.edu/archives/spr2010/entries/wittgenstein/ accessed on 05/01/11.
Blackmore, S.J. (1982) *Beyond the body: An Investigation of Out of the Body Experiences*, London: Heinmann.
Blackmore, S.J. (1993) *Dying to Live*, London: Grafton.
Blackmore, S.J. (1997) Meme, myself and I, *New Scientist*, **2179** (13 March), p. 40.
Blackmore, S.J. (1999) *The Meme Machine*, Oxford: Oxford University Press.
Blackmore, S.J. (2003) *Consciousness: An Introduction*, London: Hodder & Stoughton.
Blackmore, S.J. (2005) *Conversations on Consciousness*, Oxford: Oxford University Press.
Blackmore, S.J. (2007) Living happily and morally without free will, in Evatt, C. (ed.) *The Myth of Free Will*, Princeville, HI: Café Essays.
Blakemore, C. (1990) *The Mind Machine*, London: BBC.
Block, N. (2005) Two neural correlates of consciousness, *Trends in Cognitive Sciences*, **9**, pp. 46–52.
Block, N. (1991) Troubles with functionalism, in Rosenthal, D.M. (ed.) *The Nature of Mind*, pp. 211–228, Oxford:Oxford University Press.
Bohm, H. (1983) *Wholeness and the Implicate Order*, London: Ark.
Bohr, N. (1949) Discussions with Einstein on epistemological problems in atomic physics, in *Albert Einstein: Philosopher-Scientist*, Cambridge: Cambridge University Press.
Bolender, J. (2003) A farewell to isms, in Walter, S. & Heckmann, H. (eds.) *Physicalism and Mental Causation*, pp. 109–128, Exeter: Imprint Academic.
BonJour, L. (2010) Against materialism, in Koons, R.C. & Bealer, G. (eds.) *The Waning of Materialism*, Oxford: Oxford University Press.
Bor, D. (2010) The mechanics of mind reading, *Scientific American Mind*, (July/August), pp. 52–57.
Borges, J.L. (1964) *Labyrinths*, New York: New Directions.
Bostrom, N. (2003) Are you living in a computer simulation?, *Philosophical Quarterly*, **53**, pp. 243–255.
Bradbury, R. (1998) *Quicker than the Eye*, London: Earthlight.
Brass, M. & Haggard, P. (2007) To do or not to do: The neural signature of self-control, *Journal of Neuroscience*, **27**, pp. 9141–9145.

Braude, S.E. (1981) The holographic analysis of Near-Death Experiences: The perpetuation of some deep mistakes, *Essence*, **5**, pp. 53–63.

Braude, S.E. (1983) Radical provincialism in the life sciences: A review of Rupert Sheldrake's *A New Science of Life*, *Journal of the American Society for Psychical Research*, **33**, pp. 63–78.

Braude, S.E. (1987) Psi and our picture of the world, *Inquiry*, **30**, pp. 277–294.

Braude, S.E. (1995) *First Person Plural: Multiple Personality and the Philosophy of Mind*, Lanham, MD: Rowman & Littlefield.

Braude, S.E. (2002) *ESP & Psychokinesis: A Philosophical Examination*, (rev. ed.), Parkland, FL: Brown Walker Press.

Braude, S.E. (2003) *Immortal Remains*, Oxford: Rowman & Littlefield.

Brockman, M. (2009) *What's Next: Dispatches on the Future of Science*, London: Random House.

Brooks, R.A. (1991) Intelligence without representation, *Artificial Intelligence*, **47**, pp. 139–159.

Brown, A. (1997) *The Darwin Wars*, London: Simon & Schuster.

Bruce, V., Green, P.R. & Georgson, M.A. (2003) *Visual Perception: Physiology, Psychology & Ecology*, (3rd ed.), London: Psychology Press.

Buddhaghosa (1920) *Althasalini (The Expositor)*, Tin, M. (trans.), London: Oxford University Press.

Burke, J. (1985) *The Day the Universe Changed*, London: BBC.

Cabeza, R. & Nyberg, L. (2000) Imaging cognition II: An empirical review of 275 PET and fMRI studies, *Journal of Cognitive Neuroscience*, **12**, pp. 1–47.

Carr, B. (2008) Worlds apart? Can psychical research bridge the gulf between matter and mind?, *PSPR*, **59**.

Carter, R. (2002) *Exploring Consciousness*, Berkeley, CA: University of California Press.

Carter, R. (2008a) *Multiplicity*, London: Little, Brown.

Carter, R. (2008b) Letter, *New Scientist*, **2678** (15 October).

Cartwright, N. (1999) *The Dappled World: A Study of the Boundaries of Science*, Cambridge: Cambridge University Press.

Chalmers, D. (1996) *The Conscious Mind*, Oxford: Oxford University Press.

Chalmers, E.F. (1999) *What is this Thing Called Science?* (third ed.), Maidenhead: Open University Press.

Chomsky, N. (2003) *Understanding Power*, London: Vintage.

Chrisley, R. (2009) Artificial intelligence and the study of consciousness, in Bayne, T., Cleeremans, A. & Wilken, P. (eds.) *Oxford Companion to Consciousness*, Oxford: Oxford University Press.

Chrisley, R. & Sloman, A. (1999) How Velmans' conscious experiences affected our brains, *Journal of Consciousness Studies*, **9** (11), pp. 58–63.

Churchland, P.M. (1984/1994), *Matter and Consciousness* (rev. ed.), Cambridge, MA: MIT Press.

Churchland, P.M. (1986) *Neurophilosophy: Towards a Unified Theory of Mind/Brain*, Cambridge, MA: MIT Press.

Churchland, P.S. (1995) *Engine of Reason, Seat of the Soul*, Cambridge, MA: MIT Press.

Clarke, A.C. (1999) *Profiles of the Future*, London: Indigo.

Cohn, N. (1975) *Europe's Inner Demons*, London: Plume.

Colborn, M.L.C. (2007) The decline effect in spontaneous and experimental psychical research, *JSPR*, **71**, pp. 1–22.

Collins, H. & Pinch, T. (1982) *Frames of Meaning*, London: Routledge.
Collins, H. & Pinch, T. (1998) *The Golem: What you Should Know About Science* (second ed.), Cambridge: Canto.
Corliss, W.R. (1994) *Science Frontiers: Some Anomalies and Curiosities of Nature*, Glen Arm, MD: Sourcebook Project.
Crabtree, A. (1993) *From Mesmer to Freud: Magnetic Sleep and the Roots of Magnetic Healing*, New Haven, CT: Yale University Press.
Craver, C.F. (2007) *Explaining the Brain: Mechanisms and the Mosaic Unity of Neuroscience*, Oxford: Oxford University Press.
Crick, F. (1994) *The Astonishing Hypothesis*, New York: Scribner.
Crick, F. & Koch, C. (2002) The problem of consciousness, *Scientific American*, (August).
Crick, F. & Koch, C. (2003) A framework for consciousness, *Nature Neuroscience*, **6**, pp. 119–126.
Damasio. A. (1999) *The Feeling of What Happens: Body, Emotion and the Making of Consciousness*, London: Heinemann.
Daniels, M. (2005) *Shadow, Self, Spirit: Essays in Transpersonal Psychology*, Exeter: Imprint Academic.
Darwin, C. (1859) *The Origin of Species*, London: John Murray.
Davies, P. (2007) *The Goldilocks Enigma*, London: Penguin.
Dawkins, R. (1976) *The Selfish Gene*, Oxford: Oxford University Press.
Dawkins, R. (1986) *The Blind Watchmaker*, London: Longman.
Dawkins, R. (1998) *Unweaving the Rainbow*, London: Penguin.
Dawkins, R. (2004) *The Devil's Chaplain*, London: Mariner Books.
Dawkins, R. (2006) *The God Delusion*, London: Bantam.
Dehaene, S., Sergent, C. & Changeux, J.P. (2003) A neuronal network model linking subjective reports and objective physiological data during conscious perception, *Proceedings of the National Academy of Science USA*, **100**, pp. 8520–8525.
Dennett, D.C. (1978) Conditions of personhood, in *Brainstorms*, Cambridge, MA: Bradford Books.
Dennett, D.C. (1991) *Consciousness Explained*, London: Allen Lane.
Dennett, D.C. (1995) *Darwin's Dangerous Idea*, London: Allen Lane.
Dennett, D.C. (1997) Quining qualia, in Block, N., Flanagan, O. & Guzeldare, G. (eds.) *The Nature of Consciousness: Philosophical Debates*, pp. 619–642, Cambridge, MA: MIT Press.
Dennett, D.C. (2003) *Freedom Evolves*, New York: Viking.
Descartes, R. (1997) *Philosophical Writings*, London: Workman.
Dick, S.J. (1996) *The Biological Universe: The Twentieth Century Extraterrestrial Life Debate and the Limits of Science*, Cambridge: Cambridge University Press.
Donaldson, D.I. (2004) Parsing brain activity with fMRI and mixed designs: What kind of state is neuroimaging in?, *Trends in Neuroscience*, **27**, pp. 442–444.
Drachman, D. (2005) Do we have brain to spare?, *Neurology*, **64**.
Dreyfus, H. (1992) *What Computers Still Can't Do*, Cambridge, MA: MIT Press.
Dupré, J. (1993) *The Disorder of Things: Metaphysical Foundations of the Disunity of Science*, Cambridge, MA: Harvard University Press.
Dupré, J. (2001) *Human Nature and the Limits of Science*, Oxford: Oxford University Press.
Eccles, J.C. (1994) *How the Self Controls its Brain*, Berlin: Springer-Verlag.

Eckert, R., Randall, D., Burggren, W. & French, K. (1997) *Animal Physiology*, Cranbury, NJ: W.H. Freeman & Co.

Edelman, G.M. & Tononi, G. (2000) *A Universe of Consciousness : How Matter Becomes Imagination*, New York: Basic Books.

Edge, H. (2002) Dualism and the self: A cross-cultural perspective, in Steinkamp, F. *Parapsychology, Philosophy and the Mind: Essays Honouring John Beloff*, pp. 33–56, London: McFarland.

Edge, H. (2008) There is no mind–body problem in parapsychology, in Roe, C.A., Kramer, W. & Coly, L. (eds.) *Proceedings of an International Conference in Utrecht II: Charting the Future of Parapsychology*, pp. 421–462, New York: Parapsychology Foundation.

Edwards, P. (1996) *Reincarnation: A Critical Examination*, Amherst, NY: Prometheus.

Ellenburger, H.F. (1970/1994) *The Discovery of the Unconscious*, London: Allen Lane.

Elsasser, W.M. (1998) *Reflections on a Theory of Organisms: Holism in Biology*, Baltimore, MD: Johns Hopkins University Press.

Elsdon-Baker, F. (2009) *The Selfish Genius*, London: Icon Books.

Engel, A.K., Roelfsema, P.R., Fries, P., Brecht, M. & Singer, W. (1997). Role of temporal domain for response selection and perceptual binding. *Cerebral Cortex*, **7**, pp. 571–82.

Ertel, S. (1997) Morphische Resonanz auf dem Prüfstand des Experiments/Morphic resonance under exeprimental scrutiny, in Dürr, H.-P. & Gottwald, F.T. (eds.) *Rupert Sheldrake in der Diskussion. Das Wagnis einer neuen Wissenschaft des Lebens*, pp. 115–140, München: Scherz.

Eysenck, H.J. & Sargent, C. (1993) *Explaining the Unexplained: Mysteries of the Paranormal*, London: Prion.

Fairley, J. & Welfare, S. (1985) *Arthur C. Clarke's World of Strange Powers*, Glasgow: Collins.

Feyerabend, P.K. (1963a) Materialism and the mind–body problem, *Review of Metaphysics*, **17**, pp. 49–66.

Feyerabend, P.K. (1963b) Mental events and the brain, *The Journal of Philosophy*, **LX**, p. 11.

Feyerabend, P.K. (1975) *Against Method*, London: Verso.

Feyerabend, P.K. (1978) *Science in a Free Society*, London: Verso.

Feyerabend, P.K. (1987) *Farewell to Reason*, London: Verso.

Flanagan, O. (1992) *Consciousness Reconsidered*, Cambridge, MA: MIT Press.

Flew, A. (ed.) (1964) *Body, Mind and Death*, New York: Macmillan.

Fodor, J.A. (1972) Some reflections on Vygotsky's 'Thought and Language', *Cognition*, **1**, pp. 83–95.

Fodor, J.A. (1983) *The Modularity of Mind*, Cambridge, MA: MIT Press.

Fort, C. (1974) *The Complete Books of Charles Fort*, New York: Dover.

Frankl, V. (1992) *Man's Search For Meaning*, London: Rider.

Frith, C. (2008) No one really uses reason, *New Scientist*, (26 July), p. 45.

Froese, T. (2007) On the role of AI in the ongoing paradigm shift within the cognitive sciences, in Lungarella, M., Iida, F., Bongard, J. & Pfeifer, R. (eds.) *Proceedings of the 50th Anniversary Summit of Artificial Intelligence*, Berlin: Springer-Verlag.

Froese, T. & Di Paolo, E.A. (2008) Can evolutionary robotics generate simulation models of autopoiesis?, *CSRP*, **598**.

Fromm, E. (1955/1991) *The Sane Society*, London: Routledge.
Gardner, H. (1985) *The Mind's New Science*, London: Basic Books.
Gauld, A. (1968) *The Founders of Psychical Research*, London: Routledge & Kegan Paul.
Gauld, A. (1982) *Mediumship and Survival*, London: William Heinemann.
Gauld, A. (1992) *A History of Hypnotism*, Cambridge: Cambridge University Press.
Gauld, A. (2008) Reflections on the life and work of Ian Stevenson, *Journal of Scientific Exploration*, **22**, pp. 18–35.
Gazzaniga, M.S. (2005) *The Ethical Brain*, Chicago, IL: University of Chicago Press.
Gleik, J. (1987) *Chaos*, London: Vintage.
Goleman, D. (ed.) (2003) *Destructive Emotions and How we can Overcome Them*, London: Bloomsbury.
Goodwin, B. (1994) *How the Leopard Changed its Spots*, London: Wiedenfeld & Nicholson.
Gould, S.J. & Lewontin, R.C. (1979) The spandrels of San Marco and the panglossian paradigm: A critique of the adaptationist programme, *Proceedings of the Royal Society B*, **205**, pp. 581–598.
Granger, R.H. & Hearn, R.A. (2007) Models of thalamocortical system, *Scholarpedia*, **2** (11), p. 1796. Revision #59677.
Gribbin, J. (1984) *In Search of Schrodinger's Cat*, London: Bantam Books.
Griffin, D.R. (1997) *Parapsychology, Philosophy & Spirituality: A Postmodern Exploration*, Albany, NY: SUNY Press.
Griffin, D.R. (1998) *Unsnarling the World Knot: Consciousness, Freedom and the Mind–Body Problem*, Eugene, OR: WIPF & Stock.
Griffin, D.R. (2001) *Animal Minds*, London: University of Chicago Press.
Guyton, A. (1981) *Basic Human Neurophysiology*, New York: W.B. Sanders.
Gwinn, T. (2006) *Robert Rosen – Complexity in a Nutshell*, [Online], www.panmere.com accessed on 14/04/10.
Halpern, M. (2006) The trouble with the Turing Test, *The New Atlantis*, **11** (Winter), pp. 42–63.
Hameroff, S. (2010) The 'conscious pilot' — dendritic synchrony moves through the brain to mediate consciousness, *Journal of Biological Physics*, **36**, pp. 71–93.
Hamilton, T. (2009) *Immortal Longings: FWH Myers and the Victorian Search for Life After Death*, Exeter: Imprint Academic.
Hanson, G.P. (2001) *The Trickster and the Paranormal*, Bloomington, IN: Xlibris.
Harré, H.R. & Madden, E.H. (1975) *Causal Powers*, Oxford: Blackwell.
Harrison, T. (1994) *Stigmata: A Medieval Mystery for a Modern Age*, London: Fount.
Harvey, I. (2002) Evolving robot consciousness: The easy problems and the rest, in Fetzer, J.H. (ed.) *Evolving Consciousness*, Advances in Consciousness Research Series, pp. 205–219, Amsterdam: John Benjamins.
Harvey, I. (1997) Cognition is not computation: Evolution is not optimisation, *ICANN '97 Proceedings of the 7th International Conference on Artificial Neural Networks*, London: Springer-Verlag.
Hasker, W. (2010) Persons and the unity of consciousness, in Koons, R.C. & Bealer, G. (eds.) *The Waning of Materialism*, pp. 175–190, Oxford: Oxford University Press.

Hassabis, D., Chu, C., Rees, G., Weiskopf, N., Molyneux, P.D. & Maguire, E.A. (2009) Decoding neuronal ensembles in the human hippocampus, *Current Biology*, **19**, pp. 546–554.

Hayes, N. (1995) *Psychology in Perspective*, London: Macmillan.

Heap, M. (2000) Let's wave goodbye to the subconscious mind, *The Tri-Annual Congress of the International Society of Hypnosis*, Munich, October 2000, [Online], http://www.mheap.com/letswave.html accessed on 18/10/10.

Heath, D. & Boreham, J. (1999) *Introducing Romanticism*, London: Icon Books.

Heeger, D.J. & Ress, D. (2002) What does fMRI tell us about neuronal activity?, *Nature Neuroscience*, **3**, pp. 142–151.

Heil, J. (2004) *Philosophy of Mind: A Contemporary Introduction*, London: Routledge.

Heil, J. (2003) Multiply realized properties, in Walter, S. & Heckmann, H. (eds.) *Physicalism and Mental Causation*, pp. 11–30, Exeter: Imprint Academic.

Henry, R.C. (2005) The mental universe, *Nature*, **436**, p. 29.

Ho, M. (2008) *The Rainbow and the Worm: The Physics of Organisms*, London: World Scientific.

Hodgson, D. (2005) A plain person's free will, *Journal of Consciousness Studies*, **12** (1), pp. 3–52.

Hofstadter, D.R. (1979) *Godel, Escher, Bach*, London: Penguin.

Hofstadter, D.R. (2007) *You are a Strange Loop*, New York: Basic Books.

Hofstadter, D.R. & Dennett, D.C. (eds.) (1981) *The Mind's I*, New York: Basic Books.

Holmes, R. (2008) *The Age of Wonder: How the Romantic Generation Discovered the Beauty and Terror of Science*, London: HarperPress.

Hope, R. & Van Loon, B. (1994) *Introducing Buddha*, London: Icon.

Horgan, J. (1999) *The Undiscovered Mind*, London: Phoenix.

Horgan, J. (2004) The myth of mind control: Will anyone ever decode the human brain?, *Discover Magazine*, (October).

Hothersall, D. (2004) *History of Psychology* (Fourth edition), London: McGraw Hill.

Huxley, A. (1947) *Science, Liberty and Peace*, London: Chatto & Windus.

Huxley, T.H. (1887/1892) *Essays Upon Some Controverted Questions*, London: Macmillan.

Huxley, T.H. (1901) *Methods and Results*, New York: Appleton.

Hyman, R. (2010a) Meta-analysis that conceals more than it reveals: Comment on Storm *et al.* (2010b), *Psychological Bulletin*, **136**, pp. 486–490.

Hyman, R. (2010b) The demise of parapsychology (1850–2008), *The Skeptic* (US), **22** (2), pp. 17–20.

Hyman, R. & Honorton, C. (1986) A joint communiqué, *Journal of Parapsychology*, **50**, pp. 351–364.

Inglis, B. (1992) *Natural and Supernatural*, Bridport: Prism-Unity.

Ishai, A., Ungerleider, L.G., Matin, A., Schouten, J.L. & Hacby, J.V. (1999) Distributed representation of objects in human visual pathway, *Proceedings of the National Academy of Sciences USA*, **96**, pp. 9379–9384.

James, O. (2008) *The Selfish Capitalist*, London: Vermilion.

James, W. (1890) *The Principles of Psychology* (2 Vols.), New York: Henry Holt.

James, W. (1892/1992) *Psychology: The Briefer Course*, in *William James: Writings 1879–1899*, New York: Library of America.

James, W. (1902/1985) *The Varieties of Religious Experience*, London: Penguin.

James, W. (1909) *A Pluralistic Universe*, London: Harvard University Press.
James, W. (1912) Does consciousness exist?, in *Essays in Radical Empiricism*, pp. 1–38, New York: Longman Green and Co.
John, E.R. (2001) A field theory of consciousness, *Consciousness and Cognition*, **10**, pp. 184–213.
John, E.R. (2005) From synchronous neuronal discharges to subjective awareness?, *Progress in Brain research*, **150**, pp. 143–171.
Jones, R. (1982) *Physics as Metaphor*, London: Abacus Ed.
Joyce, J. (1986/1922) *Ulysses*, London: Penguin.
Juarrero, A. (1999) *Dynamics in Action: Intentional Behaviour as a Complex System*, Cambridge, MA: MIT Press.
Kanwisher, N. (1987) Repetition blindness: Type recognition without token individuation, *Cognition*, **27**, pp. 117–143.
Kanwisher, N. (1991) Repetition blindness and illusory conjunctions: Errors in binding visual types with visual tokens, *Journal of Experimental Psychology: Human Perception and Performance*, **17**, pp. 404–421.
Kanwisher, N. (2001) Neural events and perceptual awareness, *Cognition*, **79**, pp. 89–113.
Kanwisher, N., McDermott, J. & Chun, M.M. (1997) The fusiform face area: A module in human extrastriate cortex specialized for face perception, *Journal of Neuroscience*, **17**, pp. 4302–4311.
Kaufmann, S.A. (1993) *The Origins of Order, Self-Organization and Selection in Evolution*, Oxford: Oxford University Press.
Kaufmann, S.A. (1995) *At Home in the Universe: The Search for the Laws of Complexity*, London: Viking.
Kellis, S., Miller, K., Thomson, K., Brown, R., House, P. & Greger, B. (2010) Decoding spoken words using local field potentials recorded from the cortical surface, *Journal of Neural Engineering*, **7**, pp. 1741–2560.
Kelly, E.F. (2003) Review of Wegner, 2002, *Journal of Scientific Exploration*, **17**, pp. 166–171.
Kelly, E.F., Kelly, E.W., Crabtree, A., Gauld, A., Grosso, M. & Greyson, B. (2007) *Irreducible Mind: Toward a Psychology for the 21st Century*, Lanham, MD: Rowman & Littlefield.
Kihlstrom, J.F. (1993) Discussion, in Bock, G.R. & Marsh, J. (eds.) *Experimental and Theoretical Studies of Consciousness*, p. 215, Chichester: John Wiley.
King, R. (2008) Introduction, in Gill, R. (ed.) *Doctor Faustus* by Christopher Marlowe, London: Methuen.
Klein, N. (2007) *The Shock Doctrine*, London: Allen Lane.
Koch, C. (1997) Computation and the single neuron, *Nature*, **385**, p. 207.
Koch, C. (2004) *The Quest for Consciousness: A Neurobiological Approach*, Englewood, CO: Roberts & Company.
Koch, C. & Hepp, K. (2006) Quantum mechanics in the brain, *Nature*, **400**, pp. 611–612.
Koestler, A. (1967) *The Ghost in the Machine*, London: Hutchinson & Co.
Koons, R.C. & Bealer, G. (eds.) (2010) *The Waning of Materialism*, Oxford: Oxford University Press.
Korzybski, A. (1994) *Science and Sanity: An Introduction to Non-Aristotelian Systems and General Semantics*, New York: Institute of General Semantics.
Kosslyn, S.M. (1994) *Image and Brain: The Resolution of the Imagery Debate*, Cambridge, MA: MIT Press.

Kosslyn, S.M. (1999) If neuroimaging is the answer, what is the question?, *Philosophical Transactions of the Royal Society B*, **354**, pp. 1283-1294.

Kriegeskorte, N., Lindquist, M.A., Nichold, T.E., Poldrack, R.A. & Vul, E. (2010) Everything you never wanted to now about circular analysis, but were afraid to ask, *Journal of Cerebral Blood Flow and Metabolism*, pp. 1-7.

Kuhn, T.S. (1957) *The Copernican Revolution*, London: Harvard University Press.

Kuhn, T.S. (1996/1962) *The Structure of Scientific Revolutions* (Third ed.), Chicago, IL: University of Chicago Press.

Kurzweil, R. (2005) *The Singularity is Near*, London: Gerald Duckworth.

Lancaster, B.L. (2004) *Approaches to Consciousness: The Marriage of Science and Mysticism*, Basingstoke: Palgrave Macmillan.

Lashley, K. (1929) *Brain Mechanisms and Intelligence*, Chicago, IL: University of Chicago Press.

Lawton, G. (2009) Uprooting Darwin's tree, *New Scientist*, (24 January), p. 34.

Le Grand, H.E. (1988) *Drifting Continents and Shifting Theories*, Cambridge: Cambridge University Press.

Le Guin, U.K. (2004) *The Wave of the Mind: Talks and Essays on the Writer, the Reader and the Imagination*, Boston, MA: Shambala.

Le Malefin, P. (1995) Sciences psychiques, metaphysiques et psychologie. Cotoiement et divorce: historie d'un partage, *Bulletin de psychologie*, **48**, pp. 624-630.

Levine, B. (2001) *Commonsense Rebellion: Taking Back your Life from Drugs, Shrinks, Corporations, and a World Gone Crazy*, London: Continuum.

Lewis, D.K. (1986) *On the Plurality of Worlds*, Oxford: Blackwell.

Libet, B. (2004) *Mind-Time*, Cambridge, MA: Harvard University Press.

Libet, B., Gleason, C.A., Wright Jnr., E.W. & Pearl, D.K. (1983) Time of conscious intention to act in relation to onset of cerebral activity (readiness potential): The unconscious initiation of a freely voluntary act, *Brain*, **106**, pp. 623-642.

Llináo, R., Ribary, U., Contreras, D. & Pedroarena, C. (1998) The neuronal basis for consciousness, *Philosophical Transactions of the Royal Society of London B*, **353**, pp. 1841-1849.

Logothetis, N.K. (2008) What we can do and what we cannot do with fMRI, *Nature*, **453**, pp. 869-878.

Margulis, L. & Sagan, D. (2002) *Acquiring Genomes: A Theory of the Origins of Species*, New York: Basic Books.

Marshall, P. (2005) *Mystical Encounters with the Natural World*, Oxford: Oxford University Press.

Martin, B. (1979) *The Bias of Science*, Canberra: Society for Social Responsibility in Science.

Martin, B. (1999) Supression of dissent in science, in Freudenburg, W.R. & Youn, T.I.K. (eds.) *Research in Social Problems and Public Policy* Vol. 7, pp. 105-135, Stamford, CT: JAI Press.

Martinez-Conde, S. (2004) Review of Koch, C. (2004) *The Quest for Consciousness*, *Psyche*, **10**, [Online], http://psyche.cs.monash.edu.au/ accessed on 23/11/09.

Maturana, H.R. & Varela, F.J. (1980) *Autopoiesis and Cognition: The Realization of the Living*, Dordrecht: Kluwer Academic Publishers.

Maxwell, M. & Tschudin, V. (1990) *Seeing the Invisible*, London: Arkana.

McCarthy, G., Puce, A., Gore, J. & Allison, T. (1997) Face-specific processing in the human fusiform gyrus, *Journal of Cognitive Neuroscience*, **9**, pp. 605-610.

Meixner, U. (2010) Materialism does not save the phenomena - and the alternative which does, in Koons, R.C. & Bealer, G. (eds.) *The Waning of Materialism*, pp. 417–437, Oxford: Oxford University Press.

Melnyk, A. (2003) Some evidence for physicalism, in Walter, S. & Heckmann, H. (eds.) *Physicalism and Mental Causation*, pp. 155–172, Exeter: Imprint Academic.

Metzinger, T. (2009) *The Ego Tunnel*, London: Basic Books.

Michie, D. (1994/5) Consciousness as an engineering issue, parts1 & 2, *Journal of Consciousness Studies*, **1** (2), pp. 182--95 and **2** (1), pp. 52--66

Midgley, M. (1992) *Science as Salvation*, London: Routledge.

Midgley, M. (2001) *Science and Poetry*, London: Routledge.

Midgley, M. (2003) *Myths We Live By*, London: Routledge.

Mill, J.S. (1859) *On Liberty*, London: Longman, Roberts & Green.

Milton, J. & Wiseman, R. (1999) Does psi exist? Lack of replication of an anomalous process of information transfer, *Psychological Bulletin*, **125**, pp. 378–391.

Minsky, M. (1986) *The Society of Mind*, New York: Simon & Schuster.

Minsky, M. (1998) *Consciousness is a Big Suitcase: Interview with Marvin Minsky*, [Online], www.edge.org/3rd_culture/minsky/minsky_p2.html accessed on 22/06/10.

Monod, J. (1972) *Chance and Necessity*, London: Collins.

Moravec, H. (1988) *Mind Children*, Cambridge, MA: Harvard University Press.

Mormonn, F. & Koch, C. (2007) Neural correlates of consciousness, *Scholarpedia*, **2** (12), p. 1740. Revision #68928.

Morowitz, H.J. (1978) *Foundations of Bioenergetics*, New York: Academic Press.

Murphy, M. (1992) *The Future of the Body: Explorations into the Further Evolution of Human Nature*, New York: Tarcher Putnam.

Murphy, N. & Brown, W.S. (2007) *Did My Neurons Make Me Do It?*, Oxford: Oxford University Press.

Myers, F.W.H. (1903) *Human Personality and its Survival of Bodily Death* (2 Vols.), London: Longmans Green.

Myers, F.W.H. (1903/2001) *Human Personality and its Survival of Bodily Death* (abridged version), Charlottesville, VA: Hampton Roads.

Nagel, T. (1974) What is it like to be a bat?, *Philosophical Review*, **83**, pp. 435–450.

Nichols, M.J. & Newsome, W.T. (1999) The neurobiology of cognition, *Nature*, **402** (Supp. 2 December), pp. 35–37.

Noakes, R. (2007) Review of *Ghost Hunters: William James and the Scientific Proof of Life After Death*, JSPR, **887**, pp. 106–109.

Noë, A. (2002) *Is the Visual World a Grand Illusion?*, Exeter: Imprint Academic.

Nordberg, R.B. (1999) Review of Griffin, D.R., 1998, *Journal of Scientific Exploration*, **13**, pp. 121–131.

O'Shea, M. (2008) *Science Made Simple: The Brain* (booklet distributed free with the *Independent* newspaper in association with Oxford University Press).

Owen, A.M., Cleman, M.R., Boly, M., Davis, M.H., Laureys, S. & Pickard, J.D. (2006) Detecting awareness in the vegetative state, *Science*, **313**, p. 1402.

Pandeya, R.C. (1964) *The Madhyamika Philosophy: A New Approach* Philosophy East & West, Vol. 14, pp. 3–24, Honolulu, HI: University of Hawaii Press.

Pauen, M., Staudacher, A. & Walter, S. (2006) *Journal of Consciousness Studies: Special Issue on Epiphenomenalism*, Exeter: Imprint Academic.

Pelvig, D.P., Pakenberg, H., Stark, A.K. & Pakenberg, B. (2008) Neocortical glial cell numbers in human beings, *Neurobiology of Aging*, **29**, pp. 1754–1762.
Penrose, R. (1989) *The Emperor's New Mind*, Oxford: Oxford University Press.
Penrose, R. (1994) *Shadows of the Mind*, Oxford: Oxford University Press.
Penrose, R. (2004) *The Road to Reality*, Oxford: Vintage.
Pinker, S. (1998) *How the Mind Works*, London: Allen Lane.
Pinker, S. (2002) *The Blank Slate: The Modern Denial of Human Nature*, London: Allen Lane.
Polyani, M. (1964) *Personal Knowledge*, New York: Harper Torchbooks.
Popper, K.R. (1959) *The Logic of Scientific Discovery*, London: Routledge.
Popper, K.R. & Eccles, J.C. (1977) *The Self and its Brain*, London: Springer International.
Port, R. & van Gelder, T. (1995) *Mind as Motion: Explorations in the Dynamics of Cognition*, Cambridge, MA: MIT Press.
Presman, A.S. (1970) *Electromagnetic Fields and Life*, New York: Plenum Press.
Putnam, H. (1967) Psychological predicates, in Capitan, W.H. & Merril, D.D. (eds.) *Art, Mind and Religion*, pp. 37–48, Pittsburgh, PA: University of Pittsburgh Press.
Putnam, H. (1998/1988) *Representation and Reality*, Cambridge, MA: MIT Press.
Radin, D.I. (1997) *The Conscious Universe*, San Francisco, CA: HarperEdge.
Radin, D.I. (2006) *Entangled Minds*, London: Paraview.
Rado, A. & Scott, A.C. (1996) Is there a binding problem?, [Online], http://www.math.arizona.edu/~rado/bp4_new/bp4.html35
Rao, K.R. (2002) *Consciousness Studies: Cross-Cultural Perspectives*, London: McFarland.
Raymont, P. (2003) Kim on overdetermination, exclusion and nonreductive physicalism, in Walter, S. & Heckmann, H. (eds.) *Physicalism and Mental Causation*, pp. 225–242, Exeter: Imprint Academic.
Read, N. (2005) *Sick and Tired: Healing the Illnesses and Doctors Cannot Cure*, London: Weidenfeld & Nicholson.
Reed, G. (1988) *The Psychology of Anomalous Experience*, Buffalo, NY: Prometheus.
Revonsuo, A. (2005) *Inner Presence: Consciousness as a Biological Phenomenon*, Cambridge, MA: MIT Press.
Rhine, L. (1966) Review of Stevenson, 1966, *Journal of Parapsychology*, **30**, pp. 263–272.
Rhine, L. (1981) *The Invisible Picture: A Study of Psychic Experiences*, Jefferson, NC: McFarland.
Rhodes, R. (1986) *The Making of the Atomic Bomb*, New York: Simon & Schuster.
Richards, J.R. (2000) *Human Nature After Darwin*, London: Routledge.
Rinbochay, L. (1980) *Mind in Tibetan Buddhism*, London: Rider.
Roe, C. (2010) When is evidence sufficient?, *The Skeptic* (US), **22** (2), pp. 24–28.
Roney-Dougal, S. (2006) Taboo and belief in Tibetan psychic tradition, *JSPR*, **885**, pp. 193–210.
Rorty, R. (1979/2009) *Philosophy and the Mirror of Nature*, Princeton, NJ: Princeton University Press.
Rose, S.P.R. (1997) *Lifelines*, London: Allen Lane.
Rose, S.P.R. (2005) Human agency in the neurocentric age, *EMBO reports*, **6**, pp. 1001–1005.
Rose, S.P.R. (2006) *21st Century Brain*, London: Allen Lane.

Rose, H. & Rose, S.P.R. (2001) *Alas, Poor Darwin: Arguments Against Evolutionary Psychology*, London: Vintage.

Rosen, R. (1991) *Life Itself*, New York: Columbia University Press.

Rosenblum, B. & Kuttner, F. (2006) *Quantum Enigma: Physics Encounters Consciousness*, New York: Duckworth.

Rucker, R. (1997) *Infinity and the Mind*, London: Penguin.

Russell, B. (1946/2004) *History of Western Philosophy*, London: Routledge.

Ryle, G. (1949) *The Concept of Mind*, London: Hutchinson.

Sagan, C. (1994) *Pale Blue Dot: A Vision of the Human Future in Space*, New York: Random House.

Sagan, C. (1995) *The Demon Haunted World*, New York: Random House.

Sahtouris, E. (1999) *Earth-Dance*, New York: Springer.

Sahtouris, E. (2008) Towards a future global science: Axioms for modelling a living universe, *World Future Review*, (December).

Schrödinger, E. (1944) *What is Life?*, Cambridge: Cambridge University Press.

Scruton, R. (2009) More than meets the MRI, *Sunday Times Magazine*, 5 July, p. 9.

Searle, J.R. (1997) *The Mystery of Consciousness*, London: Granta Books.

Searle, J.R. (2007) *Freedom & Neurobiology*, New York: Columbia University Press.

Seth, A. (2007) Models of consciousness, *Scholarpedia*, **2** (1), p. 1328, [Online], http://www.scholarpedia.org/article/Models_of_consciousness accessed on 23/11/09.

Shannon, C. (1991) Representations: senses and reasons, *Philosophical Psychology*, **4**, pp. 355–373.

Sheldrake, R. (1981/2009) *A New Science of Life* (third ed.), London: Icon Books.

Sheldrake, R. (1988) *Presence of the Past: Morphic Resonance and the Habits of Nature*, London: HarperCollins.

Sheldrake, R. (2009) *The Credit Crunch for Materialism*, [Online], http://www.sheldrake.org/Articles&Papers/articles/RS_2009.html accessed on 08/10/09.

Simon, H. (1995) Artificial Intelligence: An empirical science, *Artificial Intelligence*, **77**, pp. 95–127.

Sloman, A. (2009) Virtual machines and the metaphysics of science, Conference paper, [Online], http://www.cs.bham.ac.uk/research/projects/cogaff/misc/vms-and-metaphysics-of-science.html accessed on 22/11/2010.

Sogyal Rinpoche (1992) *The Tibetan Book of Living and Dying*, London: Random House.

Spanos, N.P. (1982) Hypnotic behaviour: A cognitive, social psychological perspective, *Research Communications in Psychology, Psychiatry and Behaviour*, **7**, pp. 199–213.

Spanos, N.P. (1996) *Multiple Identities and False Memories: A Sociocognitive Perspective*, Washington, DC: American Psychological Association.

Spanos, N.P., Weekes, J.R. & Bertrand, L.D. (1985) Mutiple personality: A social analysis of cognitive skill training for the enhancement of hypnotic susceptibility, *Journal of Abnormal Psychology*, **95**, pp. 350–357.

Sparks, J. (1982) *The Discovery of Animal Behaviour*, London: Collins/BBC.

Stapp, H. (2007) *Mindful Universe: Quantum Mechanics and the Participating Observer*, London: Springer-Verlag.

Bibliography

Stapp, H. (2009) Reply to Koch and Hepp, [Online], http://www-physics.lbl.gov/~stapp/stappfiles.html accessed on 06/01/2011.

Steele, E.J., Lindley, R.A. & Blanden, R.V. (1998) *Lamarck's Signature: How Retrogenes are Changing Darwin's Natural Selection Paradigm*, Sydney: Allen & Unwin.

Steinkamp, F. (2002) *Parapsychology, Philosophy and the Mind: Essays Honouring John Beloff*, London: McFarland.

Stevenson, I. (1966) *Twenty Cases Suggestive of Reincarnation*, Charlottesville, VA: University Press of Virginia.

Stevenson, I. (1967) Letter, *Journal of Parapsychology*, **31**, pp. 145–155.

Stevenson, I. (1997) *Reincarnation and Biology: A Contribution to the Etiology of Birthmarks and Birth Defects* (2 Vols), Charlottesville, VA: University Press of Virginia.

Stokes, D.M. (2007) *The Conscious Mind and the Material World*, Jefferson, NC: McFarland.

Storm, L., Tessoldi, P.E. & Di Risio, L. (2010a) Meta-analysis of free-response studies, 1992–2008: Assessing the noise reduction model in parapsychology, *Psychological Bulletin*, **136**, pp. 471–485.

Storm, L., Tessoldi, P.E. & Di Risio, L. (2010b) A meta-analysis with nothing to hide: Reply to Hyman, *Psychological Bulletin*, **136**, pp. 491–494.

Strawson, G. (1994) *Mental Reality*, Cambridge, MA: MIT Press.

Tallis, R. (2004) *Why the Mind is not a Computer*, Exeter: Imprint Academic.

Tart, C. (1972) States of consciousness and state-specific sciences, *Science*, **176**, pp. 1203–1210.

Tart, C. (2009) *The End of Materialism*, Oakland, CA: New Harbringer Publications.

Taton, R. (1964) *The Beginnings of Modern Science*, New york: Basic Books.

Taylor, C. (1975) *Hegel*, Cambridge: Cambridge University Press

Toulmin, S. (1990) *Cosmopolis*, Chicago, IL: University of Chicago Press.

Trungpa, C. (1973) *Cutting Through Spiritual Materialism*, London: Shambala.

Truzzi, M. (1987) Zetetic ruminations on skepticism and anomalies in science, *Zetetic Scholar*, **12/13**, pp. 7–20.

Tsuchiya, N. & Koch, C. (2009) The relationship between consciousness and attention, in Laurys, S. & Tononi, G. (eds.) *The Neurology of Consciousness*, pp. 63–77, Amsterdam: Elsevier.

Tucker, J.B. (2005) *Life Before Life: A Scientific Investigation of Children's Memories of Previous Lives*, New York: St Martin's.

Turing, A.M. (1950) Computing machinery and intelligence, *Mind*, **59**, pp. 433–460.

Uttal, W.R. (2001) *The New Phrenology: The Limits of Localizing Cognitive Functions in the Brain*, Cambridge, MA: MIT Press.

Uttal, W.R. (2005) Can high-level cognitive functions be localized?, *TICS Article*.

van Gelder, T. (1998) The dynamical hypothesis in cognitive science, *Behavioral and Brain Sciences*, **21**, pp. 615–665.

Varela, F.J. & Shear, J. (eds.) (1999) *The View from Within*, Exeter: Imprint Academic.

Varela, F.J., Thompson, E. & Rosch, E. (1991) *The Embodied Mind: Cognitive Science and Human Experience*, Cambridge, MA: MIT Press.

Velmans, M. (1991) Is human information processing conscious?, *Behavioural & Brain Sciences*, **7**, pp. 131–178.
Velmans, M. (2000) *Understanding Consciousness*, London: Routledge.
Von Neumann, J. (1955/1932) *Mathematical Foundations of Quantum Mechanics*, Princeton, NJ: Princeton University Press.
Vul, E., Harris, C., Winkielman, P. & Pashler, H. (2009) Puzzlingly high correlations in fMRI studies of emotion, personality and social cognition, *Perspectives on Psychological Science*, **4**, pp. 274–290.
Wallace, B.A. (2000) *The Taboo of Subjectivity: Towards a New Science of Consciousness*, Oxford: Oxford University Press.
Wallace, B.A. (2009) Achieving free will: A buddhist perspective, *Mandala*, (January/ March), pp. 55–58.
Wallace, B.A. & Hodel, B. (2008) *Embracing Mind: The Common Ground of Science and Spirituality*, Boston, MA: Shambala.
Walter, S. & Heckmann, H. (eds.) (2003) *Physicalism and Mental Causation*, Exeter: Imprint Academic.
Warren, J. (2008) *Head Trip: A Fantastic Romp Through 24 Hours in the Life of Your Brain*, Oxford: Oneworld.
Watt, C. (2010) Putting things in perspective, *The Skeptic* (US), **22** (2), pp. 22–24.
Wegner, D.A. (2002) *The Illusion of Conscious Will*, Cambridge, MA: MIT Press.
Weizenbaum, J. (1984) *Computer Power and Human Reason*, London: Pelican.
Wertheim, M. (1997) *Pythagoras' Trousers*, London: Fourth Estate.
Wertheim, M. (1999) *The Pearly Gates of Cyberspace*, London: Virago.
Wheeler, J.A. & Zurek, W.H. (1983) *Quantum Theory and Measurement*, Princeton, NJ: Princeton University Press.
Whitby, B. (2003) The myth of AI failure, *CSRP*, **568**.
Wiener, N. (1950) *The Human Use of Human Beings*, Jackson, TN: Da Capo Press.
Wiener, N. (1961) *Cybernetics* (2nd ed.), Cambridge, MA: MIT Press.
Wilber, K. (2000) *A Brief History of Everything*, Boston, MA: Shambala.
Wiseman, R. (2010) Put up or shut up, *The Skeptic* (US), **22** (2), pp. 21–22.
Wittgenstein, L. (1953) *Philosophical Investigations*, London: Prentice Hall.
Wozniak, R.H. (1995) *Mind and Body: Rene Déscartes to William James*, [Online], http://serendip.brynmawr.edu/Mind/ accessed on 29/09/09.
Yates, F.A. (1964) *Giordano Bruno and the Hermetic Tradition*, Chicago, IL: Chicago University Press.
Zeki, S. (1999) Splendours and mysteries of the brain, *Philosophical Transactions of the Royal Society B*, **354**, p. 2054.

Index

Abbott, D., 06, 116
Abernathy, J., 35
Achromatopsia, 147
Adam & Eve (Bible story), 19
Aeroplane defence of science (pragmatic utility argument), 93
Aggregate individuals, 209, 210, 213, 244
Akinetopsia, 147
Aleksander, I.126-128, 147
Alexander, S., 199
Algorithms, 59, 98, 123, 203, 205
Allison, T., 146
Allopoiesis, 107, 116, 137
Altered states of consciousness, 150, 245
Alvarado, C.S., 48, 53
Anarchism, epistemological, 87
Anaximander, 211
Angel, L., 258
Animism, 19, 22, 27, 123, 274
Anomalistic psychology, 249, 252
Anomalistics, 250, 252
Anterior cingulate cortex (ACC), 163
Anterior insula, 164
Anterior medial cortex, 221
Anthropic principle, 199, 206, 211
Appleyard, B., 23, 114
Aristotelian causation, 13, 23-4, 25, 26, 27, 106, 114
Aristotelian logic, 12, 13, 217
Aristotle, 12, 13, 21-25, 114, 242
Artificial Consciousness, 16, 126, 127

Artificial Intelligence (AI), 13, 25, 60, 99, 100, 107, 113, 123-126, 133, 137, 138, 139, 162, 204, 206, 213, 240
Artificial life, 137
Artificial neural networks, 130, 133
Astrology, 142
Atomism, 13, 56, 64,
Atomistic reductionism, 224, 225
Attention, 127, 128, 143, 145, 146, 155, 183, 239, 240
Auschwitz, 2
Austin, J.H., 195
Autoerythrocyte sensitization (AES), 255
Automatisms, 50, 218, 233, 234, 236, 243,
Autonomy, 99, 106, 107, 119, 136-7, 251
Autopoiesis, 106, 137, 211, 224,
Axioms of consciousness (Aleksander), 126-127
Axon, 128

Baars, B., 5, 76, 127, 146, 149, 180, 215
Bacon, F., 24, 28
Bacon, R., 24
Baconian empiricism, 24
Balloon view of science, 96-7
Barrow, J.D., 19, 29, 75, 77, 198, 199, 207, 208, 211
Bauer, H., 99, 250-252, 268
Bealer, G., 71, 80, 271
Beauregard, M., 275
Beer, R.D., 133
Behaviourism, 12
Beloff, J., 34, 35, 81

Bem, D., 256, 261
Bennett, M.R., 8, 10, 61, 76, 91, 136, 170, 171, 183-185, 191, 222, 226, 240
Bergson, H., 38, 73, 81, 116, 171, 207, 211
Beyond Freedom and Dignity, 55
Big Bang, 10, 200
Binding problem, 119, 134-6, 146, 148, 276
Biletzki, A., 92
Biological causation, 16, 105, 115, 223, 270, 271, 283
Blackmore, S.J., 5, 6, 59, 60, 75, 79, 80, 81, 100, 116, 134, 144, 149, 150, 151, 159, 160, 189, 195, 202, 215, 216, 219, 220, 231, 253, 279
Blakemore, C., 3, 5-6
Blank slate theory of human nature, 36, 54, 64, 203
Blindsight, 218, 226
Block, N., 61, 186
Bohm, D., 172, 262
Bohm's Implicate/explicate order (psi theory), 262
Bohr, N., 108, 109, 113, 191
BOLD (Blood Oxygen Level Dependent) contrast, 160-1, 164
Bolender, J., 72.
BonJour, L., 191
Bor, D., 162
Borges, J.L., 74
Bostrom, N., 75
Bower, G., 215
Bradbury, R., 234
Brain holists versus localizer debate, 63
Brain language, 168,170
Brain's blueprint, 281
Brain-body dualism (Bennett & Hacker), 222
Brass, M., 221
Braude, S., 81, 82, 95, 99, 111, 152, 153, 187, 236, 244, 247, 258, 263, 264
Broca, P., 38, 63
Broca's area, 38, 63
Brockman, M., 3
Broughton, R., 261
Brown, A., 202
Brown, W.S., 15, 192, 197, 208, 216-217, 223-228
Bruce, V., 129
Bruno, G., 21, 22
Buddha, 16, 192, 246
Buddhaghosa, 180

Burrus, A., 254

Cabeza, R., 161
CADBLIND, 3
Calvin,J., 216
Cameron, E., 55
Capacities, 61, 84, 98, 99, 100, 105, 106, 111, 120, 149, 164, 184, 213, 225, 226, 229, 231, 239, 244, 245, 247, 263
Carey, J., 55
Carr, B., 262
Carter, R., 76, 78, 79, 109, 110, 127, 153, 159, 160, 168
Cartesian Dualism, 8, 25-8, 80-81, 89, 229, 240, 270
Cartesian method, 109, 126, 143, 149, 175, 274
Cartesian Mirror, 89, 240
Cartwright, N., 15, 88, 96-100, 107, 111, 150, 157, 225, 247
Causal redundancy argument, 79-80, 86
Central state theory see identity theory
Cerebral cortex, 63, 146, 164, 166, 220
Cerebroscope, 145, 159, 175
Cetaceans, 206
Ceteris Paribus ('all other things being equal or held constant'), 97, 103, 173
Chalmers, D., 10, 75, 76, 80, 199
Chalmers, E.F., 93, 94, 95, 102, 124
Chapin, J., 167
Chomsky, N., 95, 205
Choomaliaiwong, C., 257
Chrisley, R, 126, 128, 133, 229
Chun, M.M., 145
Churchland, P.M., 3, 76,144, 159, 181, 185, 186
Churchland, P.S., 76, 79, 144, 159
CIA, 55
Clairvoyance, 34, 35, 50, 82, 243, 253, 256, 263
Clarke, A.C., 249
Classical physics, 9, 15, 72, 120, 153, 172, 239, 263
Clifford, W.K., 4
Clinton, W., 170, 171, 172, 174
Clockwork universe, 28, 29, 64, 85, 155, 199, 205, 212, 218
Closure principle, 73, 75, 155, 157, 227, 254, 263, 271
Coe, W.C., 236
Cognitive architecture of brain, 160
Coleridge, S.T., 32

Collins, H., 4, 71, 230, 251-252, 262
Colonization problem, 276
Coma, 150, 167
Compatibilists (free will), 217, 223-7, 230
Complementarity (Velmans' version), 228
Complementarity, Generalized, 109, 180, 191
Complementarity, quantum theory, 108, 109
Complexity, as boundary condition, 98, 105
Compound individuals, 209-210, 213, 247, 265
Computational Model of Mind, 58, 123-124, 131, 133, 139
Concept of Mind, The, 56
Conditioned realities, 193
Conjectural explanations, 85, 86, 93,
Consciousness
  As mapping problem, 190-1
  As theoretical entity, 92
  Definitions of, 13, 141, 143, 147, 151, 170, 190, 193, 206, 234, 235, 242, 273,
  Neurobiological theories of, 141-153
  Quantum theories of, 116, 141, 153-157
  Theories of, 1, 96, 105, 109, 128, 142-145, 151, 180, 186, 188, 191, 267, 269
Consciousness Explained, 124, 135
Consciousness studies, 12, 13, 106, 109, 268, 276, 281
Consensus, scientific, 70, 113, 134, 141, 163, 251, 267-268, 280
Continental drift debate, 233
Conventional compatibilism (free will), 223-224,
Copenhagen Interpretation, quantum theory, 109, 154
Copernicanism, 21-22
Copernicus, 21, 22
Corliss, W., 219
Cosmogony, 200
Crabtree, A., 33, 34, 124, 150, 234, 236-237
Crane, 205
Craver, C.F., 143, 169, 225
Creationism, 199, 200
Creative selection, principle of, 110
Creativity, 110, 182, 197, 222, 245, 283
Crick, F., 11, 76, 146-148,153, 273

Crisis apparitions, 51
Crystal gazing, 51
Cybernetics (book), 58
Cybernetics, 58, 133, 144, 226

Dalai Lama, 195
Damasaio, A., 76, 135, 143, 180
Daniels, M., 77, 143, 183
Dante Alighieri, 21
Darwin, C., 38, 39, 40, 197, 201, 202, 203, 204, 205, 212, 264
Darwin, E., 38
Darwin's Dangerous Idea, 203
Darwinism, 39, 79, 148, 197, 201, 202, 205
Davies, P., 199, 206, 211, 212
Davy, H., 32
Dawkins, R., 4, 10, 32, 93, 110, 114, 116, 146, 198, 202, 224
De Chardin, T., 38, 77, 199
De Revolutionibus, 22
de Stael, Madame, 49
Deacon, T., 208, 226
Deep consciousness, 235
Dehaene, S., 147
Dendrites, 128
Dennett, D.C., 3, 5, 61, 76, 116, 124, 128,135, 136, 138, 141, 151, 186, 187, 197, 201-206, 212, 223, 224, 240, 243, 244, 279
Descartes, R., 8, 25-28, 31, 40, 41, 44, 46, 64, 71, 80, 89-90, 107, 205, 229, 238, 240
Determinism, 7, 14, 99, 153, 157, 169, 215-7, 218, 222, 224, 225, 226, 228, 229, 239, 246, 270, 279
Di Christina, M., 166
Di Paulo, E.A., 137
Di Risio, L., 257
Dialectical materialism, 169
Dick, S.J., 261
Digital computers, 57, 59, 128
Digital machine, 58, 128
Disintegrations of personality, 243, 244
Dissipative structures, 118
Dissociation, 150, 236
Dissociative Identity Disorder (DID), 233, 236, 237,243, 244,
Distinct apperceptive centres, 244
Divided consciousness, 34
Divine Comedy, the, 21
Doctrine of final causes (see teleology)
Donaldson, D.I., 165

Downwards causation, 224-226
Drachman, D., 154
Dreams, 20, 51, 146, 150, 243
Dreisch, H., 35
Dreyfus, H., 25, 124
Druses, 257
Dualism, 8, 9, 47, 48, 70, 73, 75, 80-82, 84, 119, 123, 132, 153, 156, 157, 181, 183, 184, 187, 191, 206, 209, 222, 224, 228, 247, 262, 263, 269, 270, 275
Duhkha (suffering), 193
Dupré, J., 88, 99, 205, 225, 227
Dynamic core model, 147-148, 226,
Dynamical systems approach, 116, 123, 132-133, 134, 136, 137, 138, 139, 144, 179, 240
Dyson, F., 72

Ebbinghaus, H., 44
Eccles, J., 6, 9, 10, 25, 26, 28, 36, 40, 69, 77, 79, 81, 83, 84, 85, 207, 272
Eckert, R., 129, 130
Edelman, G., 147, 226
Edge, H., 182, 262, 263, 275
Edwards, P., 258
Efficient causation, 23, 114, 217
Ego tunnel, 234
Ego Tunnel, the, 238
Einstein, A., 109, 271, 274
Elan Vital, 207
Electrodynamic definition of life, 116, 117-118
Electroencephalograms (EEG), 160, 220
Eliminative materialism, 76, 274
Elsasser, W., 11, 87, 107-112, 113, 119, 120, 148, 191, 271, 272-273
Elsdon-Baker, F., 203
Emergent property, consciousness as, 73, 195, 198, 200,
Emergentism, 191, 206, 213
Emotion, 26, 27, 28, 44, 78, 79, 100, 126, 163, 165, 180, 220, 242, 255
Empyrium, 21
Engel, A.K., 167
Engineering, biology as, 13, 202, 204, 205, 223,
Enlightenment (Buddhist), 192, 194
Enlightenment (social/philosophical movement), 25, 28, 31, 32, 36, 83, 138
Epiphenomenalism, 76, 78-9, 80, 190, 200, 219, 220, 228, 247
Epistemology, 15, 16, 41, 86, 87, 90, 102, 281

ESP, 82, 150, 253, 263, 264
Essay on the Principle of Population, 39
Essential tension (Kuhn), 141
Essentialism, 12, 85, 270,
Evangelism, 49
Evo-Devo, 203
Evolution, 5, 19, 38, 39, 50, 79, 113, 114, 119, 180, 190, 198, 200-208, 211, 213, 216, 223, 264
Evolutionary cosmologies, 50, 211
Evolutionary psychology, 203, 250
Expanded science compatibilism (free will), 224, 227
Extrastriate cortex, 145
Extreme states of consciousness, 150
Eysenck, H.J., 56, 254, 256

Fairley, J., 254
Falsificationism, Popperian, 124
Far-from-equilibrium engines, living things as, 117
Ferrier, D., 63
Feyerabend, P.K., 10, 12, 15, 19, 70, 76, 77, 87, 88, 97, 100, 101, 102, 107, 142, 172, 173, 181-2, 189, 191, 199, 230, 262, 271, 274, 277-278, 280
Ficino, M., 22
Field theories of consciousness, 148
Fields and forces worldview, 8, 103, 273
Filter dualism, 47, 73, 81, 82, 116, 246
Flanagan, O., 273
Flatland holism (Ken Wilber), 175, 179
Flourens, M.P., 36-7
fMRI (functional Nuclear Magnetic Resonance), 14, 63, 112, 160-165, 170, 181, 219, 245,
Fodor, J., 62, 95
Folk psychology, 182, 218, 275
Fort, C., 249, 250, 265
Frankenstein, 33
Frankl, V., 2, 281
Franklin, B., 34
Franz, S. I., 62
Free Agency, 217, 223, 224, 230,
Free will, 4-8, 14, 16, 45, 81, 99, 155, 182, 215-217, 222, 223, 224, 228, 230, 231, 237, 239, 279
Freedom Evolves, 223
Frege, G., 69, 84
Freud, S., 53, 146
Fringe of consciousness, 146
Frith, C., 215

Froese, T., 133
Fromm, E., 280
Functionalism, 55, 61, 128
Fusiform Face area (FFA), 145, 166

Gage, P., 37
Gall, F., 37
Galvini, L., 32
Ganzfeld (telepathy experiments), 83, 255-256, 259, 261
Gardner, H., 56, 57, 58, 60, 61, 62, 63, 99
Gauld, A., 33, 34, 35, 48, 49, 50, 51, 81, 111, 146, 150, 161, 236, 237, 242-244, 264, 275
Gazzaniga, M., 15, 215, 230
General Semantics, 12-13
Genes, 13, 37, 100, 107, 147, 201, 202, 224,
Genius, 50, 243
Georgeson, M.A., 129
Ghanem, S., 257
Gleik, J., 95
Global workspace theories, 118, 127, 145
God, 20, 21, 27, 74, 75, 197, 216, 230
Gödel, K., 188
Gödel's incompleteness Theorem, 188
Goleman, D., 195
Goodwin, B., 106, 116
Gould, S J, 79
Gravitation, 28, 81, 92, 97, 205
Great Chain of Being, 20
Great Mind (God), 74, 198
Greek rationalism, 24
Green, P.R., 129
Gribbin, J., 48, 55, 70, 71
Griffin, D. (Donald), 200, 206
Griffin, D.R. (David Ray), 170, 198, 206-210, 212, 213, 217, 250, 263

Hacker, P.M.S., 8, 10, 61, 76, 91, 136, 170, 171, 183-185, 191, 222, 226, 240
Haggard, P., 221
Hallucinogenic drug, 3
Halpern,M., 125, 138
Hammeroff, S., 141, 156
Hamilton, T., 48-49, 51
Hard problem, 10, 133, 194, 276
Harpaz, Y., 145
Harré, H.R., 106
Harrison, T., 255
Hartley, D., 25
Harvey, I., 132, 133

Hasker, W., 247
Hassabis, D. 161
Hayes, N., 44, 53, 54, 55, 62, 131, 138
Heap,M., 235
Hebb, D., 63,168
Heckmann, H., 70, 219, 229
Heeger, D.J., 160, 162
Heil, J., 79, 80, 151, 219, 229
Henry, R.C., 71, 75, 188, 241
Hepp, K., 141, 155, 156
Hidden/abstract entities, 86, 90-93, 102
Higher order thought (Ned Block), 186
Ho, M.W., 116-119,149, 224, 226
Hobbes, T., 28
Hodel, B., 8, 40, 46, 194
Hodgson, D., 224, 227
Hofstadter, D.R., 60,142, 240
Holistic biology, 175, 179
Holistic memory, principle of, 110, 111
Holistic properties of organisms, 208
Holographic theory of memory, 81-82
Holophysicalism, 246
Honorton, C., 256, 261
Hope, R., 194
Horgan, J., 124, 133, 167, 170, 171
Horizontal Gene Transfer, 203
Hothersall,D., 36, 37, 38, 43, 45, 53, 55, 63
Human Personality and its Survival of Bodily Death, 48, 49, 241, 243
Hume, D., 25, 92, 190, 192, 193
Husserl, E., 90, 188
Huxley, A., 100
Huxley, T. H., 39, 40-41, 51, 76, 78
Hydesville, New York State, 49
Hylomorphism, 23-24, 207, 270, 271
Hyman, R., 256-257, 259-261
Hypnosis, 51, 150, 234, 236-238, 255
Hypnotic phenomena, 150, 234, 236-237
Hysteria, 237, 243

Idealism, 73, 74-75, 191, 271
Identity theory, 76, 79-80, 147
Ideological imperialism, 182
Illusion arguments, 5-8, 75, 78, 80, 93, 101, 133, 135, 170, 173, 193-194, 207, 227, 229, 230, 235, 248
Incompatibilists (free will), 216, 217
Indeterminism, 217, 223
India, 257
Incffability problem, 151
Information Integration theories, 148

Information processing, 14, 16, 95, 123, 128-133, 135, 136, 138-139, 142, 144, 164, 169, 170, 172, 179, 180, 192, 199, 202, 234, 235, 246, 267, 269, 270, 271
Information theory, 157, 202
Inglis, B., 33, 49
innere Wahrnehmung (internal perception), 43
Intelligent Design, 114, 115,119,199,200
Intentional stance, 61, 146
Intentionality (of consciousness), 61, 84, 123, 155, 204, 223, 271
Interaction problem, mind-body, 26, 80, 182
Intersubjective knowledge, 70, 229, 241
Introspection, 43, 46, 53-55, 183, 185, 206, 244
Introspectionist school, 44
Ishai, A., 145, 153

James, O. 248
James, W., 1, 2, 9, 41, 45-48, 51, 53, 55, 73, 81, 88, 102, 116, 146, 148, 155, 171, 180, 181, 208, 210, 211, 231
Jamesian 'Permission' Dualism, 47, 73, 81
John, E.R., 118, 148, 149
Jones, M.C., 53
Jones, R., 28, 85
Journal of Consciousness Studies, 10, 11, 56, 70, 111
Joyce, J., 1, 2
Juarerro, A., 226
Jung, C.G., 53, 146

Kant, I., 89, 240
Kanwisher, N., 145, 153, 166, 169
Kaufmann,S.A., 116, 117, 118
Keats, J., 32
Kellis, S., 160
Kelly, E.F., 4, 40, 50, 61, 82, 111, 134, 148, 150, 161, 166, 174, 175, 219, 234, 236, 237, 242, 245, 254
Kelly, E.W., 40, 50, 242, 255
Kepler, J., 22
Kim, J., 80
King, R., 216
Klein, N., 55
Knowledge monopolies, 277
Koch, C., 9, 11, 14, 72, 76, 109, 130, 141, 142, 143, 146-148, 153, 155, 156, 166, 167, 171, 205, 273
Koestler, A., 54, 56, 57, 73, 138

Koestler's dualism, 73
Koons, R.C., 71, 80, 271
Korzybski, A., 12, 13, 188, 204
Kosslyn, S.M., 5, 152, 163, 169, 183
Kriegeskorte, N., 163
Kuhn, T., 21, 22, 65, 101, 138, 141, 142, 156, 253, 267
Kurzweil, R., 14, 60, 131
Kuttner, F., 71, 109, 252

L'Homme Machine, 36
La Mettrié, J.O., 36
Lamarckism, 204
Lancaster, B.L., 245-246
Lancet, The, 255
Language, 13, 20, 36, 38, 57, 60, 62, 63, 87, 146, 181, 183, 188, 223, 226, 267, 273, 280
Language, brain, 168, 170
Language, mind, 168
Laplace's demon, 29
Lashley, K., 62, 63
Lawrence, W., 35, 36
Laws of aerodynamics, 125
Laws of nature, 15, 88, 107, 224, 250, 271
Laws of planetary motion, 22, 97
Le Grand, H.E., 233
Le Guin, U.K., 276
Le Malefan, P., 53
Learning as general capacity, 98
Lebanon, 257
Legallis, J.C., 36
Leibniz, G., 28, 76, 77
Leipzig University psychology department, 44
Levine, B., 152
Lewis, D.K., 69, 70, 84
Lewontin,R.C., 79
Leyden jar, 32
Libertarians (free will), 217, 230
Libet, B., 78, 220-222, 238
Lieberman, P., 3
Liebig, J., 36
Life principle, 209, 212
Life, nature of, 32, 35, 41, 107, 112-113, 115-117, 119, 137, 151, 198, 204, 206
Lightning as electrical charge, 144
Linnaeus, 49
Liquid crystal and organisms, 118
Living Universe model, 77, 211-212
Llinàs, R., 149
Locke, J., 25, 28, 36, 240

Logos (order), 24, 114-115
Logothetis, N.K., 164, 169
Lord Byron, 33

Mach, E., 173, 271
Machine metaphor, 123
Macrocosm (outer universe), 26
Madam de Stael, 49
Madden, E.H., 106
Magnus (robot), 127
Malthus, T., 39
Man's Search for Meaning, 2
Marshall, P., 74, 85
Martin, B., 268, 277, 280-281
Martinez-Conde, S., 143
Marxism, 169
Matar, A., 92
Material cause, 23, 114
Materialism, 4, 9, 28, 36, 48, 58, 65, 73, 76, 90, 169, 207, 274
Maturana, H.R., 106
Maxwell, M., 2
McCarthy, G., 145
McDermott, J., 145
Medical iatrogenesis, 236-237
Medieval cosmos, 20
Meditation, 150, 195
Mediumship, 43, 82
Medulla oblongata, 36, 234
Meixner, U., 184
Memes, 10, 13, 100, 202,
Memoire pour servir à l'histoire et à l'établissement du magnétisme animal, 34
Memory traces, 26, 110, 153
Memory, 26, 27, 34, 37, 44, 62, 77, 81, 85, 87, 95, 110-112, 118, 119, 124, 146, 152-153, 161, 168-169, 171, 207, 242, 271, 281
Mental Causation, 40, 45, 80, 83, 115, 155, 195, 254
Mental content, 95, 167, 245
Mental monoculture, 277
Mesmer, F.A., 33, 34, 275
Mesmerism, 15, 33-35, 65, 278
Metaphors, 2, 13, 14, 33, 46, 47, 51, 60, 62, 64, 71, 85, 86, 112, 114, 123, 124, 128, 131, 132, 135, 138, 146, 150, 170, 171, 172, 183, 199, 202, 205, 212, 226, 234, 240, 248, 262, 267, 272
Metaphysics, 11, 70, 74, 147, 170, 171, 174, 175, 245, 264
Methodism, 49

Metzinger, T., 41, 90, 91, 101, 149, 150, 151, 226, 234-235, 238-241, 246, 247-248
Michie, D., 109
Microcosm (inner universe), 26
Middle Way (Madhyamika), 46, 188, 193-195
Midgley, M., 2, 4, 19, 22, 24, 27, 56, 57, 70, 72, 75, 79, 94, 186, 190-191, 199, 202, 211
Military-industrial-academic complex, 268
Mill, J.S., 277
Milton, J., 254
Mind,
   As computation, 128
   As function/aggregation, 56-57, 93, 98, 213
   As theoretical entity, 92
   Definitions of, 13, 85, 194
Mind-body problem, 182
Mind language, 168
Mind's eye, 5, 183
Minsky, M., 60, 124, 159, 213
Modular view of brain/mind, 7, 160, 165, 166
Molecular cascades, 117
Monism of kinds, 74
Monism, 9, 72, 73, 85, 209, 269
Monistic Idealism, 73, 74
Monistic Materialism, 73
Monod, J., 198, 212
Moravec, H., 60, 131, 132
More, H., 49
Mormonn, F., 141, 142, 143, 167
Morowitz, H.J., 117
Morphic fields, 111, 119
Motor cortex, 63, 222
Murphy, M., 275
Murphy, N. 15, 192, 197, 208, 216-217, 223-228
MVPA (multivariate pattern analysis), 162
Myers, F.W.H., 38, 47, 48-51, 65, 81, 148, 150, 174, 233-235, 241-245, 247, 248
Mysterianism, 269, 273
Mystical experience, 2, 49, 74
Mythology, 64
Myths, 19-20, 34, 56, 64, 83, 123, 125, 269, 279

Nagel, T., 180

National Science Foundation (NSF), 58
Natural selection as algorithm, 203-4
Natural selection, 5, 38-39, 40, 78, 110, 114, 115, 197-198, 201, 203, 211
Naturalism, 48, 82, 147, 224, 245, 246, 262, 271, 281
Nature (journal), 142, 156, 252
Near-Death Experiences (NDEs), 82, 150
Negentropy, 117
Neo-Darwinism, 201-202
Neodissociationists, 236
Neoparapsychologists, 259, 260
Nerve terminal, 154
Neural code, 160, 167, 171, 172, 174-175, 281
Neural correlates of consciousness, 144, 145
Neural Darwinism, 147
Neural representation, 127, 135, 169
Neurath, O., 15, 96, 97
Neuroarthistory, 159,
Neuroethics, 159
Neuroimaging, 14, 15-16, 145, 159, 160, 165, 168, 170, 175, 248, 271, 272
Neuron, 15, 128-129, 130, 131, 134-135, 142, 146, 147, 148, 153-4, 162, 164, 167, 170, 174, 215, 222, 224
Neurophenomenology, 189
Neurophilosophy, 159
Neurotransmitters, 129, 154, 156
Neutral monism, 73, 85, 270
Newsome, W.T., 163, 229
Newton, I., 28, 29, 65, 71, 85, 92, 97, 98, 173
Newton's laws of motion, 28, 29, 92, 97, 115, 173, 175, 225
Newtonian epistemology, 41
Nichols, M.J., 163, 229
Noë, A., 135
Nomological machines, 97-99, 100, 101, 102, 107, 225, 250
Non-fractionable aspects (complex systems), 113
Nonmechanistic biology see holistic biology
Non-physical property, consciousness as, 184, 191, 192, 271, 275
Nordberg, R.B., 207
Normocentric thinking, 150
Nothing but thinking, 7, 13, 36, 69, 74, 100, 115, 116, 171, 185, 215
Nyberg, L., 161, 162

Objectivism, 72, 189, 228, 274
Observational theory (psi theory), 262
Observer problem, 240
Obsessive-Compulsive Disorder (OCD)
Occult view of mind, 4, 25
One-size fits all theory (consciousness), 267, 269
Ontological reduction, 76, 79, 224
Ontology, 27, 69-71, 73, 79, 83, 85, 86, 87, 90, 91, 192, 241, 270, 281
  dualistic, 73, 80
  monistic, 72, 73
  trialist, 73, 83
Organicism, 179, 247, 282
Organization of Behaviour, The, 63
Organized scepticism, 252
O'Shea, M., 3, 100
Ouija board, 218, 233, 243
Out of Body Experiences (OBEs), 149, 150, 174, 239, 248
Owen, A.M., 167

Paley, W., 198, 205
Palmer, J., 261
Pandeya, R.C., 193
Panexperientialism, 197, 208, 209, 210, 213
Panpsychism, 75, 76-77, 197, 198, 200, 210, 211
Paradigmic thinking (David Ray Griffin), 250
Parahippocampal place area (PPA), 145
Parallelism, Mind/body, 26, 210
Paramecia, 207
Paranormal, 34, 35, 48, 50, 234, 242, 243, 248, 250, 253, 260
Paraphenomena, 252
Past life memories, 83, 257, 258
Pavlov, I., 54, 57
Pauen, M, 78
Pelvig, D.P., 154
Pendulum, motions of, 132, 156
Penrose, R., 59, 69, 72, 84, 92, 116, 123, 124, 141, 153, 156, 205
Perkins, W., 216
Permission/transmission theories of mind/consciousness, 47, 73, 81
Personal experiences of consciousness see subjective experience
Phaedo, 23
Phantasms of the Living, 49

Phenomenological Self Model (PSM, Metzinger). 238
Phenomenology, 92, 147, 172, 188-189
Philosophical Investigations, 92
Philosophical Lectures, 32
Photons, 108
Phrenology, 15, 37, 38, 65, 278
Physicalism, 9, 10, 16, 70, 71, 72, 75, 79, 80, 81, 85-86, 90, 120, 171, 179, 188, 191, 192, 193, 194, 195, 200, 217, 224, 228-230, 262, 263, 270, 271, 272, 274, 275, 282
Physiognomics, 25
Pierre-Simon, Marquis de Laplace, 29, 218
Pinch, T., 4, 71, 230, 251-252, 262
Pinker, S., 95, 131, 202, 203
Place, U.T., 144
Placebo effect, 82, 254
Plato, 21, 22, 23, 24, 83, 84, 91, 189
Platonic mind, 91
Platonic self, 51, 81, 233, 234-235, 241-242, 244-245, 247
Platonic token (memory), 92, 152, 153, 187
Platonism, 13, 21, 25, 27, 81, 83, 84, 92, 116, 152, 153, 189, 193, 208,
Pluralism
 epistemological, 15, 46, 70, 77, 87-88, 102, 143,
 methodological, 169
 property, 8, 180, 184, 191, 270, 272, 274, 282
Polyani, M., 142
Popper, K., 6, 9, 25, 26, 28, 36, 40, 69, 73-81, 83-85, 93, 127, 207, 208, 210, 272
Popperian property Dualism, 73
Port, R., 111, 132-133
Position Emission topography (PET), 160, 163
Positivism, 14, 86, 90, 93, 143, 157
Pragmatic information theories (psi theory), 262
Precognition, 253, 264
Predestination, 216
Presentism, 124
Primates, 206
Principle of the internal mechanism, 152
Principles of Psychology, 1, 45
Private experiences, 90, 133, 181, 183, 184, 187,

Process 1/Process 2, 155-157, 229
Process and Reality, 208
Process dualism (Stapp), 154
Progress in evolution, 39, 49-50, 208, 211
Progressivism, 38, 50
Promissory materialism, 206, 208
Protagoras, 16, 189, 273
Protestantism, 216
Pseudoscience, 15, 37, 65, 251, 252
Psi, 10, 81, 82, 111, 252-254, 256, 257, 258, 259-260, 262-263, 283
Psychic experiences, 249
Psychical Research, 15, 47-48, 53
Psychokinesis (PK), 82, 254
Psychons, 10
Psychophysics, 44
Psychophysical influences, 82
Psychophysical Unitarianism (Hacker), 184
Pulses of consciousness (William James), 148
Purpose, 5, 24, 36, 37, 64, 100, 114, 115, 136, 198, 204, 272
Putnum, H., 60, 272
Puységur, Marquis de, 33, 34
Pyramid view of science, 96, 97
Pythagoras, 23, 91
Pythagoras' theorem, 23
Pythagorean soul, 132

Qualia, 3, 5, 61, 76, 144, 148, 149, 151, 179, 180, 185-187, 188, 204, 227-228, 239-240
Quantum biology, 105
Quantum physics, 10, 16, 69, 75, 93, 105-109, 116, 118, 120, 134, 141-142, 153, 154-157, 172, 188, 199, 205, 225, 229, 241, 252, 262, 263, 269, 271, 272
Quantum Zeno effect, 155
Quest for certainty, 28
Quintessence, 74, 205

Race, V., 34
Rashevsky, N., 112
Radical materialism see eliminative
Radical novelty, 197, 207-208, 213, 224, 246
Radin, D., 10, 181, 253, 256, 262
Rado, A. , 135
Rainbow and the worm, The, 117
Rao, K. R., 61, 123, 179, 180, 192, 193, 228, 229

Raymont, P., 80
Rationalism, 22, 24, 32, 75, 241, 252, 255, 272-4, 279
Read, N., 237
Realism (epistemological), 88, 93, 94-96, 102, 274
Reductionism, 28, 76, 79, 87, 107, 143, 151, 160, 185, 224, 225, 231, 263
Reed, G., 249
Reflex arc, 54
Reflexive view of consciousness (Velmans), 228
Regeneration, 106-107, 119
Reincarnation, 194, 257-258, 263-4
Relational biology, 112
Relativism, 93-94, 182, 195, 270, 274-275
Renouvier, C., 45
Representation, 14, 23, 63, 81, 89-90, 127, 147, 152, 153, 161, 169, 170, 171, 172, 173, 194, 241, 269
Representational theory of mind, 25, 62, 81, 89-90, 124, 127, 128, 133-134, 135, 157, 169-170, 171, 174, 179, 226, 240-241
Research cartels, 268, 277
Ress, D., 160, 162
Reticular activating system, 167
Revonsuo, A., 149
Rhine, J.B., 253
Rhine, L., 258, 265
Rhodes, R., 58
Richards, J.R., 20, 197, 201, 202
Ridley, M., 202
Rinbochay, L., 180
Robertson, C., 254-255
Roe, C., 257, 260-261
Rogue phenomena see paranormal phenomena
Romanticism, 32, 49
Roney-Dougal, S., 195
Rorty, R., 76, 87, 89, 90, 91, 92, 181, 281
Rose, H., 203, 250
Rose, S.P.R., 8, 37, 107, 110, 116, 120, 126, 134, 159, 168-169, 170, 201, 202, 203, 209, 217, 223, 224, 250
Roseannean complexity, 113-115, 126, 247, 272
Rosen, R., 8, 11, 41, 105, 112-115, 120, 125, 270, 271
Rosenblum, B., 71, 109, 252
RP (Readiness potential, volition), 221
Rucker, R., 72, 188
Rule-based systems in AI, 99

Rupa (sensory data), 192
Russell, B., 23, 85, 90
Ryle, G., 56-57, 61, 76, 92, 98, 133, 181, 213

Sagan, C., 83, 203, 276-277
Sagan, D., 203
Sahtouris, E., 26, 77, 137, 189, 211
Sankhara (volition), 192-193
Sanna (perception/sensation), 192-193
Sarbin, T.R., 236
Sargent, C., 254, 256
Scholasticism, Medieval, 8, 24, 86
Schrödinger, E., 117
Schwartz, J., 275
Science (journal), 142, 252
Scientific Materialism, 8, 15
Scientific method, 230, 260, 261-262, 268-269
Scientism, 4, 57, 174
Scott, A.C., 135
Scruton, R., 159, 215
Searle, J., 7, 8, 71, 84, 103, 147, 191, 205, 269
Second scientific age (nineteenth century), 31-32
Self, 'deep', 16, 235, 241, 242, 245, 246
Self, 'shallow', 16, 235, 238
Self, 2, 5, 6, 7, 16, 20, 51, 81, 143, 149, 180, 182, 192, 194, 195, 202, 215, 223, 233, 234-235, 238-244, 246, 247, 248, 275, 278, 283
Self, medieval views, 20
Self, virtual, 234, 238, 245
Selfish replicators, 116, 119, 202, 209
Seth, A., 109, 134, 144, 145, 148
Shannon, C., 58, 111
Shaw, G. B., 39
Shear, J., 2, 14, 146, 187, 189
Sheldrake, R., 79, 111, 119, 281
Shelley, M., 33
Shins, 10
Sidgwick, H., 48
Signal sensitivity of organisms, 117
Simon, H., 60, 125
Simulation models, 73
Skandhas (aggregates), 192
Skeptic magazine (US), 252, 253, 258
Skinner, B.F., 55-56
Skyhooks, 205
Sleep, 2, 36, 47, 150, 167, 210, 234, 237, 243, 256,
Sleep, magnetic, 34

Sloman, A., 131, 149, 229
Social science, 95, 99, 203, 250-251, 261, 277
Society for Psychical Research (SPR), 48
Sociocognitive school, 234, 236-237, 243
Sogyal Rinpoche, 11
Soma, 128
Somnambulism (sleep-walking), 33
Soul, 1, 20-21, 23-24, 25-26, 31, 35-36, 46, 51, 132, 151, 182, 241, 245
Spandrel, evolutionary (consciousness as), 79
Spanos, N.P., 236-237
Sparks, J., 26, 44, 54
Spencer, H., 40, 50
Spinoza, B., 76-77
Spirit possession, 218, 233
Spiritualism, 48-49
Split brain (commissurotomy), 218, 247
Spurzheim, J., 37
Stapp, H., 9-10, 46, 72, 73, 124, 142, 153-157, 208, 229, 262
Stapp's dual-process theory, 73, 142, 153-157, 262,
Stapp-von Neumann model (psi theory), 262
Steele, E.J., 203
Stevenson, I., 257-258, 264
Stigmata, 82, 254-255
Stimulus-Response (S-R) unit, 54
Stokes, D., 10
Storm, L., 257
Staudacher, A., 78
Strawson, G., 207, 217
Structural theory of science, 94-95
Subjective experience, 1-2, 3, 5, 7, 8, 10, 16, 47, 57, 76, 86, 91, 123, 134, 135, 143, 144, 153, 157, 170, 174-175, 179, 180-181, 184, 186-190, 194, 197, 219, 221, 227-228, 238
Subliminal mind, 49, 50, 81, 174, 234, 242
Sunyata (unconditioned realities), 193
Supernormal phenomena, see paranormal phenomena
Super-psi hypothesis, 263
Survival of bodily death, 248
Symbiogenesis, 203
Synaptic cleft, 129, 156
Synchronized neurons, 167
Systema Naturae, 49

Tachistoscope, 44
Tallis, R., 3-4, 62, 90, 170-171
Tart, C., 150, 248
Tatchell, P., 56
Taton, R., 74, 205
Taylor, C., 20
Technocracy, 57, 64
Teleology, 24, 115, 197-200, 204, 208, 212, 213,
Teleonomy, 198
Telepathy, 43, 50, 82, 83, 243, 253, 263
Telos (final cause), 114, 119
Thailand, 257
Thalamocortical rhythms theory, 148
Thalamocortical system, 141-142, 148, 166
Thalamus, 142
Theaetetus, 189
Theological argument for design, 198
Theory of everything, 41, 69, 74
Thermodynamics, 116-117
Tipler, F.J., 75, 198-199, 207-208, 211
Tononi, G., 148
Tressoldi, P.E., 257
Tropoi (causes), 114
Trungpa, C., 188
Truzzi, M., 252
Tschudin, V., 2
Tsuchiya, N., 143
Tucker, J., 257, 258
Turing machine, 59, 126
Turing test, 124
Turing, A., 59-60, 99, 113, 124-126, 247
Turner, F., 48
Twenty Cases Suggestive of Reincarnation, 258
Two-sphere Universe, 21-22, 29
Ultra-Darwinists, 202
Ulysses, 2
Unfathomable complexity, 108, 110, 153, 213
Unified field theory, 74
Universalism, 269, 270, 274
University of Virginia, 257
Uploading the mind, 131
Uranus, 97-98
User illusion, self as, 235, 247-248
Uttal, W., 14, 63, 110, 162, 165-166

Van Gelder, T., 111, 132-133
Van Loon, B., 194
Varela, F., 2, 14, 106, 133, 146, 186, 189
Vendana (feeling), 192-193

Vendanta school, 77
Vestiges of the Natural history of Creation, The, 38
Veto phenomenon (free will), 221-222
Vinanna (consciousness), 192-193
Virtual Machine, consciousness as, 131, 149, 179
Visual cortex, 5, 129, 134-135, 147, 167, 171-172
Visual illusions, 6
Vitalism debate, 32, 35
Vitalism, 32, 35, 81, 107, 115, 209
Von Neumann, J., 154-156, 262
Voodoo death, 82
Voxels (volumetric pixels), 161-163
Vul, E., 161, 163,

Walden Two, 55
Wallace, B.A., 8-9, 14-15, 44, 46, 170, 186, 191, 194, 198, 208, 246
Walter, S., 70, 78, 219, 229
Warren, J., 150, 152
Watchmaker theory, 198
Watson, J.B., 53-56, 62, 76, 107
Watt Governor, 133
Watt,C., 260-261

Wave-particle duality, 108
Weak-quantum theory (psi theory), 262
Weaver, W., 58
Wegner, D., 5, 76, 78, 99, 101, 215, 217-221, 227, 229-230, 233, 235, 238
Weizenbaum, J., 60, 100, 137
Wertheim, M., 21, 24, 74, 132
What is Life?, 117
Whitby, B., 125
Whitehead, A.N., 23, 208, 211
Whole-part relation, 192, 226
Wiener, N., 58, 128-129
Wilber, K., 77, 179
Wiseman, R., 256, 259-261
Wittgenstein, L., 15, 89, 92, 133, 181, 193
Wozniak, R.H., 31
Wundt, W., 43-44, 46, 53, 55

X Club, 39-40

Yates, F., 21, 24

Zeki, S., 91
Zombies (philosophical), 151, 199, 227